POWER/GENDER

INQUIRIES IN SOCIAL CONSTRUCTION

Series editors
Kenneth J. Gergen and John Shotter

This series is designed to facilitate, across discipline and national boundaries, an emergent dialogue within the social sciences which many believe presages a major shift in the western intellectual tradition.

Including among its participants sociologists of science, psychologists, management and communications theorists, cyberneticists, ethnomethodologists, literary theorists, feminists and social historians, it is a dialogue which involves profound challenges to many existing ideas about, for example, the person, selfhood, scientific method and the nature of scientific and everyday knowledge.

It has also given voice to a range of new topics, such as the social construction of personal identities; the role of power in the social making of meanings; rhetoric and narrative in establishing sciences; the centrality of everyday activities; remembering and forgetting as socially constituted activities; reflexivity in method and theorizing. The common thread underlying all these topics is a concern with the processes by which human abilities, experiences, commonsense and scientific knowledge are both *produced in*, and *reproduce*, human communities.

Inquiries in Social Construction affords a vehicle for exploring this new consciousness, the problems raised and the implications for society.

Also in this series

Psychology and Postmodernism
edited by Steinar Kvale

Constructing the Social
edited by Theodore R. Sarbin and John I. Kitsuse

Conversational Realities
Constructing Life through Language
John Shotter

POWER/GENDER

Social Relations in Theory and Practice

EDITED BY

H. LORRAINE RADTKE
and HENDERIKUS J. STAM

SAGE Publications

London • Thousand Oaks • New Delhi

SAGE Publications Ltd
6 Bonhill Street
London EC2A 4PU

SAGE Publications Inc
2455 Teller Road
Thousand Oaks, California 91320

SAGE Publications India Pvt Ltd
32, M-Block Market
Greater Kailash – I
New Delhi 110 048

British Library Cataloguing in Publication data

Radtke, H. Lorraine
  Power/Gender: Social Relations in Theory
  and Practice. – (Inquiries in Social
  Construction Series)
  I. Title II. Stam, Henderikus J. III. Series
  305.4

ISBN 0–8039–8674–2
ISBN 0–8039–8675–0 (pbk)

Library of Congress catalog card number 93–086424

Typeset by Mayhew Typesetting, Rhayader, Powys
Printed in Great Britain by Biddles Ltd, Guildford, Surrey

Contents

PART III: POWER AND THE SOCIAL
CONSTRUCTION OF GENDER

PART IV: STUDIES IN THE PRACTICE OF
POWER AND GENDER

Acknowledgements

While preparing this volume, the editors were supported by Sabbatical Leave Fellowships from the University of Calgary. We would like to express our deep appreciation to members of the Vakgroep Vrouwenstudies Sociale Wetenschappen and the Sectie Theoretische Psychologie, Vakgroep Psychonomie and the University of Utrecht for their hospitality during our work on this book. They provided us with the space and resources we needed, not to mention the *gezelligheit, hartelijk bedankt*. We would also like to thank Ken Gergen and John Shotter, the series editors, for their enthusiastic encouragement and advice throughout the project. Sue Jones, Ziyad Marar and Rowena Lennox of Sage gave advice and invaluable assistance in all stages of the editorial work, making it look easy. Thanks also to Mary Gergen for her helpful comments on an earlier version of the manuscript.

Notes on Contributors

R. W. Connell is Professor of Sociology at the University of California, Santa Cruz. His recent research concerns masculinity, sexuality, education and social theory, and his books include *Gender and Power* and *Schools and Social Justice*.

Karlene Faith teaches criminology at Simon Fraser University in British Columbia, Canada. Her research interests include women and criminal justice, and she is the author of *Unruly Women: The Politics of Confinement and Resistance* (1993).

Michelle Fine is Professor of Psychology at the City University of New York Graduate Center and Senior Consultant at the Philadelphia Schools Collaborative. Recent publications include *Beyond Silenced Voices: Class, Race and Gender in American Schools* (1992) and *Framing Dropouts: Notes on the Politics of an Urban High School* (1991).

Marilyn French received her doctorate from Harvard University and has taught at Hofstra, Harvard, and the College of Holy Cross. She has written several volumes of literary criticism and three novels, including *The Women's Room* (1977). She is also the author of *Beyond Power: On Women, Men, and Morals* (1985) and *The War Against Women* (1992).

Nancy M. Henley is Professor of Psychology at the University of California, Los Angeles. She is the co-editor of *Language and Sex: Difference and Dominance* (with Barrie Thorne, 1975) and of *Language, Gender and Society* (with Barrie Thorne and Cheris Kramarae, 1983), and of numerous articles and chapters on language, nonverbal communication, power, and gender.

Wendy Hollway is Senior Lecturer in Women's Studies at the University of Bradford. Her research domains are the self in social relations (particularly sexual and gender relations) and the production of psychological knowledge, particularly related to work and management.

Deborah Kerfoot is Lecturer in Organizational Behaviour in the School of Business and Economic Studies at the University of Leeds. She is an associate editor of the journal *Gender, Work and Organization*. Her research interests and publications are in the areas of work and organization, and gender and sexuality.

Celia Kitzinger teaches social psychology and women's studies at Loughborough University, UK. She is the author of *The Social Construction of Lesbianism* (Sage, 1987) and *Changing Our Minds: Lesbian Feminism and Psychology* (with Rachel Perkins, 1993). She co-edited (with Sue Wilkinson) *Heterosexuality: a* Feminism and Psychology *Reader* (Sage, 1993).

David Knights is Professor of Organizational Analysis at the Manchester School of Management, UMIST, Manchester and co-editor of a new international journal, *Gender, Work and Organization*. He co-authored *Managing to Discriminate* (1990) with D. Collinson and M. Collinson.

Marianne LaFrance is Professor of Psychology at Boston College in Chestnut Hill, Massachusetts. Her research is concerned with the relationships among gender, language, and nonverbal communication.

Jean Lipman-Blumen is the Thornton F. Bradshaw Professor of Public Policy and Professor of Organizational Behavior at the Peter F. Drucker Graduate Management Center, The Claremont Graduate School, Claremont, California. She is the author of *Gender Roles and Power* (1984).

Hilary M. Lips is Professor of Psychology and Director of the Center for Gender Studies at Radford University. She is the author of several textbooks on the psychology of gender, including *Women, Men and the Psychology of Power*.

Pat Macpherson taught English at Germantown Friends School in Philadelphia for thirteen years and now writes full-time. Her publications include *Reflecting on Jane Eyre* and *Reflecting on the Bell Jar* for Routledge's *Heroines?* series.

H. Lorraine Radtke is Associate Professor of Psychology at the University of Calgary. Her current research interests include the relationships among gender, understandings of knowledge and experience at university, as well as the relationships between mothers and sons.

Eliane Leslau Silverman is Professor and head of the Women's Studies Program at the University of Calgary. She is a historian committed also to interdisciplinarity and has written on frontier women, adolescent women, and historiography. She has been active in the women's movement since 1970.

Henderikus J. Stam is Professor of Psychology at the University of Calgary. His research interests focus on the historical and theoretical foundations of psychology. He is the editor of the journal *Theory & Psychology* and co-editor of the third volume of *Recent Trends in Theoretical Psychology*.

Jill Vickers is Professor of Political Science and Canadian Studies at Carleton University in Ottawa. She has published many articles and books on various aspects of women's involvements in and exclusions from power. Most recently she co-authored *Politics As If Women Mattered* (1993). She has also been active in the English-Canadian women's movement for many years, as President of the Canadian Research Institute for the Advancement of Women and as Parliamentarian of the National Action Committee on the Status of Women among other roles.

Lorraine Weir is Professor of English and Women's Studies at the University of British Columbia, Vancouver. Her research interests include contemporary literary theory and twentieth century literature, and she is the author of *Writing Joyce: A Semiotics of the Joyce System* (1989).

1

Introduction

H. Lorraine Radtke and Henderikus J. Stam

Power and gender are terms so commonly conjoined that their combined invocation has almost ceased to be indexical. Feminism initially alerted us to the fact that gender inequality is not natural, that women speak from unique worlds, and that their gender is (at least to a large extent) a cultural incarnation. Power is both the source of oppression in its abuse and the source of emancipation in its use.

But as there are many and varied voices within feminism, so there are multiple contexts for the use of power. Is power a thing/property/attribute to be feared/used? Is power inherent in social structures, language, bodies, relationships? Is it the very foundation of social life or, at the least, emergent from those foundations?

Without seeking a univocal solution, we believe that it still matters how we come to engage in discourses of power. If power is not to be viewed as an entity, as so many analyses of a post-Foucauldian nature proclaim, then how do we obtain it? And if it is so diffuse as to be inscribed on our very lives, our bodies, at every turn, then how do we know we have it?

These are questions which seek not answers but possibilities. And while it is difficult not to discuss forms of power in questions of gender, it still matters in the practice of changing social life how we conceive of power. Rather than solutions there are emerging dialogues and an engagement between authors who adhere to one or another version of the notion of power. Hence our not very subtle paraphrase of Foucault's problematic into one of power/gender. For feminists it is not only knowledge that is required for the diffusion and understanding of power – it is the realization of an embodied, gendered life. Power is inscribed in the rituals and practices of gender yet it is both more or less than gender. It is more in so far as these practices can be deliberately refused as well as explored. It is less because gender is not always and only a social practice. In the discussions of power and gender which make up this volume, both terms are thoroughly evaluated and revitalized.

The multifaceted problems raised by power are explored here from multiple angles, positions, practices and disciplines. Yet, none of our authors is unaware of the lived practices to which their analyses must eventually turn. Premature foreclosure on the question of power and gender would be foolhardy just as endless evocation is debilitating. But let the reader decide.

In what follows we would like to frame the text by raising major elements of the discussions in this volume. Given the multidisciplinary nature of the collection, we will begin with the problematic nature of the notion of power and then discuss how our authors bring their views of power to bear on the conceptions, problems, cases and analyses of gender.

The Definition of Power

How then to conceive of a term which has been labelled 'essentially contested' (Lukes, 1974)? Authors in the social sciences often argue a 'best' definition of the term relying on different criteria for evaluating various meanings. This comparative process resists the label 'objective'; rather, the many definitions of power may be seen to reflect varying moral and political assumptions. Much of the concern in the literature on power has been to identify and analyse the implications of conceptualizations of power. What practices flow from these conceptions? How does one oppose unjust power? How does one exercise power if one is marginalized and oppressed? What is the personal/social/political basis of power? What are the limits of power? Theorists of power have recognized the relevance of these definitional matters for questions of human agency and justice within the complexity of social structures which presumably have been created to serve human needs and interests.

It was Foucault who alerted us to the economic or essentialist base of traditional conceptions of power. Power, like an entity, may be ceded from one person to another and may be acquired by virtue of one's position within a social hierarchy or through sheer brute force. Analyses based on this traditional model focus primarily on access to resources and strategies of influence, and frequently an underlying liberal philosophy in such accounts requires that power be one of the essential characteristics of individuals. Exemplars of this traditional view, three of which are illustrated here, can be found throughout the social sciences.

One such view which has commanded considerable influence within psychology is McClelland's notion of the power motive, the goal of which is to feel powerful and to act powerfully. The thrust of McClelland's research is to find out 'what goes on in a person's head when the power motive is present' (1975: 6) and to examine the implications of this internal state for behaviour. The emphasis is intrapersonal and endogenous. The expression of the motive is linked to ego development, enabling McClelland to classify American males (the object of his studies) according to their type of power orientation. Thus, power is construed as an entity that can be categorized/known and delimited to individual motives.

Within sociology, Blau has defined power as the 'ability of persons or groups to impose their will on others despite resistance through deterrence either in the form of withholding regularly supplied rewards or in the form of punishment, inasmuch as the former as well as the latter constitute, in effect, a negative sanction' (1964: 117). The exercise of power is then placed within the context of social exchange theory, and therefore at its most fundamental level involves independent individuals whose actions are motivated by the returns expected from others. Such models of power are classified by Lukes (1974) as 'behavioural'.

Our third example comes from the economist Kenneth Boulding, who defined power in its broadest sense as 'a potential for change' (1989: 15). Superficially this definition appears to undo the narrow economic or behavioural metaphors which dominate the social sciences, yet at the level of the individual Boulding sees power simply as 'the ability to get what one wants' (1989: 15). A threefold classification of power follows and includes the stick (threat power), the carrot (economic power) and the hug (integrative power). These are in turn related to the power to destroy, the power to produce and exchange, and the power to create relationships. Whatever the merits of this assessment (and there are several which we cannot elaborate on here), power itself is associated with individuals and their personal resources.

Power has also been construed as a relational entity that is diverse and active. It is not only the possession of an individual but a process occurring within relationships between individuals. For example, Bachrach and Baratz (1970) describe a power relationship as one which exists when there is a conflict of values or course of action between two people, and one person complies with the other's wishes out of fear of deprivation of the values or things valued. Although this is still relatively individualistic, Bachrach and Baratz (1970) argued that non-decision-making or inaction also constitutes an exercise of power. Lukes, pursuing this line, includes the role of social structures ('collective forces and social arrangements', 1974: 22) in controlling the political agenda and the consequences of this for one's 'real' interests. Moving away from the individualistic, voluntaristic assumptions embedded in most theories of power, he sought to emphasize the role of social structures in creating subjective interests. Power and responsibility are intimately linked for Lukes. He argues that power is exercised only when the individual or group exercising power can be held responsible for the consequences. When no attributions of responsibility can be made, the outcomes are attributed to 'fate'. Although these points of view were early attempts to move away from traditional, positivist-bound economic views of power they retain certain characteristics of that model. In particular, conflicts of interest continue to be seen as essential components of the exercise of power (Hartsock, 1985). The more radical move to alternative conceptions of power would follow the appearance of post-modernism and feminism which hastened the 'death of the subject'.

While the Foucauldian legacy is undergoing something of a re-evaluation in the social sciences, his studies of the regimes of power/knowledge have had a profound impact on the way we have come to view power. Foucault identifies a non-economic form of power which is closely related to epistemic concerns and subjectivity:

> Power must be analysed as something which circulates, or rather as something which only functions in the form of a chain. It is never localised here or there, never in anybody's hands, never appropriated as a commodity or piece of wealth. Power is employed and exercised through a net-like organisation. And not only do individuals circulate through its threads; they are always in the position of simultaneously undergoing and exercising this power. They are not only its inert or consenting target; they are always also the elements of its articulation. In other words, individuals are the vehicles of power, not its points of application. (1980: 98)

The important insight here is that the exercise of such power requires no external surveillance or coercion; rather, because the individual is constituted through power, the exercise of power can occur through a process of self-discipline or self-regulation. Moreover, the exercise of power is implicated in the mechanisms and procedures for producing knowledge, and hence, in knowledge itself. Consequently, all social practices are shaped by power, including, at least according to some authors, the reproduction of traditional gender arrangements.

Feminist authors engaged in rethinking the utility of traditional concepts of power have reacted to Foucault's understanding of power in diverse ways, reflecting their concern with the nature of patriarchal forms of power, their use and abuse, and the need to revise and rethink power so that it serves an emancipatory role in the lives of women. Robin Morgan makes the point succinctly:

> Patriarchal power . . . requires the monopolizing of power, which in turn requires the monodefining of power as a static and singular object, the better to monopolize it. Fluid, multiple powers cannot be employed to such an end because they are not so controllable, because the more powers there exist, the more likely they are to be distributed via many vehicles and channels . . . Recognizing these qualities of power/powers is a political act. (1989: 325)

Analysing power is akin to understanding the deep meaning of patriarchy; feminism has by its very nature grappled with the politics, the practice and the experience of power. Gender is inextricably bound to questions of power and through their conjunction the understanding of both has been deeply transformed, although the evaluation of that transformation remains for feminists a contentious topic (for example Fraser, 1989; Sawicki, 1991). It is our hope that this volume captures a broad cross-section of these transformations.

Gender and Power

The power dynamics inherent in traditional conceptualizations of gender was theorized in the writings of those who noted that 'difference' was often equated with women's subordination or inadequacy (see Davis, 1988; Grosz, 1990, for summaries). Ironically, those most interested in gender have had to rely largely on theories of power which were not specifically developed to account for female–male power relations. Indeed, in some cases, the theorists of power appear to be blind to women's experience (for example, see Grosz's (1990) discussion of the ideas of Althusser, Lacan, Foucault and Derrida). As a consequence, the application of theories of power to research problems focused on gender has been problematic, requiring a cautious and critical approach (for example, the papers in the collection edited by Davis et al., 1991). The meaning of power has undergone considerable analysis by those who wish specifically to include women's experience within its scope. It is these developments that make up the core of this section of the book.

The chapters in the first section of this volume are devoted to the project of theorizing power in a way that can do justice to gender relations. Two of these draw on Foucault, who remained ambivalent about the uniqueness of gendered power relations.

Karlene Faith offers a very detailed analysis of the utility of Foucault's ideas about power for feminists who aim to alter power relations. She uncovers a number of ideas central to Foucault's theorizing about power, focusing particularly on the notion of resistance, and shows how they can be applied to the feminist project. Following such an account, feminists are seen to be engaged in the project of resisting dominant discourse and promoting 'subjugated knowledges'. By calling into question the discourses that privilege men (and these include discourses about the 'nature' of gender), Faith notes that feminists have shifted (and can continue to shift) power imbalances that disadvantage women. Thus, despite his apparent gender blindness, Foucault's account of power can be helpful in theorizing gender relations.

In their chapter Deborah Kerfoot and David Knights turn to Foucault for an analysis of power and the reproduction/ maintenance of gender inequality and men's domination. They explicitly move away from the debate about the underlying reasons for men's domination and its reliance on the traditional, economic model of power. Instead, they wish to establish a non-essentialist account of this domination. Drawing on Foucault, they argue that gender relations are a reflection of gendered subjectivities which in turn are constituted through power relations. The maintenance of gender inequalities does not require continual external coercion but can be achieved through the actions of gendered individuals who 'choose' to act in ways that reproduce male domination. Here, then, an important link is established between the 'nature' of gender and power relations; gender is a product of power relations. None the less, Kerfoot and Knights also see radical possibilities for change in the prevailing system of men's domination through the effects of the local, marginalized 'subjugated knowledges' of women.

Jean Lipman-Blumen seeks to explore what it is in the nature of the human condition that produces power relationships. She takes the relationships between the genders as a paradigm case, that is, gender relations serve as a useful context in which to examine the workings of power, not because of their uniqueness *per se*, but because of 'their marked intransigence to efforts to recalibrate the power relationships they represent' (p. 109). Power is a process that characterizes virtually all social relationships, both between individuals and between larger social units. Power relationships allay our existential anxiety by creating the illusion that things are under control. Thus, we willingly enter into power relationships and indeed need such relationships in order to stave off anxiety. According to Jean Lipman-Blumen, only by directly confronting our existential fears can we alter the importance of power within social relationships.

Others have argued that the social position of women in relation to men is sufficiently unique to require special consideration in any account of power. For example, Hartsock (1985) advocates a standpoint epistemology aimed at generating a theory developed from the point of view of the dominated (that is, a theory of power *for* women). In the introduction to their volume entitled *Gender, Power and Sexuality*, Abbott and Wallace note that 'Sexuality emerges repeatedly as the instrument by which power over women is maintained and exercised because it serves to define them in particular ways' (1991: xii). This includes women's roles in the reproductive process (for example, O'Brien, 1981).

Such 'standpoint' strategies have resulted in the broadening of existing theoretical frameworks. For example, drawing on Lukes, Duffy (1986) notes that through their involvement in organizations such as cultural associations, the Planned Parenthood Association, charity groups, and so on, women too 'have affected the basic parameters of social existence – values, tastes, attitudes, behaviour ... [and] have, in the course of these efforts, significantly altered the life experiences, social perception, and public options of large numbers of individuals' (1986: 38). Similarly, Janeway (1980) identified the 'powers of the weak', as the power to disbelieve, the power to come together as a group to further its own ends, and the power to organize for action. Thus, even the dominated are conceptualized as actors who, despite their disadvantage, have some chance of influencing those 'in control'. Such ways of talking about power highlight its productive nature and expand the definition to include not only coercion and domination but also power as the expression of a capacity to act (see also, French, 1985; Miller, 1986). Indeed, Hartsock (1985), citing examples such as Hannah Arendt, Dorothy Emmet and Hanna Pitkin, notes that women's writing on power tends to emphasize power as capacity, energy and potential. Through this definition of power, women have been recast as active participants in their social world, striving to cope with their subordination in the most effective way possible, rather than as passive victims of their oppression.

Marilyn French's chapter can be situated within the tradition of 'woman-centred' theorizing about power. She questions the naturalness of existing social arrangements and seeks to explain the roots of male domination. She suggests that power became linked to domination and control with the construction of a male identity designed to compensate for the ambiguous and limited role of men in the reproductive process. In her view, this particular definition of power is a dangerous one that threatens our very existence because it is 'unnatural'. She seeks to alter the moral order through a redefinition of power that emphasizes the value of human needs and recognizes domination as negative. As gender is created in response to power relations and in turn influences the way in which power is exercised, changing power relations will also change the 'nature' of gender.

Hilary Lips defines power as 'the capacity to have an impact or produce an effect' (p. 90), a definition which is drawn from the psychological literature and is consistent with a 'woman-centred' approach to power. She is interested primarily in the apparent choices of gendered individuals and how they may be linked to social practices. Her thesis is that girls are 'actually prepared' to behave in powerless ways and to acquiesce to the powerlessness. Through a 'micro-accumulation of broadly supported interaction patterns', they fail to take control of their own lives and to develop confidence in their abilities. Consequently, they make gender-appropriate choices and do not consider non-traditional alternatives. Thus, gender as constructed under existing social arrangements serves to maintain female powerlessness and hence maintains existing gender relations.

Gender, Power and Politics

In his book *Gender and Power*, Bob Connell (1987) argues that gender relations are structured in three different ways: by the division of labour, by power and by emotional attachments. All three structures constrain social practices related to gender. Power is defined in a variety of ways to include force, being relatively advantaged, unequal access to resources and the control of the definitions and understanding of situations. He identifies a core in the power structure of gender (for example, the military, the high-technology industry, the working-class milieu) where legitimate power or authority is unquestionably connected to masculinity and a periphery (including the family) where power is contested. Because gender relations exist in every institution and in many cases constitute a fundamental structure within the institution, 'sexual politics' affect social practices in many different domains. He refers to the 'state of play in gender relations in a given institution' as its 'gender regime' (1987: 120), and the gender regimes contained within various institutions are themselves related within a 'gender order'. It is at the level of the gender order that the 'macro-politics' of gender are played out. This macro-politics is historically dynamic and affects not only institutional and state powers but also the constitution of gender.

Following from this, in his chapter in this volume Bob Connell argues for the importance of theorizing the relationship between gender and the state. On his account, the construction of the state is influenced by gender and gender relations, but while the state regulates gender relations, it also influences the transformation of gender relations. Hence, concerns focused on gender inevitably involve concerns of the state. Both the state and gender relations are conceptualized as dynamic and responsive to the forces of history. Although by virtue of concrete social practices the state historically has been patriarchal, he argues that spaces for change are opened up whenever there are crises within the gender order or contradictions within the state patriarchy.

Jill Vickers too argues that gender arrangements and political arrangements are inextricably intertwined. To maintain their existence as political entities, social groups must reproduce themselves both physically and in terms of their social identity. As Vickers points out, women are at the centre of this reproductive activity, and it is the need to control this process that is at the heart of patriarchal gender arrangements. Her analysis acknowledges the significance of procreation in helping to understand women's power and the differences in the reactions of dominant and minority groups to political conflict. The significance of reproduction does not have fixed meaning, however, but varies with the socio-historical context. Thus, sex/ gender arrangements, as 'technologies of social organization and control', will also vary.

The Social Construction of Gender

All of the chapters in this volume share (sometimes implicitly) the understanding that gender is a social product; how gender is related to the biological organism which achieves that gender is a matter of continuing debate. Regardless of how 'it' connects with the differing reproductive contributions of women and men, it is generally agreed upon that gender reflects a whole variety of consequences, the majority of which bear little obvious connection to reproduction or sexuality. What is more, there is general agreement that gender is constituted within a particular set of power relations and hence reflects those power relations. That which is considered to be female and male reflects the subordinate–dominant relationship of female and male, and when we 'do' our gender appropriately, we act to maintain that relationship. In this sense power is both productive and oppressive, creating and constraining our social practices of gender.

Two of the chapters explicitly deal with the constructed nature of gender and sex and how power is implicated in the constructive process. Celia Kitzinger focuses on sexuality and concludes that sex, both heterosexual and lesbian, embodies heteropatriarchal norms of dominance–submission. In effect, sexual pleasure has been constructed as 'eroticized power differences'. On her account, power is productive. It shapes the social representations of sexuality, prohibits certain sexual activities, and influences sexual practice. Hence, patriarchal social arrangements do not simply promote heterosexuality, they influence the very nature of sexual pleasure, which is manifested as 'eroticized power differences', regardless of the choice of sexual partner. She suggests that only through altering the socio-political context will alternative constructions of sexuality emerge.

Lorraine Weir contrasts Judith Butler's constructionist position, and with it those of other post-modern feminists, to Adrienne Rich's hermeneutics of experience. By making 'gender trouble', however, Butler is seen to rely on an old foundation, the very hermeneutics she has rejected. Weir argues that the 'subversive laugh' of Butler and the call to presence of Rich require each other, are implicated in the other, 'and both are formed through the technology of hermeneutics which, as successfully as ever, winds its prophetic skein around the truths it was designed to capture' (p. 217). The binary opposition between constructionism and essentialism hides a fundamental dependency, one not eradicated through gender parody.

Case Studies of Gender and Power

Recent feminist theory has emphasized the importance of a focus on the experience of women. Captured by the well-known phrase 'the personal is political', in practice this has meant examining the details of women's lives as told by its participants. Through analysing the experiences of 'ordinary' women, feminist scholars have developed theoretical frameworks that are often at odds with those traditionally adopted within their disciplines. Although controversial in its own right, Carol Gilligan's work (1982) on the ethic of care is one example of feminist theorizing that originated in part from a study of women confronted with an ethical dilemma (whether or not to have an abortion) and challenged the dominant thinking of the day as characterized by Kohlberg's views on moral development. Another example that is not specifically related to gender is Dorothy Smith's (1990) book *The Conceptual Practices of Power*. In this work Smith criticizes Foucault's concept of power/knowledge as too abstract, lacking any reference to the specific actions of the specific individuals involved in the social relations underlying the dominant discourses. Instead, consistent with her feminist position, she argues that

> The power of objectified knowledge arises in the distinctive organization it imparts to social relations. Knowing how to read, and reading a given factual text is to enter a coordinated set of relations subordinating individual consciousness to its objectification; subjects subdue their particularized experience to the superordinate virtual reality of the text. The factual text has power at this point of conjuncture between a reader knowing how to read it as factual and the relations of which it is a constituent. (1990: 70)

Thus, such knowledge 'subdues, discounts, and disqualifies our various interests, perspectives, angles, and experience, and what we might have to say speaking from them' (1990: 80). The power in the discourse of 'objectified knowledge' lies in the suppression of the particular 'truths' revealed in our everyday experience. None the less, such texts do not necessarily serve the 'relations of ruling', but may stand in opposition to them. This latter possibility however does not free us from the problem of the masking of individual experience.

In this volume there are four chapters that follow this general approach by examining the connection between power and gender as they are practised in the specific contexts of women's lives. It is such studies that provide tentative answers to questions such as: Where are there spaces that permit resistance? What sorts of changes might be envisioned?

Talking with four female adolescents, Michelle Fine and Pat Macpherson sought to analyse the discourses of adolescence, power and feminism. Their 'body talk' revealed a struggle with gendered power that varied along racial and class lines. Although their female gender meant that the bodies of all four young women were subject to external surveillance and that they were vulnerable to the threat of male violence, what was taken to be normative for the body and the expression of control, management, resistance, and so on, differed depending on culture and class. While resisting the cultural prescriptions for femininity by taking up the discourse of adolescence (which is inherently male), these young women also resisted male domination. In this case, however, feminism was expressed in terms of 'equal access to being men'.

In her case study Wendy Hollway draws on the theoretical work of Foucault and Connell. She analyses the association between structures of power and gender relations in a particular organizational context with special emphasis on the multiple and contradictory nature of gender relations. Although at a formal level the organizational structure promoted gender equality, in practice power relations within the organization reflected the same gender inequities evident in the cultural context at large. Moreover, husbands actively resisted their wives' striving toward gender equality. For their part, the women used whatever sources of power were available to them, at times challenging the existing gender regime and at other times acting in ways that reproduced it. It is when contradictions among the structures of power arise, argues Hollway, that the possibility of changing social practices emerges.

Eliane Silverman examines historical changes in the way power is viewed by the leaders of a national women's organization. In general, the women viewed power in terms of their collective ability to effect improvements in the community, a form of action seen as part of their human responsibility. What changed over time was the growing comfort of the younger generation with the exercise of power, not to facilitate others' actions but in its own right. This case study underscores the creative means by which women have been able to exercise power when other routes to political action are blocked.

Marianne LaFrance and Nancy Henley critically evaluate the thesis that sensitivity to nonverbal cues is related to gender and power. They argue that women's superiority in this domain is a function of their subordinate social position and serves to maintain and reproduce the social order. Power is defined as a quality of social relations rather than as a personal attribute; nonverbal behaviours signal differences in social positioning and hence control. When treated as an individual characteristic, power as an explicit conceptual tool disappears from the analysis. Thus psychological explanations of the gender differences represent partial explanations at best, and inclusion of power in the conceptual framework enhances understanding.

Conclusion

Linking gender and power, whether the primary intent is to understand gender relations or power relations, remains contested territory. Our contributors view 'gender' and 'power' as social practices best studied in the world of human interaction. Moreover, gender and power emerge as ubiquitous aspects of social relationships. Within any given relationship, we are already and always positioned as female and male as well as being positioned within some power relation(s).

Including gender in an analysis of power leads some of these authors to definitions of 'power' that permit us to see the exercise of power where formerly we saw only passive victims of power. Power relations invariably reflect the gender(s) of the persons involved. Through these varied but more complex conceptualizations of power we also come to understand the exercise of power not simply in social practices that constrain and oppress, but also in those that enable and liberate.

Including power in an analysis of gender allows us to see how gender is constructed through the practices of power. 'Female' and 'male' are shaped not only at the micro-level of everyday social interaction but also at the macro-level as social institutions control and regulate the practice of gender. Indeed, one consequence of the analyses contained here is to say that gender relations *are* power relations.

References

Abbott, Pamela and Wallace, Claire (eds) (1991) *Gender, Power and Sexuality.* Houndmills, Basingstoke: Macmillan.

Bachrach, Peter and Baratz, Morton S. (1970) *Power and Poverty: Theory and Practice.* New York: Oxford University Press.

Blau, Peter M. (1964) *Exchange and Power in Social Life.* New York: John Wiley.

Boulding, Kenneth (1989) *Three Faces of Power.* Newbury Park, Ca: Sage.

Connell, R.W. (1987) *Gender and Power.* Stanford, Ca: Stanford University Press.

Davis, K. (1988) *Power Under the Microscope.* Dordrecht: Floris Publications.

Davis, K., Leijenaar, M. and Oldersma, J. (eds) (1991) *The Gender of Power.* Newbury Park, Ca: Sage.

Duffy, Ann (1986) 'Reformulating power for women', *Canadian Review of Sociology and Anthropology*, 23: 22–46.

Foucault, Michel (1980) *Power/Knowledge: Selected Interviews and Writings 1972–1977* (ed. Colin Gordon). New York: Pantheon Books.

Fraser, Nancy (1989) *Unruly Practices: Power, Discourse and Gender in Contemporary Social Theory.* Minneapolis: University of Minnesota Press.

French, Marilyn (1985) *Beyond Power: On Women, Men, and Morals.* New York: Summit Books.

Gilligan, Carol (1982) *In a Different Voice: Psychological Theory and Women's Development.* Cambridge, Mass.: Harvard University Press.

Grosz, Elizabeth (1990) 'Contemporary theories of power and subjectivity', in Sneja Gunew (ed.), *Feminist Knowledge: Critique and Construct.* London: Routledge.

Hartsock, Nancy C.M. (1985) *Money, Sex, and Power: Toward a Feminist Historical Materialism.* Boston, Mass.: Northeastern University Press.

Janeway, Elizabeth (1980) *Powers of the Weak.* New York: Morrow.

Lukes, Steven (1974) *Power: A Radical View*. London: Macmillan.

McClelland, David C. (1975) *Power: The Inner Experience*. New York: Irvington Publishers.

Miller, Jean Baker (1986) *Towards a New Psychology of Women*. Boston, Mass.: Beacon Press.

Morgan, R. (1989) *The Demon Lover: On the Sexuality of Terrorism*. New York: W.W. Norton.

O'Brien, Mary (1981) *The Politics of Reproduction*. Boston, Mass.: Routledge and Kegan Paul.

Sawicki, Jana (1991) *Disciplining Foucault: Feminism, Power and the Body*. New York: Routledge, Chapman and Hall.

Smith, Dorothy E. (1990) *The Conceptual Practices of Power*. Toronto: University of Toronto Press.

2

Power/Sex

Marilyn French

The world we live in frequently feels insane, and most of us find ourselves questioning how its madness arose. But the assumptions that underlie the structure of human society are so ancient and so buried that our way of life appears to be 'natural', as necessary and inevitable as the wind or gravity. Suzanne Langer suggested that the business of philosophy was to make the implicit explicit.[1] This chapter is an attempt to make explicit the assumptions of civilization as it has existed for several thousand years and to offer a hypothesis for the origin of these assumptions. It also analyses how the falseness to reality of the concepts that have formed our value systems have led us to erect a factitious world – which is indeed insane. Central to our value systems is the way we conceive of sex and power (both power-to, ability, and power-over, domination). To trace this, we must return to our earliest emergence as a species.

Biology on the whole favours females. Although more males than females are conceived – about 110 males to 100 females – more die before birth: 105–106 males are born for every 100 females. And more die in the first year of life. At the end of it, the sexes are equal, 100 to 100. And if they are fed and cared for equally, more males than females die in every decade of life. When both sexes receive equal treatment, the ratio of male/female in the population is about 105–106 females to 100 males.[2] *By nature,* men, not women, are 'the weaker sex'. Men's greater vulnerability, not female inferiority, is the natural fact.

In addition, females are given by nature a powerful social role: females conceive, bear children and feed them from their bodies, and have always taken responsibility for maintaining them – that is, maintaining the entire human race. The male contribution to procreation not being obvious, no male role beyond sexual drive seems 'given' by nature. For these reasons, males far more than females have been driven to *create* an identity. However males defined themselves during the first millions of years of human occupation of Earth, within the past ten thousand years they re-defined themselves in a way that contradicted natural fact: men call themselves powerful, indeed dominant. But this definition is flung in the face of nature, not given by it. Male power is self-proclaimed, based in the word; thus it can be realized only symbolically. On this shaky foundation rests what we call civilization.

Generations of male thinkers have asserted that male dominance arises from nature. Some have attempted to prove this by showing male dominance in other animal species, in studies that falsify or slant the facts. Clearer eyes and minds have revealed that while most mammal species live in groups, most animal societies are composed only of females and their young. Lion and elephant mothers expel adolescent males from the community and live exclusively with female adults and their young of both sexes. Males of these species live as solitaries. Among some mammal species, females allow a single male to live in their otherwise all-female communities. Male ethologists often call such groups *harems*, using language to suggest that males control and have authority over females, which they do not. In no animal species but our own does one sex have authority or rights over the other sex. Recent studies also show that when dominance-ranking exists, it is not intersexual – males dominate males, females females. And most mammal females educate the entire species.

Our closest relatives are the chimpanzees – chimpanzee DNA is almost identical to human DNA, differing in only one of 100 elements. Chimp infants cling to a mother's body hair as she moves through the forest foraging for food, and remain with her until maturity – females at thirteen, males at fifteen. A mother nurses her infant, shares food, holds, rocks, and protects it; she shows affection by grooming her baby, teaching it to groom in return. She builds a nest nightly, and sleeps with the infant. Over years, she teaches it what to eat and when, what routes to take through the forest, which plants or insects or conditions are dangerous, how to build a nest, and how to make tools like the twigs female chimps strip and use to gather termites. In teaching the young how to survive in their environment and to share food and affection, *females teach the entire species what they need to survive.* Unlike other mammals, chimpanzees live in sexually integrated societies. Adult males forage for themselves, but sometimes share food with females, cuddle an infant or groom a female. Aside from their vital role in procreation, males are marginal to chimpanzee life. While most chimpanzee communities are harmonious, outsider males sometimes attack them, killing the babies.

Species of humanoids have existed for at least 3.5 million years. All walked upright, had an opposable thumb and a brain a bit larger in proportion to body mass than that of other animals. Some, like the Neanderthals, were very intelligent. Even after *Homo sapiens* emerged in Africa between 150,000 and 250,000 years ago, several humanoid species continued to coexist peacefully. There is no evidence of humanoid creatures using weapons against each other, no groups of slaughtered humanoids, no sign of war until about 10,000 years ago.

At first, humanoids probably lived much like chimps, except that their young could not grasp body hair (which had gradually disappeared) and therefore had to be carried. This deprived women of the use of one hand for foraging; they began to make containers of bark and twigs to carry their babies, eventually adapting these vessels to other purposes. Instead of foraging daily for food, eating as they went like other animals, they gathered while foraging, putting the surplus in a container for the next day. Anthropologists studying some two hundred gathering–hunting societies report that women in these groups work three or three-and-a-half days a week and feed virtually the entire community. (Men work about half that time.) Containers also made migration possible – a clan could take food and water over long distances through unknown territory.

For the first 1.5 million years of their existence, humanoids lived on vegetation; they had meat only if someone trapped a small animal in their hands. We do not know when they first began to use language, but since the ability to speak is learned early in life or not at all, language had to evolve from communication between mothers and their young. Most anthropologists agree that humanoids, like chimps, lived in small, sociable, egalitarian groups bound by blood and affection. The primary bond was between mothers and children, but adult siblings were also close. Like chimp males, hominid males probably voluntarily left the maternal group at puberty, attaching themselves to a female in another group. (Incest is uncommon in the animal world.) Boys had to break their bond to their mothers to form one with a mate; girls did not, remaining with their mothers and sisters throughout their lives.[3] Men lived with women's kin after mating (an arrangement called matrilocality). Not recognizing their role in procreation, men probably treated their sisters' children as their own, as they still do in some simple societies. The bond between mates was emotional, physical, and

practical, not political – and therefore changeable at will. Yet in
the simple matrilineal societies we know about, most unions are
happy.

Societies organized this way are not matriarchal. Matriarchy, as
indicated by its root, *arche*, means *rule by mothers*. There is no
evidence that women ever tried to rule men or claimed authority
over them *as a sex*. Women probably had authority within their
families, as women often do today. But this is personal, earned
authority, not political authority. Societies centred about mothers
are called matricentric. The greatest values in matricentric societies
were bonds of blood and affection, sharing, fruitfulness and
harmonious living-together. Humans saw themselves as part of
nature, one species among many. They probably raised their
children (as the Mbuti and others still do) to cooperate: to outdo
another is considered shameful. Conflict was resolved, as it is still
in simple societies, by diplomacy; if that fails, one antagonist
leaves the group.

Remains of societies like Catal Hüyük in Anatolia (Turkey),
and luxurious Minoan Crete suggest that up to about 10,000 years
ago humans lived in relatively egalitarian groups, in harmony with
each other and the environment. Wall paintings and sculptures
from Catal Hüyük, like those found all over the world, merge
female human with female animal forms, suggesting that people
believed females of all species created life by themselves,
autonomously. Those paintings and burials also suggest women
had higher status than men: women were buried under the main
bed, often with children; men in the corners of houses, never with
children. But women were not buried with pomp or the trappings
of rank. Societies like Catal Hüyük endured *unfortified* for
thousands of years; in none is there any sign that women used
their higher status as producers of life to claim authority or hold
economic prerogatives over men.

Anthropologists who have studied societies that retain some
matricentric ways find them happier and more harmonious than
our own. And matricentric values kept our race alive for 3½
million years – which *Homo sapiens* may not achieve. The vital
difference between matricentric and male-dominated societies lies
in their division of power: in matricentry the sex that takes
most responsibility for group well-being has a major voice in
group decisions. In male-dominated societies, power is reserved
to those who take less responsibility for the well-being of the
group.

In gathering–hunting societies, women provide 80 per cent of
the group's food, do all preparation of food and most care of the

young; in many of these groups, women also build the shelters, fish, hunt and manufacture objects for use or sale. Men are marginal in gathering–hunting societies: they spend less time hunting or fishing than the women do gathering, and are often unsuccessful – no matter how skilled, a hunter returns empty-handed when game is not running. Even in societies in cold regions which depend mainly on meat for survival and in which men do almost all the hunting, men spend most of their time sitting around the settlement making or polishing weapons, gambling, gossiping, tending the children (for example, Gould, 1969; Sharp, 1981).

This division of labour persists in male-dominated societies. If you visit rural India, Greece, Turkey, or many African countries, you see men sitting idle under trees, in tavernas or coffee-houses or soda shops or pubs, while women walk for miles bent under burdens of faggots fetched for fuel, vegetation for fodder or with heavy water jugs on their heads. Women do a day's work in the fields or a factory, and still entirely maintain the household. This is also the case in so-called advanced industrial societies. But in male-dominated societies, women's work does not give them a voice in public decisions.

Something happened to end the matricentric way of life. The catalyzing events seem to have occurred after the recognition of the male role in paternity: drawings in Catal Hüyük suggest the Anatolians of the day recognized the male role in procreation. Other groups may have recognized it earlier or later. Recognition of men's essential role does not seem to have triggered an immediate change in the structure of society. The trigger seems to be the invention of horticulture.

The Creation of Male Solidarity

No animal knows its father nor do fathers know their offspring; but in species that rear their young, mothers and offspring recognize each other. Still, in some species males help to rear the young. In extant gathering–hunting societies, men tend children lovingly. Unaware that they contributed to procreation, men may have felt marginal to human life. Procreation was far more important in the millennia when humans were a tiny host living in the vastness of nature, in which our vulnerability to weather, lack of food or water, predatory animals, and disease was obvious daily. Today our vulnerability is less visible and billions of humans occupy the globe. Once, the very survival of the species depended on producing children, which it seemed women achieved alone.

Since they produced the young, they took all responsibility for their care, as female mammals do. Males contributed food, labour, protection, or opinions as they chose and as females demanded, but the essential contribution of their sex went unrecognized. Children were named for their mothers, and people lived in matrilineal clans.

The discovery of the male role in procreation was an essential prerequisite to revalorizing maleness: men had to realize they were part of the miraculous birth process before they could claim the right to patrilineal descent. Simple societies still see maternity as a huge power given by nature to women. To feel equal to women, men needed an equal power. Learning that they participated in procreation gave them such a power, but in an indirect, unprovable way: as the old saying advises, it is a wise child who knows its father. Men may thus have felt insemination less as power-to, an ability, than as justification for power-over, domination. They probably envied pregnancy, parturition and lactation less than women's ownership of children, which in any case was the only part of mothering they could appropriate. Conceived from the first as a relation of power, fatherhood would be mainly symbolic without some realistic buttress like naming children for their fathers. But women would certainly oppose this: the second prerequisite to a new male identity was male solidarity; the third was willingness to use force to establish patrilineality, a system in which the sex less legitimately entitled to do so claims ownership of children.

Male anthropologists are fond of rooting male solidarity in the hunting group, seeing hunting as an all-male enterprise involving danger and requiring strength and cooperation. But projectiles did not appear until about 1.9 million years ago; before that, hunting was a matter of catch-as-catch-can in one's hands. And when hunting began men and women hunted together in groups. In some societies, group hunting remained the norm. In some, males gradually took it over (perhaps because of their greater upper-body strength), but women still hunt in extant gathering–hunting societies. Indeed in many women take a greater risk than men (who hunt in groups), going out alone with a dog. Hunting societies often have all-male cults dedicated to rituals intended to control the gods that govern the hunt. (Ancient sculptures of females with animals and at least one wall painting suggests that at one time the hunt was believed to be governed by a goddess.[4]) Hunting may have given men a purpose through which they forged social solidarity. But few gathering–hunting peoples had group male initiations, the primary instrument for forging male solidarity. Group male initiations are a characteristic of horticultural society.

About 12,000 years ago women in the Middle East developed horticulture, which in time spread throughout the arable world. Horticulture revolutionized human life: it lead to creation of a food surplus and a rise in population, which in turn led to a decline in game and so in hunting, which may have created shortages. In addition, farming is an isolated occupation, and requires settlement, 'owned' land. These factors may have generated the first group aggressions. Farming alone, men lost a sense of gender role; raids may have occurred, requiring defence.

Men's functions changed and they needed a new self-definition based on their new roles as farmers and soldiers. (For some reason, women, the first farmers and still the primary farmers in some parts of the world, who probably were also involved in defence, did not alter their self-image.) Horticultural rituals and myths suggest that people saw farming as a violation of the body of the mother-earth. Making war violates the age-old maternal sense of life as sacred. Men's new self-definition was as violators. (The gathering–hunting Mbuti believe humans were immortal until they began to hunt, and would be again if they could renounce hunting.) This new identity may have frightened men but they made the best of the hand they were dealt: they exalted it into a religion of power that counteracted the old sense of inferiority and integrated knowledge of paternity.

But creating a new identity not given by nature required solidarity. Solidarity is a political strategy for gaining power against a superior force. Women did not need sexual solidarity: they had as much power as they needed, since they never tried to institutionalize female authority over men. Women as a group have occasionally held great power, most notably in ancient Japan, in the Roman Empire or the great double monasteries of medieval Europe. But *never* in recorded history have women joined together to diminish or degrade men; *never* have they tried to bar men from useful activities or limit their freedoms. A group needs legislated advantage only when it is profoundly steeped in a sense of inferiority and feels equality is not possible. Male-dominance was the first affirmative action programme.

Male solidarity is created by male initiations at puberty. Male puberty rituals are artificial because a boy's maturing into manhood has no clear demarcation. Girls enter adulthood dramatically with the onset of menstruation. The growth of breasts and pubic hair may occur over years, but girls are capable of reproduction once they menstruate. In societies that practise female puberty rituals, a girl is initiated singly when her menses begin, through deprivation and isolation. In some societies, girls' genitals are mutilated at puberty; in some, this is done earlier or before marriage (which usually soon follows puberty).[5]

Puberty in boys is signalled by the ability to have erections and is accompanied by a lowering in voice timbre and the appearance of pubic and (usually) facial hair. But boys cannot reproduce until their sperm become viable. Since this change is imperceptible, the advent of male reproductive capacity is uncertain – like fatherhood. Male puberty rites mark a *symbolic* moment, treating male maturity *as if it were* the physiological event females experience. Celebrating an appearance rather than a reality, they imitate female progress into maturity.

It would be possible to set some standard equivalent to the onset of menstruation – the end of wavering in the voice, say – to initiate a boy. The symbolic nature of the event and the fact that most societies initiate boys of different ages together indicates that the agenda behind male initiation is not merely to mark maturity. Boys are initiated in groups to inculcate sexual solidarity. Male initiations *always* forge male solidarity and the need to dominate women – in simple horticultural and in complex industrial societies (in boy's educational, military, religious and fraternal institutions, clubs, or gangs). It is essential to exclude girls from initiatory institutions: their presence would subvert the entire purpose – to divide the sexes and inculcate boys with the idea that domination is not just essential to manhood but divinely ordained. Male hierarchies imitate the female power to conceive invisibly passed from mother to daughter, by passing a mantle of symbolic power from spiritual father to spiritual son. Male initiations also imitate female parturition: they offer boys a second (brutal) birth through men to teach them that being a man requires transcending feeling, compassion and vulnerability (all associated with females), separating from women and dominating them by standing together against them. Thus, male identity is formed in imitation of a female identity given by nature, and declared *higher* than the female precisely because it is man-made, not natural.

Fatherhood is largely a matter of faith: evidence of genetic heritage – resemblance in appearance or voice – is often undetectable until a child is adult, and sometimes not even then. A man cannot be certain a child is of his body without guarding its mother's body, keeping it under surveillance. To do this, he must own her. But men's upper-body strength did not advantage them in matrilocal societies. Men could not control – guard or abuse – women who lived and worked surrounded by supportive kin. The husband might come from an alien (if related) group, and all children belonged to their mothers' clan and were named for it. To assert male parentage of children as primary required a revolutionary change in the structure of society, required overthrowing the *natural* order in favour of an artificial order.

Thus, the establishment of patriliny required a new mentality: willingness to use force against beings considered more powerful. Some thinkers believe animal husbandry inured men to the use of force: the ways human control the mating of animals can be cruel in the extreme (for example, Fisher, 1979). Myths from a host of cultures describe men seizing women's powers by force. The founding myths of Athens and Rome depict armed male attack on women (the Greek heroes against the Amazons, the Roman rape of the Sabine women). It is likely that women would not voluntarily accept the loss of power patriliny represents. What history records as happening in Africa may have occurred earlier and unrecorded elsewhere in the world: men captured and enslaved women to break their tie to their matrilineages and enlist their children in men's lineages. Many historians believe women were the first slaves: the reason may lie not in greater male strength but in the division of reproductive labour. The effort to establish patriliny, rather than horticulture, may have led to the first aggressive raids.

Patriliny required patrilocality and a further rule – exogamy – to bolster male control. In exogamy, people must marry out of their society. Invariably, it is the women who are married 'out' – sent to live among strangers. The men remain at home and marry imported brides, who come from various groups and may not even share a language. Isolated from each other, treated as subordinates by both the men of the lineage and their mothers-in-law, women in all such societies are deeply oppressed. Male solidarity may be necessary to establish and maintain male dominance, but it is not enough if men marry the women of their own groups. Only patrilineages are exogamous.

The new system took hundreds of years to spread, and never became universal.[6] Women and many men probably opposed it. To control women, a man must sacrifice mutual love, trust, fellowship and intimacy and adopt an unremitting guarded stance of domination. Many men were probably reluctant to sacrifice felicity for something as impalpable as status; and women's long struggle against the new religion earned them their reputation as subversive, deceptive, insane witches. Myths from Babylonia, Greece, the Norse, Aztec, a host of African societies and Bible tales suggest a murderous struggle between adherents of matri-

and patrilineage, mother-right and father-right. These terms are parallel but the forms are not. Mother-right involves responsibility for children and rights over them and to the fruits of the land; men are politically dominant in matrilineages but women retain these rights. Father-right involves ownership of children and women, and lineage rights to own land – political and economic dominance.

Because it reverses and was intended to overthrow the natural order of things, male supremacy always involved extreme cruelty and oppression. The rules devised by patrilineages gave men the right to exploit, pen, mate, sell or kill wives, female slaves and children. When men achieved solidarity, they used it to do to women what women had never done to men: they joined together to diminish and degrade women, bar them from useful activities, limit their freedoms, and deny them rights of ownership. Men gained much by this revolution: no longer marginal beings less necessary than women to the life of the group, they now defined themselves as transcendent, able to impregnate women without suffering pregnancy, parturition, the responsibility of nursing. They had power without responsibility: mothers still did the work of having and raising children, but men determined their fate.

Women retained some freedoms in many patrilineal societies – in some aboriginal patrilineages, for instance, female sexuality is relatively free, women may return male abuse blow for blow, and have a refuge – the *jilimi*, a women's camp. Any woman may enter and reside there, but no man is permitted to enter it. Men must often travel by long, roundabout routes in order not to pass near it. The camp is a haven for single women, widows who choose not to remarry, estranged wives of violent husbands, women visiting from other areas, women who are ill – and their dependent children. Married women come for a day's visit; a woman may live in the camp and occasionally return home to spend time with a man or men (Bell, 1980). In some African societies before European colonization, women and men had dual political and religious hierarchies. Not until patriarchy did women lose all rights. But by creating the first stratification – male supremacy over women – patrilineality and its attendant institutions prepared the ground for patriarchy – the dominance of an elite group over all other groups.

The vanguard of patriarchy was probably a priesthood, men enchanted by the idea of power. Again, this was a long and probably erratic process: the priests posited a split between humans and nature, and cast contempt upon nature as in need of control, the realm of filth, pain, death and women (long associated with it). The priests gradually asserted the supremacy of gods over goddesses, and transformed their deities into 'high' gods, transcendent powers. Apotheosizing transcendence and domination, they legitimated male supremacy. A transcendent power stands above and apart from what it controls; it is an unmoved mover that can affect humans or nature without being affected in return. The only human power that resembles it is insemination, which causes a major event yet has no necessary effect on the inseminator. Like transcendent gods, men could affect a situation without being affected by it: this power, as miraculous as women's, did not like women's tie them to the necessary. Men were closer than women to godhead.

Emulating a god whose attributes were power and control, man could also transcend nature by winning fame and glory, immortality: domination was divine. The first rulers of states were priest-warriors (the root of hicrarchy is *hiero*, 'priest'); they 'proved' their divinity by war. While the first local wars were probably raids for women, cattle, grain or territory, large-scale war was from the first about domination: men avid for resources and fame, reputation as living gods, proof of their invulnerability, expanded their reach to dominate other men. Trying to prove themselves human (and prove women and subordinate men sub-human), they forgot their humanness and dyed rivers red with human blood. To prove the new definition of Man accurate, they introduced new elements into human life: widespread slavery, widespread bloody war, and a new crime – adultery. In Sumeria, one of the first regions to be made a state, a word for freedom was *amargi*, 'back to the mother'.

War fosters an ethic of militarism – rigid control, asceticism, hierarchy and misogyny. Women were soldiers well into historical time (among Germanic peoples and in many African societies), but men seem always to have been the major fighters, perhaps because it is harder to get women to fight: they tend to feel they owe their first allegiance to their children. Without this profound commitment, the human race would long since have died out. Women took almost all the responsibility for children and all or a large responsibility for feeding society. Men were more expendable. However, they were also unwilling to fight. War is cruel and terrifying; people prefer not to risk their lives unless they are immediately threatened or bullied or coerced into fighting. To build a willing corps of soldiers, leaders developed an ideology in which fighting signalled male superiority and in all early states gave male soldiers rewards of women, loot, and land.

When the first states emerged about 6,000 years ago, patriarchy was born. Patriarchy extended the ideology of domination to elevate one clan (later, an elite) over others and create class. Patriarchy, a realization of the male dream of centrality, is a political arrangement designed to create the illusion that some men are gods. Patriarchy was spread as a religion dedicated to domination as *the* male principle.

Men could only dominate women because they could not feel equal to them. Power-over is not equatable with power-to but can annul it. Domination can cancel women's biological advantage by enabling men to live longer and better than women. By appropriating rights over children, fathers could insert themselves between mother and child; by making women and children dependent on men, men can force women to serve them and focus on them. But for an elite to dominate, patriarchists had to legitimate the right of a small group to rule others. The first step in such legitimation is victory in war. When almost everyone believed deities showed favour by answering appeals, victory in battle was seen as a sign of divine approval. Once a war was won, the conquerors built male solidarity by exercising power over the women of conquered groups, and rewarding obedient men with power over women. In places in which some record of state formation exists (like the Andes, the Valley of Anahuac, and Dahomey), the winners appropriated the women of conquered groups to solidify their control of conquered men.[7] The tactic of sexual division was particularly brilliant because the claim of male solidarity disguised the fact that a few men had power over the rest. By nature, patriarchists insisted, all men were equal in that all were superior to women.

All slave societies devise ideologies to convince the enslaved they deserve their subordination. No elite can rule without such justification, which must perpetually be reinforced by propaganda – through religion or secular mass media. Patriarchy is an ideology justifying slavery – it divides Man from Nature and sets Man above Nature by defining nature as a slough of filth and vileness, a realm of meaningless flux to be approached warily and controlled if possible. Nature could be made innocuous only by priestly intervention. And women were part of nature. The central chapters of Leviticus, for instance, conflate rules for eating and sex – the two activities in which the male body intersects with foreign bodies. Some versions of patriarchy held men depraved by nature since they emerge from women's bodies, but allowed that certain men (like Macduff in Shakespeare's *Macbeth*) escape the general curse by having Caesarean delivery, the vaginal canal apparently being more polluted than the womb. But obedience to the god allows men, not women, to transcend the general curse. Women are of another species from men: part of nature, by nature inferior, 'mutilated' men as Aristotle named them, bound to the necessary, men's servants. Once this is established, further subdivision is easy: men of nationalities, races, or religions other than the dominant one can also be declared inferior.

The ideology of male supremacy devised by patriarchists informs every world religion from Hinduism through Buddhism, Judaism, Christianity, and Islam – although at least the last two of these religions started with a different message. It informs Western thought from Hesiod on and appears full-blown in the *Politics*, in which Aristotle locates mechanics and labourers among the necessary conditions of the state and distinguishes them from free males of property who, because they do not work, have the leisure to dedicate themselves to ruling all others. Aristotle tacitly posits two realms of existence, the necessary and the volitional. The former contains slaves, mechanics, labourers, and women; the latter contains free propertied men only. The division implies that women and working men exist *for* the elite – the few free males in society (6 per cent of Aristotle's Athenians) – that the function of the mass of humanity is to provide the elite with the leisure and education to pursue 'higher' things. Aristotle's division has for centuries been accepted as a law of nature by Western societies, all of which granted an elite rights to property and the labour of women and men of other classes and treated the leisure class not as a parasite but the show flower of civilization.[8]

The elite, those who may properly be called citizens, are in some way free of necessity. Now, for Aristotle, this probably meant simply that being male they were free from bondage to bodily processes like menstruation, pregnancy, parturition and lactation; and being propertied, they were freed from bondage to physical labour. The one physical occupation acceptable to the elite is war. Soldiers were defined as men able to transcend, to deny bodily need and fight with courage despite wounds, blood, fear of death. Thus, Aristotle and generations of thinkers who followed him implicitly claim that one class of men is *by nature* created able to achieve freedom from bodily and emotional demands, from necessity, a class haloed with an inherent superiority over other mortals. In time, philosophers postulated male freedom from all external circumstances: Ernst Cassirer in *An Essay on Man* insists that self-knowledge required the denial and destruction of the objective certainty of the outside world and of all externals.

We must try to break the chain connecting us with the outer world in order to enjoy our true freedom . . . All which befalls man from without is null and void. His essence does not depend on external circumstances; it depends exclusively on the value he gives to himself. Riches, rank, social distinction, even health or intellectual gifts – all this becomes indifferent. What matters alone is the tendency, the inner attitude of the soul, and this inner principle cannot be disturbed. (1944: 1, 7)

This position is cruel (consider judging an inhabitant of a Nazi death camp by its tenets) and morally insidious: to live in superb indifference to the external world is to live in narcissistic isolation and madness and to forfeit the world to the power-hungry. It is also false: all humans are bound to necessity, equally subject to pain, sorrow, loss, delusion, illness and death. *Natural* superiority of some men over others does not exist outside value systems. When anthropologist Colin Turnbull – male, white, tall and British-educated – went to live among the Mbuti, he was seen as a child and assigned a mother to teach him how to survive in the jungle, find food and handle his excreta. As kindly as they could, the Mbuti discouraged him from joining them on hunts because his size made him noisy in the jungle and his body smell alerted the animals (Turnbull, 1961, 1983). Only when maleness, whiteness, height and abstract intellect further one's chances of survival is one endowed with those characteristics superior to others. 'Human superiority' can only mean greater natural ability to survive. Value systems inhere not in nature but culture; all superiority is contingent.

Aristotle and his fellows were probably too down-to-earth to deny that elite men have bodies that define and control their minds in that, like other creatures, they require food, sleep, excretion of wastes, sexual release, bodily and mental stimulation. Yet Chaga men must be down-to-earth and they claim that after being initiated as men they no longer need to defecate. In endowing propertied males with superiority, Aristotle was not seeking to discover or communicate truth but to justify a claim to prerogatives by a particular group, to defend its right to privilege. Only 'natural' superiority can morally justify privilege in a particular group of humans, for only inborn capacities do not change. But to claim superiority is automatically to degrade all others, assigning them a subhuman category. To claim natural superiority for a class or caste, one must postulate two human kinds, two different *species* with differing genetic structures and capacities. Limited creatures born into the realm of necessity are locked there forever and, moreover, are contented there, for, as

Aristotle points out, a person with the soul of a slave can tolerate slavery.

But no matter how powerful a master class or how pervasive its propaganda, the claim that humans are of two species is always difficult to substantiate: it is always obvious that some members of any elite are stupid or inept while some commoners are intelligent and competent. Natural gifts and disabilities shine even through culturally produced differences in education and training. They even shine through the manufactured split between men and women, when women are (as they were in Aristotle's Athens) underfed, imprisoned, uneducated, without rights and married off in adolescence to men of thirty who valued them only as servants and means to procreate sons.

Because all claimed superiorities are contingent and shaky, they must be backed by extraordinary measures, both institutional and ideological. To bolster claims of a profound split between elite and working men, Aristotle and others resorted to mystery and posited a 'natural' split among human capacities, a division between mind and body that varies between the sexes and among classes. To claim mind and body are separate is to establish a hierarchy between them. Someone, Derrida perhaps, remarked that all dualities are inequities. I would amend this: all dualities are created to justify and bolster inequity. If mind is superior to and governs body, it is right and proper that those possessed of greater mental power rule over those whose power is limited to the body. Since education and training profoundly influence the development and assertion of mental power, the desiderated proposition – that propertied men are by nature superior to other men and all women – can be transformed into fact.

Stratifications can be multiplied and arranged in a pattern of analogy: Man is essentially different from and superior to animals; all men are essentially different from (less subject to necessity) and superior to women; certain men are essentially different from and superior to other men; mind is essentially different from and superior to body, which is gross matter – primeval mud – requiring direction from intellect. Earth too is gross inert matter which for animation requires control by man; society is a huge slow greedy body, requiring domination by a ruling class for direction and accomplishment.

Western culture and customs subsume women as closer than men to nature, body and the necessary; men, seen as having greater intellectual power and creativity, are entitled to live volitionally. Traditional mainstream Western thought defines man explicitly as primarily a thinking animal and implicitly denies the existence of necessity for free reasonable enlightened men. In *The Wanderer and His Shadow*, Nietzsche pointed out that philosophers scorn 'everyday matters' like 'eating, housing, clothes, and intercourse', adding that 'nearly all the bodily and spiritual infirmities' of individual life derive from this failure to attend to the quotidian. Robert Paul Wolff (1976) demonstrates that Western political philosophers considered the facts of the human condition extraneous to our understanding of man as a political actor.

Philosophy ignores the basic facts of everyday existence – rising, washing, dressing the body, the pleasures of eating and excretion, the agony of starvation. Philosophers ignore the subtle emotional interplay that penetrates human interactions even of the most superficial sort, and pretend that tiredness from labour, the sorrow of loss, or being overwhelmed by the clamorous claim of children upon us, do not exist. Nor do children, wives and mothers exist in philosophy, although hatred of women does. Indeed, philosophy ignores the most profound truths of human existence – birth and death: Wolff writes that philosophers treat death as accidental to life, something that terminates but does not 'infiltrate' it.

Man – and the noun used in philosophy is gender-specific – exists in isolation, dealing with others only by contract, as it were, as an individual, self-made, self-defined and self-referential. The ideal man is *not* dependent, *not* governed by emotion, but is in complete control of his body and his life. In our deep-rooted conceptual life, man lives in volition, a being with control. His life is subject to his will, which philosophy holds is guided by reason – narrowly perceived as the logical operation of an intellect uncontaminated by emotion or the senses – and is concerned only with his own best interest. He seeks his good in isolation and, philosophy suggests, can find it there. He is free because he is not subject to necessity. Thus he incarnates power.

Woman, however, incarnates responsibility. She, not man, is held responsible for sexual behaviour: prostitutes, not the men who rent them, are considered criminals and arrested and imprisoned; when men rape women, it is women, not men, who are responsible because their dress was provocative, they were out alone, out in public, their shades were not drawn. For centuries, men could freely buy condoms but women were either denied birth control devices or forced to request them from a controlling male. Societies have permitted abortion and infanticide only when men controlled them.[9] Women, not men, are held responsible for children and, in the West, blamed for their fates. So we have smothering mothers, schizophrenigenic mothers, mothers who cause autism, male homosexuality, female eating disorders, and all varieties of neurosis and psychosis.

And despite decades of feminist agitation, women are still expected to provide the necessary without pay, pension, or a day off. Women's work is decreed *non-work*: everywhere.[10] Even if they labour outside the home for wages, women are supposed to do the work of the home as well – to cook, launder, clean, market and tend children, to maintain society. Men who follow such occupations are paid for their work and are considered professionals. Occupations involving control and instrumentality are associated with men. (Horticulture, farming done by hand, is women's work. Agriculture, farming with machines, is men's. This division remains constant in societies that practise both types of farming.) This sexual division of power and responsibility remains intransigent to change.

The mind–body duality was devised for political reasons, to legitimate stratification and parasitism. But it has another purpose, which I will call spiritual. A mind–body duality allows men to *transcend* nature as saints by asceticism, as soldiers by toughness, or as superior intellects. Antony drinks the stale of horses; Coriolanus does not feel his wounds. Since sexual desire seems to be men's most powerful tie to the external world, *transcending* sex is the mark of the hero. To prove dedication to a 'higher' good, a Hindu, Christian, or Marxist man must scorn women and sex; the true holy man is also indifferent to bodily comfort and appearance. Contempt for the body is a magical formula for immortality: to defeat nature is to defeat death and achieve what the Greeks sought in fame, Hindus in Nirvana, Christians in heaven, and communists in a utopian world. (Women too adopt this attitude.) Our sacrifice bribes the god to give us invulnerability, im*preg*nability.

Despite the male ability to procreate without responsibility, transcendence is the most unrealistic concept men ever devised. The power to affect things without being affected by them is not a possibility. All one can achieve is the appearance of transcendence, trappings of rank and office that symbolize superhuman power, but that cannot annul the hold of nature on the human body–mind. Nor can we manufacture an artificial environment to substitute for nature without risking its destruction. Transcendence is an illusion. Even masculine projects like psychology and science regularly produce evidence of the interconnection of body and mind, yet scientists and psychologists continue to separate them. Sub-atomic phenomena are not transcendent nor does domination characterize natural processes: all phenomena are interrelated.

Humane thinkers and writers have insisted for centuries that all things are connected, all bells toll for all of us. In the long term, transcendence is not a human possibility.

We have dragged our ancient associations into the modern world. We worship transcendence, an illusion. We worship domination, a political position guaranteed to thrust the dominator into untrusting competitive isolation (that is, unhappiness) or the paranoia that has characterized many world leaders. We divide humans by sex, class, colour, insisting on innate differences that do not exist; we separate body from mind and humans from nature and spend our energy trying to prove that these separations exist. (Part of what Derridean deconstruction reveals is the intricate web of lies philosophers weave to create an appearance of transcendent existence, birth through the male.) We live by lies.

Living on lies drives one mad, yet religious and political leaders continue to insist those lies are truths. The great irony is that even as patriarchy teaches that power is the highest value, it demands fear and obedience. It asserts men are gods but requires them to kneel. And in actuality, few men have the opportunity to command: most live and die at the lower end of hierarchies. But in return for fear and obedience – deference – now called 'fitting in' – all men, even those lowest on the ladder, are granted superiority over women. Women have protested being locked in the necessary and excluded from the public realm ever since a public realm was created. They have protested it in writing at least since Christine de Pisan in the fourteenth century. Since the late eighteenth century and Mary Wollstonecraft, women have protested on grounds of human rights. And they have gained some access to power-seats within some institutions. But their gains come slowly and are impeded at every step by the conscious will and the unconscious fears of men.

Men live in the terror of confronting the fraudulence of their self-definition and hate and fear women as subversive agents who might expose the truth. Men are not in control even of themselves at all times – no one can be. A man may have enormous control over others yet see it vanish in a moment – witness the Shah of Iran, Nixon, Duvalier, Marcos, the collapse of the Soviet bloc and the swift descent of Gorbachev, or the recent downfall of some hugely rich investment brokers. Power is not a substance, something you can hold in your hand like its symbol, the sceptre. Power is a fragile dynamic interaction. The patriarchal system placed some responsibilities upon men, rewarding them by creating legal structures that forced women into economic, physical and political dependency on men –

something they would not have had to do if women were truly inferior by nature. Yet despite all these controls, at no time have men felt in control of women. Men continue to fear and hate women, to discriminate against them economically and politically and to strike out at them physically (French, 1992). The only way men can free themselves of fear and hate and an unhappy relation to others is to admit that they are not in control and in fact do not need to be in control to be men.

The first lie, the assertion that the human species and nature were two separate entities, enabled men to claim to be of a different species (human) from women (nature); the second lie, that the father was the primary parent, was bolstered by the establishment of patrilineality. Those two lies generated others to bolster patriarchy, stratification, the mind–body split, and above all, to deify domination. Our formative texts, many considered sacred, describe the proper human relation to nature as domination, the dominion over fish, flesh and fowl that God grants 'men' in the book of Genesis. Francis Bacon and Karl Marx – to leap through time – made the same assumption: Man must dominate Nature. To build a morality that can foster human well-being we must value human needs – from the most basic to the most exalted. We must re-define *human* and learn that domination is not only not divine, but malign. To build a sane and felicitous world, we must revise our associations with power and sex, reintegrating our experience. We must, simply, stop lying.

Notes

1 'Philosophy . . . is the study of the conceptual framework in which all our propositions, true or false, are made' (Langer, 1953: 3).

2 However, males and females are not fed and cared for equally: as of 1990, there are more males than females in the world according to the 1991 UN publication, *The World's Women: 1970–1990.*

3 There are societies in which men go on living with their mothers throughout life, and only visit their wives in the evenings.

4 For female sculptures, see Marija Gimbutas (1974). See William Irwin Thompson (1981) for a sketch of a North African rock painting showing a man about to shoot an arrow into an animal. A line is drawn to his penis from the vulva of a naked women who stands behind him, hands outstretched as if she were transmitting energy to him.

5 Female genital mutilation may seem exotic to a Western reader, but over 20 million women worldwide are genitally mutilated, most in Africa and Asia. For further information on this subject, see Fran Hosken (1979); Hanny Lightfoot-Klein (1989); and Lilian Passmore Sanderson (1981).

6 Many societies in Africa, Australia, Southeast Asia, the Americas, and elsewhere were matrilineal when Europeans or Muslim Arabs invaded them; many remain matrilineal to this day.

7 For information on the Inca appropriation of the women of conquered groups, see Irene Silverblatt (1987). On Aztec treatment of women, see Marysa Navarro (1988); Ferdinand Anton (1973); Burr Cartwright Brundage (1979); June Nash (1978, 1980); and June Nash and Ruby Rohrlich (1981). For the treatment of women by Dahomey, see Robin Law (1986, 1989) and Edna G. Bay (1983).

8 These and the following ideas also appear in French (1986).

9 In Ancient Assyria, infanticide, especially female infanticide was common, and abortion was permitted if a man commanded it. However, a woman who aborted herself or helped another to abort was punished by being impaled – the most severe punishment, the punishment for treason.

10 Women's work in the household is not counted in the GNP or GDP.

References

Anton, Ferdinand (1973) *Women in Pre-Columbian America.* New York: Abner Schram.

Bay, Edna G. (1983) 'Servitude and worldly success in the palace of Dahomey', in Claire Robertson and Martin Klein (eds), *Women in Slavery in Africa.* Madison, Wis.: University of Wisconsin Press, pp. 240–67.

Bell, Diane (1980) 'Desert politics: choices in the marriage market', in Mona Etienne and Eleanor Leacock (eds), *Women and Colonization.* Brooklyn, NY: J.F. Bergin, pp. 239–69.

Brundage, Burr Cartwright (1979) *The Fifth Sun.* Austin, Tex.: University of Texas Press.

Cassirer, Ernst (1944) *An Essay on Man.* New Haven, Conn.: Yale University Press.

Fisher, Elizabeth (1979) *Women's Creation: Sexual Evolution and the Shaping of Society.* Garden City, NY: Anchor Press/Doubleday.

French, Marilyn (1986) 'Self-respect', *The Humanist.* 46(6): 18–23.

French, Marilyn (1992) *The War Against Women.* New York: Summit Books.

Gimbutas, Marija (1974) *The Gods and Goddesses of Old Europe.* Berkeley, Ca: University of California Press.

Gould, Richard A. (1969) *Yiwara.* New York: Charles Scribner's Sons.

Hosken, Fran (1979) *The Hosken Report: Genital and Sexual Mutilation of Females.* Lexington, Mass.: Women's International Network News.

Langer, Suzanne (1953) *Feeling and Form.* New York: Charles Scribner's Sons.

Law, Robin (1986) 'Dahomey and the slave trader: reflections on the historiography of the rise of Dahomey', *Journal of African History*, 27: 237–67.

Law, Robin (1989) 'Slave-raiders and middlemen, monopolists and free-traders: the supply of slaves for the Atlantic trade in Dahomey c. 1715–1850', *Journal of African History*, 30: 45–68.

Lightfoot-Klein, Hanny (1989) *Prisoners of Ritual: An Odyssey into Female Genital Circumcision in Africa.* New York: Harrington Park Press.

Nash, June (1978) 'The Aztecs and the ideology of male dominance', *Signs*, 4(2): 349–62.

Nash, June (1980) 'Aztec women: the transition from status to class in empire and colony', in Mona Etienne and Eleanor Leacock (eds), *Women and Colonization*. Brooklyn, NY: J.F. Bergin, pp. 134–48.

Nash, June and Rohrlich, Ruby (1981) 'Patriarchal puzzle: state formation in Mesopotamia and Mesoamerica', *Heresies*, 13(4): 60–5.

Navarro, Marysa (1988) 'Women in pre-Columbian and colonial Latin America', in *Restoring Women to History*. Bloomington, Ind.: Organization of American Historians.

Sanderson, Lilian Passmore (1981) *Against the Mutilation of Women*. London: Ithaca Press.

Sharp, Henry S. (1981) 'The null case: the Chipewyan', in Frances Dahlberg (ed.), *Woman the Gatherer*. New Haven, Conn.: Yale University Press.

Silverblatt, Irene (1987) *Moon, Sun, and Witches: Gender Ideologies and Class in Inca and Colonial Peru*. Princeton, NJ: Princeton University Press.

Thompson, William Irwin (1981) *The Time Falling Bodies Take to Light*. New York: St Martin's Press.

Turnbull, Colin (1961) *The Forest People*. New York: Simon and Schuster.

Turnbull, Colin (1983) *The Human Cycle*. New York: Simon and Schuster.

Wolff, Robert Paul (1976) 'There's nobody here but us persons', in Carol C. Gould and Max W. Wartofsky (eds), *Women and Philosophy*. New York: G.P. Putnam's Sons, pp. 128–44.

3

Resistance: Lessons from Foucault and Feminism

Karlene Faith

Since the mid-1960s, thousands of writers and scholars, generally but not always female, have brought competing or complementary perspectives to analyses of gender construction. Within this burgeoning body of work one finds an impulse toward locating and building on convergences between feminist thought and other critical approaches. Michel Foucault (1926–1984) is prominent among twentieth-century Western male scholars whose analyses, despite androcentricities, are complementary to or evocative of feminist perspectives.[1]

Evolving out of the French structuralist tradition (though defying its methods), Foucault (1984: 56) examines the dynamics through which power relations are engendered. He fails, however, to identify the centrality of gender in the power relations he analyses. Nevertheless, feminist scholars, who have found links between their own insights and perceptions and Foucauldian thought, have entered into critical dialogue with the tone of having located a useful ally as well as a sparring partner (see, for example, Butler, 1987, 1990; Cocks, 1989; Diamond and Quinby, 1988a; Eisenstein, 1988; Fraser, 1989; Fuss, 1989, 1991; Morris and Patton, 1979; Sawicki, 1988; Smart, 1989). In acknowledging male/female power differentials, Foucault says that 'Men think that women can only experience pleasure in recognizing men as masters' (1988b: 300). He also tells us that 'Where there is power there is resistance' (1980b: 95).

Before his death in 1984, Foucault was taking an interest in feminism and women as subjects, but his published work is conventionally androcentric, with only fleeting or incidental references to women. His work reflects male dominance but without presuming male superiority. He engulfs the reader in a patriarchal voice critically and instructively reflecting on its own uses of power, the very forms of power to which feminism, among many progressive movements, offers resistance. He nevertheless presents illuminating accounts of how power creates itself, and the political uses that can be made of it.

As Diamond and Quinby point out, Foucault 'proposes that ethics should be grounded in resistance to whatever form totalitarian power might take, whether it stem from religion, science, or political oppression' (Diamond and Quinby, 1988a: xiii; see Foucault, 1988b: 225–67). He examines, as a scholar, how dominant discourses, through which power and knowledge are inextricably connected, are dispersed through the social and individual body. At the same time, as an ethicist, he understands power/knowledge to be a political dynamic and, therefore, specific transformations are both desirable and possible. Diamond and Quinby observe that, 'Foucault's analytics of power reminds us that we are not totally encapsulated by the prevailing discourse' (1988b: 201; also see Foucault, 1988b: 123).

Beginning in the 1960s with the anti-psychiatry movement, Foucault served as a perhaps inadvertent inspiration for various political activist groups. With his colleague Deleuze, he came to liken his published work to 'little tool boxes', which readers could use as they wished to draw on ideas which could short-circuit, discredit and otherwise challenge systems of power (Eribon, 1991: 124–5, 237). It is in this spirit that I look at Foucault's work, to consider processes of feminist resistances as a forging of ethical and political challenges. I am interested in links between resistance and power as mapped out by Foucault and as lived by feminists.[2] For this purpose I focus on the concepts of marginalization, individuality and collectivity, exclusion, power relations, the state and rights discourse, the idea of truth and finally the female body as a strategic site of power and resistance.

From the Margins

Feminism, as I know it, is resistance to invisibility and silencing. It is the recognition that resistance to gendered power relations is both integral to and distinct from all other resistances to global injustice. Feminism is a willingness to reckon with gender disparities as a universal but 'unnatural' power reality, a structural process affecting both male and female, which can be deconstructed through consciousness-raising and social change. Feminist resistance is articulated through women's movements and through individual actions, including refusals and separations.

Foucault insists that one is never outside power, that power is 'always already there', and that there are no 'margins in which those in rupture with the system may gambol' (Foucault in Morris and Patton, 1979: 55). He is not suggesting that we are in all times and places totally trapped by an omniscient binary power structure, the one side dominating, the other dominated. Rather, power relations take multiple forms. We are all subject to normalizing judgements which are associated with particular forms of power/knowledge, and we do not stand apart from those issuing judgement. Both acquiescence and resistance are inherent to, not outside of, power relations.

In the amorphous realm of identity politics, including certain forms of feminism, resistances are indeed formed from margins, from points of view that are disqualified by dominant discourses. Diana Fuss, in discussing gay and lesbian identity, warns against romanticizing marginalization: 'To endorse a position of perpetual or even strategic outsiderhood (a position of powerlessness, speechlessness, homelessness . . .) hardly seems like a viable political program' (1991: 5). However, it is often from real or perceived margins that one finds a metaphorical home, one's own voice, a sense of individual and collective empowerment which, at the same time, produces resistance to marginalization itself. Contemporary feminist methods of resistance include an assertive revision of 'his'-stories and rejection of the androcentric, white supremacist hierarchies and interpretations they spawned. The margins which signify disqualification from dominant discourses are also locations from which transformative points of view and social action coalitions can be generated.

Locating Resistance

Bartkowski observes that 'We have long listened to power explaining and justifying itself in economic, biological, and sociological terms; what has been spoken in recent years is the history of the resistance that confronts power everywhere' (Bartkowski, 1988: 46). Disciplinary forms of power, in Foucault's conception, permeate the body politic and the literal body of the individual, which is inscribed with the imperatives attached to it by the knowledge regimes in which it is submerged and through which it is subordinated. This is not a one-way trajectory of power, however. Those who resist are likewise 'inscribing ourselves in culture, making ourselves historical' (Adams, 1991: 22). Wherever power is infused across the range of disciplinary sites, there it simultaneously intersects with the force of resistance, even at the most microscopic, cellular and capillary levels of existence.

Resistance cannot simply defeat, overturn or suddenly transform disciplinary power. Such powers circulate independently of particular authorities who institutionalize and claim them for themselves (and who, theoretically, as mere carriers, can themselves be turned around). Resistance can, however, resituate the problematic of power abuse. That is, resistance weakens processes of victimization, and generates personal and political empowerment through the acts of naming violations and refusing to collaborate with oppressors. Feminist resistance, in particular, begins with the body's refusal to be subordinated, an instinctual withdrawal from the patriarchal forces to which it is often violently subjected. Resistance is formed on the most visceral, personal level, and the compelling 'No!' which it incites is a political act.

This act of resisting incursions into the body may be conscious, thoughtful, deliberate and/or ideologically situated, or it may be a primitive act of survival. Whether or not a response of counter-force to power abuse is planned and intentional, it is within this realm of the body that the personal becomes political and the individual becomes the collectivity. The female body, as a central, socially invested site of male domination, renders virtually all women vulnerable to the fear if not the actuality of violation. It is especially within the realm of sex, the most private intimacy, that power is made most public and resistance is most socially engaged. 'In establishing the self/body/politics/violence nexus, feminism has set an agenda for the sociology of the body' (Frank, 1989: 132).

Resistance may take the explicit form of a counter-force doing political battle, a strategic play of forces: this is what is generally meant by resistance throughout this chapter. Whether on the legal and political-negotiation levels of seeking or defending group rights, or on the individual level of physically defending one's self against constraint or violence, aggressive resistance may be necessary. Resistance may also be a choreographed demonstration of cooperation. The 'willing victim' may be operating from the vantage of strategic resistance, watching for openings and coalescing the fragmentary forms of resistance which, in combination, articulate a potential challenge to the status quo. The subject may know the experience of being in charge even as she is liable to the disciplines which claim her subjection. Foucault likens this process to the martial art of judo, proposing that sometimes 'the best answer to an adversary maneuver is not to retreat, but to go along with it, turning it to one's own advantage, as a resting point for the next phase' (Baudrillard, 1987: 65).

Individuality and Collectivity

During the early 1970s, 'counterculture' and 'politico' feminists debated whether (a) social change occurs because individuals change their consciousness and therefore their lives, or whether (b) individual consciousness is altered as a result of strategic structural change. The first position privileged the subjective, intuitive and spiritual elements of women's experience; the second, following Marx's class analysis, adhered to the materialist position that held the conditions of one's life responsible for one's relations within and understanding of the world. In Marx's own words 'It is not the consciousness of men that determines their social existence, but, on the contrary, their social existence determines their consciousness' (Tucker, 1972: 4). Each position dichotomizes reality – ideational/material, subjective/objective, spiritual/secular – so as to privilege one form of reality over the other.

Foucault joined the French Communist Party in his young adult years, and interpreted the events in France of May 1968 as a time of intensified class conflict. By the late 1970s, however, he had become a self-declared non-Marxist (Dews, 1986: 102; Merquior, 1985: 157–9). Although holding Marx to be an exalted 'founder of discursivity', Foucault declared in 1983 'I have never been a Marxist', to emphasize his refusal to be identified with dogma (1984: 114; 1988b: 22).

Marxist principles are not, however, abandoned by Foucault. Rather, he critically resituates class struggle within a broader view of power relations. Foucault certainly recognizes that capitalism exploits working people, and creates oppressed under-classes; however, his work gives focus to forms and patterns of domination that cannot be readily explained by labour theory. With feminists, civil rights and aboriginal activists, anti-racism movements, religious freedom movements, political prisoners, environmentalists, lesbian and gay rights movements, and so on, he demonstrates that the emancipation of the working class is a key facet of human liberation struggles but it does not encompass all others. Further, even Marx, as Foucault observed in 1982, 'would be horrified by Stalinism and Leninism' (R. Martin, 1988: 10), which altogether subordinated individual and minority group rights to the powers claimed by the state. Marx himself conveyed concern for the individual within the collectivity, as in his work with Engels on alienation (Marx and Engels, 1985[1846]: 82–6), but it was still 'Man's' status as a worker that defined 'His' human identity.

Foucault takes a broader view of social structures and institutions, examining how they shape the individual (the Self), and how these institutions have themselves been constituted by discourses of power (Poster, 1984). He suggests that neither the subjective nor the objective circumstance can produce or determine the other in the absence of their mutual unfolding, whether toward totalitarianism or freedom. There is no individual or collective identity prior to history; yet, history does not determine our identity, but rather charts it (see Foucault, 1973). Identity, then, is both socially constructed and the consequence of individual and collective choices within the parameters of regulated freedoms. Yet, in the world Foucault constructs, 'subjects become obliterated or, rather, recreated as passive objects, a world in which passivity or refusal represent the only possible choices' (Hartsock, 1990: 167).

In Deleuze's reading of Foucault, 'The struggle for modern subjectivity passes through a resistance to the two present forms of subjection, the one consisting of individualizing ourselves on the basis of constraints of power, the other of attracting each individual to a known and recognized identity, fixed once and for all' (Deleuze, 1988: 105–6). Deleuze does not have women in mind. Rather, he is discussing the subject as male, as the historically specific (elite-class European-heritage) male for whom power and knowledge are individualized and constantly recreated, but for whom subjectivity is obfuscated. As Foucault puts it, 'We have to promote new forms of subjectivity through the refusal of this kind of individuality which has been imposed on us for several centuries' (Foucault, 1982: 216).

Woman, conversely, from a feminist perspective, has been seen by male knowledges to be constituted by nature as an essentially subjective species, appropriate to the processes of subjection and subjectivity, but without the individual voice of an active human subject. In this deterministic paradigm, women must struggle to locate themselves in the world as individuals, and men must struggle to create, locate or re-member the feelings and perceptions which link them to the collectivity. Women may strive to distinguish themselves apart from the collectivity of women, but there is no escape from masculinist epistemologies without transforming them. For example, when in 1929 the British Privy Council overturned the Canadian Supreme Court's ruling that women were not 'persons', it was a victory in the symbolic sense that women could now, theoretically, be appointed to the Canadian Senate. But it did not represent the beginnings of significant structural change.

The early second-wave feminist slogan 'sisterhood is powerful' is affirmation, revelation, inspiration, consolation and a way of resisting the feminine. With this assertive recognition of female group strength, the collectivity is informed of itself, reassured of its own value and empowered to name itself and to act on that identity. The individual feminist who searches for identity in the man's world, as distinct from identifying with women, remains unprotected. To assimilate as 'one of the boys' is to resist exclusion from systems of domination but it is also to enter the practice of domination itself, which is the antithesis of resistance.

If political resistance against oppression by class, racial designation, sex/gender, nationality, ethnicity, physical ability, age, language and so on is one's *raison d'être*, one is less likely to be compelled to separate one's Self from one's own group(s). Rather, the issues are how to achieve solidarity, how to minimize difference in the process of cohering fragmented resistances, and how to challenge the status quo towards systemic change while, at the same time, recovering or sustaining cultural particularity and specificity.

Their emphasis on difference ensures radical women's position at the margins, but margins of their own making, both as re-action and re-creation. Deleuze suggests that social change, such as shifts in capitalism, 'find an unexpected "encounter" in the slow emergence of a new Self as a centre of resistance' (Deleuze, 1988: 115). Radical feminist movements make his point, but not in the individualizing way he intends.

Words such as 'radical', 'feminist', 'movement', 'sisterhood' and even 'women', in this context, connote an activist, political commitment to challenging patriarchal political relations, despite the differences which preclude unity. The essence of each of those words is resistance to individualized, hierarchial arrangements of judgement and decision-making power. Certainly many self-defined feminists are participating in those arrangements to their individual advantage; however, traditional femininity is not geared toward the individuation valued by the public male-dominant worlds of competitive, capitalist societies. Rather, the purported reason for being female, across cultures, has been to give and, if necessary, to sacrifice one's self to the needs of those reliant on one's care and labour, namely men, children, sick people and the aged. Among feminists are many women who explicitly resist, who refuse to wear His Name as their own, whose individuation is both a political act and a statement of selfhood: 'The subject becomes an active agent, a point of intelligibility, a self that constitutes itself in relation to history' (Poster, 1989: 61).

Marx reveals the material production of exploitation, alienation and revolt. Foucault recognizes, with the anarchist-metaphysicians, that 'There is always something in the social body, in classes, in groups, in individuals themselves, which in a certain way escapes relations of power' (quoted in Dews, 1986: 100). In a Western capitalist context, one cannot simply transcend the material reality in which one is situated. Yet subjectivity accounts for resistance beyond that which is articulated, observable or politicized. It is a more primal and revolutionary resistance, and it cannot be contained by or narrowly attributed to struggles of ascribed class, race, gender or any other discriminatory category. This force is not androgynous because it does not explain itself in terms of, or attempt to resolve, dualistic divisions. Such a force can be accountable only to itself, springing from the individual or the group but not necessarily under the command or call of its carrier, its conduit. Differences and exclusion may call forth such resistance, and Foucault argues that 'Difference can only be liberated through the intervention of an acategorical thought' (Foucault, 1977: 186). The uncategorizable is the inexplicable rebellion which cannot be normalized, routinized, classified, controlled or disciplined. It is the pre-dogma generating spirit of political movements.

Defying Exclusions

Foucault's work illustrates that when a group of people are separated from society it is not a random affair. They are discerningly divided off from the population, through discursive and exclusionary exercises of sovereign power, and subjected to disciplinary techniques which classify and control them through strategic power relations. Or, to rephrase from a feminist perspective, Western and most other women were (ideally) kept at bay in the private sphere, subject to patriarchal discourses and practices, and socialized into and restricted by class, race and gender classifications asserted through both formal and informal social control techniques and mechanisms. Any exception to or interference with that formula has signified resistances at work.

Empathy shown by feminist scholars toward Foucault's method of analysis may be in part attributed to his lived betrayal of masculine gender prescriptions. As an openly gay man whose intellect and political sensibility nevertheless defy marginalization, he finds the 'homosexual' to be 'an inadequate category' (1988b: 292), and much of his later work focuses on how, through the complex construction of Self, man is constituted as a sexual being.

In considering male/female differences, Foucault remarks admiringly on the congenial physical ease shared by women in the settings of female friendship (1989: 208), as cultivated in gender segregated societies (1988b: 299; 1989: 205, 227). In his brief diagnosis of modern exclusions and sexual normalization of women, he focuses on medical discourse (1986; 1988b: 10–11, 286–303):

> [Psychiatrists] tried to pin women to their sex. For centuries they were told: 'You are nothing but your sex.' And this sex, doctors added, is fragile, almost always sick and always inducing illness. 'You are man's sickness.' And toward the 18th century this ancient movement ran wild, ending in a pathologization of woman: the female body became a medical object *par excellence*. But the feminist movements responded defiantly. (1988b: 115)

A conversation entitled 'The Confession of the Flesh' (recorded in 1977 prior to the onslaught of AIDS, from which he died in 1984), gives focus to Foucault's respect for and understanding of the positive ethics of women's liberation movements. He discusses how apparatuses of sexuality have served as instruments of subjection, and says of women's movements that their 'real strength' is having 'departed from the discourse conducted within the apparatuses of sexuality' (1980a: 219–20). He goes on, in comparing the political movements of American (male) homosexuals and feminist women, inclusive of lesbians:

> Like women, [the homosexuals] begin to look for new forms of community, co-existence, pleasure. But, in contrast with the position of women, the fixing of homosexuals to their sexual specificity is much stronger, they reduce everything to the order of sex. The women don't. . . . [T]he homosexual liberation movements remain very much caught at the level of demands for the right to their sexuality, the dimension of the sexological. . . . Women on the other hand are able to have much wider economic, political and other kinds of objectives than homosexuals. (1980a: 220)

Foucault does not reckon here with the negative, inhibiting effects of patriarchal impositions on female sexuality, but his history of male sexuality clearly describes the paradigm of father-right. The ancient Athenian bourgeois male who indulges sexual proclivities with boys also maintains his authority as head of the wife-children-servants household. He is not betraying his loyalty to the patriarchal ideal (as would be true of the contemporary gay man who lacks such a household) but rather is fulfilling it, and is therefore not excluded from the dominant discourses.

In Foucault's discussion, the Greek (male) citizen was more concerned with food and his dietary health than with sex

(Foucault, 1988a). Modern Western societies, by contrast, have been excessively concerned with normalizing and restricting sex. The Victorians silenced women, and put screens around both 'normal' and 'deviant' sex, while moralists and psy-professionals thought, talked and wrote about sex incessantly, as a sin, sickness and danger, a public secret. Women attempted to accommodate their voicelessness to the dark confessional. Ricci, in discussing women as 'forced to the margins of discourse' is concerned that a

> thoroughly Foucauldian analysis [of women and power] would have to proceed at the level of the 'micro-techniques of power' through which woman has not only been silenced, but *constituted* as object of power and knowledge, much as delinquents, the insane and the sexually perverse have become 'species' which power has used for its own ends. ... A Foucauldian history of women, then, would begin at the point where 'woman' is revealed to be a social construction. (Ricci, 1987: 14–15)

Clearly sex affects everything, and clearly it is objectively unrelated to many aspects of life which it deeply affects. The question of whether a woman has the skill and competence to perform a traditionally male activity in the workplace, for example, is not about sex, except in so far as someone wants to invest that question with sexual meaning as a political strategy (for example, to prevent women from competing with men occupationally). For a woman to betray her social assignment is resistance to a gendered distribution of labour and income, and resistance to gender itself.

Power Relations

Foucault emphasizes the 'relational character' of power, whose 'existence depends on a multiplicity of points of resistance' (Foucault, 1980b: 95). He rejects any notion of top-down, totalizing, unobstructed power, and he mediates the importance given by Marxist or Gramscian theorists to the functions of (false) consciousness, or ideological hegemony, to explain submission to sovereign power. Strategic power relations, in his view, are constituted through disciplinary techniques, and resistance is a key feature of these relations. From Foucault's perspective, instead of examining power as the key to understanding and dismantling subordinations, we might better examine resistance and struggle (Smart, 1985: 135). Like power, resistance is not a homogeneous, fixed phenomenon: it is pluralized, 'diverse in form, heterogeneous, mobile and transitory' (Cousins and Hussain, 1984: 242). Power relations, thus, are not inevitable, unchanging, unalterable.

Many women came to North American feminism in the 1960s from leftist and civil rights movements with slogans such as 'Power to the People' and 'Black Power', objectifying power as something obtainable through adversarial politics – something that could be possessed, something concrete to be claimed and exercised, something over which one must struggle, something which a coterie of 'white capitalist-imperialist male pigs' was trying to monopolize. We the People would overcome, and a clenched fist was a common symbol of that determination. As Foucault characterized, women's liberation and parallel social movements,

> Such struggles are actually involved in the revolutionary movements to the degree that they are radical, uncompromising and nonreformist, and refuse any attempt at arriving at a new disposition of the same power with, at best, a change of masters. (Foucault, 1977: 216)

With the advent of a new stage of feminism in the 1960s, it was seen that all those revolutions in the past had not altered male/ female power relations, and had reinforced hierarchical structures which ensure the subordination of human groups. Feminist resistances, which begin with the body and a woman's right to choose how it is or is not to be used, extend through the social field of the body's existence, through all of Life as it has been imbued with patriarchal powers. Familial, social and intimate relationships, public and private agencies and institutions, the economy, government, media, education, science/medicine, churches, literature, music and the visual arts, the ecosystem: in its myriad forms, the feminist project resists patriarchal presumptions within every niche and at every level of contemporary Western society. The holistic gaze of the feminist eye produces its potentiality for transformative power.

Although explicit feminist identity represents a minority of women, broad-based liberal reforms that result from specific resistances provide openings for a more radical feminist critique. In turn, society's most conservative voices are raised in defence of traditional social divisions and values, with the predictable effect of deepening the levels of resistance, and exposing the political connections between oppressive divisions. Anachronistic power relations perpetuate categorical subordinations based on the fictions of race, sex and so on. The dissolution of these epistemological categories is implicit to post-modern feminist agendas, and this can occur only through challenge to the specific hierarchical material realities which the categories represent.

Foucault does not examine specific resistances; rather, again and again, he stresses in passing the importance of resistance as a conjunct of power. In discussing Foucault's view of resistance, Dreyfus and Rabinow summarize as follows:

> Foucault holds that power needs resistance as one of its fundamental conditions of operation. It is through the articulation of points of resistance that power spreads through the social field. But it is also, of course, through resistance that power is disrupted. Resistance is both an element of the functioning of power and a source of its perpetual disorder. (1982: 147)

Feminist resistance challenges prevailing discourses and de-legitimizes presumptions of female inferiority in local and specific ways. As resistance, feminism is the power of women disrupting patriarchal truths – which may both loosen some holds and invite re-entrenchment of others. Feminist disruptions produce backlash effects which, in turn, compel new strategies of resistance.

Foucault suggests that an analysis of power relations is served by investigating

> the forms of resistance against different forms of power . . . so as to bring to light power relations, locate their position, find out their point of application and the methods used. Rather than analyzing power from the point of view of its internal rationality, it consists of analyzing power relations through the antagonism of strategies, . . . forms of resistance and attempts made to dissociate these relations. (Foucault, 1982: 211)

Feminism is both a spontaneous reaction against and a strategic resistance to existing power relations. The project is not to overturn one system of dominance for another, but rather to deconstruct power relations by transforming or reconstructing social values and institutions. The feminist movement serves to refract and highlight significant features of power relations, and to expose how hierarchies, built on divisions created according to discursive categories of difference, have destructive effects on the dominant as well as on the subordinated.

Foucault has aligned himself with political struggles such as prisoners' rights, but his refusal to carry ideological banners is at the heart of his analysis, and is akin to the critical/post-modern feminist impulse against totalizing doctrines or explanations. The binary opposition model which necessitates a belief in a singular Enemy – the family, the state, parents, capitalists, white people, straight people, the devil or whomever – does not square with Foucault's recognition of networks of interlinked power relations.

Among early radical feminists, in the mid-1960s and into the 1970s, virtually all grown men were seen as the enemy, as identifiable perpetrators of sexism. In the 1990s, feminists would generally recognize that women as well as men can be carriers for patriarchal values and customs, and that the enemy cannot be reduced to a single totalizing entity or system, much less overthrown with one revolutionary turn of events. However, persistent feminist resistances speak of optimism fuelled by visions of a world transformed, which problematizes the post-modern rejection of progress. As Sawicki similarly observes of Foucault, he 'holds onto his hope without anticipating the emergence of a better time, basing [hope] instead on the many sites of resistance to forms of domination in the social body' (1987: 171). The pragmatic, historical reality of shifts in discursive power relations, and the clear absence of permanent political structures, give reason to hope.

Radical feminists seek not to rearrange the hierarchy, but rather to dismantle the structural and discursive girdings upon which hierarchies stand. They seek to stop the violences which subordination invites, and to rectify economic imbalances which create and reinforce female dependency. To the extent that women have only resisted their exclusion from dominant discourses, they have served to reinforce the legitimacy of those discourses. As a political act, and consistent with Foucault's perspective (1982: 211), feminist movements resist both the power of discourses which define top-down (elite-male) truths, and the relational systems of privilege awarded to and by those who possess these truths and the powers which they signify.

Foucault tells us that 'At every moment the relationship of power may become a confrontation between two adversaries' (Foucault, 1982: 226). However, in his historical analyses Foucault does not position his understanding of adversarial confrontation within defined political terrain, nor does he offer a strategic blueprint (Weeks, 1989: 49). As Ray complains, 'while Foucault correctly says that sites of power become sites of resistance, he leaves out of the picture the sociological dynamics of struggle' (1988: 98). Fraser says of Foucault that he lacks the 'critical resources necessary to sustain a viable political vision' (1989: 64). Rajchman observes that 'his contributions to the politics of prisoners, mental patients, or homosexuals would seem to require *some* conception of a *political* freedom' (1985: 45). And, in Hunt's view, Foucault analyses power relations according to dominant strategies, but he looks to 'strategy without strategists: strategies emerge as outcomes of combinations of agencies, with unintended consequences' (Hunt, 1991).

One might indeed expect Foucault to speak more directly to political strategy, given his focus on power relations and his association with the struggles of silenced groups (Eribon, 1991; Simons, 1991). However, one recognizes with Foucault how every moment of resistance devises its own strategy, according to local and specific conditions and resources but with global linkages. Whereas some resistances effectively cause certain positive shifts in particular power relations, others are benign or counter-productive. As Foucault surmises, 'There is no universal (or continuous) history, there is no completely free society, and there is no destiny of a people' (Rajchman, 1985: 62). There are, however, particular strategies that extend from shared, generalizable identities, across borders and boundaries, and create international alliances among workers, peoples of African or Jewish heritage, aboriginal peoples and so on. Feminists might argue that, like other groups, women are globally destined to liberation not due to teleological inevitability but due to their own blood, sweat and tears, as a visceral, human imperative.

The State

Speaking of Western resistances, Minson asks whether 'the movements of women, blacks, prisoners, anti-psychiatry and so on are necessarily furthered by their being as easily subsumed as they currently are within party-political programmes' (1986: 145). This is a dilemma for feminism. To the extent that resistance can be absorbed by the liberal state, and its multifarious agencies, ministries, parties and so on, the demands for structural change can be obfuscated and compromised beyond recognition. The institutionalization of feminist issues is a likely means of diluting and distorting them, as well as avoiding the relation of women to capital.

The modern state has been a conglomerate of social and legal agencies which hold women subject to hegemonic-patriarchal authority. However, both criminal and civil law also have been the sites of openings for feminist action. Foucault decentred the state as The Site of conflict, viewing the state rather as a mediating apparatus which connects innumerable sites of power struggles and competing discourses. As Eisenstein comments, 'Through his decentering of the state, Foucault points us in the direction of a radical pluralist epistemology of power relations'. She also observes that Foucault errs in failing to show the 'connections between sites of power ... Without some notion of unity and centrality, we cannot conceptualize hierarchy or the inequality of difference(s)' (Eisenstein, 1988: 10, 19).

The global effects of women's liberation and other resistance movements, combined with the re-entrenchment of rights discourses, have produced legal shifts in gender relations which cannot be readily reversed, such as the equality provisions in the Canadian Charter of Rights and Freedoms, which read:

> Section 15(1) Every individual is equal before and under the law and has the right to the equal protection and equal benefit of the law without discrimination and, in particular, without discrimination based on race, national or ethnic origin, colour, religion, sex, age or mental or physical disability.

> Section 28 Notwithstanding anything in this Charter, the rights and freedoms referred to in it are guaranteed equally to male and female persons.

These are reassuring promises; however, the substantive value of such rights is dubious. For example, of the 591 constitutional decisions under the equality provisions between 1983, when the rights were entrenched, and 1986, less than 10 per cent were concerned with discrimination according to sex (Brodsky and Day, 1989: 49). The balance of the cases were brought by men in conflict with other men and corporations. (In one case, for example, the manufacturers of aluminum softdrink cans believed they were being discriminated against *vis-à-vis* manufacturers of steel softdrink cans) (Brodsky and Day, 1989: 3). Men have also successfully used equality provisions in such areas as abortion and custody to reinforce father-right presumptions inherent in customary and modern law (Boyd, 1991; Crean, 1988; Delorey, 1989).

It is too soon to predict the long-term effects of contemporary women's exercise of enshrined individual legal rights. As a precedent-setting strategy, entering the courts may prove to be of more value to women in the future than in the present. Currently, few women have the knowledge or resources to pursue legal protections or redress, and, within the courts, rights discourses can be readily turned against women's interests.

Female victims of male violence, a frequently studied example of gendered injustice, have traditionally been revictimized by the criminal justice system, which has discouraged women from reporting offences.[3] The focus of the rape trial has not been on the offence or the offender but on the sexual history or reputation of the victim – who, by the harm done to her, is transformed into a defendant, an accused. Relatedly, the demand by feminists for state-supported transition houses for battered women resulted in the state assuming control of shelters and imposing a traditional familial ideology to their governance (Faith, 1993).

Contrarily, since the practice and interpretation of law is not universally monolithic or rigid, some judges and jurisdictions do take seriously the validity and urgency of women's demands, and progressive public opinion is sometimes reflected in legal judgments and social service policies. With uneven results, the state, in its broad network of constituent disciplinary parts, 'holds open or radically shuts down the possibility of local resistance', and that is the risk of political action (Walzer, 1986: 66; also see Barnsley, 1985; Faith, 1993).

The liberal feminist emphasis on legal rights has drawn cautionary analyses from critical scholars who demonstrate the contradictions inherent in a patriarchal juridical system (Eisenstein, 1988; Smart, 1989). As Foucault observes, 'the state can only operate on the basis of other already existing power relations' (1984: 64). Smart, while acknowledging the historical necessity for women to demand legal rights and protections in such areas as reproduction, observes that equal rights is tantamount to competing rights, and that women are not commonly in a favourable position to compete with men. Disagreeing with Foucault's decentring of the law as a primary site of power relations, Smart (1989) illustrates, through discussion of the medicalization of the female body, ways by which dominant discourses such as medicine join with the law to exert compounded disciplinary technologies on the population.

Taking Smart's lead, and contrary to Foucault, the law's power is strengthened, not weakened, by the interjection of complementary or competing discourses. Legalism, as a broad strategy, is futile, but ignoring the law's relationship to other discourses is foolhardy. The individual rights and adversarial approaches of Western legal systems have not invited examination of the lived experiences of women as women. This could change over time, coincident with more women entering law and judgeships, but fundamental epistemological assumptions would have to be successfully challenged if women were to claim substantively equitable space in judicial territory.

Meanwhile, criminal and civil law have provided limited protections for and defences of women's rights both as women and as equal human beings, and these rulings have set precedents for more advanced, transformative challenges. The process of placing issues before the courts, publicly reported as news, is a vital educational mechanism. It serves as both a tool and barometer of social change; as cases accumulate, female subordination becomes apparent to a broader public and that awareness may have some effect. For example, the vast North

American populations that are united by television networks are no longer presented with prime time sitcoms that make light of wife abuse as a comical theme.

A critical point of feminist socio-legal deconstruction is to demonstrate that law is itself a social construct, protected by a state whose 'reasonable person' standard is a privileged male standard (Razack, 1991). Resistance to the law requires new definitions, and challenges to mutually reinforcing networks of discursive formations. Feminist projects include the deconstruction of these discourses, and the juxtaposition of alternative visions which take group rights and historical injustices into account.

In the realms of the home, the political economy, the social and the private, women have been historically situated as the Other to men. Whether defending equal rights on the grounds of sameness, or pleading special protections on the grounds of difference, women have had to prove themselves in terms of their likeness to or difference from men; the standard has been male, by definition. As feminists have illustrated, this dualistic paradigm has produced untenable contradictions, given that women generally cannot be other than women, and that women are very diverse in their human composition and behaviours, as are men.

Truth

In Foucault's model, 'regimes of truth' in Western society are inextricably bound up with forms of sovereignty and domination. He demonstrates how discourses assume proprietary holds on knowledges and on the power relationships which are imbued with those knowledges. None of these elements are static: a regime of truth in one era may be dismissed as myth or falsehood in the next; and no single group or discourse dominates without internal and external challenges to its ever-shifting powers.

Power relations are at all times in flux and subject to resistant strategies; within the discursive spaces that resistances create, disqualified knowledges can be made audible. Feminism is not simply a matter of superimposing female truths on the traditional grid, or of decentring the male and putting the female at the centre. Collectively, various forms of feminism signify a process of weeding out retrogressive and deafening knowledges that stifle growth around them.

The techniques and procedures which Foucault documents as the means to acquiring 'truth', and thereby confirming power (Foucault, 1980a: 109–33), relate to the institutionalization and professionalization of discursive truths. Truth is regulated within the networks of authority which operate under state legitimation and on which the state depends for its own legitimacy. 'In the last analysis [in modern capitalist society], we must produce truth as we must produce wealth' (Foucault, 1980a: 93).

To pursue truth has been to pursue totalization, an essential, all-encompassing epistemology or complementary sets of realities which accommodate the smooth functionings of existing power relations and belief systems. 'Who says the truth? Individuals who are free, who arrive at a certain agreement and who find themselves thrust into a certain network of practices of power and constraining institutions' (Foucault, 1988c: 17). To reject the dominant (master's) truth is to reject the basis of the relationship; it is to resist subordination to that fabricated truth.

Resistance is itself an exercise of power, as a projection of alternative truths. The myriad variations on the feminist theme preclude the unity from which political revolutions expect to be won, despite the manifold resistances by women across the globe. Indeed, 'Foucault identified liberation with resistance rather than revolution', the acting out of refusal at multiple points of power relations (Wolin, 1988: 181). And as Foucault states, 'The problem is not changing people's consciousnesses – or what's in their heads – but the political, economic, institutional regime of the production of truth', at the bio-power levels through which local resistances are induced (1980a: 133; 1984: 74).

Feminisms produce a mosaic of resistances which address the family, language, courts, churches, media, welfare, educational and health institutions, violence against women, political economy, heterosexism, colonization, racism, imperialism and all other impositions of patriarchal truths. The targets of feminist wrath and appeal are vast, deep, intricate and constantly shifting. Whereas individual feminist voices may convey a dogmatic certitude of analysis, as a broad and internally diverse social movement feminism moves beyond the model that would simply replace one regime of truth with another. Feminisms are local in their expressions and global in their collective, potential force.

As Foucault speaks of the 'insurrection of subjugated knowledges', feminist cultural scholars and activists assert and celebrate the emergent Woman's voice, the reconstruction of 'her-story', the re-birthing of Woman which eons of patriarchal relations have silenced or substituted with the quiet voice of the disempowered Feminine. The restoration of Woman as active, historical agent is necessary to a feminist challenge to the silencing of women. The process, however, is laden with essentialist inferences that there is An original and abiding female voice. This transcendent Woman precedes culture, class and socialization, and can be sustained or recovered despite the ways by which females have been distorted by patriarchal knowledges and desires. And we should assume that males are likewise distorted and by no means always privileged by those same gendered knowledges and desires which defy but are promoted as nature.

The uncertainty of things dissuades Foucault from any essentialist tendency and his scepticism towards dogma is inclusive of scientific discourses. As discussed by Morris, Foucault displaces the 'problematics of science and ideology' by looking instead at the ways that power/knowledge is transformed by the 'revolts of disqualified knowledges'. This displacement 'could permit a more productive approach to the articulation – and extension – of the struggles of those resistant objects of knowledge, "women"' (Morris, 1979: 159). Foucault demonstrates how bodies (and 'souls') are constituted according to strategic knowledge/power relations, and how they are likewise invested with those relations (Foucault, 1979). From this perspective, Morris concludes

> what becomes possible in relation to 'women' [who comprise a] special category in the catalogues of the human sciences, is something more than a history of a 'construction': it is rather the possibility of a history of a strategic *specification*, and at the same time, a history of that in women which *defies* specification, which escapes its hold; the positively *not* specific, the unwomanly in history. (1979: 159)

When assigned gender is resisted or betrayed by scattered individuals, it is an act of defiance that may be accepted as anomaly, rebellion or eccentricity, or it may signify social failure. When 'compulsory' gender roles are consciously resisted by millions of people, men as well as women, in homes, professions, workplaces, social life, government, or as a life style, it is a serious social movement with political implications for gendered 'truths', and this has been an outcome of 'second-wave' (mid-1960s) feminist politics.

Women in Canada, and other countries, have not become voting blocs, which is reflective of real differences among them as well as cynicism or apathy across that broad population that does not vote at all. Nor have women succeeded in transforming fundamental structures and ideologies which create and sustain patriarchically tainted status quos. There is no evidence of the lessening of violence against women. Women and children dominate poverty statistics, women of colour predominate in the lowest-paid and least-valued occupations, and in most countries there is no affordable childcare. Feminist movements, then, have had very marginal or no material effect on most women's lives. At the same time, feminism poses alternative discourses which result in the weakening of specific, local expressions of patriarchal hegemony, and a radical shift in the way many women (and men) regard themselves in relation to intimate others, the law, their culture and their society. Feminism is an assertive network of movements which resist the 'negative conception of power as exclusion, concealment or repression, as a force exercised over the body which denies or perverts its "essence"' (Smart, 1983: 86). Rather, both power and resistance are understood as productive expressions which have the capacity to facilitate human freedoms.

In examining Foucault's analysis of power and resistance, Sawicki observes that in his work,

> freedom lies in our capacity to discover the historical links between certain modes of self-understanding and modes of domination, and to resist the ways in which we have already been classified and identified by dominant discourses. This means discovering new ways of understanding ourselves and each other, refusing to accept the dominant culture's characterizations of our practices and desires, and redefining them from within resistant cultures. (1988: 186)

Those who, from within resistant cultures, are redefining their practices and desires, are themselves exercising power, leading with vanguard voices which characterize movements and by which they are judged into the future. Foucault strained to convey that power is not *de facto* a negative force, that power is productive; indeed, it produces reality. The ultimately radical feminist project would be to produce a reality in which power more clearly facilitates everyone's human freedoms, as opposed to privileged people exercising powers which delimit other people's human freedoms. The praxis of that project is not to overthrow every existing truth and expression of power, but rather to deconstruct the fundamental bases of 'he-man' claims:

> First question: who is speaking? Who, among the totality of speaking individuals, is accorded the right to use this sort of language? . . . Who is qualified to do so? Who derives from it his own special quality, his prestige, and from whom, in return, does he receive if not the assurance, at least the presumption that what he says is true? (Foucault, 1972: 50)

The Female Body as a Strategic Site

Feminist resistance is the antithesis of female-victim identity, although privileging of the victim was one of the unintended early outcomes of second-wave feminist writing and activism. Violence against females was (and is) endemic and a perpetual emergency, and public outcry increased the perception of women as powerless. That is, women's actual, material subordination was exposed, and although no longer objectified as male property, Woman was re-objectified as Victim. The victim characterization conflicts with demands for equality: How can those who need special protections, because they are unable to defend themselves in the 'real' world, be equal? Feminists were derided for attacking the status quo, but feminists understood that disempowerment accrues from the absence of resistance, the succumbing to conditions as they are or appear to be.

The Panopticon design conceived by Jeremy Bentham in 1787 as a model (male) penitentiary fascinates Foucault as both a graphic model and a metaphor for strategic social controls. The Panopticon has a guard tower in the centre of tiered individual cells in a circular rotunda arrangement. In this 'laboratory of power', as Foucault put it, the cells are lighted so as to ensure that the guard can at any time look into the cell of any prisoner, and the prisoner can see no one. Aware of the possibility of being observed at any moment, prisoners internalize the surveillance and each becomes their own best guard. Everyone is supervised and watched, including the guard, by an actual or symbolic authority in the anonymous 'uninterrupted play of calculated gazes' (Foucault, 1984: 193).

Foucault judges such techniques of surveillance to be 'the discovery of population as an object of scientific investigation' (1984: 65), and he asks, 'Is it surprising that prisons resemble factories, schools, barracks, hospitals, which all resemble prisons?' (1979: 228). Surveillance accomplishes its purpose when the observed internalizes the sense of being watched, and behaviours are accordingly circumscribed and thereby normalized. Practices of modern femininity attest to female acquiescence invoked by the knowledge which requires obeisance. Indeed, male prisoners tellingly complain of being 'treated like a woman', made to be quiet, compliant and obedient.[4] Through what Foucault calls 'the infinitely minute web of panoptic techniques' (1984: 213), human beings are examined, classified, watched and disciplined even as they may be resisting those very processes.

As Smart comments on Foucault, his work 'has revealed the complex multiple processes from which the strategic constitution of forms of hegemony may emerge' (Smart, 1986: 160). Foucault's interest in sovereign power and dominant discourses is, in certain senses, complementary to Gramsci's theory of hegemony, in explaining why people may appear to adapt to subordination within power relations (Gramsci, 1971). In speaking of sovereign powers and social cleavages, Foucault notes that 'Major dominations are the hegemonic effects that are sustained by all these confrontations' (1980b: 94). Gramsci, like Foucault, is interested in political and cultural resistances: neither observes humankind as lacking in initiative, nor do they observe static power relations. Rather, in combination, they demonstrate means by which dominant or hegemonic discourses are transmitted through political economies and cultures, and encompass life itself. A key difference between them, as noted by Cocks, is that 'Foucault's answer to what criticism and resistance should aim at is very far from Gramsci's . . . [Foucault has] no trust in power emergent that seeks to replace power entrenched' (Cocks, 1989: 74).

Feminists have successfully challenged some of the laws, institutions and agencies which sustain gender hierarchies, and result in the shaping of bodies, but they have only just begun to resist the modes of rationality, individual ownership and authority on which modern patriarchal realities were constructed. And, according to Walzer, a critic of Foucault, resistance that has 'only just begun' is not of consequence. He comments,

As the conventional disciplines are generated and validated by the conventional uses of power, so Foucault's antidiscipline is generated by the resistance to those uses. But I don't see, on Foucault's terms, how [antidiscipline] can be validated by resistance until the resistance is successful (and it's not clear what success would mean). (Walzer, 1986: 65)

However, resistance, like power, is not static, monolithic or chronological; there is no one resistance, but rather infinite multiplicities of strategic resistances. As Hoy summarizes Foucault's analyses, 'Change does not occur . . . by transforming the whole at once but only by resisting injustices at the particular points where they manifest themselves' (Hoy, 1986: 143).

One key strategy, namely networking, has produced strategic patterns among feminist communities across regional boundaries. During the early 1970s, rape crisis centres were established throughout and beyond North America, most of them operating on a collectivist model. Annual candlelight Take Back the Night demonstrations, protesting pornography and violence against women, spread across nations. Women in many communities set up childcare cooperatives. Networking processes resulted in considerable sharing of information and experiences among women involved in such projects. National and international associations, such as those representing pro-choice movements, and feminist publications, provide some organizational coherence and symbolic unity. However, the initiatives and methods of political challenges are invariably shaped by local environments and the communities directly affected by specific actions.

Walzer emphasizes the ambiguity of the effects of resistance on or its importance to power, unless there is some signifier of 'success'. It would be generally agreed among feminists that some successes have occurred, on certain issues in certain times and places, but they are neither finite, permanent, nor universal, and cannot be objectified as singular revolutionary moments.

Historically and metaphysically, the emancipation of 'women' is contingent on the emancipation of *all* women, and all peoples, whereas specific, local and temporized successes are signifiers of particularized strategic gains. The strategy, for example, may be to advance opportunities for already-privileged women, with the rationale that they will open doors for other women, and serve as worthy role models. This may indeed produce the result of opening some doors for other women, but it may also have the effect of reinforcing power relations based on class, colour, professionalism and other non-gender bases for discrimination.

Resistance to power is resistance to specific strategies by which power relations are patterned. Gendered power relations are specifically organized according to interplay among the traditional discourses which have controlled women's bodies. Consider religious, economic and familial ideologies through which women have been physically and sexually subservient; legal, medical and welfare discourses which pathologize the female body, and exercise state-sanctioned (expert, professional, primarily male) authority over its reproductive functions; psychiatry and other 'psy' professions, which similarly issue policy and treatment which sexualize the female, who is viewed as an unfortunate product or victim of her biology in the ways it affects her psyche; the law, for its part, has criminalized female sexuality and sexualized female criminality. The strategic relations between and among these discourses, and the institutions which pronounce and certify them, determine how, by whom and for what purpose the female body can be classified, confined and turned into capital.

The fashion, beauty, media, entertainment and, of course, the pornography and other sex industries exploit and disperse representations of idealized females. Commercialized images serve to objectify, normalize and regulate the female body, promoting a form of compulsory, fashionable heterosexuality, or sexual hegemony, and establishing correct sexual appearances and behaviours in a distinctly he-man world. Resistances have converged in recognition of the diversities and positivities of sexuality and sexual relations as shifting social constructs: 'though power produces instances of sexuality that reshape, constrain, and oppress human beings, it can also be said to generate new forms of pleasure and new positions from which to resist' (Woodhull, 1988: 168).

Foucault, through his study of the birth of the nineteenth-century prison (1979), discusses how this modern institution resulted in an ostensible shift from punishments directed against the body, to punishment which keeps the body entrapped but which is aimed at the soul or psyche of the prisoner. Modern penal discourse 'individuates, normalizes, and mobilizes human bodies; it operates on bodies not through direct physical cruelty, but via a gaze that has its effects on the soul, via the "bad conscience" which is attached to bodies' (Lash, 1990: 58). This does not signify humanitarian progress, and physical cruelties are by no means everywhere abandoned, but notions of a 'soul' and a 'conscience' amplify a new acknowledgement of the (male) individual behind the label 'criminal'. Even as Man was increasingly subjected to 'scientific' scrutiny, so was He credited with a subjectivity allowing for choice, ethics and Self-Identity.

In the larger society, it is still on the crudest level of physicality that females are most earnestly moulded (Bartky, 1988: 61–86), as candidates for contemporary afflictions such as anorexia (Bordo, 1988: 87–117). Among women globally we see the atrocities of, and resistances against, dowry burnings in India, cliterodectomies in West Africa, rapes in Great Britain, foot-bindings in China, sexual slavery in Thailand, wife-battering in Canada . . . These are all clearly linked, a patchwork of myriad cultural forms and meanings which all illustrate how sovereign power facilitates violent controls over subjects.

Specific practices and resistances cannot be equated and must be contextualized non-linearly from one time and region to another, so as to preclude generalizations about violences against women. At the same time, the relations of power which produce these customs do share in common the virtually universal phenomenon of male violence against females. Although most men are not violent toward women, and many women, in their way, are violent against men, most Western societies have specifically facilitated and created rationales for female victimization. By enshrining male dominance in law, economy, science, medicine, religion, social policy and in the family, females are reduced to their sex and to a class-based feminine gender standard which tyrannizes most females. As stated by Lash,

> The effects of such structuration have been, arguably, to invent a female sexuality and subjectivity (and the inventors surely have been men) which in turn acts as a bad conscience or 'soul', as a 'prison-house' on the bodies of women. (Lash, 1990: 76)

Feminists have produced a pot-pourri of counter-strategic grassroots resistance and reconstruction movements on the level of the body. Significant examples include: rape crisis centres; battered women's shelters; anti-pornography campaigns; women's health centres; prisoners' rights; community midwifery services; child sexual abuse recovery counselling; and, persistent lobbying in the courts to ensure women's rights to decisions concerning their own bodies. It remains a property question: who owns it? Rights discourse has been a logical channel through which to resist unwarranted claims on the female body. However, as a legal process, rights discourse invokes the contradiction of using a privileged male system of power to challenge a privileged male system of rights.

One could interpret specific setbacks and obstructions to feminist goals as proof that heavy power imbalance overcomes resistance, but with Foucault 'power is defined in such a way that resistance of "freedom's refusal to submit" constitutes a condition of [freedom's] very existence' (Smart, 1986: 170). Women exercise their powers in many ways to create overt or subversive strategies, and, in Foucault's view, 'if there are relations of power throughout every social field it is because there is freedom everywhere' (1988c: 12). It is the positivity of resistance, as a dynamic and productive feature of power relations, rather than any transregional, transhistorical consensual strategy or goal, which gives impetus to feminist action and initiatives. Martin suggests that the fiction of the unity of Woman, in tension with the global effects of patriarchal relations, 'has created a space for us from which to interpret as well as to speak' (B. Martin, 1988: 16).

Conclusion

Colin Sumner likens Foucault to liberal feminism, because his thought 'addresses issues of discrimination but not the deeper structural condition of hegemonic masculinity. A realistic or historically accurate critique must attend to the gendered character of all censures and the censorious character of gender constructs' (Sumner, 1990: 39). In this critique Sumner is taking a feminist point of view. That is, gender is a fundamental factor in power relations – between men, between women, between men and women. Gender is a primary feature of the constitution of the Self, and the basic choices are either to accommodate the culturally specific and historically situated assignments for members of one's sex or to resist.

Foucault had embarked, at the time of his death, on the study of the history of female hysteria and the medicalization of women, and he might well have been on the verge of a deeper analysis of the construction of gender. As it is, Foucault has been of interest to many feminist thinkers for other reasons: his method of understanding power relations complements feminist analyses; he illuminates ways by which dominant discourses produce power imbalances; he starts from the point of difference, the Other – leper, madman, prisoner and other confined beings, to include women; he demonstrates, through the Greeks, the means by which sexuality is constructed through discourse; and, he shows that changes brought about by resistances occur with historical shifts in knowledges.

Resistances are not placed on the surfaces of Foucault's work on ancient and modern techniques in the constitution of the self. He makes regular reference to resistance as both the directive and target of power, but he does not let us see what resistance looks like from the inside out. Foucault is himself part of the problem that feminists resist, in so far as he is dismissive of gender in examining discursive bases of power relations – thereby representing and contributing to the androcentricity of dominant discourses. Feminist resistances offer clear examples of the strategic struggles that accrue when spaces are created, through liberal discourse, for seeking democratic rights (and rites) and political empowerment.

Feminism is a massive re-education project. Feminist resistances challenge patriarchal power/knowledges and challenge institution-alized silencing of alternative discourses. Feminist resistances are community-based, from the grassroots, and are grounded in diverse women's beliefs in their rights, but even more in their *needs*, to transform the society in which they live, to change their relationships, home life and/or workplaces. Foucault was not optimistic, yet he affirmed political struggle and expected his work to lead his readers to 'pessimistic activism' (Poster, 1989: 114). Because he does not accept totalizing theories or strategies, he does not anticipate a glorious Freedom Day, but rather continuing, shifting struggles. What he has not envisioned, except as an idealization, is a revolutionary movement which does not as its goal reproduce the modern hierarchial structure of power relations.

The anarchist impulse in both Foucault and strands of feminism converge in a world whereby Authority and Truth are abandoned, and such a world can be reached only to the extent, to paraphrase Foucault, that subjugated groups find their voices and insurrect or generate their knowledges. Women are doing this, and with some effect. We see continuing violence and discrimination, which cannot be prevented until the majority of men agree that it cannot go on. The law continues to be a dubious ally to women's interests. The economy still does not accommodate women's need for living wages. At the same time, many people across cultures, since the 1970s, have changed their behaviours and ways of thinking about sex-roles and gender. Middle-class women are enjoying certain structural improvements in their lives. Some legislatures, courts and institutions in Western nations have made decisions which acknowledge women's human rights. However, formalistic remedies do not signify a straight line towards progress, and progress, like rationalism, is itself a discredited, modernist concept. Nevertheless, on Foucault's own evidence, there is no more reason for pessimism than for optimism, as we proceed day by day, in all our diversities, searching out strategies to effectively resist violences, and to transform the hierarchical knowledges, material conditions and relations of power through which they are produced.

Notes

I am grateful to friends and colleagues John Lowman, Colin Sumner and Mimi Ajzenstadt for stimulating my interest in Foucault some years ago, and to Liz Elliott for her welcome assistance, knowledge and collegiality. Special thanks and appreciation to the J.S. Woodsworth Resident Scholar Program, at the SFU Institute for the Humanities, and especially to Advisory Board Member Andrea Lebowitz, Director Jery Zaslove and Coordinator Christine Goodman. This chapter is one outcome of the Institute's 1990 sponsorship of a public symposium, and a weekly Humanities seminar, on 'Foucault, Feminism and Power'. Finally, my thanks to John Lowman, Shauna Butterwick and Pamela Sleeth, for their helpful comments on an earlier draft.

1 Michel Foucault, who was born in Poitiers and died in Paris in 1984, at age 57, was considered by that time to be 'France's leading intellectual' (Sheridan, 1989: 41). His prodigious work, spanning the humanities and social sciences, was published in many languages. He served on numerous faculties in Europe, and from 1970 onward he held the title Professor of the History of Systems of Thought, a singular position created for him at the Collège de France. For an excellent biography, see Eribon (1991).

2 There are several terms in this essay which require qualifiers to avoid universalizing very particular identities or concepts. Post-modern feminists recognize identity difference and power differentials, and avoid speaking with authority for 'women' or for 'feminists'. This is not to say that one can never generalize within a given context, but when I have in this essay resorted to generalization it has been with caution and generally in a Western context. Just as there is no single definition of 'feminism' (Descarries-Belanger and Roy, 1991), nor is there a single definition of 'woman'. Another term that causes difficulty is 'patriarchy' (Cocks, 1989: 209), which suggests both centralized and localized male power, unchallenged, and a clearly defined private/public split. The patriarchy as such does not exist. I do, however, speak in various ways of patriarchal relations, as a vestigial, hierarchical form of structuring power and authority, including the regulation, discipline and surveillance of female persons.

3 Examples of book-length Canadian research on violence against women and children include the following: Boyle (1984); Clark and Lewis (1977); Cole (1989); DeKeseredy and Hinch (1991); Sleeth and Barnsley (1989); Walker (1990). Also see Price (1989).

4 This analogy was repeated to me numerous times during the 1970s and 1980s, in conversations with men in several West Coast prisons in the USA and Canada.

References

Adams, Kathleen (1991) 'Bad sisters: punk culture and feminism', *FUSE*, 14(5–6): 22–7.

Barnsley, Jan (1985) *Feminist Action, Institutional Reaction: Responses to Wife Assault*. Vancouver: Women's Research Centre.

Bartkowski, Frances (1988) 'Epistemic drift in Foucault', in Irene Diamond and Lee Quinby (eds), *Feminism and Foucault*. Boston, Mass.: Northeastern University Press, pp. 43–58.

Bartky, Sandra Lee (1988) 'Foucault, femininity, and the modernization of patriarchal power', in Irene Diamond and Lee Quinby (eds), *Feminism and Foucault*. Boston, Mass.: Northeastern University Press, pp. 61–86.

Baudrillard, Jean (1987) *Forget Foucault*. New York: Semiotext(e).

Bordo, Susan (1988) 'Anorexia nervosa: psychopathology as the crystallization of culture', in Irene Diamond and Lee Quinby (eds), *Feminism and Foucault*. Boston, Mass.: Northeastern University Press, pp. 87–117.

Boyd, Susan (1991) 'Some postmodernist challenges to feminist analyses of law, family and state: ideology and discourse in child custody law', *Canadian Journal of Family Law*, 10(1): 79–113.

Boyle, Christine L.M. (1984) *Sexual Assault*. Toronto: Carswell.

Brodsky, Gwen and Day, Shelagh (1989) *Canadian Charter Equality Rights for Women: One Step Forward or Two Steps Back?* Ottawa: Canadian Advisory Council on the Status of Women.

Butler, Judith (1987) 'Variations on sex and gender: Beauvoir, Wittig, and Foucault', in Seyla Benhabib and Drucilla Cornell (eds), *Feminism as Critique*. Minneapolis: University of Minnesota Press, pp. 128–42.

Butler, Judith (1990) *Gender Trouble: Feminism and the Subversion of Identity*. New York: Routledge.

Clark, Lorene and Lewis, Debra (1977) *Rape: the Price of Coercive Sexuality.* Toronto: Women's Press.

Cocks, Joan (1989) *The Oppositional Imagination: Feminism, Critique, and Political Theory.* New York: Routledge.

Cole, Susan (1989) *Pornography and the Sex Crisis.* Toronto: Amanita Enterprises.

Cousins, Mark and Hussain, Athar (1984) *Michel Foucault.* New York: St Martin's Press.

Crean, Susan (1988) *In the Name of the Fathers: the Story Behind Child Custody.* Toronto: Amanita Enterprises.

DeKeseredy, Walter S. and Hinch, Ronald (1991) *Woman Abuse: Sociological Perspectives.* Toronto: Thompson Educational Publications.

Deleuze, Gilles (1988) *Foucault.* Minneapolis: University of Minnesota Press.

Delorey, Anne Marie (1989) 'Joint legal custody: a reversion to patriarchal power', *Canadian Journal of Women and the Law/Revue juridique la femme et le droit (Women and Custody),* 3(1): 33–44.

Descarries-Belanger, Francine and Roy, Shirley (1991) *The Women's Movement and its Currents of Thought: a Typological Essay.* Ottawa: Canadian Research Institute for the Advancement of Women.

Dews, Peter (1986) 'The Nouvelle Philosophy and Foucault', in Mike Gane (ed.), *Towards a Critique of Foucault.* London: Routledge and Kegan Paul, pp. 61–105.

Diamond, Irene and Quinby, Lee (eds) (1988a) *Feminism and Foucault: Reflections on Resistance.* Boston, Mass.: Northeastern University Press.

Diamond, Irene and Quinby, Lee (1988b) 'American feminism and the language of control', in I. Diamond and L. Quinby (eds), *Feminism and Foucault: Reflections on Resistance.* Boston, Mass.: Northeastern University Press, pp. 193–206.

Dreyfus, Hubert L. and Rabinow, Paul (1982) *Michel Foucault: Beyond Structuralism and Hermeneutics,* 2nd edn, Chicago: University of Chicago Press.

Eisenstein, Zillah R. (1988) *The Female Body and the Law.* Berkeley, Ca: University of California Press.

Eribon, Didier (1991) *Michel Foucault* (trans. Betsy Wing). Cambridge, Mass.: Harvard University Press.

Faith, Karlene (1993) 'State appropriation of feminist initiative: Transition House, Vancouver, 1973–1986', in Karlene Faith and Dawn Currie (eds), *Seeking Shelter: a State of Battered Women.* Vancouver: Collective Press, pp. 1–36.

Foucault, Michel (1972) *The Archaeology of Knowledge.* New York: Pantheon Books.

Foucault, Michel (1973) *The Order of Things.* New York: Vintage Books.

Foucault, Michel (1977) *Language, Counter-Memory, Practice* (ed. Donald F. Bouchard). Ithaca, NY: Cornell University Press.

Foucault, Michel (1979) *Discipline and Punish.* New York: Vintage Books.

Foucault, Michel (1980a) *Power/Knowledge: Selected Interviews and Writings 1972– 1977* (ed. Colin Gordon). New York: Pantheon Books.

Foucault, Michel (1980b) *The History of Sexuality,* vol. I: *An Introduction.* New York: Vintage Books.

Foucault, Michel (1982) 'On the genealogy of ethics: an overview of work in progress', in Hubert L. Dreyfus and Paul Rabinow (eds), *Michel Foucault: Beyond Structuralism and Hermeneutics.* Chicago: University of Chicago Press, pp. 229–52.

Foucault, Michel (1984) *The Foucault Reader* (ed. Paul Rabinow). New York: Pantheon Books.

Foucault, Michel (1986) *The History of Sexuality*, vol. II: *The Use of Pleasure*. New York: Vintage Books.

Foucault, Michel (1988a) *The History of Sexuality*, vol. III: *The Care of the Self*. New York: Vintage Books.

Foucault, Michel (1988b) *Politics, Philosophy, Culture: Interviews and Other Writings 1977–1984* (ed. Lawrence D. Kritzman). New York: Routledge.

Foucault, Michel (1988c) 'The ethical care of the self as a practice of freedom' (trans. J.D. Gauthier), in James Bernauer and David Rasmussen (eds), *The Final Foucault*. Cambridge, Mass.: MIT Press, pp. 1–20.

Foucault, Michel (1989) *Foucault Live: Interviews 1966–1984* (trans. John Johnston, ed. Sylvere Lotringer). New York: Semiotext(e).

Frank, Arthur W. (1989) 'Bringing bodies back in: a decade review', *Differentia: Review of Italian Thought*, No. 3–4 (Autumn).

Fraser, Nancy (1989) *Unruly Practices: Power, Discourse and Gender in Contemporary Social Theory*. Minneapolis: University of Minnesota Press.

Fuss, Diana (1989) *Essentially Speaking: Feminism, Nature and Difference*. New York: Routledge.

Fuss, Diana (1991) *Inside/Out: Lesbian Theories, Gay Theories*. New York: Routledge.

Gramsci, Antonio (1971) *Selections from the Prison Notebooks* (eds Q. Hoare and G.N. Smith). New York: International Publishers.

Hartsock, Nancy (1990) 'Foucault on power: a theory for women?', in Linda J. Nicholson (ed.), *Feminism and Postmodernism*. New York: Routledge, pp. 157–75.

Hoy, David Couzens (ed.) (1986) *Foucault: a Critical Reader*. New York: Basil Blackwell.

Hunt, Alan (1991) 'Why did Foucault get law so wrong?', Public lecture, Simon Fraser University, Vancouver, 8 April.

Lash, Scott (1990) *Sociology of Postmodernism*. New York: Routledge.

Martin, Biddy (1988) 'Feminism, criticism and Foucault', in Irene Diamond and Lee Quinby (eds), *Feminism and Foucault*. Boston, Mass.: Northeastern University Press, pp. 3–19.

Martin, Rux (1988) 'Truth, power, self: an interview with Michel Foucault', in Luther H. Martin, Huck Gutman and Patrick H. Hutton (eds), *Technologies of the Self: a Seminar with Michel Foucault*. Amherst, Mass.: University of Massachusetts Press, pp. 9–15.

Marx, Karl and Engels, Frederick (ed. C.J. Arthur) (1985[1846]) *The German Ideology, Part I*. New York: International Publishers.

Merquior, J.G. (1985) *Foucault*. Berkeley, Ca: University of California Press.

Minson, Jeff (1986) 'Strategies for socialists? Foucault's conception of power', in Mike Gane (ed.), *Towards a Critique of Foucault*. London: Routledge and Kegan Paul, pp. 106–48.

Morris, Meaghan (1979) 'The pirate's fiancee: feminists and philosophers, or maybe tonight it'll happen', in Meaghan Morris and Paul Patton (eds), *Michel Foucault: Power, Truth and Strategy*. Sydney: Feral Publications, pp. 148–68.

Morris, Meaghan and Patton, Paul (eds) (1979) *Michel Foucault: Power, Truth and Strategy*. Sydney: Feral Publications.

Poster, Mark (1984) *Foucault, Marxism and History*. Cambridge: Polity Press.

Poster, Mark (1989) *Critical Theory and Poststructuralism: In Search of a Context*. Ithaca, NY: Cornell University Press.

Price, Lisa (1989) *Patterns of Violence in the Lives of Girls and Women: a Reading Guide*. Vancouver: Women's Research Centre.

Rajchman, John (1985) *Michel Foucault: the Freedom of Philosophy*. New York: Columbia University Press.

Ray, Larry (1988) 'Foucault, critical theory and the decomposition of the historical subject', *Philosophy and Social Criticism*, 14(1): 69–111.

Razack, Sherene (1991) *Canadian Feminism and the Law*. Toronto: Second Story Press.

Ricci, N.P. (1987) 'The end/s of woman', *Canadian Journal of Political and Social Theory*, 11(3): 11–27.

Sawicki, Jana (1987) 'Heidegger and Foucault: escaping technological nihilism', *Philosophy and Social Criticism*, 13(2): 155–73.

Sawicki, Jana (1988) 'Identity politics and sexual freedom: Foucault and feminism', in Irene Diamond and Lee Quinby (eds), *Feminism and Foucault*. Boston, Mass.: Northeastern University Press, pp. 177–91.

Sheridan, Alan (1989) 'Michel Foucault: the death of the author', in Lisa Appignanesi (ed.), *Ideas from France: the Legacy of French Theory* (ICA Documents). London: Free Association Books.

Simons, Jon (1991) 'From resistance to polaesthics: politics after Foucault', *Philosophy and Social Criticism*, 17(1): 41–55.

Sleeth, Pamela and Barnsley, Jan (1989) *Recollecting Our Lives: Women's Experience of Childhood Sexual Abuse*. Vancouver: Women's Research Centre.

Smart, Barry (1983) *Foucault, Marxism and Critique*. London: Routledge and Kegan Paul.

Smart, Barry (1985) *Michel Foucault*. London: Routledge.

Smart, Barry (1986) 'The politics of truth and the problem of hegemony', in David Couzens Hoy (ed.), *Foucault: a Critical Reader*. New York: Basil Blackwell, pp. 157–74.

Smart, Carol (1989) *Feminism and the Power of Law*. New York: Routledge.

Sumner, Colin (1990) 'Foucault, gender and the censure of deviance', in Loraine Gelsthorpe and Allison Morris (eds), *Feminist Perspectives in Criminology*. Milton Keynes: Open University Press, pp. 26–40.

Tucker, Robert C. (ed.) (1972) 'Marx on the history of his opinions', from Preface to *A Contribution to the Critique of Political Economy*, in *Marx–Engels Reader*. New York: W.W. Norton.

Walker, Gillian E. (1990) *Family Violence and the Women's Movement: the Conceptual Politics of Struggle*. Toronto: University of Toronto Press.

Walzer, Michael (1986) 'The politics of Michel Foucault', in David Couzens Hoy (ed.), *Foucault: a Critical Reader*. New York: Basil Blackwell, pp. 51–68.

Weeks, Jeffrey (1989) 'Uses and abuses of Michel Foucault' in Lisa Appignanesi (ed.), *Ideas from France: the Legacy of French Theory* (ICA Documents). London: Free Association Books, pp. 49–62.

Wolin, Sheldon S. (1988) 'On theory and practice of power', in Jonathan Arac (ed.), *After Foucault: Humanistic Knowledge, Postmodern Challenges*. New Brunswick, NJ: Rutgers University Press, 179–201.

Woodhull, Winnifred (1988) 'Sexuality, power and the question of rape', in Irene Diamond and Lee Quinby (eds), *Feminism and Foucault*. Boston, Mass.: Northeastern University Press, pp. 167–76.

4

Into the Realm of the Fearful:
Power, Identity and the Gender Problematic

Deborah Kerfoot and David Knights

A considerable amount of time and intellectual energy has been devoted to theorizing about women's social and economic position in society. Some writers have attached themselves to a strand of explanation locating the source of contemporary sex inequalities at home and in the workplace as centred on a fundamental and inescapable biological difference between men and women. This division is seen as ordering the allocation of tasks, the 'separation of spheres', and the more general form and experience of everyday life. A major concern has been to understand the operation of the capitalist economy, and its relationship to women. These, primarily Marxist, authors have opted to locate their explanation of exploitation in theories centred on the economic relations of production under capitalism. The resultant class-based theory denies specificity to women and explains their position as merely an additional manifestation of the exploitation and subordination of all propertyless labourers (Zaretsky, 1976). Here, the sex of the labourer is largely irrelevant since it is individuals' relationship to the mode of production which determines their class position, not their sex (also Hartmann, 1981): sex inequalities thus become obfuscated by and secondary to class structure.

Alongside interest in the workings of economic systems is a related concern, that of unpacking the linkages between hierarchy as women's oppression, and the development of contemporary capitalism. A debate has arisen which is geared toward discovering the 'essential origin' of women's differential position in terms of the interface of capitalism and patriarchy. Engaging with a Marxist account and inspired by what are regarded as deficiencies in the 'class first' approach of many authors, others have sought to explore the root cause of sex inequality in terms of women's relationship to the family as a social institution. This group of largely Marxist feminists adapt Marx's categories to retain a basic premise of inequalities generated by the mode of production, but allow for what they regard as the distinctiveness of women's experience. They see women's relationship to capital as one grounded in their primary link with the family: from this perspective, the subjugation of the female sex is due to the existence and form of the family unit, and the sexual divisions of labour associated with it.

A further group of writers declare dissatisfaction with theories that privilege one locus of explanation over another in this either/or manner. Preferring instead to offer explanations grounded in a synthesis of the economic and the domestic sources of female subordination, they envisage capitalism and patriarchy as 'dual systems' which require separate theorizing, either as completely detached, fully autonomous entities (for example, Mitchell, 1975); as discrete but interlocking in mutual accommodation (Hartmann, 1979); or as separate and in conflict (Walby, 1986). In any event, authors of this persuasion suggest that to include a theoretical analysis of both capitalism *and* patriarchy simultaneously provides an escape from the difficulties encountered in elevating one theoretical pole, capitalism above patriarchy or vice versa, and from the reductionism whereby the subordination of women occurs as a by-product of material class relations.

However, we would suggest that the fundamental mistake is to seek out a singular all-embracing cause which, whether ideological, material or a synthesis of the two, attempts to provide a 'total' explanation of sex inequality. Part of our critique here is that, in their attempt to explain both the separation of the sexes, and the reproductive responsibilities and divisions of labour between them, these writers take for granted part of what they seek to explain. Furthermore, despite claims to the contrary, they are in danger of explaining social divisions through an essentialistic view of male domination, structured around the binary opposition between ideology and materialism.

Our approach differs in that we are concerned to explore 'gender differentiation', defined as the social construction of sexual difference. In other words, our interest is to address how sex-based specificities come to be maintained, rather than why or from what point of origin women's oppression supposedly emanates. The purpose in this chapter then is twofold; to offer an account of how the division of labour has remained so stable, within the context of a discussion of gender and sexuality; and, following Game (1991: 36) a second purpose is to stimulate debate – to begin to address the question 'how are we constituted now, and how might we be otherwise, *now*?' In so doing, we draw on an understanding of critical analysis as the production of a dialogue occasioning the possibility of a more creative engagement with, or perhaps even subversion of, the practices sustaining socially constituted sexual differences at the level of their discursive production.

The chapter is informed primarily by a critical reading of Foucault, drawing on his analysis of power and subjectivity as grounded in the exercise of power through social practices in which subjects are embedded. As is argued in section three, this notion of the 'discursive production of subjects' within and between power relations can provide a way of reconciling the material/ideological dualism that informs much writing on women's oppression, but moreover, can open up the possibility for a theoretical space in which to conceive of a challenge to those mechanisms and operations of power, productive of sexual divisions. It is our contention that a conception of power and its operation informed by a reading of Foucault provides an escape from what we regard as the dualistic thinking of many Radical and Marxist feminists, and may lead us towards an understanding of how sex inequality and male domination are perpetuated.

The chapter is divided into four sections. The first outlines our theoretical perspective by developing an analysis of power, subjectivity and self that is capable of advancing a view of sexuality and gender inequality which escapes the problems of a disembodied dualism and essentialism found evident in the literature. The second section then provides an account of a pre-eminent Anglo-American debate on women's oppression which we conclude falls precisely into these dualistic and essentialist traps. We turn in section three to an examination of post-structuralist analyses of power and identity in order to illuminate some of the problems of theorizing from a position of 'fixed' meanings, and to illustrate how this forecloses on an analysis of the problems of sex inequality and of gender differentiation. This leads in section four to our discussion of a selection of French feminist literature, in an attempt to elaborate the potential of post-structuralist accounts to address the problems of the reproduction of gender inequality and sexual difference *without* resort to dualist or essentialist arguments. In the summary and conclusion we return to our opening analysis and assess the potential of a discourse on power, subjectivity and self to open up a dialogue on gender and sexuality that has been conspicuous by its absence, in all but a very narrow range of literatures.

For the moment, several points are salient pertaining to the theoretical position we adopt; one, on the theoretical conception of power; a second on the status of the subject; a third on the implicit conception of 'the self' within theories of women's oppression. These points are elaborated in the first section, to which we now turn.

Power, Subjectivity and Self

Explorations of patriarchy or women's oppression as a topic of analysis assume a conception of power as a commodity disproportionately held by some groups, and wielded over or used against others. For feminists concerned to theorize women's differential social and economic position in terms of patriarchy, this translates as men 'having power over' women, regarded as manifest in a variety of institutional forms, patriarchal practices and relations acting to oppress the female sex. The feminist political project is then one of a transformation of society, of these historically entrenched (unequal) relations, and a 'redistribution' of power. Indeed, the notion of achieving sex equality is in part conditional upon the acquisition, or seizure, of mutual and equal access to material resources and 'fairer shares' in what is held to be the zero-sum game of power. This understanding of power as the property of some to the exclusion of others, and outside of and beyond the individual, sets up a dichotomous relationship between the individual and the social world, between powerful men and powerless women as largely internally undifferentiated categories, and imputes a passivity to all women.

An alternative theorization (Foucault, 1980a, 1982) is to conceive of power as existing only in its exercise, operating through the production of particular knowledges – around discourses of gender and sexuality, pleasure and morality, sanity and madness, and the law for example. From this perspective, power is neither one-directional, nor does it flow from a single source to shape, direct, or constrain subjects. Rather, power is in reciprocal relation to subjectivity, where subjectivity can be defined as individual self-consciousness inscribed in particular ideals of behaviour surrounding categories of persons, objects, practices or institutions. Subjectivity is constituted through the exercise of power within which conceptions of personal identity, gender and sexuality come to be generated. Men and women actively exercise power in positioning themselves within, or of finding their own location amongst, competing discourses, rather than merely being 'positioned by' them. This leads to our second point on the status of the subject.

Where subjectivity is constructed in and through discourse, the gender identity of men and women as masculine and feminine subjects is socially constituted in and through certain sites, behaviours and practices at any one time. We regard gendered subjectivities therefore as fractured, historically shifting, constantly unstable and potentially multiple. This idea of the 'precariousness' of identity exists in contrast to that 'solidity' implied in conceptions of the subject as existing prior to, or outside of the operation of power, and which presuppose a seamless rationality on the part of self-conscious individuals. Thus, we see that gender identity must be worked at, acquiring the status of a 'personal project' to be achieved and requiring continual accomplishment. Consequently and flowing from this, we regard gender relations as open to contestation, to moments of resistance and, more importantly for our purposes here, to *change*, rather than in any way fixed or pre-existing.

A third point relates to the conception of 'the self' within theories of women's oppression. Our concern here could perhaps best be summarized by posing the question: what's 'there' to be oppressed? Proposals for a feminist transformation are predicated on the belief that a 'true self' of women will be freed once the sites of, and structural institutions for, patriarchal oppression are located, unravelled and thence, overturned. Yet it is this essentialist underpinning to 'the self' with which we wish to take issue here. The notion of the continuity and inevitability of self, and the language of 'liberation' in which it so frequently finds expression, is of course by no means peculiar to feminist writings on contemporary social divisions. The notion of a fundamental inviolability and constancy of self finds equal resonance, for example, in state regulation of social policy, in contemporary approaches to criminality, deviance and punishment, and in domestic and international health and welfare provision, in turn underpinned by debates over 'rights' and 'citizenship'.[1]

Yet in the context of women's position, to invoke the 'essential self' argument is to impose a fixity and ahistorical unity to the experience of all women (see, for example, Wilson, 1982; also de Beauvoir, 1984[1949]). Moreover, this is to create a false separation between the body, as biologically sexed flesh, and the 'self' of a person (also Pateman, 1988) where the self is conceived of in exteriority to and above social relations. Here we follow Game in questioning both the potential of a feminist social science 'concerned to free truth from power', to sustain a politics of social transformation, based on the theoretical fiction that a new subject might be freed if liberated from the constraints of patriarchal power; and in questioning 'whether the conditions of production are themselves free from patriarchal power and knowledge' (1991: 15).

This leads us to consider the implications of our theorizing for a sexual politics of change. While recognizing that women are often subjugated as a result of the exercise of power, Foucault's work neither confronts the problem of material inequality, nor the production of hierarchical divisions between the sexes, between masculinity and femininity, and between management and labour. In *The History of Sexuality* (Foucault, 1980b) he neglects sexual inequality in favour of developing a thesis on sexual *identity*, and the regulatory and productive potential of power at the level of the body: in so doing he is said to overlook the differentiation between male and female sexualities (Mort, 1987; Nead, 1988). From this then, there would seem to be little to glean for the development of a radical feminist transformatory project. Indeed a common criticism is that his analysis lacks both the propensity for political engagement and a 'coherent' normative framework because, although suggestive of alternatives, it never fully specifies them (Fraser, 1989: 17–34, especially 27–33).

Yet in our view, Foucault's conception of power and of sexual subjectivity could facilitate the possibility of a feminist politics that avoids the sexual divisiveness of gender essentialism, and the disembodied discourse of deconstruction theory. While we would refrain from prescribing the content of a 'more effective' alternative, or of improving 'the formula' of an existing politics for action, an argument of this chapter is that a re-appraisal of the gender problematic in the context of a discussion of power and subjectivity may provide the conditions in which an alternative gender politics may emerge. We believe our analysis has value in its potential to advance a non-essentialist and embodied account of gender relations. Accordingly, this chapter is concerned to examine a selection of French feminist literature in so far as it allows us to tease out the potential for a non-dualistic and non-essentialist account of sex inequality and gender differentiation.

Radical and Marxist Feminism

In the 1960s and early 1970s much feminist debate was instigated by radicals (dalla Costa and James, 1972; James, 1972) who had a major task in shaking Marxists out of their gender myopia. Like other institutions, Marxism responded to the general impact of feminist debates in attempting to take account of sex as well as class inequality. It largely failed in this attempt other than by a reductionism in which issues of sex, whilst acknowledged, suffered a theoretical eclipse behind the edifices of class structure determined by the forces and relations of production. Accordingly, the radical feminist critique of Marxism as either sex-blind or reductionist was firmly upheld. In the 1980s, however, a Marxist feminism emerged concerned with the task of producing a critical analysis of sex and class inequality that eschewed any such one-sided reductionism.

In Britain, it revolved around a debate over Barrett's (1980) attempt to bridge the theoretical polarization between material and ideological explanations of sexual inequality and women's oppression (Armstrong and Armstrong, 1985a, 1985b; Barrett, 1984; Brenner and Ramas, 1984; Lewis, 1985; Weir and Wilson, 1983). Here, she attempts to bridge the divide between radical feminists' stress on gender ideology and Marxists' concentration on material class relations as explanation of inequality and oppression. Barrett focuses her attention on the sexual division of work within the household, tracing the historical development of the organization of domestic labour under capitalism. She identifies a material source of the development of domestic labour in the economic dependency of women on men within households, and an ideological source in the moral and symbolic power surrounding the institution of the family within which women are effectively constrained (also Barrett and McIntosh, 1980, 1982).

Barrett traces the development of the sexual division of labour in the household under capitalism, noting two sources of the current organization of domestic divisions; one linked to the economic dependence of women on men (cf. Beechey, 1977, 1987); another to a socially developed ideology which acts as an effective constraint over all women. It is primarily an 'ideology of familialism' (Barrett, 1980: 206) rather than the form of the family (see Engels, 1972) which sustains the sexual division of labour and material inequalities. Further, this ideology is simultaneously both pervasive and prescriptive in invoking the moral desirability of 'family life' which 'assigns financial support to the husband and father, sexual fidelity to the wife and mother, and obedience to the children' (1980: 223). Barrett places considerable theoretical weight on this ideology in accounting for the reproduction of the 'family-household system', sex-specific divisions of labour, and women's unpaid acceptance of the responsibility for childcare and domestic tasks.

Women find themselves the objects of the ideology of familialism, and as men's dependants, due to a combination of forces acting against their interests in the last century. Of primary significance were the regulation of labour by craft unions and state interventions through legislation. Barrett argues that male craft workers tried to exclude women by preventing female recruitment entirely, or by denying women access to socially valued technical skills within occupations. Moreover, in the same period, legislation effectively removed from women the same labour market choices as were available to men, although designed initially to protect the physical, moral and material conditions of women and children (cf. Humphries, 1981). None the less, the effect was to reinforce the domestic role of women and to promote a hidden yet rigid system of job segregation in employment.

One critique (Brenner and Ramas, 1984) centred on the failure to escape the dualism between ideology and material class relations, identified as the major obstacle to the development of Marxist-feminism. It was argued that Barrett had neglected the economic inequality of the sexes in the labour market, seen as deriving from women's child-bearing and rearing responsibilities, which rendered women at a disadvantage *vis-à-vis* men in the labour market. Barrett's argument appears sophisticated in that it offers an account of ideology grounded in material reality, rather than conceptualizing ideology as theoretically separate or in some way detached from people's lived experience. Yet she in no way explains the practice of reproducing sex inequality, and how, rather than why, a supposedly sex-blind capitalist system facilitates the maintenance of sex inequality and exploitation (Brenner and Ramas, 1984). In other words, 'how is it possible, given the capitalist drive to accumulate and to use up labour power, that women are left out of capitalist production and remain in the home to the extent that they do?' (1984: 37).

Brenner and Ramas's critique stems from what they regard as Barrett's failure to transcend the dualism of ideology and material class relations. They take issue with Barrett's evidence on male trade union members' exclusion of women, and on state intervention through protective legislation to conclude that she demonstrates '[no] material basis for the historical development and reproduction of the family-household system, the sexual division of labour, and women's oppression in capitalism' (1984: 47).

In place of Barrett's stress on 'the ideology of familialism', Brenner and Ramas suggest an interpretation placing considerable emphasis on women's role in biological reproduction. More specifically, their concern is with how far biological differences condition women's participation in economic and political life under capitalism, given that 'relationship between the natural and the social must be built into the analysis' (1984: 47). In sum, Brenner and Ramas construct a case for women's responsibility for child-rearing and domestic labour in capitalism as stemming from the biological facts of reproduction 'in so far as they conditioned both sexual divisions of labour *and* power balances between men and women' (1984: 48, emphasis in original).

Yet the aim of both parties in this debate, briefly described above, is to explain the operation of the capitalist economy in its relation to women as stemming from a fundamental point of origin from which inequality springs. In their quest for monocausal explanations, the authors begin with a conception of male and female positions in the sexual division of labour as observed in the contemporary capitalist economy. From this observation, both seek to explain the material and social inequalities experienced by women as if all men and women were firmly and permanently anchored to segregated sex roles in domestic and paid work. Barrett focuses on the sexual division of labour in the household, explaining domestic labour divisions as derived from a combination of women's economic dependency on men, and the social ideology of familialism – as if the product of this synthesis was a given role or position which *all* women, for the purpose of Barrett's analysis, are seen to occupy. Thus Barrett begins with a framework of analysis which assumes a stereotypical position for its object. Her mission is then to explain how and why this role occurred.

Similarly, Brenner and Ramas look at the fact of women's role in biological reproduction as, to a greater extent, determining the conditions under which sex segregation and material and social inequality come about. In their analysis, segregation in the labour market stems from women's poor bargaining position, shaped by historically developed domestic responsibilities, and primarily, the responsibility for childcare. Yet this depends on a leap from female reproduction to the social organization around that reproduction, as if an understanding of the experience of all women could be extrapolated from the fact of childbirth. No consideration is offered of how and in what way childbirth becomes conflated with childcare. It seems inadequate to suggest that in the case of childcare, 'capitalists are not willing to make such expenditures' (Brenner and Ramas, 1984: 48) and that, as a result, women find themselves on the receiving end of the responsibility for domestic tasks. Consequently, any potential for exploring the link between women and childcare as a social construct, or men's absence from child-rearing, is lost.

The interstices between sexed bodies and forms of social organization simply become dissolved by the permanent fusion of sex and category, women/children/home and men/job/work, and the social generation of these categories is thus either negated or denied. In their search for an origin these authors simultaneously create and impose 'fixed' meaning on their categories in self-sustaining momentum. At once, they create and give life to totalizing explanations of complex social processes. What we would argue limits both sets of accounts is a conception of gender as self-evident and undifferentiated, of power and knowledge as primarily the prerogative of men and an absence of, or silence around, sexuality. Within post-structuralism and the feminisms influenced by it, universal and 'fixed' meanings are problematized in such a way as to render power, gender and sexuality open to critical reflection and re-examination. It is to this literature that we now turn in our pursuit of a non-essentialist and embodied analysis of gender and sexual inequality.

Post-structuralism and Feminism

Borrowing from the structural linguistic analyses of Saussure and Lévi-Strauss, Derrida (1976, 1978) argues that modern Western thought or metaphysics is based on a false assumption that 'true' meaning is inherent in the spoken utterance (the logos). Western metaphysics assumes that signifier (the word) and signified (the meaning we attach to the word) are immediately present at the moment of the speech act. So for example, to use the word 'man' would be always, consistently and universally, to invoke the same fixed meaning. However, Derrida's work focuses on deconstructing this privileging of self-evident 'presence' of meaning, in other words, he alerts us to what is missing, what is either denied or disregarded in the process of signification. In our example, what is missing is 'woman' and yet it is precisely 'her' absence that constitutes the meaning 'man', for without the contrast, 'man' does not exist. Derrida's critique is thus that in privileging what is present, the process of signification in effect denies what is absent.

He shows that its reliance on a fixed source of undifferentiated meaning (the 'transcendental signified') is simply an arbitrary or random closure upon the infinite number of potential inter-pretations. Returning to our example, the word 'man' could be seen to connote numerous either positive or pejorative meanings; interpretations differ according to the context of the utterance and the meaning systems which actors themselves bring to the utterance. More important for our argument here is Derrida's assertion that this random closure on interpretations secures meaning through the *suppression* of what is absent.

Similarly, Lacan (1977) suggests that 'woman' is what cannot be conceptualized, that which is outside of and beyond purely a simplistic biological description of flesh. In reinterpreting Freud's notion of the development of human consciousness, Lacan is concerned to provide a psychoanalytic account of the development of human subjectivity that is informed by structuralist conceptions of language. He suggests that the point at which human beings become 'self-conscious' occurs when the child recognizes itself as separate from the 'other' or where the rule of the father displaces the symbiotic unity of the mother and child. It is the moment of entry to the symbolic realm of language and discourse which is dominated by the phallus,[2] and where 'woman' does not exist.

If we combine Derrida's deconstruction of presence with Lacan's notion of 'woman' as that which can never be envisioned, it can be seen that masculine meaning is constructed through reference to, and an interplay with, what differs from it but must defer to it. Thus masculine meaning (phallogocentricism) defined as the rational logic that is dominated by the desire for a return to the symbiotic unity of a pre-oedipal existence, can be seen as a form constructed and held in position by its own shadow. Derrida uses the term 'differance', with an 'a', to capture significations such as those relating to what is feminine and whose difference is suppressed through exclusion yet rendered deferential to an all-pervading masculine presence. Phallogocentric discourse and practice quite clearly reflects and reproduces differance in regard to women and their significations. Indeed, men at least in part secure the meaning of their masculine existence, of what it means and how it feels to be 'a real man', through the negation of women or the feminine (Kerfoot and Knights, 1993). This is so readily discernible in the advertising and news media and in commonsense conversation.

In sum, Derrida and Lacan appear to coincide in their views about phallogocentric discourse wherein women or the feminine occupies a space which is both differential and outside of language such that it cannot be spoken about. Lacan appears to subscribe to an essentialism regarding the phallocentric nature of the symbolic order (Fraser, 1992: 58), from which there is no escape. By contrast, the deconstructionism of Derrida does offer an alternative, indeed continuous alternatives, to the privileging of masculine meanings, albeit in the abstract and disembodied terminology of the structuralism that his (post-structural) theory seeks to transcend. But even Derrida refuses to accept that there is any escape from the desire for fixed or self-identical meaning which presumably derives from the Lacanian principle that underlying phallocentric discourse or the symbolic order is a self-defeating desire for the symbiotic unity of pre-symbolic existence.

In spite of the pessimism of Derrida and Lacan, some feminists apply the work of these post-structuralists in searching for a transformation of the logocentric and phallocentric discourse. These mainly French feminists believe in the possibility of thinking and acting in regard to gender in ways which release women from 'the negative pole of a binary opposition (masculine–feminine)' (Duchen, 1986: 76–85). In so doing, French feminism attempts to disrupt the complacency that allows our entire cultural framework to be 'predicated on the indifferentiation of gender, on the repression/suppression of the feminine' (1986: 76–85).

Our major concern in providing here a brief summary of three French feminists is to abstract from these writings those aspects which we believe extend post-structuralist theory in ways that advance non-essentialist and embodied analyses of gender relations. An additional concern is that these analyses can inform debate on a politics for challenging conventional social relations with respect to gender and sexuality. To some degree, however, this necessitates a departure from traditional Marxist-inspired conceptions of a collective politics that requires for its effectiveness precisely the unity, linearity and stability of meaning associated with the phallogocentric and patriarchal discourse and practice to which French feminist philosophy directs most of its criticism. It is by way of this challenge that we seek to address the latter part of Game's (1991) original question posed earlier, in exploring the possibility of thinking 'how might we be otherwise, *now?*'

Perhaps the most virulent opponent of patriarchal language is Irigaray (1980), who argues that the first task is to expose the masculinity of language from behind its appearance as a universal and neutral phenomenon. While the basic preoccupation of the masculine is to order, categorize, rationalize, stabilize and unify, Irigaray characterizes the feminine as multiple and diffuse. Concentrating on the feminine libidinal economy she argues that women in contrast to men experience 'jouissance', defined as the multiplicity of corporeal, sexual and bodily pleasures. This falls in line with her overall project to explore women's sexual autonomy and their sexual specificity as a mark of sexual difference from men, rather than sameness (see, for example, Grosz, 1989). Further, her argument is that women experience a way of being in the world that disrupts the linear logic and the limits on meaning which phallogocentric discourse imposes on our culture. While drawing upon the language and discourse of Lacan and Derrida, she refuses to concede that the feminine is that which cannot be conceptualized or reflects merely the absence or differance which provides the conditions of possibility of masculine dominance.

The political challenge to the symbolic order of patriarchal domination takes the form of a celebration of women's 'alterity' in writing and in female sexual autonomy. Having taken on Lacan and Derrida's account of the absence of women from masculine phallic discourse, Irigaray is convinced that progress can only be made by beginning from elsewhere – in the body. But in writing, there is a contradiction, for as Felman (1975: 3) has argued, when discussing Irigaray's work: 'if "the woman" is precisely the other of any conceivable Western theoretical locus of speech, how can the woman as such be speaking in this book?' Irigaray's answer is to refrain from posing the question 'what is woman?' but instead to engage repeatedly in interpreting the way 'the feminine finds itself determined in discourse – as lack, default or as mime and inverted reproduction of the subject' (1980: 75–6). Her concern is to elevate the feminine in opposition to what is defined as monolithic patriarchal oppression. But as Moi (1985: 147) points out, 'the paradox of [Irigaray's] position is that while she strongly defends the idea of "woman" as multiple, decentred and undefinable, her unsophisticated approach to patriarchal power forces her to analyse "woman" (in the singular) throughout as if "she" were indeed a simple, unchanging entity'.

This essentialist trap is an outcome of developing uncritically Lacan's theory in the direction of transcending his political pessimism. For, in treating the sexes themselves as so distinct and seeking to elevate the fluidity, multiplicity and plurality of the feminine, theorists are engaged precisely in attributing essential characteristics to the woman in the same way that patriarchal discourse does to the man.

In an attempt to avoid the essentialism of Lacan, Helene Cixous (see Conley, 1984) follows Derrida's deconstructionism more closely than Irigaray. She therefore seeks to 'split open' the closure of meaning where the privileging of masculinity within a conventional binary opposition inflicts upon femininity a negative, inferiority or 'other' status. One of the escapes from this essentialism is achieved through separating the sex of discourse from the sex of its author. Feminine writing, which can be written by men as well as women, is that which, through a continuous play on difference, undermines phallogocentric domination. This anti-essentialism, however, is achieved at the cost of a feminist utopia where female spontaneity and creativity are realized through a flight from the material reality of the Symbolic into the Imaginary ideal of the original unity 'between male and female, father and mother, subject and object, body and soul' (Moi, 1985: 122). In other words, rather than struggle with power, Cixous escapes into a self-expressive, but necessarily individualistic, poetic ecstasy that is non-essentialist only by virtue of having no relationship to material existence. While appropriating imagination and the pleasure principle for women, indeed to the extent of elevating precisely those emotional intuitive and irrational characteristics imposed by 'the very patriarchal ideology she denounces' (Moi, 1985: 123), Cixous's analysis remains equally as disembodied as the discourse of Derrida from which she draws her inspiration.

There are parallels in the work of Kristeva (1980, 1981), in that she also celebrates the poetic and subversive power of marginality where her conception of 'semiotics', as 'the expression of libidinal drives' (Fraser, 1992: 63) associated with femininity is the source of a material and revolutionary rejection of the dominant symbolic, rule-bound order of paternalism and masculinity. Following Derrida, Kristeva refuses to accept any positive definition of 'woman' since 'she' is outside discourse, existing only as an absent opposition to that phallogocentric order through which her negativity is defined. Rather than counter this marginal and negative image by proposing an alternative positive feminine identity, Kristeva celebrates marginality as a strategy for disrupting and undermining 'the phallocentric order that defines woman as marginal in the first place' (Moi, 1985: 163).

Her theory of language supports this dissident politics for she argues that the semiotic or inter-contextuality of meaning, although marginal and heterogeneous, has the capacity to subvert the structures of traditional linguistics. Moreover, this subversion will facilitate a breakdown of gender divisions since the semiotic, as the pre-figuring of symbolic meaning, develops prior to the phallogocentric discourse which creates the Symbolic Order. For it is associated with the pre-oedipal mother where opposition between masculine and feminine has not yet emerged. Here Kristeva develops Lacan's theory without falling into the trap of elevating some pure conception of femininity. Instead, her emphasis on marginality means that the negation of what is feminine is not a question of women's essential nature but of their *position* within patriarchal power relations.

In contrast to Lacan's view of 'woman' as that which cannot be known, Kristeva sees women as representing a limit of the symbolic order, a frontier between phallogocentric discourse and chaos – neither known nor unknown, inside or outside the dominant male culture. It is for this reason, she argues, that women are often viewed by men as either 'seductive temptresses or innocent virgins', as 'wicked whores or heavenly creatures'. In both cases, women are seen to protect patriarchal power and its symbolic order from the imaginary chaos which lies beyond their limit (Moi, 1985: 167).

Of these three authors, Kristeva makes the best use of post-structuralist theory, not least because she challenges it theoretically as well as politically. Unfortunately, and this may be a result of her concern for semiotics, context and specificity, she does not appear to advance a political practice that is realistic in the sense of it expanding beyond a celebration of marginality. Indeed, this romanticization of marginality elevates individuality to the exclusion of any collective organization. In her empathetic criticism, Moi (1985: 171) agrees that women are rendered marginal by phallogocentric discourse. However, from a material position concerning the reproduction of the species, women are absolutely central.

Two significant problems arise with this critique of Kristeva. First, Moi drifts into a conventional Marxist fallacy of reifying the ruling order when she seeks to explain the marginalization of labour and women. Without the continued exploitation and oppression of these groups, she argues, the status quo could not be maintained. Accordingly, the ruling order 'seeks to mask [women's] central economic role by marginalizing them on the cultural, ideological and political levels' (1985: 171). Having continuously and vigorously criticized feminists for falling into an essentialist trap in restoring a positivity and presence for the 'woman', Moi ends up attributing a self-preserving essence to an abstraction like the ruling order. In order to avoid the slide into such essentialism, an analysis of power has to be developed that escapes locating it as a property of abstract categories, whether these be phallogocentric discourses or ruling orders. Conversely, if we are to avoid the 'conspiracy trap', we must refrain from treating power as the property of the agents of capital or patriarchy and instead demonstrate how it resides not so much in persons as social relations and practices.

This takes us to the second problem implicit in Moi's critique which is the slippage into dual systems theory where distinctive explanations are given for the marginalization of labour and women which reinforce, rather than undermine, the prevailing economic and gendered segregation of production and reproduction. It is not mere coincidence, however, that the method proposed for resolving the problem of essentialism may be suggestive of a solution to this drift into dualism which is characteristic of Marxist feminism. As we have already seen, in rejecting an essentialist conception of feminine or masculine identity and proposing that, in their position of marginality, women can subvert or disrupt the male-dominated symbolic order, Kristeva displays a kindred spirit with Foucault. She does not, however, engage with his discourse on power and therefore cannot develop it for purposes of advancing her non-essentialist feminist politics.

In our view it is the absence of an analysis of power relations and conceptions of subjectivity that reflect and reinforce them which leaves French feminists falling back either on essentialist definitions of the distinctiveness of the 'woman' and/or utopian escapes from phallogocentric reality. In sum, despite recognizing how the projection of fixed and unitary meanings reproduce phallogocentric power, these theorists find it difficult to resist the promise of symbiotic unity that may be attained through securing themselves in a feminine identity. By way of attempting to rectify this shortcoming, the following section develops our analysis of power, sexuality and gender subjectivity.

Exploring Power and Sexuality

There is a potential in Foucault's analysis of power and sexuality that has not as yet been explored by feminists. This could be explained by the fact that, as we have already noted, Foucault had a blind spot in terms of problems of sex inequality and women's subordination. He concentrated his analysis not on relations between the sexes so much as upon the effects of power in constituting sexuality as the very truth of subjective being (Foucault, 1979). However, this focus on sexual subjectivity can be turned to 'good' effect in terms of establishing a feminist politics that avoids the sexual divisiveness of gender essentialism or the disembodied discourse of deconstruction theory.

Of most importance for our purposes is his identification of power and subjectivity. In broad outline, here power is an effect of strategies and mechanisms embedded in social practices which are themselves the consequence of the operation of previous power/ knowledge relations and apparatuses. This is to suggest that power has a history, albeit often discontinuous. In its exercise, however, power is targeted upon bodies and social relations in such a way as to discipline individuals and regulate populations. The work on discipline (Foucault, 1977) identifies hierarchical surveillance, normalization procedures and 'the examination' as the three most dominant strategies or instruments of power in modern society. The power of each of these strategies lies in their effect not just in constraining subjects through external observation, segregation and judgement of populations but also in producing a subjectivity that generates its own self-discipline internally, within people. In other words, the concern is with how subjectivity is produced – how individuals come to recognize themselves as subjects and, in turn, are recognized by others.

It is the interest in uncovering the extent to which power/ knowledge relations are constitutive of subjectivity in what he calls a positive and productive sense that leads him to study the 'history of sexuality'. Freud's theory of sexual repression is said to have concealed the reality of a proliferation of discourses on sexuality. Sexual identity, then, has become the most dominant mode of self-discipline for subjects yet, at the same time, a predominant source of anxiety and insecurity. Foucault (1982) concentrates his attention on how the power of discourse has turned subjects in on themselves, making them increasingly dependent on some form of self-discipline in conforming to, and revealing the truth of, their own sexual identities. In particular, this power has turned subjects back in on themselves through a process of individualization wherein they have to develop 'techniques of the self' for purposes of managing the effects of various power/knowledge strategies.

The creation of sexual difference can be seen then, on the one hand as a mechanism of power where subjects are divided between 'the good and the bad', citizens and criminals, the normal and the deviant. On the other hand, and most importantly for our purposes here, the creation of difference occurs with respect to men and women, and also to masculinity and femininity. These dividing practices and effects of power are routine and voluntary, undertaken by large numbers of the population attempting to achieve and secure subjective identity through a process of negating the threat of the 'other'. What Foucault does not examine is the interdependence of power within and between the techniques of self-management and dividing practices such that, for example, sexual difference as a dividing practice can be seen as a condition of the struggle over sexual identity and vice versa. Thus, for example, in negating homosexuality and homosexual men, in talk of 'pansies', 'poofs' or 'queers', heterosexual males deny the 'other' of sexuality in an attempt to secure their own sexual identities, and to deny the threat which gay men present to the subjectivities and identities of heterosexuals. It can be seen here how both power strategies and the techniques of managing subjective identity embrace the same stereotyping discursive and non-discursive practices which, in turn, constitute subjects whose mode of maintaining a sense of security depends on the very system of domination that is their global outcome.

Summary

In this chapter, we have concentrated on the theoretical analysis of power and identity for purposes of illuminating the problems of gender inequality, and gender differentiation. Beginning with the debate in Anglo-American Marxist feminism concerning the origin of women's oppression, our analysis turned to the work of the French post-structuralists and feminists in search of a non-dualistic account of gender relations. Despite the Anglo-American commitment to break away from dual systems theories, wherein women's oppression is seen to originate with patriarchal power on the one hand and class domination on the other, it was concluded that the very search for origins forces analysis back into the dualism, either privileging ideology or material existence. Clearly, the recent phase of analysis has become more sophisticated than the original debate where the response to Hartmann's view that class and patriarchy are separate, yet interrelated systems, was simply to assert, rather than demonstrate, a unity between the capitalist structure and gender ideology in creating and sustaining sex inequality and women's oppression (1981: 366). In the main, though, the development has been that of accumulating historical evidence ostensibly to display the interpenetration of gender ideology, as a legacy of pre-capitalist patriarchal structures, and class or economic power, as the medium of capitalist social organization.

In examining the various competing, historical arguments, it became increasingly uncertain as to whether the problem of dual systems theory was ever likely to be resolved through these methods. Not least, we argued, this is because historical analysis invariably slips into a search for origins – a project that rests ultimately on the classical philosophical conception of a trans-cendental subject (for example, God, the Sovereign, Man) to whom the source of all meaning can be traced (see also Hekman, 1990). Although of a higher order of abstraction than the patriarchy–class dualism, it amounts to the same in as much as there is a dualistic separation between the subject and object of meaning. Only by focusing upon the constitution, reproduction, deconstruction and transformation of meaning in both discourse and practice, can we approximate a dissolution of accounts that shift dualistically between material (class or biological) and ideological (patriarchy or family system) explanations of sex inequality.

Accordingly, our analysis turned to the post-structuralists and French feminists who have concentrated attention on the psycho-analytic formation of gendered sexuality and the deconstruction of the phallogocentric discourse and practice that is its contemporary condition and consequence. Examining first the work of Lacan and Derrida, it was argued that beneath the obscure abstractions lay respectively a gendered essentialism and a disembodied discourse. This essentialism and/or disembodiment resurfaces in the work of Cixous and Irigaray but less so in the analyses of Kristeva. None the less, each of these feminist writers articulates a significant reversal of masculine logocentric domination and, by contrast with the others, Kristeva achieves this neither by resorting to a gendered essentialism nor in producing a highly disembodied text. Indeed, although committed to a socio-political transformation, she criticizes 'any libertarian movement, feminism included, [that] does not analyze its own relationship to power and does not renounce belief in its own identity' (Kristeva, 1980: 141).

In our view, Kristeva's concern to dissolve identity, or what we would argue is the false security of the 'closure on meaning' that comes from an attachment to either sexual or oppositional identities, is necessary if resistance is not to replace the domination it struggles against with an equally repressive structure of subjugation. As far as can be seen, however, her politics, although subversive, lack mobilization thus remaining marginal for want of collective agency. Partly this stems from a tendency to romanticize the marginal and hence ultimately to celebrate individual difference in advance of any potential for communal or collective solidarity.

We concluded by focusing on Foucault, not because he resolves the problem of transforming marginal subversion into collective resistance. Rather, our interest in Foucault concerns the extent to which his work dissolves conventional dualisms at the same time as it avoids both the gendered essentialism and disembodied abstractions of his post-structuralist compatriots. Moreover, he concentrates specifically on how the constitution of sexual subjectivity and identity has, through the proliferation of discourses on sex, generated the very truth of what it is to be human under modern power/knowledge regimes.

For our purposes, what is particularly valuable is the way in which this dissolves conventional dualistic discourse. So, for example, by focusing on the *truth* effects upon practices and subjectivities of power/knowledge relations that in themselves are claimed to be neither true nor false, he collapses the dualism between reality and ideology. At the same time, through identifying the target of the mechanisms, technology and strategies of power in the minds and bodies of subjects, he escapes the problems stemming from either materialistic or idealistic forms of analysis. Finally, he demonstrates how power/knowledge relations are dispersed much like a relay throughout the social body such that their mechanisms may just as well be colonized by, and produced through, the more global strategies. Here the dualism between structure and action is broken down. Moreover, its methodological injunction is to concentrate analysis on the more localized mechanisms and practices since, in contrast to the global power that embraces them, they are amenable to empirical examination and investigation.

All of these methods facilitate an analysis of the social production of sexual divisions which discloses its conditions of possibility without resort to essentialist origins or disembodied abstractions. Most importantly, it focuses our attention on the way in which power and identity prevail upon social relations creating or sustaining systems of sex inequality. Finally, we believe this analysis is not devoid of a 'radical' and practical potential. Within the interstices of power relations exist a whole series of localized yet subjugated knowledges, which intimate considerable potential for resistance. In line with the views of many French feminists, we suggest that, although marginalized by the dividing practices of phallocratic discourse, the subjugated knowledges of 'woman' and 'the feminine' are specifically capable of subverting and disrupting prevailing masculine-dominated power relations.

Notes

1 Drawn from within political theory (see for example, Paine, 1969[1791]; Rawls, 1972), the residual legacy of which forms a bedrock to contemporary social regulatory state practices. For a discussion of 'needs' and rights in a contemporary capitalist context, see also Nancy Fraser (1989), especially chapter 8.

2 This is a reading of Lacan which coincides with that of Fraser (1992: 56), and which she argues could be seen as 'exaggerating the centrality of phallocentricism to [his] view of the symbolic order'. However it is a reading that exposes how the attempts of post-structuralism 'to break free of structuralism only render them all the more bound to it' (1992: 56).

References

Armstrong, P. and Armstrong, H. (1985a) 'Beyond sexless class and classless sex: towards Marxist feminism', in P. Armstrong, H. Armstrong, P. Connelly and A. Miles (eds), *Feminist Marxism or Marxist Feminism: A Debate*. Toronto: Garramond Press, pp. 1–38.

Armstrong, P. and Armstrong, H. (1985b) 'More on Marxism and feminism: a response to Patricia Connelly', in P. Armstrong, H. Armstrong, P. Connelly and

A. Miles (eds), *Feminist Marxism or Marxist Feminism*. Toronto: Garramond Press, pp. 63–8.

Barrett, M. (1980) *Women's Oppression Today: Problems in Marxist Feminist Analysis*. London: Verso Press.

Barrett, M. (1984) 'Rethinking women's oppression: a reply to Brenner and Ramas', *New Left Review*, No. 146 (July/August): 123–8.

Barrett, M. and McIntosh, M. (1980) 'The family wage: some problems for socialists and feminists', *Capital and Class*, No. 11: 51–72.

Barrett, M. and McIntosh, M. (1982) *The Anti-social Family*. London: NLB Press.

de Beauvoir, S. (1984[1949]) *The Second Sex*. Harmondsworth: Penguin.

Beechey, V. (1977) 'Some notes on female wage labour in capitalist production', *Capital and Class*, No. 3, pp. 45–66.

Beechey, V. (1987) *Unequal Work*. London: Verso.

Brenner, J. and Ramas, M. (1984) 'Rethinking women's oppression', *New Left Review*, No. 144 (March/April): 33–71.

Conley, V.A. (1984) *Helene Cixous: Writing the Feminine*: London: University of Nebraska Press.

dalla Costa, M. and James, S. (1972) *The Power of Women and the Subversion of the Community*. Bristol: Falling Wall Press.

Derrida, J. (1976) *Of Grammatology* (trans. G.C. Spivak). London: Johns Hopkins University Press.

Derrida, J. (1978) *Writing with Difference*. Chicago: University of Chicago Press.

Duchen, C. (1986) *Feminism in France*. London: Routledge and Kegan Paul.

Engels, F. (1972) *The Origins of the Family, Private Property and the State*. London: Pathfinder Press.

Felman, S. (1975) 'The Critical Phallacy', *Diacritics*, Winter: 2–10.

Foucault, M. (1977) *Discipline and Punish: the Birth of the Prison*. London: Allen Lane.

Foucault, M. (1979) *Power, Truth, Strategy* (eds N. Morris and P. Patton). Sydney: Federal Publications.

Foucault, M. (1980a) *Power/Knowledge: Selected Writings and Interviews 1972–77* (ed. Colin Gordon). Brighton: Harvester Press.

Foucault, M. (1980b) *The History of Sexuality*, vol. I: *An Introduction*. New York: Vintage Books.

Foucault, M. (1982) 'The subject and power', in H. Dreyfus and P. Rabinow (eds), *Michel Foucault: Beyond Structuralism and Hermeneutics*. Brighton: Harvester Press.

Fraser, N. (1989) *Unruly Practices: Power, Discourse and Gender in Contemporary Social Theory*. Oxford: Blackwell.

Fraser, N. (1992) 'The uses and abuses of French discourse theories for feminist politics', in M. Featherstone (ed.), *Cultural Theory and Cultural Change*. London: Sage.

Game, A. (1991) *Undoing the Social: Towards a Deconstructive Sociology*. Buckingham: Open University Press.

Grosz, E. (1989) *Sexual Subversions: Three French Feminists*. Sydney: Allen and Unwin.

Hartmann, H. (1979) 'The unhappy marriage of Marxism and feminism: towards a more progressive union', *Capital and Class*, No. 8: 1–33.

Hartmann, H. (1981) 'The family as a the locus of gender, class and political struggle', *Signs*, 6(3): 366–94.

Hekman, J. (1990) *Gender and Knowledge: Elements of a Postmodern Feminism.* Cambridge: Polity Press.

Humphries, J. (1981) 'Protective legislation, the capitalist state and working class men: the case of the Mines Regulation Act', *Feminist Review*, No. 7, pp. 37–59.

Irigaray, L. (1980) 'When our lips speak together', *Signs*, 6(1): 69–79.

James, S. (1972) *Women, the Unions and Work.* London: Notting Hill Workshop Group.

Kerfoot, D. and Knights, D. (1993) 'Management, masculinity and manipulation: from paternalism to corporate strategy in financial services', *Journal of Management Studies*, 30/41 July, pp. 659–77.

Kristeva, J. (1980) *Desire in Language.* New York: Columbia University Press.

Kristeva, J. (1981) 'Women's time', *Signs*, 7(1): 13–20.

Lacan, J. (1977) *Ecrits: A Selection* (trans. A. Sheridan). London: Tavistock.

Lacan, J. (1978) *Four Fundamental Concepts of Psychoanalysis.* Oxford: Blackwell.

Lewis, G. (1985) 'From deepest Kilburn', in L. Heron (ed.), *Truth, Dare or Promise: Girls Growing Up in the Fifties.* London: Virago, pp. 213–36.

Mitchell, J. (1975) *Psychoanalysis and Feminism.* Harmondsworth: Penguin.

Mitchell, J. and Rose, J. (eds) (1982) *Feminine Sexuality: Jacques Lacan and the Ecole Freudienne.* London: Macmillan (reprinted 1985).

Moi, T. (1985) *Sexual/Textual Politics: Feminist Literary Theory.* London: Routledge.

Mort, F. (1987) *Dangerous Sexualities: Medico-Moral Politics in England Since 1830.* London: Routledge and Kegan Paul.

Nead, L. (1988) *Myths of Sexuality: Representations of Women in Victorian Britain.* Oxford: Blackwell (reprinted 1990).

Paine, T. (1969[1791]) *The Rights of Man.* Harmondsworth: Penguin.

Pateman, C. (1988) *The Sexual Contract.* Cambridge: Polity Press.

Rawls, J. (1972) *A Theory of Justice.* Oxford: Clarendon Press.

Walby, S. (1986) *Patriarchy at Work.* Cambridge: Polity Press.

Weir, A. and Wilson, E. (1983) 'The British Women's Movement', *New Left Review*, No. 148: 74–103.

Wilson, E. (1982) 'Interview with Andrea Dworkin', *Feminist Review*, No. 11, pp. 73–81.

Zaretsky, E. (1976) *Capitalism, the Family and Personal Life.* London: Pluto Press.

5

Female Powerlessness: a Case of 'Cultural Preparedness'?

Hilary M. Lips

For the past several years, I have been engaged in two projects that, though separate, continually produce overlapping themes. One is a study of the academic choices young women and men make with respect to mathematics and science (Lips, 1989, 1992), the other is a synthesis of research on gender and power (Lips, 1991).

Though I did not particularly look for it, the theme of power and powerlessness often echoes through the data I gathered on the academic choices and career plans made by college students. With regard to mathematics, the physical sciences and, especially, engineering, female students often show a lack of confidence in their ability that belies strong past performance – equal to or exceeding that of their male peers. More generally, a surprising number of graduating female students, when asked to list their career goals, leave the space for their answer blank – as if the space itself represents the horizon they see. I have been struck by the repeated observation that, in an era when there is an abundance of talk about choices for women, women of college age often do *not* take control of their lives, avoid making strong choices, and project a stunning lack of security in their own abilities.

It appears that girls and women are at high risk, first as targets of a 'wisdom' that clips their wings, and then, eventually, as recipients of a strong message that a powerless stance works best for them in many situations. This is not a new insight. What it lacks, however, is an analysis of the means whereby this clipping, even crippling, is actualized: the mechanisms through which that message is conveyed and incorporated in ways to be and, especially, ways not to be. For many of us the larger factors supporting this view are obvious: sex discrimination, other forms of coercion at work, at school, at home, and the ever-present threat and reality of violence against women. What is not so obvious, however, are numerous socialization practices that enhance girls' sense of powerlessness, and the ongoing patterns of social control in ordinary interaction made possible by these practices. Thus, the focus here is on the manner in which these routine practices and controls underlie the more obvious factors and prime or prepare girls and women to accept powerlessness.

An examination of the research on social interactions reveals a theme that I have labelled 'cultural preparedness for power-lessness'. It is as if girls are taught from the start that they can exert control over a situation only in certain limited circumstances – and the message is so consistent that girls and women become increasingly *ready* to learn the lesson of powerlessness in any new situation. The effect is analogous to what psychologists have labelled 'biological preparedness' – a biologically based readiness to learn particular behaviours or associations (for example, Diener et al., 1975). In a similar fashion, my reading of the research on social interaction suggests, early and continuing socialization 'primes' girls and women to accept powerlessness.

A generally accepted definition of power, in psychology, is the capacity to have an impact or produce an effect. Research has accumulated showing that girls receive strong and consistent indications of their powerlessness in two major areas of power: mastery over tasks and influence over other people.

Childhood Socialization: Mastery vs Helplessness

Much of the research evidence suggests that, from childhood onward, females, in contrast to males, are taught that their actions frequently do not make a difference. Jeanne Block (1984), summarizing a lifetime of longitudinal research into the socialization of girls and boys, characterized the difference thus: girls, she said, were encouraged to develop *roots*, boys were taught to develop *wings*. Girls, in other words, were given few chances to master the environment, and their socialization tended toward 'fostering proximity, discouraging independent problem solving by premature or excessive interventions, restricting exploration, and discouraging active play' (Block, 1984: 111). Boys, on the other hand, were encouraged to 'develop a premise system that presumes or anticipates mastery, efficacy, and instrumental competence' (1984: 131). Recent research supports Block's claim: parents and teachers, often unwittingly, are teaching girls not to try things (because their efforts either do not make any difference or may result in failure or danger) and not to speak (because no one will pay serious attention to them). Boys, by contrast, are being taught that their outcomes depend on their own efforts and that their concerns are taken seriously by adults.

Parents
While parents do encourage their female and male children to engage in sex-typed activities, they do not treat their sons and daughters as differently, at least during childhood, as gender norms might suggest (Lytton and Romney, 1991). However, small differences in the early childhood treatment of girls and boys may lay the groundwork for the construction of far larger gender differences. The projection of small early differences in treatment to equally small later consequences implies a perhaps unjustified assumption of linearity in the relationship between socialization and outcomes. With the emergence of chaos theory and non-linear modelling, evidence is growing, within psychology as in other social sciences, that linear relationships between behavioural antecedents and consequences may be the exception rather than the rule (for example, Chen, 1988; Grebogi et al., 1987; Guastello, 1988; Mende et al., 1990; Richards, 1990; Sterman, 1988). Seen within the framework of non-linear dynamics and catastrophe theory, the presence of small, seemingly trivial, differences in the initial positions and development of two groups (in this case, females and males) does not imply continued similarity of paths in later stages of development. Thus, a mild or modest differential emphasis on mastery may foster subsequent gender divergences totally disproportionate to initial treatment differences.

To this point, parental behaviour shows a relationship to the development of mastery, and that relationship may differ for female and male children (Yarrow et al., 1984). From the time when parents describe newborn infant daughters as 'softer' and 'finer' than their newborn infant sons who are comparable in size and strength (Rubin et al., 1974), to the times when young boys are given toys that require skill and perseverance to assemble and use while girls are given dolls (Miller, 1987; Rheingold and Cook, 1975), the message sent by parents to their children is that boys can make things happen and can take care of themselves, while girls cannot. This message is underlined in early adolescence when girls' dating behaviour is watched and circumscribed while that of boys is granted more latitude (Katz, 1986).

Studies of parent–child interactions show quite consistently that parents are more likely to encourage dependency in daughters than in sons (Lytton and Romney, 1991). In one study (Frankel and Rollins, 1983), parents worked with their 6-year-old children on jigsaw puzzle and memory tasks. The parents of sons and daughters used different strategies: parents of sons were more likely to suggest general problem-solving strategies and let the boy figure out how to apply them to the task at hand; parents of girls were more likely to suggest specific solutions rather than waiting for their daughters to work out the solutions themselves. With a daughter, parents were more likely to work cooperatively; with a son, they were more likely to remain physically uninvolved but to praise him for good performance and scold him for inattention. The parents in this study offer an example of the different messages about mastery that are communicated to girls and boys: it is communicated more strongly to the sons than to the daughters that it is important for them to learn to solve this problem and others like it – and that they do it, as far as possible, on their own.

The pattern described here may emerge very early. A study of parents attempting to teach their 8-month-old infants to put a small cube into a cup showed differences in the behaviour they directed at females and males (Brachfield-Child et al., 1988). Parents were more directive of their female than their male infants. They aimed more utterances, particularly negative, imperative and exhortative utterances, at girls than boys. Another study, focusing on parents' involvement in communication between their children, also showed parents of very young children being more directive of daughters than sons. Parents made more utterances encouraging girls than boys to interact with a sibling (Austin, Summers and Leffler, 1987). In this study, which included pairs of siblings aged 18–26 months and 4–6 weeks, fathers were especially active in directing the interactions between their children, particularly the interactions involving girls.

Although parents in various cultural groups differ in the rules they attach to gender, it is not unusual to find that parents, particularly fathers, pay more attention to boys than to girls, and emphasize cooperation and nurturance more for girls and achievement and autonomy more for boys. For example, Phyllis Bronstein (1984) showed, in a study of Mexican families, that when interacting with their school-aged children, fathers listened more to boys than to girls and were more likely to show boys than girls how to do things. These fathers treated their daughters especially gently, but they seldom gave them their full attention and were quick to impose opinions on them. These fathers too were communicating a message of mastery to boys and help-lessness to girls: what boys have to say is more important than what girls have to say, and boys are more capable than girls of learning new skills.

This conclusion is reinforced by findings that parents react to the achievements of their daughters and sons differently. For example, they tend to credit their sons' success at mathematics more to talent and their daughters' success more to effort (Yee and Eccles, 1988). A longitudinal study linking the influence of mothers to the academic expectations of young children illustrates that, particularly in middle-class families, mothers may unwittingly produce gender differences in their children's expectations for success (Baker and Entwisle, 1987). The effects of mother's expectations are generally positive for boys and tend to favour boys over girls in arithmetic and in beginning reading. It appears that mothers, through their day-to-day interactions with their young children, subtly support the creation of a gender-differentiated academic self-concept by giving girls and boys different messages about the perceptions and expectations they should have of themselves. This process, note the researchers, is distinct from the abstract opinions mothers have about gender, which tend to be egalitarian.

Parents, through their encouragement of sex-typed activities, may encourage girls less than boys toward the sense of power that accompanies physical self-efficacy. Girls learn that they are weaker than boys, that they cannot depend on their bodies for certain strength-related tasks. They are less likely than boys to be steered towards sports. These messages to girls continue despite research suggesting that some of the female–male strength disparity that appears in adolescence is due to a lack of sufficient muscle use by females (Roundtable . . . 1985; Wilmore, 1975). When girls do participate in strength training, they show gains in self-efficacy that generalize beyond confidence in physical ability to a sense of general life effectiveness (Holloway et al., 1988).

Especially as they approach adolescence, girls may be taught by parents to think of their bodies as sources of vulnerability and danger. Concerns about sexual activity and pregnancy often cause parents to place new restrictions on girls at adolescence so that growing up is associated with a feeling of decreasing, rather than enhanced, freedom (Golub, 1983; Katz, 1986). Moreover, for the significant minority of girls who are victims of childhood sexual abuse by a family member, sexuality as a source of vulnerability takes on a sinister aspect. For these girls, whom researchers estimate make up from 4 to 12 per cent of the female population in North America (Herman, 1981; Russell, 1983), a long-term outcome is a persistent sense of powerlessness (Briere and Runtz, 1986; Edwards and Donaldson, 1989; Lowery, 1987).

Teachers

The gender-differentiated patterns of emphasis on mastery initiated by parents may be enhanced and extended by teachers and school environments. Girls get higher grades in school than boys but show less confidence than boys in their scholastic abilities (Kimball, 1989). Even though girls *do* master academic tasks, often more quickly and easily than do boys, they are apparently led to attribute their successes to factors other than their own abilities. Preschool[1] classrooms are characterized by a greater frequency of interactions between teachers and boys than between teachers and girls; one study of 2,183 such interactions found the ratio to be 60/40 (Ebbeck, 1984). Attention and feedback in classrooms from elementary school upwards are dispensed differently to girls and boys – and the differences are such as to reinforce feelings of mastery and control in boys and helplessness in girls. Teachers pay more attention to boys than girls and allow boys to talk and to interrupt them more than they do girls (Sadker and Sadker, 1985; Serbin and O'Leary, 1975). This pattern ensures that more time will be spent on boys' than on girls' questions and that children will learn that male concerns take first priority.

Thus, though sharing instructional situations, girls and boys may nevertheless encounter very different educational experiences. For example, studies of elementary and secondary school[2] mathematics classes show that boys receive a greater share of the teachers' attention in class than do girls, are more active than girls in providing answers, have more non-academic conversational contact with teachers, and may be more likely to be considered the best, or as possessing high potential (Becker, 1981; BenTsvi-Mayer et al., 1989; Brophy, 1985; Koehler, 1986; Marshall and Smith, 1987).

These patterns are not limited to white, middle-class students. A pair of studies by Irvine (1985, 1986) show that, in the first two grades of elementary school, white girls received less total communication from teachers than did white boys or African-American children of either gender. However, as the African-American girls moved from lower to upper elementary school grades, there was a significant decline in the total amount of teacher feedback, the amount of positive feedback, and the number of opportunities they received to respond in class, culminating in a situation where they were as inconspicuous to the teachers as the white girls. African-American girls apparently enter the school system with more self-confidence, perhaps drawn from their families and communities, than do their white counterparts. However, once in the school system, they are the targets of attempts to mould them into the 'quiet girl' ideal favoured by white, middle-class culture. These attempts may succeed less well with African-American girls than with their Caucasian counter-parts. A recent survey of self-esteem among adolescent girls showed that African-American girls maintained their self-esteem at higher levels during the transition to adolescence than did white or Hispanic girls (Little girls . . ., 1991).

In addition, the patterns are not limited to elementary school. Even at the college level, the classroom atmosphere and interactions may be less comfortable in general for females than males (Constantinople et al., 1988; Crawford and MacLeod, 1990; Schnellman and Gibbons, 1984).

Research by Dweck and her colleagues (Dweck et al., 1978; Dweck and Leggett, 1988; Elliott and Dweck, 1988) shows that elementary school classrooms may introduce gender differences in the contingencies of performance feedback – with mastery orientations being more strongly encouraged for boys than for girls. The differences in feedback take three forms: the amount and diffuseness of feedback, the type of response on which the feedback is contingent, and the type of attribution for performance that is delivered along with the feedback.

Boys receive more negative classroom feedback than do girls, and that negative feedback is also more diffuse (that is, not focused narrowly on whether the answer is correct, but also on broader issues such as neatness, boisterousness, etc.). Girls, by contrast, get more, and more diffuse, *positive*, feedback than do boys. When girls get negative feedback it is usually in response to a wrong answer; when they get positive feedback it may often be for behaving well, looking nice, handing in something that is neat and attractive. By contrast, when boys get negative feedback it is as likely to be for sloppiness, inattention, or disruptive behaviour as for poor performance; when they get positive feedback, it is usually for good intellectual performance. Boys, under a steady stream of negative feedback, get used to criticism and learn not to be crushed by it. Girls, for whom negative feedback is rare, take that negative feedback to heart and maintain a sensitivity to failure.

Contributing to the tendency for girls and boys to respond differently to feedback from teachers are the explicit attributions teachers make when delivering feedback. For boys, negative feedback is often accompanied by an attribution to lack of effort or motivation. For girls, there is often no such attribution, since teachers apparently see girls as motivated and diligent. Negative feedback is often delivered to girls with *no* accompanying attribution, leaving them to infer that they are simply not very good at the task.

According to Dweck (1986), the end result of these different patterns of feedback is that girls and boys learn to make different causal attributions for success and failure. Boys are more likely than girls to learn that failure means they are just not trying hard enough. Girls are more likely than boys to learn that success means the task was easy – or that the teacher likes them. Girls learn that it is important to demonstrate their ability by performing well; they learn to avoid challenging, difficult tasks unless they are extremely confident of success – because failure threatens their own and others' opinions of their ability. Boys learn to think of their skills as improvable and to focus on that possibility of improvement as a goal. They learn, in other words, that their efforts make a difference, that, by trying harder, they can master a difficult situation.

Reinforcing the conclusions reached by Dweck and her colleagues are a variety of other findings. For example, teachers' judgements of girls' intellectual competence is predicted by girls' compliance to the teacher; however, teacher ratings of boys' competence is unrelated to compliance (Gold et al., 1987). Even in the first grade, girls and boys indicate that they have learned different things about what is important in school: boys' academic self-concept includes a strong focus on being able to learn quickly; girls are focused on the importance of obeying the rules and being honest (Entwisle et al., 1987). Such teacher influences may provide some of the underpinnings for the frequently reported observation that girls enter many achievement situations with lower expectations of success than do boys (Crandall, 1969; Parsons and Ruble, 1977).

Dweck (1986) has argued that the different patterns of feedback for girls and boys may lead to a differential emphasis in academic development. The pattern encourages boys toward the belief that their abilities are not fixed, but incremental, and helps them to focus on mastery-driven achievement goals. Girls, by contrast, are encouraged towards 'fixed ability' beliefs, an orientation to achievement that emphasizes performing well in order to demonstrate their ability, and a sensitivity to failure feedback. The result may be a stronger predisposing tendency for females to seek favourable judgements of their competence and avoid negative judgements – by avoiding the risks associated with publicly trying to master difficult material. Indeed, one study suggests that by the time students are in college, females and males show differences in their approach to learning that appear to reflect Dweck's predictions. Female college students report an emphasis on demonstrating that they know the material; male students focus on the challenge of learning and emphasize feedback and exchange with the instructor (Magolda, 1990).

Such differential beliefs and orientations may have no obvious consequence in a number of classroom settings. However, they may cause girls and young women to be more vulnerable to uncertainty and failure when specific competencies are challenged and confused. In intellectual achievement situations fostering confusion and uncertainty about success, girls' self-views of abilities suffer and confidence falls; difficulty and confusion are interpreted as failures documenting an inadequate and unchangeable ability (Dweck et al., 1980). When vulnerable individuals with performance-orientated achievement goals lose confidence in their level of ability, the result is a 'helpless pattern' (Dweck and Leggett, 1988; Dweck and Licht, 1980).

Given these predisposing differences in implicit ability beliefs and motivational goals, boys may tend to display more confidence than girls in academic areas where opportunities for success seems most uncertain (Dweck and Licht, 1980). Such expected differences in confidence are in agreement with earlier work showing that girls' lower confidence is most likely to emerge on tasks that are unfamiliar and for which no clear feedback has been given about previous performance (Lenney, 1977), and at times when success is very uncertain (Licht et al., 1989). Congruent with the evidence concerning confidence are findings such as those by Tapasak (1990): by the eighth grade, females with mathematics averages equivalent or better than males tended to underestimate their own future performance, while males tended to overestimate theirs. Significantly more females than males exhibited a negative expectancy-attribution pattern: they attributed success in mathematics to variable factors and failure to stable factors, and were less likely than males to persist at tasks and courses in mathematics (Tapasak, 1990). As with many other studies (for example, Dweck and Leggett, 1988; Licht et al., 1989), the Tapasak study demonstrates that reported gender differences in implicit views and beliefs about ability are not merely gender differences in self-presentational style. This is accomplished by showing that females and males differ not only in their self-reports, their presentations, but also in their behaviour with respect to the achievement areas in question.

As students progress from elementary school, they face an increasingly negative instructional environment (Eccles et al., 1989). This occurs at a time when classroom environments and student–teacher relationships are salient to students and important to student achievement (Feldlaufer et al., 1988). With transfer to middle school, relative performance comparisons and self-assessments of ability intensify, effort and ability begin to be differentiated, grades tend to be lower (Feldlaufer et al., 1988). For mastery-orientated persons, the encounter with novel and confusing material in this less supportive, more uncertain climate would still remain a challenge to seek, or at least overcome; for performance-orientated persons, it would represent an increasing confusion and threat to avoid. Such situational increases in the uncertainty of success in areas such as mathematics and the physical sciences, coupled with differences in predisposing beliefs and goals may explain girls' and young women's reluctance (relative to males') to continue taking mathematics courses, even when they have done well in the past (Dweck, 1986).

Regardless of talent, as challenges and obstacles increase from late elementary school to college, females seem likely to receive less parental and teacher encouragement and support than males. As early as elementary school, female students, more than males, have been encouraged to develop and maintain implicit beliefs and motivational orientations that allow failures to have a detrimental effect on their self-perceived abilities. In contrast, more male students than females have been encouraged to develop implicit dispositions and mastery orientations that channel failures into opportunities for learning and growth. Moreover, this greater female vulnerability or sensitivity to failure will be most apparent in differing patterns of cognition, affect, behaviour displayed in transitions from success to success-uncertainty and failure; that is, those novel situations in which success is uncertain and in which they are exposed to the possibility of performance assessments and ability attributions for their outcomes. From middle school to university, mathematics and related subjects are characterized by ever new, difficult material, a shrinking ratio of females to males, and an increasing emphasis on ability. When faced with such situations, females are apparently more likely than males to expect less success, to avoid the situation if possible, and to persevere less strongly in the face of difficulties. Most disturbingly, Dweck's analysis suggests that such motivational factors are strongest, and most maladaptive, for the brightest girls – those who have had a string of early and consistent successes.

The school environment may provide females with socialization toward powerlessness not only through messages about academic success and failure, but also through messages about relationships and sexuality. A survey of more than 1,000 university science students showed that 17 per cent of the females and 2 per cent of the males reported that they had been sexually harassed by an instructor (McCormack, 1985). Other studies have found similarly high percentages of female harassment victims among college students (Adams et al., 1983; Bailey and Richards, 1985). A young woman being sexually harassed by her teacher or professor is made to feel powerless in several ways: she feels that she has little control over the relationship; she feels that her achievement-orientated behaviours will make little or no difference to the academic outcomes that are controlled by the harasser; she is aware that she is not being taken seriously as a whole person, but is being related to mainly in terms of her sexuality. Since sexual harassment of female students is not a rare event, but rather seems to affect directly at least one-sixth of female college students (and indirectly, through observation and discussion, many more), it must be regarded as part of the process through which females absorb the message of powerlessness in school situations.

Peers
What parents, teachers and school systems illustrate by example and leadership, children themselves are quick to model and reproduce. Children and adolescents apparently collude with adults in the socialization of females and males into different roles and styles when it comes to power. Clearly there are strong cognitive categorizing and social identity forces at work: children use the cultural information that surrounds them to construct gender stereotypes (Maccoby, 1988), and also to enforce them (Fagot, 1984). Messages about appropriate behaviour for males and females are absorbed from parents, teachers and other socializing agents, encoded and then re-enacted in a multitude of contexts.

Children join actively in the process of socializing one another into gender-appropriate patterns of mastery and influence. Even among toddlers, girls paired off with male playmates behave more passively than boys or than girls paired with other girls (Jacklin and Maccoby, 1978). As preschoolers, boys make more attempts than girls to influence their peers – mainly by making direct requests and giving orders (Serbin et al., 1982). As boys move from the ages of 3 to 5 years, they become increasingly likely to use direct modes of influence: orders ('give me that'), announcements ('you have to give me that'), or assigning roles ('pretend you're the doctor'). During the same time period, girls are becoming more likely to use *indirect* influence styles: implying rather than clearly stating the request ('I need that toy'), or bracketing requests in polite, deferential phrases ('May I please have that toy?'). Between the ages of 3 and 5, boys become increasingly impervious to influence attempts by their peers, while girls' responsiveness to influence attempts remains stable. It is possible that boys' decreasing responsiveness is related to the high number of influence attempts directed at them by parents and teachers.

When girls do use direct influence strategies, they are more effective with other girls than with boys. This experience, researchers suggest, helps to perpetuate both the high levels of same-gender play found in preschool and elementary school classrooms and the development of verbal influence styles that are increasingly gender-differentiated (Maccoby, 1988; Powlishta and Maccoby, 1990). These researchers note that boys, because of their higher use of power assertion and physical power, tend to get more than their share of a scarce resource in a mixed-gender, competitive situation. This disparity is attenuated in the presence of adults, because boys do not try so hard to dominate girls when adults are present. It appears that girls learn early that they are ineffective influencers with respect to boys and that they retreat to the influence styles (indirect, polite) and contexts (other females, adults) that *are* effective for them.

For girls who do not retreat into accepted styles, there are problems ahead. A study of first and second graders suggests that reactions to power holders may differ in female and male groups. Boys who were the most dominant members of their groups tended to be liked and accepted by their same-gender peers; dominant girls, on the other hand, were targets of dislike and rejection by other group members (Jones, 1983).

Extensive (self-chosen) segregation between girls and boys in elementary schools provides gender-differentiated contexts for learning the processes of power and influence. Boys obtain considerable practice in interactions that are competitive and dominance-orientated (Maccoby, 1990) and they experience the shared excitement and bonding that accompanies public transgression of rules (Thorne and Luria, 1986). Girls, on the other hand, practise interactions that are facilitative, form friendships through self-disclosure, and construct a shared identity based partly on being 'good' (Ullian, 1984). These different patterns of socialization lay the groundwork for future gender differences in power when the two groups must finally work and live together as adolescents or adults. A woman, used to a facilitative style of relating, is bound, in many contexts, to find herself at a power disadvantage when interacting with a man who has been socialized toward a more dominant, competitive interaction style (Maccoby, 1990).

Children's conversations reflect and strengthen gender differences in approaches to power. Studying children from a sample of largely white, working- and middle-class families, researchers have noted that boys are more likely than girls to 'take charge' of conversations (Austin, Salehi and Leffler, 1987). In preschool, third and sixth grades, boys were more likely than girls to initiate conversations and to use various devices, from tapping another child insistently on the arm to shouting 'Look at me', for getting attention. Girls, by contrast, were more likely than boys to try to facilitate an ongoing conversation and to use reinforcers (nodding, 'um-hm') to acknowledge a partner's speech or behaviour. This pattern is the precursor of the frequently observed pattern of male conversational dominance among adults (for example, Spender, 1989; Zimmerman and West, 1975).

In classroom situations, girls receive less information and task-related interaction from their peers than do boys (Webb, 1984; Webb and Kenderski, 1985). Furthermore, female students after being exposed for years to schooling conditions and interactions with teachers that tend to make them sensitive to negative feedback and failure, may have to face a barrage of such negative feedback from peers if they choose, in high school or university, to pursue achievement goals in areas stereotyped as masculine. Up to and including the university level, male students are more likely than females to stereotype mathematics, science, engineering and computing as male domains (Hyde et al., 1990; Lips, 1989, 1992; Temple and Lips, 1989). Such findings suggest that, like their younger counterparts, women in college mathematics, computing and science classrooms may face a more negative social context in the form of peer judgements than do men. Peer reactions are likely to be especially important among college-age students because students in college have the leeway to adjust their programmes of study if they sense peer disapproval.

Prepared for powerlessness

By adolescence, females are showing a pattern of lowered self-confidence and readiness to accept the notion that they are not capable of mastering certain situations. Female adolescents underrate their competence in a number of life skill areas (Poole and Evans, 1989). Female high school students rate themselves as significantly more powerless than do their male counterparts (Calabrese and Seldin, 1985/86). At the ages of 4, 9 and 14 years, boys control more decision outcomes than do girls; by the age of 14, girls are less likely than are their male counterparts to perceive themselves as decision controllers (Lind and Connole, 1985). One study of young African-American adolescents showed that, although females listed more successful experiences, males self-reported higher competence (Alderman and Doverspike, 1988). A large study sponsored by the American Association of University Women documents a disturbing drop in self-esteem among girls as they move from childhood to adolescence (Little girls . . ., 1991). At the age of 9 years, 60–70 per cent of girls and boys responded positively to questions designed to measure their confidence and self-esteem. However, by the age of 16, the percentage of positive responses had dropped far more dramatically for girls (to 29 per cent) than for boys (to 46 per cent).

Clearly, children are socialized into, and also construct, using the information that surrounds them, gender-differentiated perceptions of their own possibilities for power. What is being absorbed and reproduced is far less innocuous than 'pink for girls; blue for boys' or 'boys play football; girls do aerobics'. For girls, it is an abiding path of acquiescence, of relative silence in the face of uncertainty, conflict or the throes of daily testing. What is absorbed is a habit of self-doubt in the face of confusion or competition, a hesitancy that can affect a young woman's later decisions in situations ranging from speaking up with a good answer, to entering a male-dominated contest, to choosing career options, to asserting her rights strongly and publicly when faced with discrimination, sexual harassment, or abuse. In the context of current gender power relations, an implementation of alternatives to women's well-nurtured habit of silence and self-doubt is extremely difficult. Whatever the difficulties, though, this gender difference is not inevitable. If the difference in preparedness for power is fundamentally a micro-accumulation of broadly supported interaction patterns, then different patterns may be envisioned, modelled and implemented. And if non-linear dynamics are truly at play in these situations, then it is not unreasonable to expect that the un-clipped wings of a growing few can set in motion improvements in the climate for many. The changes implied by such a simple statement are far-reaching and demanding, but they begin and continue whenever women, using their own strength and the support of others, refuse, in small or large ways, to accept, for themselves or for their daughters, a silent or powerless stance.

Notes

1 Generally, preschool children are four to five years of age in North America.
2 North American elementary school children are normally six to thirteen years of age (grades one to eight) and high school or secondary school children are normally fourteen to seventeen years of age (grades nine to twelve).

References

Adams, J., Kottke, J. and Padgitt, J. (1983) 'Sexual harassment of university students', *Journal of College Student Personnel*, 24: 484–90.

Alderman, M.K. and Doverspike, J.E. (1988) 'Perceived competence, self-description, expectation, and successful experience differences among students in Grades seven, eight, and nine', *Journal of Early Adolescence* 8(2): 119–31.

Austin, A.M., Salehi, M. and Leffler, A. (1987) 'Gender and developmental differences in children's conversations', *Sex Roles*, 16(9/10): 497–510.

Austin, A.M., Summers, M. and Leffler, A. (1987) 'Fathers' and mothers' involvement in sibling communication', *Early Childhood Research Quarterly*, 2(4): 359–65.

Bailey, N. and Richards, M. (1985) 'Sexual harassment in graduate training programs in psychology', paper presented at the American Psychological Association Conference, Los Angeles.

Baker, D.P. and Entwisle, D.R. (1987) 'The influence of mothers on the academic expectations of young children: a longitudinal study of how gender differences arise', *Social Forces*, 65(3): 670–94.

Becker, B.J. (1981) 'Differential treatment of males and females in mathematics classes', *Journal for Research in Mathematics Education*, 12: 40–53.

BenTsvi-Mayer, S., Hertz-Lazarowitz, R. and Safir, M.P. (1989) 'Teachers' selection of boys and girls as prominent pupils', *Sex Roles*, 21: 231–45.

Block, J.H. (1984) 'Psychological development of female children and adolescents', in J.H. Block, *Sex Role Identity and Ego Development*. San Francisco: Jossey Bass, pp. 126–42.

Brachfield-Child, S., Simpson, T. and Izenson, N. (1988) 'Mothers' and fathers' speech to infants in a teaching situation', *Infant Mental Health Journal*, 9(2): 173–80.

Briere, J. and Runtz, M. (1986) 'Suicidal thoughts and behaviours in former sexual abuse victims', *Canadian Journal of Behavioural Science*, 18(4): 413–23.

Bronstein, P. (1984) 'Differences in mothers' and fathers' behavior toward children: a cross-cultural comparison', *Developmental Psychology*, 20(6): 995–1003.

Brophy, J. (1985) 'Interactions of male and female students with male and female teachers', in L.C. Wilkinson and C.B. Marrett (eds), *Gender Influences in Classroom Interaction*. Orlando, Fla: Academic Press, pp. 115–42.

Calabrese, R.L. and Seldin, C.A. (1985/86) 'Adolescent alienation: an analysis of the female response to the secondary school environment', *High School Journal*, 69(2): 120–5.

Chen, P. (1988) 'Empirical and theoretical evidence of economic chaos', *System Dynamics Review*, 4: 81–108.

Constantinople, A., Cornelius, R. and Gray, J. (1988) 'The chilly climate: fact or artifact?', *Journal of Higher Education*, 59: 527–50.

Crandall, V.C. (1969) 'Sex differences in expectancy of intellectual and academic reinforcement', in C.P. Smith (ed.), *Achievement-related Motives in Children*. New York: Russell Sage Foundation, pp. 11–45.

Crawford, M. and MacLeod, M. (1990) 'Gender in the college classroom: an assessment of the "chilly climate" for women', *Sex Roles*, 23: 101–22.

Diener, E., Bugge, I. and Diener, C. (1975) 'Children's preparedness to learn high magnitude responses', *Journal of Social Psychology*, 96: 99–107.

Dweck, C.S. (1986) 'Motivational processes affecting learning', *American Psychologist*, 41: 1040–8.

Dweck, C.S., Davidson, W., Nelson, S. and Enna, B. (1978) 'Sex differences in learned helplessness: II. The contingencies of evaluative feedback in the classroom. III. An experimental analysis', *Developmental Psychology*, 14: 268–76.

Dweck, C.S., Goetz, T.E. and Strauss, N.L. (1980) 'Sex differences in learned helplessness: IV. An experimental and naturalistic study of failure generalization and its mediators', *Journal of Personality and Social Psychology*, 38: 441–52.

Dweck, C.S. and Leggett, E.L. (1988) 'A social-cognitive approach to motivation and personality', *Psychological Review*, 95: 256–73.

Dweck, C.S. and Licht, B.G. (1980) 'Learned helplessness and academic achievement', in J. Garber and M. Seligman (eds), *Human Helplessness: Theory and Application*. New York: Academic Press.

Ebbeck, M. (1984) 'Equity issues for boys and girls: some important issues', *Early Child Development and Care*, 18(1/2): 119–31.

Eccles, J.S., Wigfield, A., Flanagan, C.A., Miller, C., Reuman, D.A. and Yee, D. (1989) 'Self-concepts, domain values, and self-esteem: relations and changes at early adolescence', *Journal of Personality*, 57: 283–310.

Edwards, P.W. and Donaldson, M.A. (1989) 'Assessment of symptoms in adult survivors of incest: a factor analytic study of the Responses to Childhood Incest Questionnaire', *Child Abuse and Neglect*, 13(1): 101–10.

Elliott, E.S. and Dweck, C.S. (1988) 'Goals: an approach to motivation and achievement', *Journal of Personality and Social Psychology*, 54: 5–12.

Entwisle, D.R., Alexander, K.L., Pallas, A.M. and Cadigan, D. (1987) 'The emergent academic self-image of first graders: its response to social structure', *Child Development*, 58: 1190–206.

Fagot, B. (1984) 'Teacher and peer reactions to boys' and girls's play styles' *Sex Roles*, 11: 691–702.

Feldlaufer, H., Midgley, C. and Eccles, J.S. (1988) 'Student, teacher, and observer perceptions of the classroom environment before and after the transition to junior high school', *The Journal of Early Adolescence*, 8: 133–56.

Frankel, M.T. and Rollins, H.A., Jr. (1983) 'Does mother know best? Mothers and fathers interacting with preschool sons and daughters', *Developmental Psychology*, 19(5): 694–702.

Gold, D., Crombie, G. and Noble, S. (1987) 'Relations between teachers' judgments of girls' and boys' compliance and intellectual competence', *Sex Roles*, 16(7/8): 351–8.

Golub, S. (1983) 'Menarche: the beginning of menstrual life', *Women and Health*, 8(2/3): 17–36.

Grebogi, C., Ott, E. and Yorke, J.A. (1987) 'Chaos, strange attractors, and fractal basin boundaries in nonlinear dynamics', *Science*, 238: 632–8.

Guastello, S.J. (1988) 'Catastrophe modelling of the ancient process: organizational subunit size', *Psychological Bulletin*, 103: 246–55.

Herman, J. (1981) *Father–Daughter Incest.* Cambridge, Mass.: Harvard University Press.

Holloway, J.B., Beuter, A. and Duda, J.L. (1988) 'Self-efficacy and training for strength in adolescent girls', *Journal of Applied Social Psychology*, 18(8): 699–719.

Hyde, J.S., Fennema, E., Ryan, M., Frost, L.A. and Hopp. C. (1990) 'Gender comparisons of mathematics attitudes and affect: a meta-analysis', *Psychology of Women Quarterly*, 14: 299–324.

Irvine, J. (1985) 'Teacher communication patterns as related to the race and sex of the student', *Journal of Educational Research*, 78(6): 338–45.

Irvine, J. (1986) 'Teacher–student interactions: effects of student race, sex, and grade level', *Journal of Educational Psychology*, 78(1): 14–21.

Jacklin, C.N. and Maccoby, E.E. (1978) 'Social behavior at thirty-three months in same-sex and mixed-sex dyads', *Child Development*, 49: 557–69.

Jones, D.C. (1983) 'Power structures and perceptions of power holders in same-sex groups of young children', *Women and Politics*, 3: 147–64.

Katz, P.A. (1986) 'Gender identity: development and consequences', in R.D. Ashmore and F.K. Del Boca (eds), *The Social Psychology of Female–Male Relations*. Orlando, Fla: Academic Press, pp. 21–67.

Kimball, M. (1989) 'A new perspective on women's math achievement', *Psychological Bulletin*, 105(2): 198–214.

Koehler, M.C.S. (1986) 'Effective mathematics teaching and sex-related differences in algebra one classes'. Unpublished PhD dissertation, University of Wisconsin.

Lenney, E. (1977) 'Women's self-confidence in achievement settings', *Psychological Bulletin*, 84: 1–13.

Licht, B.G., Stader, S.R. and Swenson, C.C. (1989) 'Children's achievement-related beliefs: effects of academic research area, sex, and achievement level', *Journal of Educational Research*, 82: 253–60.

Lind, P. and Connole, H. (1985) 'Sex differences in behavioral and cognitive aspects of decision control', *Sex Roles*, 12(7/8): 813–23.

Lips, H.M. (1989) 'The role of gender, self- and task perceptions in mathematics and science participation among college students', ERIC Document ED 297 945, ERIC Clearinghouse for Science, Mathematics and Environmental Education.

Lips, H.M. (1991) *Women, Men, and Power*. Mountain View, Ca: Mayfield.

Lips, H.M. (1992) 'Gender and science-related attitudes as predictors of college students' academic choices', *Journal of Vocational Behavior*, 40: 62–81.

'Little girls lose their self-esteem on way to adolescence, study finds' (1991) *The New York Times*, 9 January.

Lowery, M. (1987) 'Adult survivors of childhood incest', *Journal of Psychosocial Nursing and Mental Health Services*, 25(1): 27–31.

Lytton, H. and Romney, D.M. (1991) 'Parents' differential socialization of boys and girls: a meta-analysis', *Psychological Bulletin*, 109(2): 267–96.

Maccoby, E.E. (1988) 'Gender as a social category', *Developmental Psychology*, 24(6): 755–65.

Maccoby, E.E. (1990) 'Gender and relationships: a developmental account', *American Psychologist*, 45(4): 513–20.

Magolda, M.B. (1990) 'Gender differences in epistemological development', *Journal of College Student Development*, 31(6): 555–61.

Marshall, S.P. and Smith, J.D. (1987) 'Sex differences in learning mathematics: a longitudinal study with item and error analysis', *Journal of Educational Psychology*, 79: 372–83.

McCormack, A. (1985) 'The sexual harassment of students by teachers: the case of students in science', *Sex Roles*, 13(1/2): 21–32.

Mende, W., Herzel, H. and Wermke, K. (1990) 'Bifurcations and chaos in newborn infant cries', *Physics Letters A*, 145: 418–24.

Miller, C.M. (1987) 'Qualitative differences among gender-stereotyped toys: implications for cognitive and social development in girls and boys', *Sex Roles*, 16(9/10): 473–87.

Parsons, J. and Ruble, D. (1977) 'The development of achievement-related expectancies', *Child Development*, 48: 1075–9.

Poole, M.E. and Evans, G.T. (1989) 'Adolescents' self-perceptions of competence in life skill areas', *Journal of Youth and Adolescence*, 18(2): 147–73.

Powlishta, K.K. and Maccoby, E.E. (1990) 'Resource utilization in mixed-sex dyads: the influence of adult presence and task type', *Sex Roles*, 23(5/6): 223–40.

Rheingold, H. and Cook, K. (1975) 'The contents of boys' and girls' rooms as an index of parents' behaviors', *Child Development*, 46: 459–63.

Richards, Dianna (1990) 'Is strategic decision-making chaotic?', *Behavioral Science*, 35: 219–32.

'Roundtable: Strength training and conditioning for the female athlete' (1985) *National Strength and Conditioning Association Journal*, 7(3): 10–29.

Rubin, J., Provenzano, F.J. and Luria, Z. (1974) 'The eye of the beholder: parents' views on sex of newborns', *American Journal of Orthopsychiatry*, 44: 512–19.

Russell, D. (1983) 'The incidence and prevalence of intrafamilial and extrafamilial sexual abuse of female children', *Child Abuse and Neglect*, 7: 133–46.

Sadker, M. and Sadker, D. (1985) 'Sexism in the schoolroom of the '80s', *Psychology Today*, 19: 54–7.

Schnellman, J. and Gibbons, J.L. (1984) 'The perception by women and minorities of trivial discriminatory actions in the classroom'. Paper presented at the American Psychological Association Conference, Toronto.

Serbin, L. and O'Leary, K. (1975) 'How nursery schools teach girls to shut up', *Psychology Today*, 9(7): 56–8, 102–3.

Serbin, L., Sprafkin, C., Elman, M. and Doyle, A. (1982) 'The early development of sex-differentiated patterns of social influence', *Canadian Journal of Behavioural Science*, 14(4): 350–63.

Spender, D. (1989) *The Writing or the Sex*. New York: Pergamon.

Sterman, John D. (1988) 'Deterministic chaos in models of human behavior: methodological issues and experimental results', *Systems Dynamics Review*, 4: 148–78.

Tapasak, R.C. (1990) 'Differences in expectancy-attribution patterns of cognitive components in male and female math performance', *Contemporary Educational Psychology*, 15: 284–98.

Temple, L. and Lips, H.M. (1989) 'Gender differences and similarities in attitudes toward computers', *Computers in Human Behavior*, 5: 215–26.

Thorne, B. and Luria, Z. (1986) 'Sexuality and gender in children's daily worlds', *Social Problems*, 33(3): 176–90.

Ullian, D. (1984) '"Why girls are good": a constructivist view', *Sex Roles*, 11(3/4): 241–56.

Webb, N.M. (1984) 'Sex differences in interaction and achievement in cooperative small groups', *Journal of Educational Psychology*, 76: 33–4.

Webb, N.M. and Kenderski, C.M. (1985) 'Gender differences in small-group interaction and achievement in high- and low-achieving classes', in L.C.

Wilkinson and C.B. Marrett (eds), *Gender Influences in Classroom Interaction*. Orlando, Fla: Academic Press, pp. 209–36.

Wilmore, J.H. (1975) 'Body composition and strength development', *Journal of Physical Education and Recreation*, 46: 45–6.

Yarrow, L.J., MacTurk, R.H., Vietze, P.M., McCarthey, M.E., Klein, R.P. and McQuiston, S. (1984) 'Developmental course of parental stimulation and its relationship to mastery motivation during infancy', *Developmental Psychology*, 20(3): 492–503.

Yee, D.K. and Eccles, J.S. (1988) 'Parent perceptions and attributions for children's math achievement', *Sex Roles*, 19: 317–33.

Zimmerman, D. and West, C. (1975) 'Sex roles, interruptions, and silence in conversation', in B. Thorne and N. Henley (eds), *Language and Sex: Difference and Dominance*. Rowley, Mass.: Newbury House, pp. 105–29.

6

The Existential Bases of Power Relationships: the Gender Role Case

Jean Lipman-Blumen

Power – seeking it, using it, abusing it, decrying it, coveting it, contesting and overthrowing it – is central to the human condition. It sets a major parameter for social existence. The meaning and expression, as well as the conditions and results, of power have fascinated politicians and troubled theorists as different as Machiavelli (1961[1532]), Parsons (1953, 1954), Barnard (1964), Salancik and Pfeffer (1977), Foucault (1980, 1983), Janeway (1980), Cialdini (1984), Lipman-Blumen (1984), Bailey (1988), Fraser (1989), and Pfeffer (1992).

Some political and organizational analysts have examined the importance of the illusion, as well as the reality, of power to enhance a leader's authority (Bailey, 1988; Machiavelli, 1961[1532]). Other theorists have focused on the distinction between power and influence (Barnard, 1964; Parsons, 1953, 1954). Others suggest power is intimately related to the '"general politics of truth", that is, the types of discourse which it accepts and makes function as true' (Foucault, 1980: 131). Others have analysed the role of power in organizations (Salancik and Pfeffer, 1977), while still others have explored the relationship between leadership and power (Bailey, 1988). Ever since Rosabeth Moss Kanter (1977) first studied 'men and women of the corporation' gender relations and power within organizations have been a 'hot' topic in the organizational literature (Larwood et al., 1985, 1987; Powell, 1988; Sekaran and Leong, 1992; Stead, 1985).

Numerous gender theorists have wrestled with various aspects of the relationship between power and gender. Some gender theorists have focused primarily upon the dominant/subordinate dimension of gender roles to explore various facets of power (Bonaparte, 1982; Davis et al., 1991; Janeway, 1980; Komter, 1991; Sheppard, 1989). Others have considered the power aspects of gender roles (Fraser, 1989; Ragins and Sundstrom, 1990). Still others have concerned themselves with the differential interpretations of power and gender offered by structuralism, pragmatism and deconstructionism and their significance for feminist theory (Fraser, 1991). Although considerable attention has been given to the complex interweaving of social, political, psychological and linguistic interpretations of gender roles, few gender theorists have directed their attention to the underlying factors, embedded in the human condition, that draw human beings into power relationships. That issue – the existential bases of power relationships – will be the primary focus of this chapter.[1] I shall explore the existential bases of power relationships, or what it is about the human condition that continuously propels us to enter power relationships and then, despite protestations, perpetuate them.

Gender roles will serve as an instructive paradigm for power relationships. Gender roles are particularly useful in a discussion of power relationships because of their marked intransigence to efforts to recalibrate the power relationships they represent. Only grudgingly and very slowly do they change. Before focusing on the main concern of this chapter, however, let us turn to several prior considerations: a definition of power; the inconstancy of resources; the dual myths of powerlessness and omnipotence; and the ubiquity of power relationships.

Preliminary Considerations:

A Definition of Power
Clearly, the concept of power suffers from a plethora of definitions, a review of which could handily usurp the entire space allotted. Yet that definitional surfeit inevitably forces any discussion of power to state at the outset the conceptualization on which it is based.

Most definitions of power emphasize the ability to make others conform to one's wishes, often leaving relatively ambiguous the exact origins and nature of that capacity. Some definitions conceptualize power primarily as a style or set of strategies employed to accomplish one's goals (Maccoby, 1976). In still other treatments, power is expressed in social structure (Weber 1968a, 1968b). Salancik and Pfeffer (1977) have articulated a contingency theory of power, and more recently Pfeffer (1992) has described power as a critical factor in organizational leadership.

Some interpretations construe power as an embedded, intractable personal attribute, while others delineate it as a commodity, something to be accrued and savoured, or lost and mourned.

Michel Foucault carefully distinguishes his use of power from the repression focus of Hegel, Freud and Reich. Instead, in writings that prefigure many post-modern approaches to power, Foucault sees power as expressed in heteromorphous strategies of domination omnipresent in society and buttressed by bodies of knowledge anointed by the powerful as 'truth'. Power, for Foucault, exists in 'manifold relations . . . which permeate, characterise, and constitute the social body . . . [which] cannot themselves be established, consolidated nor implemented without the production, accumulation, circulation, and functioning of a discourse' (1980: 93). Still other definitions of power articulate an omnibus combination of attribute *cum* commodity *cum* relationships *cum* social arrangements.

In this chapter, whose definition of power departs in most major respects from a 'post-modern' orientation,[2] let us assume that power is neither an attribute of individuals, groups, or organizations, nor a commodity that can be acquired and accumulated. It does not reside in individuals, groups, organizations or States, but eventually comes to characterize the relations among them. Rather, *power is that set of **processes** whereby one party (be it an individual, group, institution, or State) can gain and maintain the capacity to impose its will repeatedly upon another, despite any opposition, by its potential to contribute or withhold critical resources from the central task, as well as by offering or withholding rewards, or by threatening or invoking punishment* (Lipman-Blumen, 1984). The results of these processes can be seen in relations among individuals, groups, institutions and nations. The dominance resulting from such access to resources eventually becomes institutionalized in quasi-permanent arrangements, including formal structures and informal practices. Moreover, the ideologies, discourses or belief systems that the currently dominant party creates or articulates constitute the prevailing 'truth' which, in turn, becomes a justification of the dominant group's hegemony.

Once power appears to be solidly entrenched, conveying the capacity to proffer contributions and rewards or impose sanctions, the powerful rarely need to resort to its use. Simply the awareness that the 'more powerful' party controls such resources, both contributory and punitive, is ordinarily sufficient to compel compliance from the 'less powerful'.

The basic characteristic of the *power process* is an *on-going negotiation*, in which *resources* figure significantly. Those players who can bring or withhold valued – better yet, scarce – resources critical to resolving important social tasks tend to tip the power relationship in their own favour. With changing circumstances, each party's resources vary in relevance to the task at hand, as well as in quantity, thereby creating the potential for a continually changing power balance among the participants. Through various strategies, including the right to define 'truth', power contenders, as we shall suggest below, act to offset, capture or nullify the opposition's resources. In the power dynamic that fuels gender roles, all of these strategies come into play.

The Inconstancy of Resources
The power balance is subject to continual recalibration stemming from fluctuations in the content, quantity and value of all parties' resources. The inconstancy of resources is particularly rooted in two, related sources. The first source of this inconstancy resides in the **definitional**, rather than the inherent, quality of resources. Each player's resources are subject to divergent definitions and evaluations, depending upon all players' perspectives and positions or status. Thus, depending upon which parties can impose their definitions and evaluations, the valuation of each party's resources varies. A familiar example is the office staff meeting, where the group may disregard or devalue a female contributor's ideas, while the identical suggestions subsequently introduced by a male contributor will be accorded respect and value by that same group. Despite the inherent merit of their potential contributions, those parties whose resources are defined by the group as irrelevant or less valuable will encounter difficulty in their attempts to negotiate increased power.

Parties to a power relationship may strive mightily to redefine others' resources as less central or valuable than their own. Roland Barthes, the twentieth-century philosopher/linguist, reminds us that the powerful enjoy the prerogative of defining and labelling social phenomena (Barthes, 1957). Thus, it is not uncommon for the more powerful to define their own resources as key to the task at hand and devalue the resources of the less powerful (Salancik and Pfeffer, 1977). Those who do not recognize the processual character of power or the definitional, and therefore fluctuating, quality of resources are likely to accept the preferential definition of the more powerful's resources – be they physical strength, talent, or money – at face value. This, in turn, leads to a self-fulfilling prophecy, whereby the very act of defining transforms the definition into a reality (Merton, 1957).

The resources of opposing parties may be quite different in their nature, and often the very existence of a difference is used to resolve the power balance in favour of the more powerful, without systematic scrutiny of the actual innate content of that difference. Gender roles again illustrate our point. Traditionally, psychological differences between males and females have been presented as evidence of masculine superiority in a variety of psychological characteristics. Thus, for many decades, males' advantage in field independence (that is, the capacity to separate background from foreground) was considered a more important analytical ability than females' advantage in field dependence (that is, the capacity to integrate all aspects of a visual field, or, put differently, to see the 'big picture'). Males' alleged 'analytical' predilections commonly are valued more highly than females' presumably more 'intuitive' approaches. It is rarely noted that when male decision-makers describe crisis decisions based on 'gut reactions' (as then Chrysler Chairman Lee Iacocca did in a televised interview conducted by Tom Brokaw), we probably are witnessing intuition moving to a lower portion of the human anatomy.

The second, related source of inconstancy in the value of resources is **situational**. Few resources, beyond good health and life (which themselves may be sacrificed willingly for a superordinate goal)[3] are valued in all situations. Even money, ordinarily desired as a valuable resource, can lose its appeal when other resources appear more essential to success or survival. When the social context in which ongoing negotiations are embedded changes, previously critical resources may lose their centrality or, alternatively, gain even greater significance. The relative power positions of their controllers ebb and flow accordingly.

Sometimes, the crystallizing effects of crisis reveal the previously overlooked value of the 'less powerful's' potential contribution. Many aspects of crisis – from the redefinition of norms and values, to the displacement of major, by minor, ideologies, to the destabilization of the stratification system, to the emergence of new leaders – create opportunities for previously ignored resources to be re-evaluated more positively (Lipman-Blumen, 1973). Moreover, since crisis inevitably requires not only the re-allocation, but often the generation of new resources, it is not surprising that we reappraise resources during periods of social disequilibrium.[4] Social roles, themselves (including gender roles), become newly regarded as resources to be differently, often more positively, valued.

For example, despite their valuable contributions to the labour force during the First World War, American women's efforts to participate in the paid labour force were largely denied, obstructed, or ignored in the years between the two world wars. In the drastically changed social context following the Japanese attack on Pearl Harbor, in 1941, American women were actively recruited, not simply into the general labour force, but even into various sectors (for example, manufacturing) ordinarily reserved for men (Wool and Pearlman, 1947).

Circumstances also change when those involved in power relationships attempt to commandeer the other party's resources. Parties locked in power struggles usually strive to seize or nullify one another's resources, as in wartime efforts to capture or destroy the opponent's personnel and weapons. The ongoing abortion rights battle provides an interesting example of a small, but vocal, group's efforts to control an undeniably key resource for societal perpetuation: the reproductive capacities of the entire American female population. In an ironic twist, this unique female resource is transformed into a weapon against women, by indirectly controlling their labour force participation. Insisting that a woman bring a pregnancy to term contrary to her own judgement and needs is a poignant example of how, in a power relationship, one party may attempt to capture, curtail, or transform into a liability another party's unique capability or resource.[5]

Different social contexts, therefore, can cast varying shades of value over any specific resource. They also provide opportunities for the concerned parties to lay claim, in various ways, to one another's resources. As a result, changes in social situations provide ongoing opportunities for the less powerful to negotiate and recalibrate their power positions. Thus, it is unduly pessimistic to construe gender roles as permanently locked into their present power balance, with males, individually and in groups (and particularly as guardians of institutions), commanding the dominant position *vis-à-vis* females.[6]

The Dual Myths of Powerlessness and Omnipotence

The preceding discussion helps lay to rest the dual myth of powerlessness and omnipotence. Clearly, no individual or group is either totally powerful or completely powerless (despite the fact that we shall use those terms in this chapter to save us from the semantic awkwardness of endlessly repeating 'the more powerful' and 'the less powerful').

Even the most downtrodden and disenfranchised control some measure of resources, from personal, to social, political, financial and/or institutional, or some combination thereof. These resources figure significantly in the complex social interactions, including negotiations, we recognize as the power process. Still, as Anna Freud (1937) suggested, subordinate or oppressed parties tend to introject, or internalize, the negative characterizations that their oppressors have drawn of them. To mobilize their own resources, the less powerful must overcome the internalized barriers created by the dominant group's negative evaluations and recognize the worth of their own assets. The consciousness-raising groups of the late 1960s and early 1970s were dynamic mechanisms for changing women's self-evaluations and awareness. Foucault's concern (1980, 1983) with the political implications of discourses and the relationship between power and knowledge (that is, 'pouvoir/savoir') offers valuable insight into the complex processes by which truths and definitions, including evaluations of resources, are socially constructed and linked to power.

The perceived omnipotence of those currently in power is equally mythical and seriously immobilizing to the less powerful. It is the mythic proportions, however, that tend to keep the less powerful intimidated. Identifying the mythical character, as well as the social construction, of these perceptions is one strategy for reducing the potency of the powerful's dominance and freeing up the less powerful to act on their own behalf.

The Ubiquity of Power Relationships

Power relationships are virtually ubiquitous. The most casual observer will note that almost all relationships, from child/parent, to student/teacher, to worker/boss, to wife/husband, to minister/congregant, are structured as power relationships. Few relationships escape the stain of power.[7]

Yet, both the powerful and the powerless complain about the constraints and burdens of their particular positions. The powerful argue that they bear the burdens of responsibility for the powerless and all aspects of society that the powerless are unable to handle. The powerful lament that they receive precious little gratitude for their unrelenting efforts to deal with the complicated societal dynamics that keep society afloat. Befuddled or cynical, the powerful, none the less, rarely rush to relinquish their position of privilege.

The powerless, on the other hand, insist that the powerful deprive them of the freedom to make and act upon their own choices and that they must sip relentlessly from the bitter cup of oppression. Lacking adequate resources to resist, the powerless remain enslaved, to various degrees, by the powerful. Worse yet, the overall effect on the powerless includes a profound loss of efficacy and identity.[8]

So why, we must ask, do people everywhere, as individuals and as groups, continue to enter either the dominant or the subordinate end of power relationships? And why, despite their genuine distress and protestations, do both the powerful and the powerless perpetuate these or substitute analogous relationships? We must seek the answer to these questions in the very nature of the human condition and the institutions and practices society has created and maintained.

Existential Anxiety – the Foundation of Power Relationships

One fundamental and immutable aspect of human existence is its uncertainty and unpredictability. Existential uncertainty,[9] that troubling inability to predict, much less control, events from one moment to the next, silently colours every aspect of our lives, awake or asleep. As noted earlier, the process by which we engage, rebalance and maintain our position in power relationships depends upon the resources we are able to develop and legitimate in the eyes of those with whom we must negotiate. Existential uncertainty, however, is the driving force that propels us, in the first instance, to seek out power relationships as a means of quelling the deep-seated anxiety that arises from this unsettling condition.

Existential uncertainty, our human inability either to know or control our destiny, is deeply disturbing to our sense of mastery and efficacy. It illuminates the limits of our autonomy and reminds us that life, itself, is only marginally within our control. The daily evidence of life's existential uncertainty appears in the media with their reportage of unpredicted earthquakes, volcanic eruptions, plane crashes, automobile accidents, muggings and murders. Closer to home, in the lives of family and friends, we see events we never would have predicted.

Recognizing and focusing upon our ultimate impotence to predict or control future events threatens to immobilize us, since the dire possibilities that could emerge are both limitless and terrifying. Without the twin capacities of prediction and control, we must acknowledge the ever-present possibility of danger, even death. Clearly, the people whose lives have been changed, even snuffed out, by the catastrophic incidents reported on the evening news would never have risen from the comfort of their beds that morning if they could have foreseen the fate imminently awaiting them. Yet, to focus on this profoundly disconcerting aspect of the human condition brings our anxiety to consciousness and crystallizes in immobilizing conflicts. To maintain our capacity to act and protect ourselves, we rely on the illusion of control that power relationships provide and to which the manifold apparatuses of society lend legitimacy.

Zilboorg (1943) saw the fear of death as necessary both to our normal functioning and our constant alert to self-preservation. Becker (1973) viewed humans' terror of death as 'one of the great rediscoveries of modern thought' and agreed with Shaler's (1900) turn of the century observation that our search for heroism, within ourselves and in others, was a 'reflex' of that terror. Recognizing that we can neither control nor predict what the future holds for us, our existential uncertainty leads to a deep disquietude, an existential anxiety, which constantly percolates just below the level of consciousness.[10]

To allay this existential anxiety, we attempt to create for ourselves the *illusion* that life is under control,[11] if not under our own control, at least under something's or someone else's. Therein lies the major attraction of power relationships, despite their admitted drawbacks. When we enter either the dominant or subordinate end of a power relationship, we generate the illusion (for ourselves and others) that someone, something, maybe even we, will keep life on an even keel. Becker provides a partial description of the process by which those who accept the subordinate position sustain that illusion:

> What is more natural to banish one's fears than to live on delegated powers? And what does the whole growing-up period signify, if not the giving over of one's life-project? . . . man cuts out for himself a manageable world: he throws himself into action uncritically, unthinkingly. He accepts the cultural programming that turns his nose where he is supposed to look; . . . he learns not to expose himself, not to stand out; he learns to embed himself in other-power, both of concrete persons and of other things and cultural commands; the result is that he comes to exist in the imagined infallibility of the world around him. He doesn't have to have fears when his feet are solidly mired and his life mapped out in a ready-made maze. All he has to do is to plunge ahead in a compulsive style of drivenness in the 'ways of the world' that the child learns and in which he lives later as a kind of grim equanimity – the 'strange power of living in the moment and ignoring and forgetting' – as James put it. (1973: 23)

There is more to the story, however. First, the complex social context – composed of multiple institutions and interactions, rules and relationships – creates a set of 'truths' that gives meaning and legitimacy to the process of engaging in power relationships. The complicated way in which the components of the social context are interwoven infuses those meanings with a moral force that increases the likelihood of their acceptance as 'natural'. As Durkheim suggests, social force acts through individuals:

For the collective force is not entirely outside of us; it does not act upon us wholly from without; but rather, since society cannot exist except in and through individual consciousness, this force must also penetrate us and organize itself within us; it thus becomes an integral part of our being and by that very fact this is elevated and magnified. (1915: 209)

Secondly, the resulting illusion of control provides a sense of activity, enabling us to go about the business of living our daily lives, but it carries a hefty price tag. The cost is compliance with the dictates of those who assume the burden of responsibility, those who occupy the dominant position in the power balance. The cost further requires that the less powerful, without rebelling, take their specified places within societal institutions and acquiesce to the complicated arrangements and practices that signify their subordinate position.

Yet, our deference to the power and superiority of that dominant force, entity, individual or group has some less obvious benefits. The demands of the dominant party usually create a framework that delineates how we must indicate our compliance. Meeting these requirements, be they the catechism of the Catholic Church or the behaviours and rituals embedded in the marital relationship, may be simultaneously painful and reassuring.

The pain lies in our recognition that, indeed, we are the less powerful and, therefore, must subordinate our own will to the dominant party's. The reassurance stems from the realization that we now have an algorithm, a 'recipe', if not an iron-clad guarantee, for predictability and security.

The belief that following the prescribed social dicta provided by the powerful will result in automatic success occasionally reveals itself as little more than magical thinking. Despite the most rigorous adherence to the prescribed behaviour and beliefs, the results are not always what we have been led to expect. For example, many traditional wives who meticulously fulfilled their husbands' expectations, none the less, found themselves transformed into 'displaced homemakers'.

Moreover, circumstances change in ways that may make it quite impossible for us to follow the prescribed course and practices articulated by the discourse guiding the life we previously accepted. For example, in the tumultuous 1960s and 1970s, many Catholic priests and nuns discovered that the changing social context called into question the previously believed religious discourse that had served as the fulcrum of their lives. As a result, many nuns and priests found themselves in profound disagreement with their church. Either by their own choice or through the church's action, many disaffected participants in religious orders ultimately abandoned or severely altered their relationship with the church.

Five Strategies for Reducing Existential Anxiety
There are at least five distinct, but related, strategies for reducing our existential anxiety:

1. Submission to a sacred force or being.
2. Allegiance to a secular, usually political, ideology.
3. Subordination to a secular institution.
4. Subjugation to a human ruler, benign or otherwise.
5. Assumption of control over other individuals, institutions, situations, and/or resources.

These strategies are not mutually exclusive. For example, one could believe devoutly in God, be a church deacon, strongly support the Republican Party, work as a loyal IBM employee, follow the dictates of the American President, and serve as chair of the local Neighborhood Emergency Association.

1. Submission to a Sacred Force or Being   For a large portion of the human race, submission to a sacred deity or force provides a fulcrum of life. The major religions, which provide such a pivotal force, count millions among their followers. Even in this post-modern age of sophisticated science and high technology, the appeal of organized religion appears to be increasing. For example, Islam, which accounted for 17.7 per cent of all religious believers in 1991, is on the rise world-wide, with 935 billion adherents – and still counting (*The Britannica Book of the Year*, 1991). The ranks of Born Again Christians have also swelled in recent decades. Women, for reasons whose complexity transcends the limitations of this chapter, outnumber male believers, at least in terms of church attendance and self-reports of religiosity. Still, however, the formal leadership of the major religions remains dominated by men. Even as this chapter was being written, American Catholic bishops voted to reject the possibility of female priests after considering the issue for seven years.

Paradoxically, to reduce the anxiety born of a sense of powerlessness, this first strategy demands that the followers consciously affirm both their powerlessness and their submission to the sacred force or deity. Only by surrendering and admitting their dependence are the followers granted membership in the community of believers.

In exchange for this confession of weakness, believers receive the tools to structure their lives for all eventualities, the tools that reassure believers that life now will be secure. The major element in this tool kit is the sacred force's message, a message formulated as an ideology or belief system, replete with rituals, norms and values. Adherence to a religious ideology provides a central set of beliefs intended to inform all the believer's decisions and behaviours. Following the rituals, norms and values linked to the central beliefs brings a sense of order and control over what otherwise might be perceived as disintegration into chaos.[12]

The believer may feel constrained, even occasionally oppressed, by the demands of the deity and the formal institution charged with implementing the deity's requirements. Still, submission to an omnipotent deity and the structuring of life entailed in that dependence bring a sense of relief and security.[13] The relief emanates from relinquishing and entrusting the burden of concern and responsibility to the omnipotent force; the security comes from a belief that the bargain (that is, submission and obedience in exchange for security) will protect the faithful from the vicissitudes of life.

For most of the major religions, the gender relationship is the earthly or secular expression of the sacred relationship between human subjects and their deity.[14] Invested with this sacred character, the traditional gender relationship, in which men assume dominance and women subordination, resists change. Few religious believers are willing to violate what they perceive to be a divine mandate. Thus, traditional gender roles express and maintain a powerful force in their own right, and, in turn, become the tangible human model on which all other power relationships are fashioned.

Believers, from cult members to congregants in world-wide religions, draw additional support for their convictions from the evidence that others share their point of view. Moreover, the community of believers acts to reinforce the norms, values and rituals that represent the deity's dictates and to censure violations. Opposing what the mass of believers accepts both as the mandate of their sacred ruler and the basis for structuring their own lives poses awesome difficulties. As a result, those men and women who have laboured to recalibrate the power dynamic of gender roles often have met with profound resistance from others whose *raisons d'être* and very identities were founded on submission to a sacred being.

2. Allegiance to a Secular Ideology The second strategy – allegiance to a secular, often a political ideology – shares certain features with the first approach. It subjects the individual or group to a belief system that gives structure and meaning to life. Ideology, whether sacred or secular, offers an explanation for the reality we confront, for the societal arrangements that provide the context of our lives. It provides a rationale for why we are poorer than our neighbours, why our son was killed on the battlefield, why our daughter died from an illegal abortion, why we are starving in a Third World desert. In each case, there is an explanation, the specifics depending upon the given ideology: the existing political system created an unequal and unjust income distribution; our son died fighting for an honourable cause; the entrenched political system denied our daughter access to legal abortion; a lack of adequate and legitimate government has created a lawlessness that disrupts the infrastructure of the society.

Allegiance to a secular belief system or ideology also creates the illusion of control, because, if the ideology is correct, then life will work itself out to its predicted outcome. Believers attribute an inevitability to events. Eventually, the ideology will prevail and a new age will dawn. Secular ideologies – from democracy and socialism to environmentalism and feminism – provide their own idiosyncratic eschatologies, which their followers interpret as inevitable. In the American Colonies, the authors of the Declaration of Independence struggled to formulate the structure for a democratic society based on equality and inalienable rights, including life, liberty and the pursuit of happiness. Marx and Engels, along with Lenin, fervently believed that socialism was the road to equality and justice. Feminists, for their part, expect that, in a world structured in accordance with feminist precepts, peace, justice and equality would prevail. So, it is clear that believers in secular ideologies, regardless of the specific belief structures involved, expect that, when their ideology attains complete fruition it ineluctably will lead to a safer, better world. Can they all be right?

Secular ideologies share with their sacred counterparts a community of believers, which has several related functions. First, it tends to reinforce the adherents' confidence in the legitimacy and correctness of their beliefs. Secondly, it reinforces believers' conformity to the related norms, values and expected behaviours. Furthermore, when secular ideologies (for example, political belief systems) expand their followership, the adherents' expectation that their ideology will prevail over competing belief systems is enhanced. As the institutional structure (for example, the political party and its candidates) that represents the secular ideology gains ascendancy, the followers are encouraged. Followers interpret each political success as proof of the ideology's eschatology, that is, that their group will inevitably prevail because of the appropriateness, moral rectitude, timeliness etc., of its beliefs and practices. Of course, repeated failures to institutionalize the ideology (for example, through losses at the voting booth or political coups) can disillusion all but the most ardent believers.

Finally, the leadership of secular belief systems is an important factor in the promulgation of secular, particularly political, ideology. Depending upon the quality of leadership and the leader's capacity for compelling, even charismatic, action, the community of followers expands or declines. The emergence of a strong, convincing leader who addresses the central concerns of the followers is likely to attract new believers and energize the lagging faithful. We shall address this in greater detail when we turn to the fourth strategy, subjection to a human ruler.

Secular belief systems, unlike their sacred counterparts, are more vulnerable to failure and dissolution. This is true, in part, because they address our political, social and economic conditions, which can change with dramatic speed. Moreover, the degree to which secular belief systems are able to fulfil their promises is tangible and measurable, while sacred ideologies tend to hold out hope of spiritual fulfilment, a subjective phenomenon far more difficult to observe and measure. The convergence of complex social, economic and political factors can destroy even robust political systems and disillusion their constituents. The falling dominoes of Eastern bloc political systems, linked by a common political ideology, is vivid evidence that even a seemingly entrenched secular belief system can founder. When this occurs, the followers' sense of security may suffer a serious blow.

None the less, for many believers, an ideology that has given structure and meaning to their lives is difficult to relinquish, even in the face of dramatic evidence of its intellectual bankruptcy. Once they have accepted a belief system and integrated their lives around that particular definition of reality, ardent, if perhaps unsophisticated, believers reinforce their beliefs through various mechanisms. Cognitive dissonance reduction, selective listening, defensive denial and a host of other psychological and spiritual measures function to protect believers from unwelcome evidence. Cialdini (1984) sheds important light on the ways in which an initial commitment is likely to stimulate additional support to the same position or behaviour despite evidence that the original decision was faulty. Thus, many Eastern bloc citizens, whose own existences were suffused with a profound belief in Communism, have stubbornly clung to a belief in the ideology that formed the fulcrum of their lives.

3. Subordination to a Secular Institution   Major secular institutions, including the family, the school, the workplace and the government, provide the context of our daily lives. Like their sacred counterparts, secular institutions infuse our lives with a semblance of control and orderliness through highly structured arrangements. Hierarchy and bureaucracy are not uncommon in secular institutions, and, although we complain about them, they clarify our relative position in the world. They dissolve the ambiguity surrounding our status and, in conjunction with the ideological strategy described above, present an explanation for our own situation.

Institutions embody values, and they are designed, replete with norms, rewards and sanctions, to ensure that participants uphold those values. The aura of institutional control and predictability – meals served at the dining room table, homework, tests and grades given in school, work assignments and pay cheques provided by employers on the last Thursday of the month – serves as substantial evidence of existential order and stability. Institutional control that dictates what time we must appear at the office, what time we may leave, even what dress code must be observed offers a tangible substitute for the elusive individual existential control we seek.

The structure of institutions, with each role differentiated according to gender, age, race, ethnicity, educational level etc., creates a sense of order and predictability. Even as we try to loosen institutional structures to allow for more individual opportunity and greater role de-differentiation (Lipman-Blumen, 1973), we still look to institutions to provide that sense of stability and control over the uncertainties of life.

Traditionally, in Western societies, males and females controlled different institutional domains: males in the public arena of corporations, legislatures, hospitals, and banks; females in the private or domestic sphere of the family. The past few decades have brought visible and important changes to the two spheres of male and female domination. Many more females have entered the ranks (but not necessarily the leadership) of executives, physicians and lawyers, and more husbands discharge domestic and parental responsibilities. Yet, the overall pattern remains essentially unchanged, with significantly more men than women in public leadership positions, and women still primarily responsible for, if not altogether dominant in, the private or domestic sphere.

Besides providing structure, stability and predictability, secular institutions also inject meaning into our lives. When our institutional roles within which we have lived our lives disappear, as in the case of the male retiree or the displaced homemaker, confusion and anomie fester. The displaced homemaker, who has devoted several decades to nurturing her children and husband, finds the transition to 'single' life a major trauma. The male retiree, who, for years, has spent eight or more hours a day in his office among familiar staff and colleagues, finds the loss of an institutional affiliation equally difficult. In different ways, both displaced homemakers and traditional male retirees must confront redefining and restructuring their lives outside of the work institution they have called 'home' (pun intended) during most of their adulthood.

4. Subjugation to a Human Ruler, Benign or Otherwise The fourth strategy for quelling our existential anxiety involves subjugation to a human ruler, benign or otherwise. In most societies, individuals and groups commonly demonstrate a predilection to subject themselves to the direction of a benevolent, wise and compassionate human ruler, even at the same time that they yearn to be free. They seek the protection of leaders whom they believe are more intelligent, more skilful, more powerful than themselves in order to avoid the burdens and responsibilities of governance, while still enjoying stability and security.

The call for leaders to grapple with followers' major concerns occurs in every country and in every organization, from the Commonwealth of Independent States to General Motors, to the local town hall. Sigmund Freud (1939, 1946) interpreted this tendency as the desire to replicate the father figures of our childhoods. The parent–child power relationship provides a ready-made mechanism by which the child can address his or her need to deal with the underlying stimulus of existential uncertainty. None the less, there are serious potential dangers in our seemingly relentless search for leaders. Erich Fromm (1941), for one, feared that the human tendency to seek strong leaders was essentially an escape from freedom that could promote the rise of totalitarian governments.

From infancy, we are imprinted for followership through our relationship with our parents. In this most obvious power relationship, we learn that the exchange of safety and care, if not stability and love, for obedience and subordination is difficult at best, particularly over the long haul. As we develop into adults, we sense that the tradeoffs are often costly, particularly when, with developing resources, we try to renegotiate the power balance. None the less, if the psychiatric evidence is to be believed, we often repeat the process with our own children and sometimes, in fact, with our choice of partners.

Even when the ruler is truly benign, the fact that one party rules and the other obeys sows the seeds for a power struggle, since few are willing to obey even the most enlightened ruler all of the time. Moreover, lack of malevolence is insufficient to ensure wise judgement. So, even when the powerful believe they have the powerless's best interests at heart, they rarely are astute enough to recognize and understand what those best interests are. The spouse who assumes all financial responsibilities to 'spare' his or her partner leaves that partner totally unprepared to deal with the difficulties of widow(er)hood. Moreover, when the powerless's best interests collide with those of the powerful, the power struggle intensifies.

Even when we call for the overthrow of a ruthless leader, we immediately install a new leader, one who, we hope, is competent and humane. We explain this search for leaders to whom we can subject ourselves as a means of meeting the societal need for organization and direction. Still, while good leaders may articulate and implement a revitalizing vision, they rarely do so without demanding compliant followers. The call for leaders is strongest in crisis, when charismatic leaders are most likely to emerge in response to their followers' distress (Weber, 1968a).

Although the human condition encourages us to seek human protectors, the choice of the specific leader or ruler may not be up to us. We have no choice in our biological parents, as the frustrated refrain of youngsters suggests: 'I didn't ask to be born'. Even at work, where we initially agree to accept a position under a particular employer or boss, jobs are not easily mixed and matched with the exact boss we would select. Moreover, organizational changes often leave us under the authority of bosses other than those we originally agreed to follow. In long-term monarchies or dictatorships, generations may be born into and die under the reign of unselected leaders. Even in more open political systems, particularly democracies with mandated periodic election of leaders, our choices remain limited by the field of candidates. The limitations in our options, however, provide a hidden benefit: we feel freer to criticize those leaders whom we did not participate in selecting.

Historically, we have few examples of relationships with leaders beyond the alternatives of subjugation or revolt. More recently there has been considerable attention focused on the possibility of sharing power with the leader, or at a minimum, keeping the leader in line by vigilant monitoring. Connective leadership, an integrative style of leadership that involves connecting the leader to constituents in a more egalitarian and innovation-producing manner, has been proposed (Lipman-Blumen, 1992). None the less, the empirical examples of leadership shared by constituents and the leader, while theoretically praiseworthy and a noble aim, remain remarkably scanty. Even efforts of co-leadership, both in the corporate and the political realm, provide few positive examples. The John Scully–Steve Jobs partnership, as well as the Gorbachev–Yeltsin collaboration were sadly short-lived.

Both historically and cross-culturally, the criteria for leadership have been surprisingly narrow, with males more often than females selected for such roles outside of the family. Legislatures, corporations, universities, law firms, hospitals, financial institutions, too, are more likely to have a male leader, further evidence of the strength of the gender–power relationship. Some observers lay the blame for this relentless usurpation of leadership roles solely with males, who are loathe to surrender the benefits they historically have enjoyed. That, however, would be an oversimplification. First, not all men are given leadership opportunities. Secondly, in the political arena, many female voters unwittingly or deliberately support the traditional gender–power balance. This is evident from the gender composition of the US Senate. Despite their strength at 52 per cent of the population, only one woman served in the US Senate until the 1992 election increased female representation to six senators (an event heralded as a major victory for women). True, more and more American women now hold elected political office at the local and state levels; however, at the national level, women politicians remain in the vast minority.

In the family, where our mythology insists women are in charge, the reality is not quite that clear-cut, either. It appears that at least our rhetoric about the equality of young partners has changed, and that, in itself, helps to move gender roles in the direction of a more equal power balance. Still, it is not always the case that behaviour matches the new rhetoric. Younger couples appear to share childcare and household tasks more than their parents did. Still, the proportion of young couples who make all major decisions based equally on both partners' career and personal needs remains relatively limited. Most American women still are held primarily responsible for the emotional well-being of their families, but we need more convincing evidence that women hold equal or greater power than men over major life decisions within the family.

The stubborn pattern of male dominance in leadership positions throughout the spectrum of social institutions suggests that the answer is far more complex than simple blame assessment conveys. The potency of the gender role blueprint affects men and women across societies and across generations. Its identification with the most primitive power relationships (that is between humans and the deities they worship) has been preserved and handed down through the pentimento of ancient gender images and myths in sacred and secular culture. From pre-Hellenic writings, through the Old and New Testaments, the Koran, to Shakespeare and Tolstoy, the images of dominant men and subordinate women have instructed generations about the dangers inherent in changing the gender–power relationship, which serves as the blueprint for all other power relationships (Lipman-Blumen, 1984).

Despite women's demonstrated ability to perform in professional, as well as domestic, roles, the cultural barriers to recalibrating the gender–power relationship are difficult to surmount. The deep-seated social reluctance to view women as competent leaders, even within the family, is evident in our attitudes towards female-headed households. Women who deliberately or inadvertently become heads of household and 'single-parent (read female-headed) families' have been the target of blame for a wide range of social ills, from juvenile delinquency and poverty to urban riots. For example, during the American presidential campaign of 1992, former Vice-President Dan Quayle sparked a national debate by focusing attention on women who undertake single parenthood. It is somewhat ironic that fathers who elect to be single parents are usually commended and rewarded for the responsibilities they shoulder and the difficulties they confront.

5. Assuming Control over Other People, Situations, Resources and Institutions   The final strategy for stilling our existential anxiety involves assuming control over others, taking charge of people, situations, resources and institutions. In the process of convincing others that we are in control, we unwittingly convince ourselves. Thus, the fifth strategy has the double advantage of convincing both the protected and the protector that the one in charge has everything under control. Although the protector's omnipotence is largely illusory, it manages, most of the time, to convince not only the protected, but the potential protector as well, that everything is under control (Bailey, 1988).

Self-discipline and self-control are fundamental prerequisites for assuming control over others. From an early age, caretakers tend to subject young males to more rigorous disciplinary regimes than females in an effort to instil a sense of self-discipline. The early childhood development literature (Maccoby and Jacklin, 1974) documents the fact that male infants and toddlers are as likely as their female counterparts to cry under similar circumstances; however, by the time they enter kindergarten, male youngsters have learned it is 'unmanly' to cry. It is through such processes that males learn to exert self-control and eventually control over others. The social arrangements augment this training by channelling males towards positions in which they exercise control over others, including weaker men and most women. These social apparatuses create the complex conditions conducive for males to gain decision-making power in most resource-laden institutions.

Those in charge have decision-making power. The powerful enjoy the prerogative of labelling and defining everything as well. The powerful design and control institutions, whose massive resources they can then use to attract and reward loyal followers or withhold from those who oppose them. Compared to the meagreness of individual resources, access to institutional resources enables the powerful to wield enormous influence both within and outside their own institution. Control over institutional resources helps the powerful to perpetuate their own power (Salancik and Pfeffer, 1977).

These are monumental powers that move institutions and the people who live and work within them. It is not surprising that the capacity to put one's desires into effect in such a grand way persuades not only the followers, but the ruler as well that he is indeed powerful, maybe even powerful enough to quell his own existential anxiety (Bailey, 1988).

Reprise and Prognosis

Reprise
Where does this analysis leave us? To summarize briefly, existential uncertainty, that is, the inability to predict or control events, produces a state of existential anxiety. Ordinarily, existential anxiety operates at the *un*conscious level, producing a tension that drives us to seek relief from its otherwise immobilizing effects. One major response to this existential uncertainty and its resultant anxiety is to enter into the cocoon of a power relationship. Power relationships create, both for the ruled and the ruler, the illusion that life is reasonably under control, at least if certain beliefs are upheld and behavioural conditions are met.

Power is a complex negotiating process in which those who can contribute or withhold important resources, thereby rewarding or punishing (or promising or threatening to do so), can impose their will on others. The complicated arrangements of control over resources – including people, social arrangements and practices, as well as institutions, and other resources – that are integral to power relationships create an illusion for all participants that life is reasonably predictable and secure, after all.

Five different types of power relationships provide a robust set of possible recourses for alleviating existential anxiety:

1. Submission to a sacred force or being.
2. Acceptance of a secular ideology.
3. Subordination to a secular institution.
4. Subjugation to a benevolent human ruler.
5. Assuming control over people, situations, institutions, and other resources.

Yet, relieving existential anxiety in these ways also tends to reinforce the existing power imbalance between men and women.

The social arrangements, socialization and historically unequal access to resources tend to predispose women and weaker men to select among the first four possibilities, all marked by submission. These same forces usually work to channel males into the fifth strategy, the control-taking initiative. The long-standing power imbalance between males and females is woven into the manifold arrangements that constitute the social context, which poses a stubborn obstacle to recalibration. The five strategies, buttressed by existing social arrangements, tend to protect the position of the entrenched power group, to wit, males, particularly the more powerful males.

Prognosis: the Bad News and the Good News
The bad news first: it seems unlikely that the uncertainty and unpredictability of human existence will diminish in any significant respect. Thus, we must expect that our bedrock existential anxiety that attracts us to power relationships will remain. Still, consciously recognizing the basis of the attraction and the alternatives available gives us some foundation for action. Confronting the irreducible fact of existential uncertainty weakens its power to drive us to unconscious remedies. Conscious choices, even when they are less than ideal, help us to transcend our sense of entrapment. Looking death in the eye and confronting existential uncertainty is hardly a joyous prospect; however, it eventually enables us to set priorities for the way in which we choose to act

out and give meaning to our lives, as any individual facing a terminal illness can attest.

Now the good news: on several other counts, there is reason for guarded optimism in this centuries-old power imbalance between males and females. First, resources, whose value is in the eye of the beholder, are subject both to definitional reappraisals and to changing situations. In turbulent times, resources undergo serious re-evaluation whereby people, talents and social arrangements previously undervalued can be redefined as crucial to resolving current problems. We have seen this occur in war and other crisis situations, when women gained access to institutional roles from which they were previously barred. The trick is to keep the new definition salient, to institutionalize the crisis-driven changes after calm returns.

Those who have perceived themselves to be completely or hopelessly powerless can begin to recognize the sources of those feelings and start to experiment with new and different strategies for reducing their existential anxiety. They can begin to form coalitions with others, pooling resources and acting to reduce their sense of powerlessness. Education and knowledge, crucial resources in most situations, go a long way towards diminishing one's sense of powerlessness. Knowledge allows the less powerful to assess the alternatives and exercise some control over choices. Abrogating one's responsibility to know, to choose, and to act rarely increases the submissive party's actual security, satisfaction, or power. Instead, relinquishing one's responsibility for self-control and self-directed action usually compounds the anxiety with the terror of being acted upon by the powerful.

One potent strategy for dealing with the powerful involves vigilantly monitoring their action or creating 'power through illumination'. Foucault's empirical study entitled *Le Regard* ('the gaze') offers important clues about the process by which unremitting observation of another's behaviour enhances the power of the observer through knowledge. Not only does the observer's knowledge translate into power over the observed, but, in addition, the observed, aware of the gaze, begin to moderate their own behaviour.[15] Living in an age of information technology suggests many complex possibilities for using knowledge gained through observation to control the powerful. An important caveat should be borne in mind, however: power through scrutiny or observation offers serious, almost unlimited possibilities for misuse both by the powerful and the subordinates.

In its most benign use, however, public vigilance by the less powerful is an important method for recalibrating the power balance represented by the gender relationship. Participating in social processes (including grassroots policy setting and policy review activities) is the first step in power through illumination or public vigilance. Such action enables the less powerful to gain sufficient knowledge to 'speak truth to power'.

What can we say to those who select the fifth strategy, that is, seizing or accepting control? First, beware of falling through the looking glass of megalomania and believing that you really are omnipotent. Resist the temptation of acting like gods in response to the urging of those who seek to calm *their* existential anxiety by placing themselves in the hands of a benevolent ruler.[16] The powerful need to exercise great caution to withstand this seductive call to usurp power.

If those who have accepted the burdens of the powerful can summon the strength to confront their own existential anxiety, they can begin to look within themselves for heroic acceptance of their irreducible human condition. Peering into the darkness of existential uncertainty is a painful, but necessary, step in reducing their own unconscious needs to use power relationships to quell their anxiety. The capacity to confront, rather than simply subvert, our existential anxiety is the first step towards a sense of equanimity, freedom and other possibilities in an uncertain world. Spreading that capacity to the less powerful, by education and example, is a major responsibility of the truly heroic leader.

Having taken steps to reduce their own unconscious need for power, the more powerful may also begin to understand that sharing the responsibilities of power can relieve the pressures and hardships of the dominant position. Neither the dominant nor the subordinate group can do it alone. Only the more and the less powerful, acting together, can hope to undertake the monumental task of resetting the gender–power balance.

Notes

1 Within most societies, the institutional arrangements and practices, formal and informal, express and legitimate existing power relationships. Although existential bases and institutional bases of power relationships are intertwined, it is beyond the scope of this chapter to delineate how the expression of power relationships becomes enmeshed in institutional arrangements, thereby fostering the perpetuation of dominant–subordinate relationships through formal structures and informal practices. For a discussion of the institutional foundations of power relationships, including an analysis of the reflexive nature of social institutions and the institutional functions of ideology, see Lipman-Blumen (1984).

2 Most post-modern writers reject the notion of power as something centred in a subject whose will is exercised. Instead, they tie power to discourse/knowledge or some other linguistic conception.

3 According to media reports, Chalad Vorachat, a 49-year-old owner of provincial cable television networks in Thailand, undertook a hunger strike that set off the May 1992 Thai democratic protest against unelected Prime Minister Suchinda Kraprayoon. When reporters probed the motivation for Chalad's dramatic vigil, he responded, 'Fighting for democracy is more important than a life' (Wallace, 1992).

4 For decades, the Brazilian rain forests were indiscriminately cut down to make way for cattle grazing. Only when the environmental crisis became apparent was the rain forest re-evaluated as a source of needed oxygen. I am indebted to Jennifer Berry for calling the relevance of this example to mind.

5 It is probably also worth noting that males frequently take the lead as TV spokespersons for the anti-abortion groups. Male usurpation of leadership within the anti-abortion group might be interpreted as a symbolic expression of one group's efforts to achieve control over another group's unique resource – the capacity to give birth.

6 This argument, rooted in the changing social context, deliberately distinguishes itself from utility theories that are conceptualized as more individualistic, asocial and acontextual.

7 Perhaps the only relationship that has a reasonable chance of avoiding the power dynamic is asexual friendship. Here, too, however, the possibility for dominance and subordination exists, at least intermittently.

8 Although some readers might feel that such a claim ideally should rest on a thorough analysis of 'identity', to do justice to such a task far exceeds the limits of this chapter. Admittedly, 'identity' has become a highly contested term in the social sciences; however, in this context, I am using it simply in the commonly understood sense. For an inquiry into the sources of modern selfhood and its relation to our long-term search for the good, see Charles Taylor (1989).

9 Although some might feel that such a claim, which serves as the underpinning for my analysis of power, should explicate systematically its definition of 'existence' or 'being', or 'self', such an extensive effort, I believe, exceeds the limits of this chapter. Let me, none the less, indicate that, following Goldstein (1939, 1940), I conceive of the self as the totality of the individual's capacities. Further, for purposes of differentiation, let me indicate that my concept of existential uncertainty, with all its associated pain, is not really akin to Søren Kierkegaard's notion of either subjective or objective dread. According to Kierkegaard, 'subjective dread is the dread posited in the individual as the consequence of his sin . . . the dread which exists in the innocence of the individual, a dread which corresponds to that of Adam and yet is quantitatively different from Adam's . . . By objective dread . . . we understand the reflection in the whole world of that sinfulness which is propagated by generation' (1957[1844]: pp. 50–1). Kierkegaard suggests an intimate connection between dread and freedom, which he defines as 'possibility' (1957[1844]: 138).

10 I use the term 'existential anxiety' to refer to *un*conscious processes, which are rarely brought directly to the surface of human consciousness. In twentieth-century literature, the works of Camus (1954[1942]), Kafka (1930, 1937) and Hermann Hesse (1947[1927]) depict anxiety as a more conscious phenomenon, in which their protagonists seek to escape their suffering induced by a sense of meaninglessness

and isolation. The poem 'The Age of Anxiety' by W.H. Auden (1947) depicts the conscious anxiety experienced by four characters during the war. Although their anxiety is related to a sense of their own valuelessness, their inability to experience love, and their loneliness, Auden indicates that the roots of anxiety are deep in the social processes evident in 'this stupid world where/Gadgets are gods'. None the less, in this same poem Auden touches on a deeper wellspring of anxiety, closer to my own concept of existential uncertainty. '. . . the fears we know/Are of not knowing. Will nightfall bring us/Some awful order?' (1947). Incidentally, it is interesting to note that the composer/conductor Leonard Bernstein translated Auden's poem into a symphony, which saw its première in 1949. See Bernstein (1949).

In modern classical and existential philosophy and religion, anxiety also represents a central concern. Spinoza's (1910[1677]) concern with fear, which he defines in contrast to hope, prefigures later work in theology and philosophy, but does not directly address the issues of anxiety. Theologians from R.F. Niebuhr (1941), to Tillich (1944), to M. Heidegger (1962[1927]) have wrestled with the role of anxiety in human existence. Tillich (1944) conceptualizes anxiety as the human reaction to the awareness of the possibility of nonbeing – a concept that itself involves not simply the cessation of physical existence, but death of spiritual and psychological meaningfulness, as well.

The concept of anxiety in twentieth-century psychological literature takes on a clinical orientation, which is related to, but clearly distinct from, the meaning presumed in this chapter. For an excellent summary of psychological theories of anxiety through mid-century, see Rollo May (1950).

11 The concept of control and the 'illusion' of control have been central, in various ways, to most of the social and behavioural science disciplines. In recent years, however, these concepts and their contextual meaning have been the subject of serious criticism. See, for example, Stam (1987).

12 Admittedly, religious experience is far more complex, with manifold nuances and subtleties, than the limitations of this chapter permit me to address; however, I have focused here on the dimensions of the religious phenomenon most relevant to power relationships and gender. For a more extensive sociological treatment of the question of whether theological thinking is possible in contemporary society, the role of the supernatural, and the rediscovery of the supernatural and its potential contribution to human existence, see Peter L. Berger (1969).

13 For an interesting discussion of Pascal's wager and the 'insurance' it provides, see Blaise Pascal (1946[1931]).

14 The recent rejection of the ordination of female priests by American Catholic bishops was based, in part, on this very argument.

15 Some observers have noted that in the wake of the home-video recording of police officers beating motorist Rodney King, during the Los Angeles riots, police behaviour was moderated by their concern about being taped on widely available home-video cameras. This is an example of the powerful controlling their own behaviour under the lamp of public scrutiny.

Foucault was particularly impressed with Jeremy Bentham's planned but never built Panopticon, an architectural structure for observing prisoners. The design featured a tower surrounded by an open space, which, in turn, was circumscribed by a circle of cubicles. Light entered each cubicle from the rear and outlined the figure of the occupant. The side of the cubicle facing the tower had a window through which the occupant could be observed by anyone in the tower. Foucault felt this method of surveillance actually complemented Rousseau's idea of a transparent society 'visible and legible in each of its parts, the dream of there no longer existing any zones . . . established by the privileges of royal power or the prerogatives of some corporations, zones of disorder'. Bentham's design stimulated enormous interest, in large part because is was applicable to many aspects of society (Foucault, 1980: 152).

16 Recently, within the medical profession, there has been a deliberate effort by physicians to involve patients in decision-making about their own treatment. Empowering patients to participate in what was previously reserved for the professional judgement of the physician has reduced the 'god-like' aura surrounding the physician and increased patients' sense of power and efficacy. No doubt some patients still wish to put themselves in the hands of a 'god-like' figure, who will magically cure them. Physicians who recognize the benefits to both parties of resetting the doctor–patient power balance are more interested in increasing the patient's knowledge about the illness and possible courses of therapy. In the long run, sharing power with patients also will probably reduce malpractice suits, which many interpret as the only expression of anger and frustration previously available to the powerless patient 'acted upon' by the omnipotent physician.

References

Auden, W.H. (1947) *The Age of Anxiety: a Baroque Eclogue*. New York: Random House.
Bailey, F.G. (1988) *Humbuggery and Manipulation: the Art of Leadership*. Ithaca, New York: Cornell University Press.
Barnard, Chester, I. (1964) *The Functions of the Executive*. Cambridge, Mass.: Harvard University Press.
Barthes, R. (1957) *Mythologies*. New York: Hill and Wang.
Becker, Ernest (1973) *The Denial of Death*. New York: The Free Press.
Berger, Peter L. (1969) *A Rumor of Angels: Modern Society and the Rediscovery of the Supernatural*. Garden City, NY: Doubleday.
Bernstein, Leonard (1949) 'Notes on "the Age of Anxiety", Bernstein's Second Symphony', in *Concert Bulletin*. Boston: Boston Symphony Orchestra.
Bonaparte, E. (ed.) (1982) *Women, Power and Policy*. New York: Pergamon Press.
The Britannica Book of the Year (1991) Chicago: Encyclopedia Britannica.
Camus, Albert (1954[1942]) *The Stranger*. New York: Vintage Books.
Cialdini, Robert B. (1984) *Influence: the new Psychology of Modern Persuasion*. New York: Quill.
Davis, Kathy, Leijenaar, Monique and Oldersma, Jantine (eds) (1991) *The Gender of Power*. Newbury Park, Ca: Sage.
Durkheim, Emile (1915) *The Elementary Forms of the Religious Life*. London: George Allen and Unwin.
Foucault, Michel (1980) *Power/Knowledge: Selected Interviews and Other Writings, 1972–1977* (ed. C. Gordon). New York: Pantheon Books.
Foucault, Michel (1983) 'Afterword: the subject of Power', in H. Dreyfus and P. Rabinow (eds), *Michel Foucault: Beyond Structuralism and Hermeneutics*. Chicago: University of Chicago Press, pp. 208–26.
Fraser, Nancy (1989) *Unruly Practices: Power, Discourse, and Gender in Contemporary Social Theory*. Minneapolis: University of Minnesota Press.

Fraser, Nancy (1991) 'The uses and abuses of French discourse theories for feminist politics', in Philip Wexler (ed.), *Critical Theory Now*. London: The Falmer Press, pp. 98–117.

Freud, Anna (1937) *The Ego and the Mechanisms of Defence*. London: Hogarth Press.

Freud, Sigmund (1939) *Moses and Monotheism*. New York: Knopf.

Freud, Sigmund (1946) *Totem and Taboo* (trans. and introduction A.A. Brill). New York: Random House.

Fromm, Erich (1941) *Escape from Freedom*. New York: Rinehart.

Goldstein, Kurt (1939) *The Organism: a Holistic Approach to Biology*. New York: American Book Co.

Goldstein, Kurt (1940) *Human Nature in the Light of Psychopathology*. Cambridge, Mass.: Harvard University Press.

Heidegger, Martin (1962[1927]) *Being and Time* (trans. John Macquarrie and Edward Robinson). New York: Harper and Row.

Hesse, Hermann (1947[1927]) *Steppenwolf* (trans. Basil Creighton). New York: Henry Holt.

Janeway, Elizabeth (1980) *Powers of the Weak*. New York: Knopf.

Kafka, Franz (1930) *The Castle* (trans. Edwin and Willa Muir). New York: Knopf.

Kafka, Franz (1937) *The Trial* (trans. Edwin and Willa Muir). New York: Knopf.

Kanter, Rosabeth Moss (1977) *Men and Women of the Corporation*. New York: Basic Books.

Kierkegaard, Søren (1957[1844]) *The Concept of Dread* (trans. Walter Lowrie). Princeton, NY: Princeton University Press.

Komter, Aafke (1991) 'Gender, power and feminist theory', in Kathy Davis, Monique Leijenaar and Jantine Oldersma (eds), *The Gender of Power*. Newbury Park, Ca.: Sage, pp. 42–64.

Larwood, Laurie, Stromberg, Anne H. and Gutek, Barbara A. (eds) (1985, 1987) *Women and Work: an Annual Review*, vols 1 and 2. Newbury Park, Ca: Sage.

Lipman-Blumen, J. (1973) 'De-differentiation as a system response to crisis: occupational and political roles of women', *Sociological Inquiry* 43(2): 105–29.

Lipman-Blumen, J. (1984) *Gender Roles and Power*. Englewood Cliffs, NJ: Prentice Hall.

Lipman-Blumen, J. (1992) 'Connective leadership: female leadership styles in the 21st century workplace', *Sociological Perspectives*, 35(1): 183–203.

Maccoby, Eleanor E. and Jacklin, Carol L. (1974) *The Psychology of Sex Differences*. Stanford, Ca: Stanford University Press.

Maccoby, Michael (1976) *The Gamesman: the Corporate Leaders*. New York: Simon and Schuster.

Machiavelli, Niccolo (1961[1532]) *The Prince* (trans. with introduction by George Bull). Harmondsworth and New York: Penguin Books.

May, Rollo (1950) *The Meaning of Anxiety*. New York: Ronald Press.

Merton, Robert K. (1957) *Social Theory and Social Structure* (revised and enlarged edition). Glencoe, Ill.: The Free Press.

Niebuhr, Reinhold (1941) *The Nature and Destiny of Man*. New York: Charles Scribner's Sons.

Parsons, Talcott (1953) *Working Papers in the Theory of Action* (joint editors Robert F. Bales and Edward A. Shils). New York: Free Press of Glencoe.

Parsons, Talcott (1954) *Essays in Sociological Theory*. New York: Free Press of Glencoe.

Pascal, Blaise (1946[1931]) *Pensées* (ed. and trans. G.B. Rawlings). Mt Vernon, NY: Peter Pauper Press.

Pfeffer, Jeffrey (1992) *Managing with Power: Politics and Influence in Organizations.* Boston, Mass.: Harvard Business School Press.

Powell, Gary N. (1988) *Women and Men in Management.* Newbury Park, Ca: Sage.

Ragins, B.R. and Sundstrom, E. (1990) 'Gender and power in manager–subordinate relations', *Journal of Occupational Psychology (UK),* 63/4: 273–88.

Salancik, Gerald R. and Pfeffer, Jeffrey (1977) 'Who gets power – and how they hold on to it: a strategic contingency model of power', *Organizational Dynamics,* 5: 3–21.

Sekaran, Uma and Leong, Frederick T.L. (eds) (1992) *Womanpower: Managing in Times of Demographic Turbulence.* Newbury Park, Ca: Sage.

Shaler, N.S. (1900) *The Individual: a Study of Life and Death.* New York: Appleton.

Sheppard, Deborah L. (1989) 'Organizations, power and sexuality: the image and self-image of women managers', in Jeff Hearn, Deborah L. Sheppard, Peta Tancred-Sheriff and Gibson Burrell (eds), *The Sexuality of Organization.* Newbury Park, Ca: Sage, pp. 139–57.

Spinoza, Baruch (1910[1677]) *The Ethics of Spinoza and Treatise on the Correction of the Intellect.* London: Everyman Edition.

Stam, Henderikus (1987) 'The psychology of control: a textual critique', in H.J. Stam, T.B. Rogers and K.J. Gergen (eds), *The Analysis of Psychological Theory: Metapsychological Perspectives.* Washington: Hemisphere, pp. 131–56.

Stead, Bette Ann (1985) *Women in Management,* 2nd ed. Englewood Cliffs, NJ: Prentice-Hall.

Taylor, Charles (1989) *Sources of the Self: the Making of the Modern Identity.* Cambridge, Mass.: Harvard University Press.

Tillich, Paul (1944) 'Existential philosophy', *Journal of the History of Ideas,* 5: 1, 44–70.

Wallace, Charles P. (1992) '"Normal guy" challenges Thai leader', *Los Angeles Times,* 23 May, p. A9.

Weber, Max (1968a) *Max Weber on Charisma and Institution Building: Selected papers* (ed. with introduction by S.N. Eisenstadt). Chicago: University of Chicago Press.

Weber, Max (1968b) *Economy and Society: an Outline of Interpretive Sociology* (ed. Guenther Roth and Claus Wittich; trans. Ephraim Fischoff and others). New York: Bedminster Press.

Wool, Harold and Pearlman, Lester M. (1947) 'Recent occupational trends', *Monthly Labour Review,* 65 (August): 139–47.

Zilboorg, Gregory (1943) 'Fear of death', *Psychoanalytic Quarterly,* 12: 465–75.

7

The State, Gender and Sexual Politics: Theory and Appraisal

R.W. Connell

A Strategic Question

The classic feminist slogan 'the personal is political' states a basic feature of feminist and gay politics, a link between personal experience and power relations. In many cases the power relations are immediately present in personal life, in matters conventionally thought 'private': housework, homophobic jokes, office sexuality, child-rearing. Yet there is also a highly 'public' dimension of these politics. During the 1970s, Western feminism made open and substantial demands on the state in every country where a significant mobilization of women occurred. So did gay liberation movements, where they developed. The list of reforms sought includes the decriminalization of abortion in France, a constitutional guarantee of equal rights for women in the United States, rape law reform in Australia, decriminalization of homosexuality in many countries; not to mention expanded state provision of childcare, non-sexist education, protection against sexual violence, equal employment opportunity and anti-discrimination measures. By the early 1980s a women's peace movement had added disarmament and feminist environmentalists had added environmental protection – neither conventionally thought of as gender politics but both now argued in gender terms.[1]

Across this spectrum of demands, the results at the end of the 1980s seemed discouraging. The Equal Rights Amendment was defeated in the United States. Abortion was decriminalized in some countries, but a powerful American movement to re-criminalize it is under way. Men's homosexuality was decriminalized in some countries and some jurisdictions, usually in a grudging and partial way, and official homophobia is on the rise again, in Britain most conspicuously. Public provision of childcare remains massively below demonstrable need. Non-sexist education policies with teeth (and funding) remain rare. Governments led by Thatcher, Reagan and Kohl, riding the neo-conservative tide, had been openly reactionary in matters of sexual politics. Those led by figures like Mitterrand and Hawke, who came to power with support from feminists, had been glacially slow to introduce the reforms feminists want, beyond the easy symbolic gestures.

Does this experience show the strategy was mistaken? If the modern state is itself 'the general patriarch', in Mies's evocative phrase (1986: 26), then demanding that the state redress injustices worked by the 'individual patriarch' in the family (or any other setting) is merely appealing from Caesar unto Caesar. Seeking reform through the state is an exercise in futility, perhaps even in deception.

What is at issue here is not just a practical appraisal of the results of a particular period of political activism. At issue is the way we think about gender and about the state. Complex theoretical questions are involved.

There is no established theoretical framework to which the appraisal can be related. In a widely read article MacKinnon ruefully remarked that 'feminism has no theory of the state' (1982, 1983).[2] This is not completely correct, but it is certain that feminism has no developed or widely agreed theory of the state. The same applies to gay liberation, and to social-scientific conceptualizations of gender. Yet the state is not blank. Many beginnings with the problem have been made.

Recent theoretical writing contains a remarkable series of sketches of a theory of the patriarchal state; at least nine have appeared in English, as essays or book chapters, since 1978.[3] Materials for developing them are available in immense volume, in practical experience and academic writing. Yet the sketches have remained sketches; there has not been a sustained *development* of theory. This suggests that we need to look carefully at the conceptual foundations of the discussion and perhaps configure it in another way. The first section of this chapter is an exploration of the main ways of thinking about gender, sexuality and the state to be found in English-language writing in recent decades. I will argue that there are indeed some problems in the theoretical bases of this literature which have severely limited it.

The second section of the chapter is an attempt to move beyond these limits by proposing, not an alternative sketch of the patriarchal state, but at a somewhat more generalized level a framework for theorizing the interplay of gender relations and state dynamics. This is meant to be systematic, though brief. It is based on the view that gender is a collective phenomenon, an aspect of social institutions as well as an aspect of personal life, and is therefore internal as well as external to the state. Put another way, the state as an institution is part of a wider social structure of gender relations. A recognition of the historicity of gender relations is the essential point of departure. Accordingly the exposition of the framework begins with the question of the historical constitution of the state. The analysis moves from this starting-point towards issues of political practice. My assumption throughout is that the point of a theory of state is a better capacity to make appraisals of political strategy.

A note about terms and scope is necessary. Sexuality is part of the domain of human practice organized (in part) by gender relations, and 'sexual politics' is the contestation of issues of sexuality by the social interests constituted within gender relations. 'Gender politics' is a broader term embracing the whole field of social struggle between such interests.

'The state' is empirically as well as theoretically complex. Actual states include local government, regional (such as provincial or state) and national levels, and there is even an international level of the state, found in international law and inter-governmental organizations like the European Economic Community and the United Nations. Drawing boundaries around 'the state' is not easy; taxation departments and courts are obviously state institutions but are medical associations? welfare agencies? universities? unions? The problem is compounded by the fact that the realm of the state as well as the form of the state changes historically.

The approach taken in this chapter, as in much modern state theory, is to emphasize the state as process rather than the state as thing. In this respect the approach parallels the work on the state and sexuality by Foucault and those influenced by him, and I have drawn on this tradition in discussing processes of regulation. But the history of gender politics requires also an analysis of the institutional apparatus of the state which makes regulation possible, and of the process of internal coordination which gives state apparatuses a degree of coherence in practice. Here I have found more helpful models in socialist state theory and in the sociology of bureaucracy. Coordination (which can be linked on the one hand to the concept of 'sovereignty', on the other to the institutional transformations that compose the structural history of the state) is the main point of reference in this chapter for marking out the sphere of the state. When I speak, to save circumlocution, of the state as an object or as an actor, I mean the set of institutions currently subject to coordination (by administrative or budgetary means) by a state directorate.

The focus of the discussion, as in most of the English-language literature, is the liberal state associated with industrial-capitalist economies in the nineteenth and twentieth centuries. Living in a semi-colonial country makes one acutely aware of the importance of imperialism in the history of modern states, and at various points I discuss divergences in gender politics between metropole and colony. I do not discuss communist states, though in principle the framework should be of use in discussing them. If it is true, as I suspect, that most communist states have little to do with socialism and in most respects are a quite familiar form of the state, a kind of military dictatorship, then their sexual politics will differ from liberal states in the way interests in sexual politics are articulated, but in other ways will be similar.

I: The Field of Argument

Mainstream State Theory and Liberal Feminism
Classical theories of the state are unhelpful in the sense that they have had little to say directly about gender. The liberal tradition that discusses citizenship, property rights and the rule of law presents the 'citizen' as an unsexed individual abstracted from social context. Socialist and anarchist analyses of the state as an agent of domination add an account of social context, but only in the form of class; the contending classes seem to be all of the same sex. So are the bureaucrats in the Weberian tradition that spawned the endless modern discussion of the state apparatus.[4]

More strikingly, the recent inheritors of these traditions also ignore gender. The neo-Marxist debate over Poulantzas's conception (1973) of the 'relative autonomy' of the state is concerned with autonomy from class interests only. As Burstyn eloquently argues (1983), the radicalism of Marxist state theory is severely compromised by its gender blindness. Skocpol's model (1979) of social revolution and the state places gender and sexual politics on the sidelines. Giddens's attempt (1985) to historicize the state in the light of structuration theory makes only passing mention of women. Poggi's (1978) neo-liberal sociology of the state as a succession of systems of rule has nothing to say about sexual dominion, with the exception of one point. It seems that the historical definition of 'the state' as an arena of discourse sharply distinct from civil society or the family is still a powerful influence on the most sophisticated modern theorists.

The exception comes where Poggi (1978) notes, correctly, that the model of bourgeois citizenship depends on the 'citizen' being supported by a functioning patriarchal household. This is a remarkable concession to make in an aside. If *citizenship* is admitted to be gendered, can we fail to explore whether *rule* is gendered? Feminists digging into the foundations of liberal power theory have uncovered a dense cobweb of assumptions about gender. Pateman (1988) argues that the fraternal 'social contract' of Rousseau and later liberalism is based on an implicit sexual contract requiring the subordination of women and regulating men's sexual access to women. This is not confined to the early stages of liberalism. As Kearns (1984) shows for the modern version in Rawls's *A Theory of Justice*, the social contract is implicitly between men, presumed to be heads of families and in charge of wives-and-children.

So the issue of gender, *formally* excluded from the discourse of state theory, is nevertheless present under the surface. State theory must deal with it somehow. The result, as seen in the liberal account of citizenship, is likely to be that an implicit sociology of gender becomes an important if unspoken part of theories of the state.

The same is true of Marxist state theory. The analysis of the state as an agency of class power is based on a specific conception of class. This arises from a political economy which excludes domestic production, therefore much of women's work, from calculation. At the same time, the concept of the state is based on a demarcation of politics from 'civil society' or from an 'ideological instance'. No prizes are offered for seeing the connection with the public/private distinction which is a major feature of patriarchal definitions of 'women's place'. In both directions the Marxist theory of the state presupposes the gender division of labour and its cultural supports.[5]

So, ironically, does neo-conservatism. The New Right envisions the state as a mindlessly expanding system of bureaucratic control, which needs to be rolled back to liberate the entrepreneurs and redistribute wealth to 'the producers'. In principle, this programme assumes that the low-paid or un-paid labour of women will always be there to pick up the pieces in terms of family life, welfare and personal survival.[6] In practice, a fair amount of neo-conservative energy is devoted to attempts to make this postulate come true.

The implicit discourse of gender in accounts of the state is brought to the surface by liberal feminism, a tradition of thought with a 200-year history embracing Wollstonecraft (1975[1792]) and Mill (1912[1869]) in Britain, Stanton (1969[1881]) and Friedan

(1963) in the United States. Liberal feminism took the doctrine of 'rights' seriously and turned it against the patriarchal model of citizenship. 'Equal rights' is more than a slogan, it is a wholly logical doctrine that is as effective against the 'aristocracy of sex' as the doctrine of the 'rights of man' was against the aristocracy of property.

The concept of rights is connected with a particular concept of the state. In this view the state is, or ought to be, a neutral arbiter between conflicting interests and a guarantor of individual rights. The right to a voice in its proceedings is given by citizenship. Liberal feminism adopts this view of the state, with one significant shift: it argues that *empirically* the state is not neutral in its treatment of women. Liberal feminism, in effect, treats the state as an arbiter that has been captured by a particular group, men. This analysis leads directly to a strategy for redress: capture it back. If women's situation is defined as a case of imperfect citizenship, the answer is full citizenship. If men presently run the governments, armies and bureaucracies, the solution is more access, packing more and more women into the top levels of the state until balance is achieved.

In its own territory this is a powerful and sharp-edged analysis. It underpins what successes the women's movement has had in dealings with the liberal state. The campaign for the suffrage itself was based on this analysis, as were the campaigns for married women's property rights last century and for equal pay in this century. More recently, liberal feminist logic has led to anti-discrimination laws, equal employment opportunity (EEO) pro-grammes, and an expanded recruitment of women in the middle levels of political power. The themes of the United Nations Decade for Women (1975–85) broadly followed liberal feminist notions of equal citizenship. Liberal feminism has developed enough leverage to receive occasional endorsement from the political leadership of the superpowers. Carter in his day endorsed the ERA; while Gorbachev sought to include liberal-feminist themes in *perestroika*:

> Today it is imperative for the country to more actively involve women in the management of the economy, in cultural development and public life. For this purpose women's councils have been set up throughout the country. (Gorbachev, 1988: 116)[7]

All that said, the liberal feminist analysis is theoretically rootless to a striking degree. In a basic sense it treats patriarchy as an accident, an imperfection that needs to be ironed out. It under-stands men as a category over-represented in the state structure.

But it has no way of explaining why that biological category should have a collective *interest* needing to be defended. Therefore, it has no way of accounting for men's resistance except as an expression of prejudice. Liberal feminists typically speak of 'sexism' not of patriarchy, and accordingly seek to change men's minds to cure the prejudice. The account of women's abstinence from the public realm is likewise based on a description of attitudes, most often on the idea that women are socialized into traditional sex roles which hamper full citizenship.

So far as liberal feminism has a social theory it is 'sex role' theory. Accordingly its analysis suffers from the well-documented shortcomings of that theory as an analysis of gender. Most pertinently it suffers from sex role theory's inability to understand the division of labour, and its evasion of the issues of force and violence. It is telling that Friedan, the most prominent figure in North American liberal feminism, finds the entry of women cadets into West Point to train for military leadership a positive move – a judgement consistent with the politics of access but horrendously at odds with recent feminist analyses of warfare. It is equally telling that Gorbachev goes on from the passage quoted above to blame Soviet social difficulties on a breakdown of family life, and to emphasize the question of 'what we should do to make it possible for women to return to their purely womanly mission'.[8]

Liberal feminism has brought to the surface the suppressed truth that the state is gendered, and has used this truth to inspire a formidable and sustained politics of access. But it has not been able to grasp the character of gender as an institutional and motivational system, nor to develop a coherent analysis of the state apparatus or its links to a social context. The underlying individualism of classical liberalism, as Z. Eisenstein argues (1986[1981]), is at odds with the social analysis required for the development of feminism. Only through a break with liberal presuppositions can these antinomies be overcome. It is, indeed, in the more radical feminisms of the 1970s and 1980s that a new concept of the state has emerged.

The Patriarchal State

Where liberal feminism sees itself as challenging prejudice, radical feminisms see themselves as contending with a social system. The name 'patriarchy' is much debated; it has been criticized in particular for a false universality, attributing modern Western patterns of men's domination over women to the rest of the world and the rest of history. If this implication is dropped, 'patriarchy' is a serviceable term for historically produced situations in gender rclations where men's domination is *institutionalized*. That is to say, men's overall social supremacy is embedded in face-to-face settings like the family and the workplace, generated by the functioning of the economy, reproduced over time by the normal operation of schools, media, and churches. Prejudice is part of this institutionalization, but only a small part of the whole.[9]

An account of patriarchy as a social system was initially modelled on socialist theories of class; feminist theorists such as Firestone adopted even the terminology, speaking of 'sex class' alongside 'economic class'. They did not at first adapt socialist theories of the state; but these existed and could be asked feminist questions.[10] In the first translations of socialist ideas into sexual politics, the state was seen as being patriarchal in order to pursue the class interests of the bourgeoisie. The ruling class through the state might seek social order by repressing homosexuality, or bolster profit by maintaining a low wage structure for women, or solve employment crises by shunting female labour between home and factory. Although some of these effects certainly occur, and are documented in research on the welfare state, the theoretical premise is untenable. As Burstyn argues, we cannot continue to see class dynamics as the ultimate cause of gender dynamics in the state. These social dynamics constantly interact, but one cannot be dissolved into the other. As this point has been increasingly accepted, a more sophisticated analysis has developed which sees the state as implicated in a class system and a system of patriarchy at the same time. Indeed, the state may be seen as the vital bridge between these two systems, as in Ursel's (1986) historical analysis of the regulation of women's labour in Canada.[11]

Socialist feminism has generally seen the link between the family and the economy as the theoretical key to women's oppression. It has therefore focused on the way the state regulates or re-structures this link. In the most sophisticated statement of this view, McIntosh (1978) sees the state intervening both in the family, and in the capitalist workplace and labour market, not to pursue immediate class interests so much as to pursue the long-term goal of securing the social conditions which allow capitalist production to continue. The moves made by the state depend on a balancing of needs and demands which may be in conflict with each other, and which certainly change historically. Thus McIntosh introduces the very important issue of the *strategic complexity* of state action in gender politics. State agencies act under contradictory pressures which often result in ambivalent policies. McIntosh emphasizes that the state's role in the oppression of women is usually indirect. It plays a part in establishing or regulating 'systems' (the family, wage labour) in which women are oppressed. But the state can appear in itself to be gender-neutral; and this is a vital aid to legitimacy.

To some extent this approach overcomes the tendency of socialist theory to prioritize class over patriarchy. But the emphasis is still on the reproduction of *capitalist* relations of production; gender relations are still conceptually derivative. The problem is only fully overcome when the analysis is generalized to the reproduction of social structure in general. Burton (1985) has proposed an 'extended theory of social reproduction' which treats the state as central. She points to the importance of state action in spheres that Marxist–feminist analysis tended to bypass, notably biological reproduction and mass education. While sociological analysis of the state, whether feminist or not, has generally seen the state as influenced by a pre-given social structure, Burton forcibly draws attention to the role of the state in *constituting* the categories of social structure. In particular she emphasizes the ways in which masculinity and femininity, and the relation between them, are produced as effects of state policies and state structures. The interplay between schools and families, for instance, is fertile ground in the making of gender.

Although this line of thought connects with the most sophisticated levels of social theory, the main line of feminist thinking has taken another path. Its point of departure is a criticism of liberal feminism for not realizing the depth at which the state is connected with men's interests. As Scutt (1985) puts it, reflecting on the defeat of feminist proposals in a process of rape law reform in Australia, 'governments and laws are established for the benefit of men, and against women'. In such a view the state is a direct expression of men's interests, it is socially masculine. The idea of the 'male state' spread in feminist writing of the later 1970s. Daly's widely read *Gyn/Ecology* (1978) spoke of the 'sado-state', assimilating the state to the destructive aspect of male sexuality. Very similar ideas became important in the feminist anti-war movement in the 1980s, which has often treated the state's military apparatus – especially nuclear weapons – as an expression of male aggression and destructiveness (for example, Stiehm, 1983).

These conceptions are close to a view of the state widespread in the early gay liberation movement, which likewise broke with a liberal politics of law reform in favour of mass mobilization and confrontation. Gay men in particular faced the state as direct oppressor since their own sexuality was criminalized. Police homophobia has been an important issue; it is significant that the gay liberation movement was triggered by a confrontation between gay men and police in New York, the so-called 'Stonewall riot' of 1969. Lesbians have experienced the state as oppressor in the courts (in custody battles, for example), in the exclusion of lesbian experience from education, and through experiences shared with heterosexual women. Gay and lesbian writers have not, however, produced much formal theorization of the state. What there is, notably the work of Fernbach, emphasizes the historical embedding of violent masculinity in the state with the creation of armies and empires.[12]

On any reading, the idea of the 'male state' commits feminism against the state. It has been, however, nuanced in two ways which imply rather different politics. The first treats the state as the hireling or messenger-boy of patriarchy, as an agent for a social interest – that of men – which is constituted outside it. Scutt's comment that governments are 'established for the benefit of men' illustrates this position. This is closer to liberal feminism, as it suggests at least a logical possibility of turning the state around. The second conception (perhaps deriving from anarchist views of the state as well as the new feminist focus on sexual violence) sees the state itself as oppressor; the state *is* the patriarchal power structure. Mies's comment on the state as 'the general patriarch' (1986: 26), quoted earlier, illustrates this idea. Here there is no political ambiguity: the state as such has got to go, in the interests of women.[13]

It is the second variant that has led to the most interesting developments, which give more bite to the conception of the state as patriarch. An influential paper by MacKinnon (1983) explores how the US legal system operates in relation to rape. Historically, rape has been constructed as a crime from the point of view of men. The legal system translates this interested point of view into impersonal procedural norms, defining (for instance) what must be proven and what is acceptable or convincing evidence. The courts are not patriarchal because they are improperly biased against women; rather they are patriarchal through the way the whole structure of rape law operates. The more *objective* they are in procedure the more effectively patriarchal they are. The norm of 'legal objectivity' thus becomes an institutionalization of men's interests.

A very similar point is made by Burton (1987) about job evaluations in Australia. 'Equal opportunity' or 'pay equity' programmes often call for an objective assessment of jobs to overcome traditional gender inequalities. But the appearance of technical neutrality is contradicted as the underlying rationale of evaluation schemes embeds patriarchal points of view, for instance in the weighting given to different aspects of a job. On a broader canvas, Grant and Tancred-Sheriff (1986) in Canada point to the arrangement of administrative units within bureaucracies as a practice embodying gender interests. Departments where women's interests are represented tend to be peripheral. Thus women's advisory units have slight organizational power compared with, say, economic policy-making units dominated by men.

What these arguments have in common is the perception that patriarchy is embedded in *procedure*, in the state's way of functioning. This perception is extremely important. It allows us to acknowledge the patriarchal character of the state without falling into a conspiracy theory or making futile searches for Patriarch Headquarters. It locates sexual politics in the realm of social action, where it belongs, avoiding the speculative reductionism that would explain state action as an emanation of the inner nature of males. Finally it opens up the question of the *state apparatus*, overlooked by liberal feminism and earlier radical feminism alike. The character and dynamics of the state apparatus, the actual machinery of government, is a major theme in non-feminist theory, and urgently needs analysis in terms of gender.[14]

The Research Agenda
These theoretical debates have been strategy-driven rather than data-driven; they respond to the feminist and gay movements' urgent needs for ideas about what to do rather than to a contemplative scientific model of theory-linked-to-research. Indeed it is not always obvious what kind of research could resolve the theoretical issues posed. Nevertheless empirical research on gender and the state has been building up at a rapid rate, mainly as a result of the impact of feminism on social science in the universities. It has taken three main forms.

First, feminist historians have traced the political history of feminism itself and its encounters with the state. Biographies of prominent feminists, such as Magarey's (1985) life of Catherine Spence, convey a great deal of information about conceptions of the state, policy debates and the tactical interplay between feminists, bureaucrats and governments. Other feminist historians have traced the state's changing regulation of women, of families, of sexual violence and so on. A notable example is Gordon's (1988) exploration of domestic violence in the north-eastern United States, studying the interplay between charity, state control and working-class women's responses. Gay historians such as Weeks (1977) in Britain and Kinsman (1987) in Canada have similarly unpacked a complex history of state regulation of homosexual practice and desire.

Secondly, the well-oiled machinery of quantitative sociology and political science is capable of sending forth, when the right button is pushed, a limitless stream of survey studies of gender and politics. One fruit of this is the debate on the 'gender gap' in voting patterns. We now have a mass of information on sex differences in voting, political participation and recruitment, attitudes, political learning and so on, in all countries where survey research is common. Most of this is quite innocent of theory, but it is not irrelevant to theory. A major finding of this research, as Epstein's recent review shows, is a broad *similarity* between women's and men's political attitudes, interests, and partisanship. This contradicts the theoretical idea that men's domination of the political apparatus arises from natural differences in motivation or outlook between the sexes.[15]

Thirdly, a fast-growing collection of feminist policy studies traces state administrative action in particular fields of gender or sexual politics. This research often illuminates the debates within the state which accompany new policies, and the limits of state interventions. Smart's study (1984) of British family law, and its ambiguous reinforcement of patriarchal domestic relationships, is a notable example. Research of this kind can, more surprisingly, also illuminate structural questions. This is shown in Ruggie's comparative study (1984) of working women in Britain and Sweden; the markedly better labour market position of Swedish women is found to be connected with the different structure of the welfare state in the two countries.[16]

This adds up to a convincing picture of the state as an active player in gender politics. Nobody acquainted with the facts revealed in this research can any longer accept the silence about gender in traditional state theory, whether liberal, socialist or conservative. The research also demonstrates that the state is, at the very least, a significant vehicle of sexual and gender oppression and regulation. The general tendency of feminist theory to move towards a conception of the 'patriarchal state' appears to be valid.

But a theory constructed on this postulate alone would give no grip on strategy. To say that 'government is women's enemy', as Presley and Kinsky (1982) do, or in Walby's more sophisticated language, 'the state represents patriarchal as well as capitalistic interests and furthers them in its actions' (1986: 57), gives no way of grasping what feminism *in practice* has seen in the state that makes the state worth addressing as a resource for progressive sexual politics. To gain some purchase on that question requires an exploration of the changing circumstances in which state instrumentalities act, the strategic problems of state directorates, and the scope and limits of the state's embroilment in gender relations.

II: A Theoretical Framework

1. The state is constructed within gender relations as the central institutionalization of gendered power. Conversely, gender dynamics are a major force constructing the state, both in the historical creation of state structures and in contemporary politics.

Many of the policy-oriented discussions of topics like 'women and welfare' take the already written history of the modern state for granted, and inquire about its consequences for women. This traps the analysis of gender politics in an external logic, most commonly in a logic of class. Rather, we need to appraise the state from the start as having a specific location within gender relations, and as having a history shaped by a gender dynamic. This is not the only basis of state history, but it is an essential and irreducible aspect of the state.

The state is a structure of power, persisting over time; an institutionalization of power relations. It is not the only institutionalization of power, nor even the monopolist of legitimate force, as some classic theory has it. Feminism points to the family as a domain of power, and to husbands' violence against wives – which survey research shows to be very widespread – as a socially legitimated use of force. Violence against gay men is also widely regarded as legitimate, and in bashings of gays, as in husbands' bashing of wives, the laws against assault are generally inactive.[17]

The state, then, is only part of a wider structure of gender relationships that embody violence or other means of control. It is a node within that network of power relations which is one of the principal sub-structures of the gender order. The state is indeed the main organizer of the power relations of gender. Its scale and coherence contrasts, for instance, with the dispersed, cellular character of power relations institutionalized in families. Through laws and administrative arrangements the state sets limits to the use of personal violence, protects property (and thus unequal economic resources), criminalizes stigmatized sexuality, embodies masculinized hierarchy, and organizes collective violence in policing, prisons and war. In certain circumstances the state also allows or even invites the counter-mobilization of power.

To speak of 'history' is to court discussions of 'origins'. Delphy has eloquently shown the traps in 'origins' arguments about patriarchy, and we should not fall into a search for a mythical 'moment of origin' of the state. It is, however, possible to launch a genuinely historical investigation of early state development. Lerner's notable study of early Mesopotamia argues that archaic states were organized in the form of patriarchy, and from the start promoted patriarchal family forms, the economic dependence of women and the control of women's sexuality. Fernbach's suggestions about the construction of a 'masculine specialization in violence' are also of interest. He argues a close link between the founding of states and the demographic and economic changes that led to the historical emergence of warfare. While serious historical investigation of such themes is still rare – most archaeology is still pre-feminist in its understanding of social structure – it seems likely that an emerging history of the state will have the gender division of labour and the institutionalization of violence as central themes.[18]

Why 'origins' arguments fail is that the constitution of the state is a continuing historical process, which creates fundamentally new forms. On a global scale, modern states were created by the dynamics of European imperialism over the past 400 years. This was a gendered, and partly gender-driven, process. There was a sharp gender division of labour in conquest, a masculine adventure perceived and motivated as such. The imperial state structures created to rule colonial empires were masculinized institutions to an even greater degree than the European states from which they grew. There might be Queens Regnant like Isabella or Elizabeth at home, but no woman was ever sent out as Viceroy of the Indies or Governor of Van Diemen's Land. When conquest was succeeded by settlement, a new gender and sexual politics arose where the state was reorganized around racist population and workforce policies. In different parts of the colonial world states changed in different directions to sustain white family settlement, Afro-American slavery, or racial bars in colonial administration. This creation of new state structures (never simply exported) could lead in unexpected directions. It is a notable fact that states on the frontier of European settlement, in the western United States and Australasia, were the first to concede woman suffrage, and some of them did so a generation before the metropolitan states.[19]

In the imperial centres the state went through a fundamental transformation between the eighteenth and the twentieth century, traced in conventional histories as a shift from the absolutist state to the liberal-constitutional state and then to the interventionist state. One of the key components of this shift, persistently missed by gender-blind research, is a politics of masculinity. The states of the *ancien régime* were integrated with, indeed operated through, a hegemonic form of masculinity which prized personal and family honour, worked through kinship and patronage obligations, and connected the exercise of authority with a capacity for violence (symbolized in the duel, and more systematically seen in the role of the landed gentry in military affairs). The creation of a liberal-constitutional order, and especially the creation of an impersonal bureaucracy in place of an administrative apparatus run by patronage, involved an attack on this form of masculinity and its ramifications, apparent in the scarifying attacks on 'Old Corruption' by English reformers in the early nineteenth century. The hegemonic masculinity of the old regime was displaced during the nineteenth century by a hegemonic masculinity organized around themes of rationality, calculation, orderliness.

This change in gender was not a *consequence* of the bourgeois revolution, it was a *central part* of it, part of the dynamic that created modern industrial capitalism as an already-gendered social order. Associated changes gradually worked through education, the arts and other spheres of culture. Thus a bureaucratized school system became a major component of the state from the mid-nineteenth century; curriculum was gradually modified to prioritize science; 'technical education' was invented. The process was far from tension-free. The creation of a 'rationalized' masculinity split off personal violence from social authority: Mr Gladstone, Mr Rockefeller and Mr Morgan did not fight duels. Violent or wild masculinities were nevertheless socially constructed on the colonial frontier, as shown in the research on New Zealand by Phillips (1980). And a calculative violence was institutionalized in the military in the wake of the Napoleonic wars. These changes came home with the terrific shock delivered to European gender orders by the First World War. The fascist movements that devastated European society in the following decades had immediate roots in the violent masculinity of the front-line soldiers of the war – one of whom was Adolf Hitler.[20]

A key part of the liberal state was the creation of a system of representation, elected parliaments and officials. This system was closely linked to an emerging distinction between a 'public' sphere, in which representation occurred, and a private sphere of domestic and personal life. Feminist historians have traced the nineteenth-century construction of a feminized 'domestic' realm, increasingly seen as the exclusive sphere of women. The link between the two, in the bourgeois ideal adopted by much of the labour movement also, was the husband/father: he was the economic actor (wage earner or property owner) and the citizen of the state.

Though powerful as ideology, this model never reflected reality. Among other things it drastically underestimated women's economic activity, and ignored women's role as cultural producers (for example, as novelists) and lobbyists in church and politics. Unless women could be absolutely controlled by a domestic patriarch, the liberal model of citizenship contained a major contradiction – forcefully pointed out by J.S. Mill. Domestic patriarchy was never up to the task. The result was deepening problems of legitimacy for the state, which gave the woman suffrage movement leverage, and drove an expansion of the system of representation towards the contemporary model of universal citizenship and plebiscitary elections (Davidoff and Hall, 1987; Mill, 1912[1869]; Zaretsky, 1976).

> **2.** As a result of this history the state is a bearer of gender (though in a much more complex way than ideas of the 'male state' suggest). Each empirical state has a definable 'gender regime' that is the precipitate of social struggles and is linked to – though not a simple reflection of – the wider gender order of the society.

It is misleading to talk of a 'male state' where millions of the state's workers are women, unless one assumes them all to have become honorary men, or assumes that their gender is irrelevant to what they do and how they do it. Rather, women and men tend to occupy particular positions within the state, and work in ways structured by gender relations. This is the 'gender regime', defined as the historically produced state of play in gender relations within an institution, which can be analysed by taking a structural inventory.[21] Three main structures can be identified.

A gender division of labour is the most obvious, and frequently documented, feature of the state's gender regime. The state directorate (the 'elites' of politics, the bureaucracy, the judiciary, the military) almost everywhere in the world is composed 95–100 per cent of men. The coercive apparatus of the state (police, military, prison officers) has a comparable percentage of men. Men's employment in infrastructural state services (railways, maritime services, power, construction) approaches these levels. Women predominate in some categories of human-service state employment (elementary school teaching, nursing). Women fill almost all secretarial positions through the administrative structure.

In other sectors (secondary school teaching, general administration, mass communication) both women and men are present in substantial numbers. Here another pattern appears, which has been documented in recent research for equal-opportunity programmes. Women predominate in the part-time, casual and unskilled positions; men in 'promotion' positions with supervisory tasks and career prospects. The predominance of men increases steadily as one works up the hierarchy of authority and income, eventually producing the lop-sided sex ratio seen among policy-making elites.[22]

As well as a gender division of labour in terms of individuals there is also a division of labour at the collective level, in terms of bureaucratic units. Grant and Tancred-Sheriff's (1986) important observation on this point has already been mentioned: women's interests are articulated in relatively peripheral parts of the state apparatus. The individual gender division of labour is both cause and consequence of a cultural differentiation of state units along gender lines. The coercive and infrastructural apparatus is strongly 'masculinized' in its ideology and practice as well as its workforce. The point is obvious in the case of armies and police forces. Equally notable is the emphasis on men's camaraderie, endurance and skill with heavy tools in the workplace culture of manual workers in the infrastructure. In the state directorate too, though the style of masculinity is more bourgeois, the few women who bring back ethnographic reports describe a milieu actively antagonistic to femininity. H. Eisenstein (1985), in her experience as an Australian 'femocrat', provides a particularly vivid account of the embeddedness of masculinity in the upper reaches of the state.[23]

Putting these points together with the useful work on taxonomy of the state apparatus in recent class-bound theory, it is possible to make a classification of the major instrumentalities of the contemporary liberal state in terms of their gender structuring. A simple model is shown in Fig 7.1. The quasi-governmental sector that Shaver (1982) has called 'the non-government state' is a particularly interesting feature of the history of the liberal state. Organizations in this sector have been the only means, until very recently, by which women have had any significant role in shaping state policy or the use of public funds. Some operate in sex-segregated fields, such as girls' schools and women's hospitals, which were important in forming and transmitting feminist traditions in the nineteenth and early twentieth centuries. A good many feminist activists of the 1970s worked in the non-government state, and feminist welfare initiatives, such as health centres and refuges, often took the shape of subsidized voluntary agencies already familiar in this sector.[24]

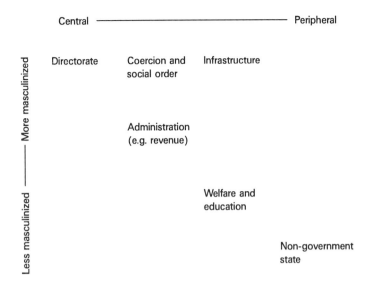

Figure 7.1 *Gender structuring of state apparatus*

The second component of a gender regime is a *structure of power*. More feminist analysis has focused on the external power relations of the state than on its internal arrangement, but there has been some discussion of the most conspicuous feature of authority in the modern state, its bureaucratization. Bureaucracy, as argued by Ferguson (1984) and Grant and Tancred-Sheriff (1986), is a 'gendered hierarchy'. Its connection with the rise of new models of masculinity in the nineteenth century has already been mentioned. The classical theory of bureaucracy developed by Weber and his followers emphasized the connection of bureaucracy with the secularization and rationalization of human relationships. Feminist research on cultural history, especially the history of science, is now showing the fundamental connections of this model of rationality with gender politics and the legitimation of men's domination over women.[25]

Yet seeing bureaucracy in direct opposition to feminism, as Ferguson (1984) does, misses key points about it. As Deacon (1989) points out, the growth of a 'white-collar' workforce as the state's administrative apparatus expanded in the late nineteenth and early twentieth centuries was a crucial means of access for women, who entered the resulting clerical and semi-professional occupations in very large numbers. Women in the bureaucracy fought, and eventually won, battles to eliminate the many organizational barriers (such as 'marriage bars') set up to restrict their access. The very 'rationalization' of practice on which bureaucracy is built is potentially subversive of patriarchy. Like the concepts of citizenship and representation, rationality implicitly contains universalizable claims; once made, these corrode the legitimacy of traditional gender inequalities. Equal employment opportunity programmes are now using this leverage to some effect.[26]

Bureaucracy is not the only feature of the organization of power within the state. The 'other side of bureaucracy' involves personal networks, factions, the informal organization of resources and contacts. Organized as networks among men, these may survive the advent of formal sex equality. The various units of the state require coordination; and the means of coordination change historically. In the 1980s a pattern of administrative coordination within state structures has been increasingly displaced by fiscal coordination, and this shift is not gender-neutral. The language of finance and 'economic rationalism' has been the vehicle for an attack on welfare ideology, and a downgrading of women's interests on a very broad front, from the abolition of women's access programmes in further education to the gutting of childcare programmes.[27] Finally, the system of representation has also been socially organized on gender lines, with the enormous majority of elected officials being men though at least half of most electorates are women. Electoral patriarchy, as we might call this situation, has been surprisingly resilient. The only part of the world where it is seriously frayed, where women are elected in substantial numbers to positions of real power, is Scandinavia.

The third component of a gender regime is the *structure of cathexis*, the gender patterning of emotional attachments. This is the side of the state we know least about, by far. There is a long tradition of psychological research on attachment to political authority, going back to early psychoanalytic speculation about political leadership, and culminating in the research on fascism that produced theories of the 'authoritarian personality'. There was almost no recognition of *gender* in this literature, though it can now be re-read as a discourse about masculinity and the ways men can be attached to political leaders; Macciocchi (1979) has explored the parallel problem for women in Italian fascism. A gender patterning of emotion may also be significant within the state apparatus. Pringle (1989) has explored the complexities of boss/ secretary relationships and suggests the importance of pleasure for understanding these workplace connections. What Hochschild (1983) calls 'emotional labour' is an important part of the labour process in some fields of state employment, such as welfare and nursing. Such work is often allocated to women, and emotion thus becomes linked into the state's gender division of labour.

One might speculate that the growth and impersonality of the state structure has created increasing problems in the management of cathexis, and that modern official nationalism is partly a response to this. There is certainly an active gender politics around nationalism. Mies has pointed to a dramatic shift in nationalist imagery in post-revolutionary states:

> In this phase, the female image of the nation, found on the revolutionary posters mentioned above, is replaced by the images of the founding-fathers: Marx, Engels, Lenin, Stalin, Mao, Ho Chi Minh, Castro, Mugabe, to name only a few. Typically, among this gallery of socialist patriarchs, there are no women. (1986: 199)

A patriarchal structure of cathexis, it appears, cannot be presumed; strenuous work goes into trying to guarantee it.[28]

> **3.** The way the state embodies gender gives it cause and capacity to 'do' gender. As the central institutionalization of power the state has a considerable, though not unlimited, capacity to regulate gender relations in the society as a whole.

This issue has been the subject of more feminist and gay discussion about the state than any other, and the contours are becoming familiar. Again we may trace this issue across the three sub-structures of labour, power and cathexis.

In terms of the gendered organization of production and the gender division of labour, the liberal state was an 'interventionist' state well before the twentieth century. 'Protective' legislation on women's work affected women's participation in wage labour and attempted to impose a nuclear-family model on the nineteenth-century working class. State control of women's wages through wage boards, arbitration, legislation and decree is now a familiar theme in economic history. The state's capacity to change its tack was shown in the shift of women into manufacturing during the world wars. A highly visible gender politics of employment re-emerged in the 1970s and 1980s, revolving around 'equal opportunity' principles and affirmative action programmes. This has carried over strongly into the international dimension of the state, with the International Labour Organization, Organization for Economic Cooperation and Development, and United Nations being forums where policy and progress around women's employment are debated. At the same time there is a system of indirect control of the division of labour, as McIntosh has argued, through welfare provision, the education system, and other machinery.[29]

The state similarly has a capacity to regulate the power relations of gender in other institutions. The most discussed case of this is marital violence, where regulation involves a violation of the cultural boundary between the 'public' and the 'private' spheres. Police reluctance to intervene in 'domestic disputes' is familiar. In effect, feminist research indicates, the state's non-intervention has tacitly supported domestic violence – which mainly means husbands battering wives – up to the point where a public-realm scandal is created and state legitimacy is at issue. At that point men as state agents will move to restrain men in households: arrests may take place, legal proceedings begin, refuges are funded. The effect of this routine of management is to construct the issue as one of a deviant minority of violent husbands, and to deflect criticisms of marriage as an institution that generates violence. Radical feminists in the 1970s used this problem of legitimacy very effectively to get funding for the women's refuge movement, but as Johnson (1980) observes of the Australian experience, they found themselves trapped in this construction of the issues of violence.[30]

Nevertheless, the fact that the state will restrain some manifestations of private-sphere patriarchy is significant. Donzelot, in a widely read book on the 'policing of families' in France (1979) suggests that the growth of an apparatus of surveillance and regulation – in what Anglo-Saxon writers call the welfare state – has generally undermined domestic patriarchy. The idea is shared by some of the American right, who wish to roll back the state in order to restore women's dependence on men ('traditional family life'). This view is exaggerated, but it is nevertheless true that the state has functioned as an alternative means of economic support for many women disadvantaged by a patriarchal economy. 'Welfare mothers' and old-age pensioners are not exactly a mass base for feminism; they are nevertheless not abjectly dependent on particular men. Defending the level of income coming to women through the state has been a key issue for feminism since the onset of the recession of the 1970s (Shaver, 1983; Sidel, 1987b).

The state has a capacity to regulate sexuality and has shown an active interest in doing so. There are legal definitions of forbidden heterosexual relationships, for instance, laws on age of consent and on incest (see *Feminist Review*, 1988). Around the prohibition of incest a to-and-fro comparable to that on domestic violence occurs. As the 1987 furore about diagnoses of incest at Cleveland in England shows, vigorous enforcement can create legitimacy problems at least as severe as non-enforcement. The state in early twentieth-century Australia banned the sale of contraceptives and introduced 'baby bonus' payments in order to increase the (white) population. The state in contemporary India and China is vigorously trying to restrain population growth. During the nineteenth and early twentieth centuries, state repression of men's homosexuality became heavier. The process escalated through criminalization of all male homosexual behaviour (for example, the Labouchère amendment in Britain in 1885) to the rounding-up of homosexual men into concentration camps in Nazi Germany.[31]

Much of this regulation can be read as an attempt to promote a particular form of sexuality in the conjugal family against a whole series of tendencies in other directions. This is not a simple matter of 'social reproduction'. Often, as population policies illustrate, the state is pursuing a *re*-structuring of the family or of sexuality. And there is no doubt that these policies have met a great deal of resistance. The criminalization of male homosexuality failed to stop male homosexual behaviour, though it drove it underground for a couple of generations. The public banning of contraceptives failed to stop the early twentieth-century decline in family size, as women found other means of regulating births. Nor are Third World governments wonderfully successful in restraining population growth at present, while children remain an important asset in peasant society and are valued in urban culture.

4. The state's power to regulate reacts on the categories which make up the structure being regulated. Thus the state becomes involved in the historical process generating and transforming the basic components of the gender order.

The masculinization of the military apparatus was mentioned earlier as an example of the gender division of labour. It is more than a statistical trend. In armies a dominance-orientated masculinity is deliberately cultivated, in the rigours of basic training and in the manners of the officer corps. The space for femininity of any kind is narrow, a point re-discovered by women recruited to the American military in the recent phase of 'equal opportunities'. But this masculinity is not all of a piece. The violent masculinity of the frontline soldier would be worse than useless in the commanding general. The most successful general of the twentieth century, Georgi Zhukov, was domineering and brutal but never fired a shot at the Japanese or Germans; he was a manager not a fighter, as is clear in his memoirs. A modern army is built around the relationships between frontline fighters, managers, supply staff and technical experts; none can function without the others. In military affairs the state apparatus is visibly constructing particular forms of masculinity and regulating the relationships between them, not as an incidental effect of its operations, but as a vital precondition of them. This part of the state operates *through* the gender relationships thus constructed.[32]

The attempts at regulating sexuality made in the core industrial states in the nineteenth century led to equally dramatic effects. As Walkowitz's research indicates, the state's intervention on the terrain of venereal disease, morality and military efficiency produced the modern socio-legal category of the 'prostitute' – creating a category out of what had been much more fluid and relational before. At much the same time, the same state apparatuses restructured the legal proscription of men's homosexuality. In combination with the medicalization of sexual 'deviance' by a state-backed medical profession, this marked off 'the homosexual man' as a distinct type of person, transforming what had been a much more fluid play of sexuality, at most a sub-cultural tendency among urban men, into a clearly-flagged social barrier (Walkowitz, 1980; Weeks, 1977, 1985).

In such cases the metropolitan state is involved in *generating* categories of gender relations. The same occurs when the colonial state, engaged in setting up institutions of permanent conquest, defines permitted sexuality. It is a notable fact that colonial systems over the long sweep of history from the sixteenth century to the twentieth, became on the whole more racist. The colonial state became more opposed to intermarriage of colonizer and colonized, came in effect to define racial categories of citizenship through its regulation of marriage. An increasing regulation of marriage developed in the metropole as well. Two centuries ago, marriage in European culture was a precipitate of kinship rules, local customs and religion. It has increasingly become a product of *contract* as defined and regulated by the state. But civil, state-regulated contract is capable of civil, state-regulated abrogation; so divorce as a social institution has developed in the wake of state regulation of marriage. Again the consequence is a new category in gender relations, the divorcee, and the reorganization of the other institutions around it (for example, the 'blended family').[33]

The state thus is not just a regulatory agency, it is a creative force in the dynamic of gender. It creates new categories and new historical possibilities. But it should not be forgotten that the state also destroys. Modern states kill on a horrific scale, and gender is central to this fact. Probably the most destructive single action in modern history was not the atomic bombing of Hiroshima, but the relatively forgotten firebombing of Dresden, a town of no military significance, by the British and American air forces in February 1945. About 135,000 civilians were burned to death in a day during an attack which followed mechanically from a bureaucratic planning process. Masculine toughness had become institution-alized in an 'area bombing' approach that delivered genocide; and no process in a military bureaucracy could stop it.[34]

5. Because of its power to regulate and its power to create, the state is a major stake in gender politics; and the exercise of that power is a constant incitement to claim the stake. Thus the state becomes the focus of interest group formation and mobilization in sexual politics.

It is worth recalling just how wide is the liberal state's activity in relation to gender. This activity includes family policy, population policy, labour force and labour market management, housing policy, regulation of sexual behaviour and expression, provision of childcare, mass education, taxation and income redistribution, the creation and use of military forces – and that is not the whole of it. This is not a sideline; it is a major realm of state policy. Control of the machinery that conducts these activities is a massive asset in gender politics. In many situations it will be tactically decisive.

The state is therefore a focus for the mobilization of interests that is central to gender politics on the large scale. Feminism's historical concern with the state, and attempts to capture a share of state power, appear in this light as a necessary response to a historical reality. They are not an error brought on by an overdose of liberalism or a capitulation to patriarchy. As Franzway (1986) puts it, the state is unavoidable for feminism. The question is not whether feminism will deal with the state, but how: on what terms, with what tactics, towards what goals?

The same is true of the politics of homosexuality among men. The earliest attempts to agitate for toleration produced a half-illegal, half-academic mode of organizing which reached its peak in Weimar Germany, and was smashed by the Nazis. (The Institute of Sexual Science was vandalized and its library burnt in 1933; later, homosexual men were sent to concentration camps or shot.) A long period of lobbying for legal reform followed, punctuated by bouts of state repression. (Homosexual men were, for instance, targeted in the McCarthyite period in the United States.) The gay liberation movement changed the methods and expanded the goals to include social revolution, but still dealt with the state over policing, de-criminalization and anti-discrimination. Since the early 1970s gay politics has evolved a complex mixture of confrontation, cooperation and representation. In some cities, including San Francisco and Sydney, gay men as such have successfully run for public office. Around the AIDS crisis of the 1980s, in countries like the United States and Australia, gay community based organizations and state health services have entered a close – if often tense – long-term relationship.[35]

In a longer historical perspective, all these forms of politics are fairly new. Fantasies like Aristophanes' *Lysistrata* aside, the open mobilization of groups around demands or programmes in sexual politics dates only from the mid-nineteenth century. The politics that characterized other patriarchal gender orders in history were constructed along other lines, for instance as a politics of kinship, or faction formation in agricultural villages. It can plausibly be argued that modern patterns resulted from a reconfiguration of gender politics around the growth of the liberal state. In particular its structure of legitimation through plebiscite or electoral democracy invited the response of popular mobilization.

This response was however, asymmetrical. In class politics the mobilization of a subordinate group, via socialist parties, was followed by a counter-mobilization of conservative parties, with remarkable success. But feminist mobilization has not been followed by a counter-mobilization of anti-feminist men. There have been some small 'men's rights' groups but they have had no mass appeal. The right-wing mobilizations that have opposed feminism, for instance on the abortion issue, are based in churches and include a large number of women.

The absence of mobilization 'from above' in gender politics raises questions about the way men's power is institutionalized, and about the connection between different sites of power. A banal but perhaps largely correct explanation is that patriarchy is so firmly entrenched in existing political institutions such as the bureaucracy, the press, and the major parties, that in the normal run of things no more is needed; state and media substitute for a mobilization of men. In some situations of crisis, however, this can break down. In European fascism in the 1920s and 1930s, and Iran in the 1980s, a political mobilization in favour of patriarchy has occurred, feminism and sexual degeneracy were denounced, and violent repression followed the seizure of state power by the movement.[36]

> **6.** The state is constantly changing; gender relations are historically dynamic; the state's position in gender politics is not fixed. Crisis tendencies develop in the gender order which allow new political possibilities.

Much social analysis seems to imply that the state directorate has it easy, that the functional thing to do is obvious and straight-forward. In reality, state elites typically face shifting situations and contradictory pressures which their strategies can only partly resolve. Their power may be destabilized by crisis tendencies arising from sources outside their control.[37]

One such is a tendency towards crisis in the legitimation of patriarchy, a breakdown of established bases of authority. The long-term decline of religion has stripped patriarchy of its main cultural defence. The rise of the liberal state gave weight to generalizable claims of equality. The use of state power must be balanced with a search for legitimation if the power is to continue, and legitimation involves the ballot-box credibility of governing parties, the willingness of citizens to pay taxes and obey officials, the discipline or compliance of state employees. Feminism lays demands on the state which may be difficult to dodge without putting legitimacy at risk. The liberal feminist platform of equal citizenship, employment rights and anti-discrimination measures is formulated in a way that maximizes this leverage on the state. That is one reason why liberal feminism on certain issues has been very effective. Even the Reagan government found it expedient to appoint women to senior levels of the judiciary.

Yet there are risks for the state here. Too close an alignment with feminism gives offence to patriarchal ideology as mobilized in the churches, and to men's employment interests as mobilized in corporate managements and male-dominated unions. There is potential for destabilizing the gender order in too vigorous an intervention in the family in pursuit of domestic violence and incest offenders, too firm a support of women's rights in divorce. A telling example is the turbulence in United States politics created around abortion after the 1973 Supreme Court decision in *Roe* v. *Wade* effectively legalized it. 'Pro-life' mobilizations have attempted to use Congress, courts and street politics to reverse this decision, resulting in a complex and bitter series of disputes about constitutional issues as well as the ethics of abortion.[38]

There are also tendencies toward crisis in the gendered accumulation process connected with the division of labour. The rising labour force participation and rising levels of education and training of women in the post-war decades, plus the dis-employment of men that has become visible in the recession (with youth unemployment, earlier retirement, ethnic minority un-employment), have not revolutionized women's economic dependence but have certainly put pressure on existing models of family economics. They create serious difficulties for state policies that are predicated on breadwinner/housewife families, including the taxation/welfare regime and the organization of elementary education. They provide an economic basis for two movements among women which threaten the power of men: the unionization of working-class women, and the emergence of second-wave feminism (whose main base is women in higher education and the semi-professions).

The recession of the 1970s triggered a change in the state's relationship to these trends. With the end of the post-war boom, buying off diverse pressure groups by expanding and diversifying state services ceased to be possible; the state directorate is now concerned to limit costs and emphasize 'efficiency'. The state itself comes under attack in the shift from Keynesian to neo-conservative economics, with heavy pressure (mostly from capitalists and middle-class men) to reduce the size of government, cut taxes and cut expenditure. With mass unemployment, policies that bring more people on to the labour market have a high political cost. They are often reconfigured around a conservative gender politics. In Australia, for instance, even under a Labour government in the mid-1980s, immigration was reorganized around 'family reunion'; the government backed off long-day childcare commitments which would support full-time employment for women; unemployment benefits for youth were cut on the grounds that families should support them.[39]

Finally there are tendencies towards crisis in the social organization of sexuality (Kinsman, 1987; Weeks, 1986). The criminalization of men's homosexuality in the late nineteenth century not only failed to repress the sexual practice, it stimulated political mobilization of gay men in the twentieth. This suggests a long-term difficulty in maintaining a policy of selective sexual repression; yet that policy is required if the state is to sustain the dominance of heterosexual masculinity. In various ways hegemonic heterosexuality is unravelling. Among women, feminism has validated the assertion of women's sexual desire in a way almost inconceivable a couple of generations ago. Among men, the fixation of desire involved in the making of hegemonic heterosexuality cannot be contained within the conjugal family. It moves on to create an externalized and alienated sexuality, now a major feature of commercial popular culture. Ehrenreich (1983) picks up an important dimension of this in her map of the post-war 'flight from commitment' by heterosexual men in the United States.

Feminist pressure on men's sexuality should not be under-estimated. Some current research on masculinity suggests it is much wider in its reach than previously assumed, though it leads to very diverse responses. Positive responses by men include attempts to create egalitarian households and sexual ethics. Negative responses include the re-assertion of a dominating masculinity that can be seen in one form in hysterical tendencies in media (such as the 'Rambo' movies), in another form in the cult of the ruthless entrepreneur in business. The state directorate may endorse neither, but will have to position itself in relation to the crisis tendencies underlying them. In the United States in the late 1980s, a serious effort was under way by the right, with the support of the Bush administration, to reimpose a primitive birth/ contraception regime. The more militant anti-abortion forces have made no secret of their intention to move on, if they succeed in overturning the *Roe* v. *Wade* decision, to further attacks on feminist gains.[40]

Appraisals

Is the state patriarchal? Yes, beyond any argument, on the evidence discussed above. It is not 'essentially patriarchal' or 'male'; even if one could speak of the 'essence' of a social institution, this would exaggerate the internal coherence of the state. Rather the state is *historically* patriarchal, patriarchal as a matter of concrete social practices. State structures in recent history institutionalize the European equation between authority and a dominating masculinity; they are effectively controlled by men; and they operate with a massive bias towards heterosexual men's interests.

At the same time the pattern of state patriarchy changes. In terms of the depth of oppression and the historical possibilities of resistance and transformation, a fascist regime is crucially different from a liberal one, and a liberal one from a revolutionary one. The most favourable historical circumstance for progressive sexual politics seems to be the early days of social-revolutionary regimes; but the later bureaucratization of these regimes is devastating. Next best is a liberal state with a reformist government; though reforms introduced under its aegis are vulnerable in periods of reaction.

Though the state is patriarchal, progressive gender politics cannot avoid it. The character of the state as the central institutionalization of power, and its historical trajectory in the regulation and constitution of gender relations, make it unavoidably a major arena for challenges to patriarchy. Here liberal feminism is on strong ground.

Becoming engaged in practical struggles for a share of state power requires tactical judgements about what developments within the state provide opportunities. In the 1980s certain strategies of reform have had a higher relative pay-off than they did before. In Australia, for instance, the creation of a network of 'women's services' was a feature of the 1970s, and the momentum of this kind of action has died away. Reforms that have few budgetary implications but fit in with other state strategies, such as modernizing the bureaucracy, became more prominent. Equal employment opportunity and anti-discrimination legislation have been highlighted; decriminalizing homosexuality is consistent with this.

Of course reform is not all in the same direction. The ascendence of market-orientated technocrats in central government leads to a re-shaping of higher education that emphasizes training for men (technology, engineering, business, physical sciences) and drains money from areas with a high proportion of women (welfare, social science other than economics, humanities). Thus new defensive battles have to be fought. Sometimes they are fought with marked success, as in the Australian 'Tax Summit' in 1985 where a coalition of women's, welfare and labour groups blocked a federal government shift to a more regressive taxation structure. (See Franzway et al., 1989; O'Donnell and Hall, 1988.)

The problem is not the fact of engagement in the arena of the state, but the shape of that engagement. For liberal feminism the state has provided leverage for reform mainly through the citizenship/legitimacy nexus. But an exclusive focus on those opportunities leads to a form of politics organized around 'representation' rather than mass participation, and emphasis on reforms such as 'equal opportunity' programmes conceived in terms of career paths. This prioritizes the interests of an educated minority of women. Working-class women do not have 'careers' and are unlikely to be picked out as 'representatives'. The strategies of liberal feminism thus risk creating a structural split between organized feminism and working-class women, the movement's potential mass base.

A more radical form of engagement in the arena of the state will have to pay closer attention to the crisis tendencies in the gender order and the contradictions in state patriarchy discussed in the previous section. Some moments in the politics of the past twenty years do seem to embody a different form of engagement with the state, more radicalizing and participatory. One is the moment of gay liberation in the first years of the 1970s, contesting the state's repression of a major form of non-conjugal sexuality. Mobilization occurred on a scale far beyond that of any previous homosexual politics, and for several years sustained a high level of political radicalism and cultural creativity. Another example is the evolution of a women's refuge documented by Johnson, set up by radical feminists in the mid-1970s making a successful claim for state funding. Feminist principles stressed a participatory style of management, which eventually led to a takeover by the working-class women whom the mainstream welfare state defined as 'clients' (Johnson, 1980; Walter, 1980).

If such a politics can be generalized – and no one should doubt the difficulty of the task – what would be its ultimate goal? Is the state as a whole capable of being transformed; or should it, as anarchist tradition prescribes, be smashed? To put the question another way, we can conceive a patriarchal state, because we have one; is a *feminist state* conceivable?

One way of answering this is to look at the 'utopias' conceived by feminist novelists. On the whole they seem to answer no. They tend to present, as an image of a society free of patriarchy, a society without the state – such as the communities in Piercy's *Woman on the Edge of Time* (1976) or Le Guin's *Always Coming Home* (1987). Or they locate a feminist state in a world fundamentally different from our own, such as the hidden world without men in Gilman's *Herland* (1979[1915]).

The problem with such a position is that it fails to deal with the sheer scale of issues in a global society requiring a decision-making and coordination capacity. We live in a world of 5,000 million people, not a world of villages, however high-tech they may become. Rather than moving to a smaller-scale political structure, it may be that a move to a *larger* scale is needed to achieve the goals of eco-feminism and the women's peace movement. An argument can be made that the nation-state as the unit of sovereignty is an institution of patriarchy, requiring – in the context of competition between sovereign states – militarization and internal hierarchy.

Another way of approaching the question is to start from existing state structures and ask how they would have to be re-shaped. Considering the gender regime of the liberal state outlined above, it is clear that the masculinized 'core' of decision-making and enforcement would have to go, replaced by demilitarization and participatory democracy. The idea of a 'representative bureaucracy' canvassed in some 1970s reform movements seems consistent with this.

However, these moves would be nugatory unless the cultural distinction which reproduces women's exclusion from state power, the distinction between public (masculinized) and private (feminized), were abolished. In one sense that seems to imply an end to the state as such, which is founded on such a distinction. In another sense it suggests an expansion of the realm to which a programme of democratization would apply. The state would become, so to speak, broader and thinner.

Gay activists and many feminists are rightly concerned about increasing the existing state's powers of surveillance and control over personal life – a point on which libertarian feminists have split with anti-pornography feminists. Yet this does seem to be consistent with the tendency of all radical feminisms to apply political criteria to events and settings conventionally defined as 'private': from unequal domestic labour through marital violence and incest to date rape and household divisions of income. A feminist state that is a structure of authority, a means by which some persons rule over others, is self-contradictory.[41] A feminist state that is an arena for a radical democratization of social interaction may be a very important image of our future.

Acknowledgements

This paper is deeply influenced by Suzanne Franzway and by the late Dianne Court; it develops in new ways ideas that went into our joint book *Staking a Claim*. Both the ideas and the writing owe an immeasurable amount to Pam Benton. My concern with the state has been stimulated and sustained by the work of Sheila Shaver. Research assistance was provided by Julienne Vennard and Jan O'Leary, and at earlier stages in my work on these questions by Tim Carrigan, John Lee, Gary Dowsett and Sandra Kessler. Typing was done by Helen Easson, Stephen and Therese Humphrey and Marie O'Brien.

My thanks to all; I am conscious of the extent to which any project like this is a collective effort over time. Participants in conferences and seminars since 1985, when I gave a primitive version of this paper, have helped to an unusual degree, pushing me towards more comprehensive, and more comprehensible, formulations. My debt to Australian feminism, gay activists and more indirectly the labour movement, will be apparent. Helpful comments were made by *Theory and Society* reviewers. Early work on these issues was funded by a grant for a project 'Theory of class and patriarchy' by the Australian Research Grants Committee, and more recent work has been funded by Macquarie University Research Grants. Continuing support has been provided by friends in several countries, by colleagues at Macquarie University in Sydney, and at the University of Southern California (Program for the Study of Women and Men in Society) in Los Angeles, where the final draft was written. This is more than a formal acknowledgement of academic neighbours. The political position of a heterosexual man pursuing feminist and gay-liberation themes is ambiguous at best, and the personal position is liable to be stressful and exposed. The political, intellectual and personal support I have had for work on these issues has been vital.

Notes

This chapter first appeared as an article in *Theory and Society*, 1990: 507–44. © 1990 Kluwer Academic Publishers. Reprinted by permission of Kluwer Academic Publishers.

1 See, for example, the narratives in Coote and Campbell (1982); Curthoys (1988); Jenson (1989).

2 The reasons for my qualification of her claim will be apparent in following notes.

3 The nine sketches, cited at various points below, are by Barrett (1980); Burstyn (1983); Burton (1985); Connell (1987); Z. Eisenstein (1986[1981]: 225–9); Knuttila (1987); MacKinnon (1982); McIntosh (1978); Walby (1986). I would be surprised if these were all.

4 Reviews of the history of 'theories of the state' by Held (1985) and Knuttila (1987) make this point about gender-blindness.

5 For these general features of Marxist theory see the classic argument in Delphy (1984); for a striking illustration, see the treatment of patriarchy in Mitchell (1975).

6 As argued by Mowbray and Bryson (1984) and Wilson (1982). It is difficult to find an intellectually substantial 'New Right' theorization of the state, most is rhetoric. De Jasay (1985) is an interesting book with some flavour of neo-conservatism; it ignores gender.

7 A particularly clear exposition of the machinery of anti-discriminatory law is Ronalds (1987); recent documentation of recruitment of women is in Epstein (1988: ch. 8).

8 For the problems of sex role theory see Connell (1987: 47–54); Edwards (1983); Stacey and Thorne (1985). For amazing scenes at West Point see Friedan (1981: ch. 5); and on truly womanly missions, Gorbachev (1988: 117–18). For more radical views, see Stiehm (1983).

9 An excellent review of the concept is Fox (1988).

10 For different versions of this modelling, see Delphy (1984) and Firestone (1971); for the persistence of the idea of sex class see Z. Eisenstein (1986[1981]: passim).

11 A clear illustration of class dynamics being presupposed is E. Wilson's important study, *Women and the Welfare State* (1977). Burstyn (1983) provides a comprehensive critique of such logic. For variations on the 'dual systems' idea, see Connell (1983); Ursel (1986: 150–91); and Walby (1986).

12 An excellent account of state controls over homosexuality is Kinsman (1987). Police homophobia in three countries is documented in Rosen (1980–81); Smith (1988); Thompson (1985). For a notable attempt to theorize the state, see Fernbach (1981).

13 The state is seen as an agent *for* men by Burstyn (1983); by Barrett (1980); more ambiguously by Scutt (1985). For the state as patriarch, see Mies (1986) and Presley and Kinsky (1982: 77–83).

14 Cf. Clark and Dear (1984). An institutional approach to the state is sketched in Connell (1987: 125–32) and pursued in much greater depth in Franzway et al. (1989).

15 A representative text is Simms (1984); cf. Epstein (1988).

16 Examples of this genre are Atkins and Hoggett (1984) and Baldock and Cass (1983).

17 For the 'monopoly' concept, deriving from Weber, see Knuttila (1987). For documentation of the scale of domestic violence, Dobash and Dobash (1979).

18 On the problem of post-structuralism, see Flax (1987) and Weedon (1987). On the questions of origins, see Delphy (1984: 199–206), Fernbach (1981), and above all, Lerner (1986), which places the issue on the terrain of genuine historiography. Coontz and Henderson (1986) is disappointing as prehistory but usefully highlights the sexual division of labour.

19 This dimension has been spectacularly absent from both Marxist theories of accumulation and from world-systems theory; though it is now beginning to be added back in by scholars such as Mies.

20 The history sketched in these two paragraphs is still mostly fragmented or unwritten; but I would draw attention to the pioneering work on the colonial frontier by Phillips (1980). Theweleit (1987) illuminates the origin of fascism.

21 The procedure of structural inventory is defined and illustrated in Connell (1987: 91ff and 119ff).

22 Dramatic statistics on sex and hierarchy are in Director of Equal Opportunity in Public Employment, Office of (1985). Sources for other details are cited in Connell (1987: ch. 1); Epstein (1988: chs 7, 8); O'Donnell and Hall (1988).

23 Patton and Poole (1985) have material on military masculinity; infrastructural masculinity is celebrated in Adam-Smith (1969). H. Eisenstein (1985) is a remarkable 'insider' account; see also Lynch (1984).

24 For 'taxonomy' see Clark and Dear (1984). For 'voluntary' sector see Shaver (1982).

25 For a useful compilation of feminist thinking on scientific rationality, see Harding and Hintikka (1983).

26 The relevance of rationalization is particularly clear at the international level of state structure, in intergovernmental organizations like the OECD (see Organization for Economic Cooperation and Development, 1980).

27 See Franzway et al. (1989); on a specific policy area, Brennan and O'Donnell (1986).

28 The classics on fascism are Fromm (1942) and Adorno et al. (1950). For newer work see Macciocchi (1979) and Theweleit (1987). Hochschild (1983) treats a related problem in the commercial sector; problems of authority are more in focus in Pringle (1989).

29 These themes are comprehensively documented for Britain: see McIntosh (1978); Ruggie (1984); Walby (1986); Wilson (1977).

30 See also, for instance, Gordon (1988); Walby (1986). Edwards (1988) is a useful survey of the regulatory apparatuses and their impact.

31 For the strange story of Australian pronatalism, see Pringle (1973) and Hicks (1978). For the Labouchère amendment, see Weeks (1977: ch. 1); for the Nazis, see Plant (1986).

32 A fascinating case study of femininity and the military is Williams (1989). I

have sketched the relationship among military masculinities in Connell (1989). Zhukov's style is well shown in his memoirs, *Marshal Zhukov's Greatest Battles* (1971).

33 This perception of the colonial state is based on discussions with Ann Stoler of the University of Wisconsin-Madison. On conceptual developments in the metropole, see Pateman (1988). On practical development, see Stoper and Boneparth (1988).

34 The story is told by Irving (1974); for an astonishing account of a survivor's experience on the ground, see Vonnegut (1969).

35 Parts of this story can be found in Altman (1982); D'Emilio (1983); Dowsett (1989); Tripp (1977). A compendium of gay history with a clear perception of the significance of the state is Greenberg (1988).

36 The most perceptive account of 'men's rights' politics is still Interrante (1981).

37 This concept of crisis is derived from Habermas (1976); for crisis in gender relations see Connell (1987: chs 7, 12).

38 The turbulence, well documented in the early 1980s by Segers (1982), reached a new peak in 1989. For the larger intentions of an anti-abortion campaigner, see 'Soldier in a holy war', *Los Angeles Times* 17 March 1989.

39 Cf. Sidel (1986) and Feminist Review (1987). The Australian developments mentioned can be traced in successive issues of *Australian Society*.

40 Positive responses to feminism are documented in some items in Kimmel and Messner (1989). For an astonishing collection of literary effusions on this theme, see Jardine and Smith (1987). The anti-feminist intention of anti-abortion forces is clear in media statements from 'Operation Rescue' in the United States in March–April 1989.

41 The libertarian feminist position on censorship, much less widely publicized than the anti-pornography position, is argued and illustrated in Ellis et al. (1988). A curious illustration of a well-known male novelist's inability to conceive feminist politics as anything but an inversion of men's dominance of women is the anti-utopia in Berger's *Regiment of Women* (1973). Not incidentally, 'Female Domination' (that is, over men) is a well-defined category of pornography, and has been since the nineteenth century.

References

Adam-Smith, P. (1969) *Folklore of the Australian Railwaymen*. Adelaide: Rigby.

Adorno, T.W., Frenkel-Brunswik, E., Levinson, D. and Sanford, R.N. (1950) *The Authoritarian Personality*. New York: Harper.

Altman, D. (1982) *The Homosexualization of America, the Americanization of the Homosexual*. New York: St Martin's Press.

Atkins, S. and Hoggett, B. (1984) *Women and the Law*. Oxford: Blackwell.

Baldock, C.V. and Cass, B. (eds) (1983) *Women, Social Welfare and the State*. Sydney: Allen and Unwin.

Barrett, M. (1980) *Women's Oppression Today*. London: Verso, ch. 7.

Berger, T. (1973) *Regiment of Women*. New York: Simon and Schuster.

Brennan, D. and O'Donnell, C. (1986) *Caring for Australia's Children*. Sydney: Allen and Unwin.

Burstyn, V. (1983) 'Masculine dominance and the state', *Socialist Register*, pp. 45–89.

Burton, C. (1985) *Subordination*. Sydney: Allen and Unwin.

Burton, C. (1987) *Women's Worth*. Canberra: Australian Government Publishing Services.

Clark, G. and Dear, M. (1984) *State Apparatus*. Boston, Mass.: Allen and Unwin.

Connell, R.W. (1983) *Which Way is Up?* Sydney: Allen and Unwin.

Connell, R.W. (1987) *Gender and Power*. Stanford, Ca: Stanford University Press, pp. 47–54.

Connell, R.W. (1989) 'Masculinity, violence and war', in M. Kimmel and M. Messner (eds), *Men's Lives*. New York: Macmillan, pp. 194–200.

Coontz, S. and Henderson, P. (eds) (1986) *Women's Work, Men's Property*. London: Verso.

Coote, A. and Campbell, B. (1982) *Sweet Freedom*. London: Pan.

Curthoys, A. (1988) *For and Against Feminism*. Sydney: Allen and Unwin.

Daly, M. (1978) *Gyn/Ecology*. Boston, Mass.: Beacon.

Davidoff, L. and Hall, C. (1987) *Family Fortunes*. London: Hutchinson.

Deacon, D. (1989) *Managing Gender*. Melbourne: Oxford University Press.

Delphy, C. (1984) *Close to Home*. London: Hutchinson.

D'Emilio, J. (1983) *Sexual Politics, Sexual Communities*. Chicago: University of Chicago Press.

Director of Equal Opportunity in Public Employment, Office of (1985) *Equal Employment Opportunity Management Plan Resurvey 1985: Preliminary Report*. Sydney: New South Wales Government.

Dobash, R.E. and Dobash, R.P. (1979) *Violence against Wives*. New York: Free Press.

Donzelot, J. (1979) *The Policing of Families*. New York: Pantheon.

Dowsett, G.W. (1989) '"You'll never forget the feeling of safe sex" AIDS prevention strategies for gay and bisexual men in Sydney, Australia' paper presented to WHO Workshop on AIDS Health Promotion Activities Directed Towards Gay and Bisexual Men, Geneva, 29–31 May.

Edwards. A.R. (1983) 'Sex roles: a problem for sociology and for women', *Australian and New Zealand Journal of Sociology*, 19: 385–412.

Edwards. A.R. (1988) *Regulation and Repression*. Sydney: Allen and Unwin.

Ehrenreich, B. (1983) *The Hearts of Men*. London: Pluto.

Eisenstein, H. (1985) 'The gender of bureaucracy: reflections on feminism and the state', J. Goodnow and C. Pateman (eds), *Women, Social Science and Public Policy*. Sydney: Allen and Unwin, pp. 104–15.

Eisenstein, Z. (1986[1981]) *The Radical Future of Liberal Feminism*. Boston, Mass.: Northeastern University Press.

Ellis, K., Jaker, B., Hunter, D., O'Dair, B., Tallmer, A. (1988) *Caught Looking*. Seattle: Real Comet Press.

Epstein, C.F. (1988) *Deceptive Distinctions*. New Haven, Conn.: Yale University Press, ch. 8.

Feminist Review (1987) 'Future insecure: women, feminism and the Third Term', Special Issue, *Feminist Review*, 27.

Feminist Review (1988) 'Family secrets: child sexual abuse', Special Issue, *Feminist Review*, 28.

Ferguson, K.E. (1984) *The Feminist Case against Bureaucracy*. Philadelphia, Pa: Temple University Press.

Fernbach, D. (1981) *The Spiral Path*. London: Gay Men's Press.

Firestone, S. (1971) *The Dialectic of Sex*. London: Paladin.

Flax, J. (1987) 'Postmodernism and gender relations in feminist theory', *Signs*, 12: 621–43.

Fox, B.J. (1988) 'Conceptualizing "patriarchy"', *Canadian Review of Sociology and Anthropology*, 25: 163–82.

Franzway, S. (1986) 'With problems of their own: femocrats and the welfare state', *Australian Feminist Studies*, 3: 45–57.

Franzway, S., Court, D. and Connell, R.W. (1989) *Staking a Claim*. Sydney: Allen and Unwin.

Friedan, B. (1963) *The Feminine Mystique*. New York: W.W. Norton.

Friedan, B. (1981) *The Second Stage*. New York: Summit, ch. 5.

Fromm, E. (1942) *Fear of Freedom*. London: Routledge and Kegan Paul.

Giddens, A. (1985) *The Nation-State and Violence*. Cambridge: Polity Press.

Gilman, C.P. (1979[1915]) *Herland*. London: Women's Press.

Gorbachev, M. (1988) *Perestroika*, new edn. London: Fontana.

Gordon, L. (1988) *Heroes of Their Own Lives*. New York: Viking.

Grant, J. and Tancred-Sheriff, P. (1986) 'A feminist perspective on state bureaucracy', paper to conference on L'Etat Contemporain, Lennoxville.

Greenberg, D.F. (1988) *The Construction of Homosexuality*. Chicago: University of Chicago Press.

Habermas, J. (1976) *Legitimation Crisis*. London: Heinemann.

Harding, S. and Hintikka, M. (eds) (1983) *Discovering Reality*. Dordrecht: Reidel.

Held, D. (1985) 'Central perspectives on the modern state', in D. Held, J. Anderson, B. Gieben, S. Hall, L. Harries, P. Lewis, N. Parker and B. Turok (eds), *States and Societies*. Oxford: Blackwell, pp. 1–55.

Hicks, N. (1978) *This Sin and Scandal*. Canberra: Australian National University Press.

Hochschild, A.R. (1983) *The Managed Heart*. Berkeley, Ca.: University of California Press.

Interrante, J. (1981) 'Dancing along the precipice: the men's movement in the '80s', *Radical America*, 15/5 53–71.

Irving, D. (1974) *The Destruction of Dresden*. Elmfield: Morley.

Jardine, A. and Smith, P. (eds) (1987) *Men in Feminism*. New York: Methuen.

de Jasay, A. (1985) *The State*. Oxford: Blackwell.

Jenson, J. (1989) 'Ce n'est pas un hasard: The varieties of French feminism', in J. Howarth and G. Ross (eds), *Contemporary France*. London: Frances Pinter.

Johnson, V. (1980) *The Last Resort*. Melbourne: Penguin.

Kearns, D. (1984) 'A Theory of Justice – and love: Rawls on the family', in M. Simms (ed.), *Australian Women and the Political System*. Melbourne: Longman Cheshire, pp. 191–203.

Kimmel, M. and Messner, M. (eds) (1989) *Men's Lives*. New York: Macmillan.

Kinsman, G. (1987) *The Regulation of Desire*. Montreal: Black Rose Books.

Knuttila, M. (1987) *State Theories*. Toronto: Garamond.

Le Guin, U.K. (1987) *Always Coming Home*. London: Bantam Press.

Lerner, G. (1986) *The Creation of Patriarchy*. New York: Oxford University Press.

Lynch, L. (1984) 'Bureaucratic feminisms: bossism and beige suits', *Refractory Girl*, 27: 38–44.

Macciocchi, M.-A. (1979) 'Female sexuality in fascist ideology', *Feminist Review*, 1: 67–82.

McIntosh, M. (1978) 'The state and the oppression of women', in A. Kuhn and A.-M. Wolpe (eds), *Feminism and Materialism*. London: Routledge and Kegan Paul, pp. 254–89.

MacKinnon, C. (1982) 'Feminism, Marxism, method and the state: an agenda for theory', *Signs*, 7: 515–44.

MacKinnon, C. (1983) 'Feminism, Marxism, method and the state: toward feminist jurisprudence', *Signs*, 8: 635–58.

Magarey, S. (1985) *Unbridling the Tongues of Women*. Sydney: Hale and Iremonger.

Mies, M. (1986) *Patriarchy and Accumulation on a World Scale*. London: Zed Books.

Mill, J.S. (1912[1869]) 'The subjection of women', in *Three Essays*. London: Oxford University Press.

Mitchell, J. (1975) *Psychoanalysis and Feminism*. New York: Vintage.

Mowbray, M. and Bryson, L. (1984) 'Women really care', *Australian Journal of Social Issues*, 19: 261–72.

O'Donnell, C. and Hall, P. (1988) *Getting Equal*. Sydney: Allen and Unwin.

Organization for Economic Cooperation and Development (OECD) (1980) *Women and Employment*. Paris: OECD.

Pateman, C. (1988) *The Sexual Contract*. Stanford, Ca: Stanford University Press.

Patton, P. and Poole, R (eds) (1985) *War/Masculinity*. Sydney: Intervention.

Phillips, J. (1980) 'Mummy's boys: Pakeha men and male culture in New Zealand', in P. Burkle and B. Hughes (eds), *Women in New Zealand Society*. Sydney: Allen and Unwin, pp. 217–43.

Piercy, M. (1976) *Woman on the Edge of Time*. New York: Knopf.

Plant, R. (1986) *The Pink Triangle*. New York: Holt.

Poggi, G. (1978) *The Development of the Modern State*. Stanford, Ca.: Stanford University Press.

Poulantzas, N. (1973) *Political Power and Social Classes*. London: NLB and Sheen and Ward.

Presley, S. and Kinsky, L. (1982) 'Government is women's enemy', in W. McElroy (ed.), *Freedom, Feminism and the State*. Washington, DC: CATO Institute, pp. 77–83.

Pringle, R. (1973) 'Octavius Beale and the ideology of the birth-rate', *Refractory Girl*, 3: 19–27.

Pringle, R. (1989) *Secretaries Talk*. Sydney: Allen and Unwin.

Ronalds, C. (1987) *Affirmative Action and Sex Discrimination*. Sydney: Pluto.

Rosen, S.A. (1980–81) 'Police harassment of homosexual women and men in New York City 1960–1980', *Columbia Human Rights Law Review*, 12: 159–90.

Ruggie, M. (1984) *The State and Working Women*. Princeton, NJ: Princeton University Press.

Scutt, J. (1985) 'United or divided? Women "inside" and "outside" against male lawmakers in Australia', *Women's Studies International Forum*, 8: 15–23.

Segers, M. (1982) 'Can Congress settle the abortion issue?', *Hastings Center Report*, June: 20–8.

Shaver, S. (1982) 'The non-government state', paper to Conference on Social Policy in the 1980s. Canberra.

Shaver, S. (1983) 'Sex and money in the welfare state', in C. Baldock and B. Cass (eds), *Women, Social Welfare and the State in Australia*. Sydney: Allen and Unwin.

Sidel, R. (1986) *Women and Children Last*. New York: Viking Penguin.

Simms, M. (ed.) (1984) *Australian Women and the Political System*. Melbourne: Longman Cheshire.

Skocpol, T. (1979) *States and Social Revolutions*. Cambridge: Cambridge University Press.

Smart, C. (1984) *The Ties that Bind*. London: Routledge and Kegan Paul.

Smith, G.W. (1988) 'Policing the gay community', *International Journal of the Sociology of Law*, 16: 163–83.

Stacey, J. and Thorne, B. (1985) 'The missing feminist revolution in sociology', *Social Problems*, 32: 301–16.

Stanton, E.C., Anthony, S.B. and Gage, M.J. (eds) (1969[1881]) *History of Woman Suffrage*, vol. 1. New York: Arno and the New York Times.

Stiehm, J. (ed.) (1983) *Women and Men's Wars*. Oxford: Pergamon.

Stoper, E. and Boneparth, E. (1988) 'Divorce and the transition to the single-parent family', in E. Boneparth and E. Stoper (eds), *Women, Power and Policy*, 2nd edn. New York: Pergamon, pp. 206–20.

Theweleit, K. (1987) *Male Fantasies*. Minneapolis: University of Minnesota Press.

Thompson, D. (1985) *Flaws in the Social Fabric*. Sydney: Allen and Unwin.

Tripp, C.A. (1977) *The Homosexual Matrix*. London: Quartet.

Ursel, J. (1986) 'The state and the maintenance of patriarchy', in J. Dickinson and B. Russell (eds), *Family, Economy and the State*. Beckenham: Croom Helm, pp. 150–91.

Vonnegut, K. (1969) *Slaughterhouse-Five*. New York: Delacorte Press.

Walby (1986) *Patriarchy at Work*. Cambridge: Polity.

Walkowitz, J.R. (1980) *Prostitution and Victorian Society*. Cambridge: Cambridge University Press.

Walter, A. (ed.) (1980) *Come Together: the Years of Gay Liberation*. London: Gay Men's Press.

Weedon, C. (1987) *Feminist Practice and Post-Structuralist Theory*. New York: Blackwell.

Weeks, J. (1977) *Coming Out*. London: Quartet.

Weeks, J. (1985) *Sexuality and its Discontents*. London: Routledge and Kegan Paul.

Weeks, J. (1986) *Sexuality and its Discontents*. London: Horwood and Tavistock.

Williams, C.L. (1989) *Gender Differences at Work*. Berkeley, Ca: University of California Press.

Wilson, E. (1977) *Women and the Welfare State*. London: Tavistock

Wilson, E. (1982) 'Women, the "Community" and the family', in A. Walker (ed.), *Community Care*. Oxford: Blackwell.

Wollstonecraft, M. (1975[1792]) *Vindication of the Rights of Women*. Harmondsworth: Penguin.

Zaretsky, K. (1976) *Capitalism, the Family and Personal Life*. London: Pluto.

Zhukov, G. (1971) *Marshall Zhukhov's Greatest Battles*. London: Sphere.

8

Notes toward a Political Theory of Sex and Power

Jill Vickers

In this chapter I will take our discussion into the realm of politics, as understood by the movers and shakers of the power order. It is ultimately my purpose, as a political scientist, to develop a theoretical framework which can link our growing understanding of reproduction and sexualities with politics, conventionally understood. In particular, I will argue that patriarchal sex/gender[1] arrangements constitute the deep structure of many political conflicts by establishing identities, maintaining group cohesion and transmitting identities and values across generations.

In this text, I am conscious of swimming against the tide of theorizing which scrupulously avoids discussion of biological difference. Since it is my thesis that the female power to reproduce identity groups, socially *and* physically, is part of what men have attempted to control in gender struggles, I must reject a naive social constructionism. Instead I will argue the value of conceptualizing sex/gender arrangements as *technologies of social organization and control*. Expanding the concept of technology to encompass these modes of social control clearly establishes that they are artefacts of human creation while retaining a firm fix on the material character of biological reproduction.

Patriarchies are also usefully seen as technologies of social organization and control. Indeed, one of the values of this approach is the possibility of developing a general theory of social organization and control capable of capturing all forms of oppression, exploitation, domination and subordination in a common framework without decontextualizing the differences among them.

To explore this general thesis I have examined competitions for power among many identity groups, usually expressed through *battles of the cradle*[2] and *battles of the nursery and of the school*. Especially in multinational states and states containing indigenous or immigrant communities striving to preserve their linguistic and cultural cohesion, these links between reproduction and political conflict are most obvious. These links between sex and power are especially evident in conflicts between nationalisms and between claims for individual rights and claims for collective rights. In the discussion which follows, I will present only a few illustrations of the many linkages to demonstrate the significance of the thesis advanced: that the relationships between sex and power are unique because only women can reproduce identity groups materially and because women have customarily been the main conduits for the replication of identities in the years of youthful dependency.

The text which follows takes the form of four notes. These are linked meditations on the problems of developing a theory of sex and power which allows us to understand politics without marginalizing reproduction, sexualities or gender struggle.

In the first note, I explore the significance of a theory which can locate sex/gender within the dynamics of politics, conventionally understood. This is a project different from attempts to integrate our understanding of gender into knowledge of the general social order or from our efforts to understand how patriarchal sex/gender arrangements affect women's political participation in politics in the sense of voting or holding office (Vickers, 1987, 1988). Important though these projects are, they fail to illuminate the political significance of difference, both in the sense of women's power to reproduce and in the sense of the different stake in power perceived by women of different classes, races, ethnicities, tribes and nations.

By conceptualizing patriarchal sex/gender arrangements as a medium through which the political conflicts of identity, territory and possession are waged, it is possible to illuminate these two dimensions of difference in feminist politics and in conventional politics. These conflicts range from the threatened break-up of my country under the force of a Quebec nationalism supported by many of my francophone feminist colleagues to the profound disagreements between some women of the aboriginal 'First Nations'[3] and of the European diaspora over individual versus collective rights in the realm of reproduction.

In the second note, I explore problems in using the concept of gender alone in a theory of politics which can recognize the centrality of reproduction. To focus on the use of sex/gender as a medium for creating, maintaining and transmitting political identities, I require a conception of the historically and situationally varying links between political power and reproductive sex. As the matrix for birthing and nurturing children, reproductive sex has often been an important source of women's political power in some historical contexts. I develop the analytic construct 'sex/gender' to accommodate this fact. Drawn from Gayle Rubin's concept of 'the sex/gender system' (Rubin, 1975), I adopt the sex/gender concept, while rejecting the universalism implied in her wider conceptualization.

Relying on earlier work (Vickers, 1980) and on the work of Nancy Hartsock (1983), I also reconceptualize the nature of power in this note to transcend the crude sense of power only as dominance and oppression and to note areas of power in which women dominate, especially in their relations with other women and with children. Opening up our ability to see the full range of power relationships in which women are involved is key to my task.

In the third note, I develop the notion of sex/gender as a technology for organizing human communities. I also present the idea of patriarchies as complex technologies in a schematic way. This note serves as a coda in which I sketch a conceptual apparatus which is, as yet, more abstract and less well-developed.

In the fourth note, I explore some of the ways in which patriarchal sex/gender arrangements underwrite identities, especially nationalisms. Part of my purpose is to highlight how feminisms, by offering alternate identities to women who are, at least potentially, the reproducers of dominated or marginalized communities can be seen as threatening their solidarity. This setting of gender struggle in opposition to race or class struggle or in opposition to the struggles between tribes and nations is poorly dealt with in feminist thought and practice. Women who believe they cannot 'afford' to disrupt the solidarity of their community in struggle are accused of 'false consciousness' or considered less feminist.[4]

Feminists who are part of a secure majority or dominant culture understand reproduction and its links to political power differently from those whose natal identity depends on the solidarity of a community not able to use state institutions for its cultural cohesion. If we can understand this link as it affects a Mohawk woman who identifies herself as powerful because she is a 'Mother of the Nation' or as it affects a Baltic, Serbian or Croatian woman during the dissolution of the old order in Eastern Europe, we will better understand the conflicts within women's movements over 'bottom line' feminist positions.

Most of the issues of conflict within women's movements revolve around 'moments' of reproductive sex (O'Brien, 1981) because women differently located, in class, race or national terms, may experience these moments differently. Hence the notion of reproductive 'rights' potentially provokes deep conflict among women differently located. For a young woman of a secure, dominant culture, it means freedom *from* reproduction through birth control, abortion, formula milk and bottles, state-funded childcare or childcare tax relief. Moreover, the dominant culture can 'afford' to lose her as a reproducer since it can easily recruit others to its language and culture. By contrast, women of threatened communities may see reproductive 'rights' as collective claims to physical and cultural survival.

In the final note, I also explore insights from several multinational states in which dominant cultures in charge of state institutions have as state policy used 'sexual politics' to undermine the cohesion of minority communities. The cases include the attack on the solidarity of families in Soviet Central Asia in the 1920s (Massell, 1974) and the shameful forced transportation of aboriginal children to residential 'Indian' schools in Canada through much of this century. (In the latter case, the sex/gender technology of many groups was so damaged that the language and parenting skills needed for the survival of the First Nations were very nearly destroyed.)

It is perhaps not surprising that the greatest felt need for a theory of politics which restores reproductive sex/gender arrangements to a central position in our explanatory schemas has arisen in a settler society like Canada on the fringes of the American empire in an era of frantic economic internationalization. In societies which have aggressively and successfully absorbed minority cultures, focusing on a single axis of difference based in gender and sexualities may work. Elsewhere, the complex, cross-cutting themes of sex/gender, sexual identities and class, race or national identities perplex us as citizens and frustrate us in our feminist politics. This points to the need for a theory of politics which can link reproductive sex with political power in a more coherent way.

Note I: About the Need to Root Thought in Concrete Experience

In this note I will explore the significance of a theory which can locate sex/gender arrangements within the dynamics of politics, conventionally understood. This is a project different from that in which feminists explored 'sexual politics', declaring that 'the personal is political', although it draws from it. It stems from my need to combine insights emerging from my academic work with responsibilities emerging from my politics. As parliamentarian of the National Action Committee on the Status of Women[5] for half a decade, I saw constantly the result of our failure to contextualize difference and reproduction adequately. We failed to link conflicts in the arena of state politics with the absences, silences and conflicts within our own, women-centred organizations.

When we ask how we can develop the kind of grounded theory we need to map a path for the changes we urgently desire in the world, we must follow Mary O'Brien's advice to develop it by '[t]hinking about the world, acting in the world, [and] getting the two together' (O'Brien, 1989: 4). In this work, therefore, my concrete experience will be the basis of my thinking about both conventional and feminist politics.

As a Canadian, I live in a settler society composed of aboriginal communities, fragments of two European nation states and many other peoples here as a consequence of the European diaspora of colonization and imperialism. It is not surprising, therefore, that our feminist organizations are often afflicted with class, race, ethnic, linguistic and national conflicts, although it comes as a shock to majority women who often see women attached to these other identities as 'less feminist' as a result.

It has been hard to witness feminists in conflict over matters considered 'bottom line' in earlier, less complex times. It has been difficult to recognize that some First Nations women reject the notion of abortion as a 'right'. Similarly, it has been hard to comprehend some immigrant women, eager to ensure that their children retain their mother-tongue, suspiciously resisting our project of state-funded childcare as an extension of the education system. Likewise, we have been perplexed when working-class and ethnic or racial minority women reject feminist critiques of 'the family' as a site of oppression, or lesbianism as a life choice.

These conflicts among women otherwise united in their desire to improve the condition of women threaten the cohesion of feminist movements in all multicultural states. This reflects the fact that the theoretical accounts of women's oppression on which majoritarian feminists in the West have relied were built on their experiences as women of dominant cultures.[6]

In our political practice, majority feminists have tried hard to 'accommodate' difference. But like men trying to grapple with women's changing expectations, we have often ended up asking 'what do minority women want?' With no theoretical guide to the significance of patriarchal sex/gender arrangements in maintaining minority community identities, how can we understand why women, who are otherwise clearly feminist, reject what are to us 'bottom line' feminist positions? We then repress our knowledge of difference and, caught in a sense of guilt about the racism, classism or other bias attributed to us, we fail to develop an effective political practice for negotiating difference and creating coalitions based on compromise.

An adequate political theory of sex and power, however, must also help explain the sex/gender elements of political conflicts, conventionally understood, from a feminist perspective. Canadian politics provide a complex case study of what I must understand and also illustrate the poverty of our current theoretical tools.

As I write, Canada faces deconstruction under the force of nationalisms as deeply felt, although I pray not as violent, as those now rampant in the former Yugoslavia and many parts of the dissolving Soviet empire. Westerners watched in amazement as the nationalisms of the Baltic states emerged, apparently intact, after half a century of foreign occupation. Even more astonishing is the emergence of a coherent nation in the Ukraine after more than a century of foreign domination. I want to be able to understand each of these political phenomena from a feminist perspective and, indeed, my embryonic theory does provide some insight.

Each of these political conflicts reveals the vigour of identity groups, especially nationalisms, even without the instruments of an autonomous state to maintain cultural cohesion. In each, combinations of patriarchal sex/gender arrangements, a common faith, language and a rich literature all played a role. We must grasp the centrality of patriarchal sex/gender arrangements in our technologies of human organization and control, however, if we are to understand politics fully from a feminist perspective. Collective identities such as tribalisms and nationalisms have been remarkably resistant to coherent analysis because of our failure to understand the importance of sex/gender arrangements to the processes of identity formation (and, therefore of cultural cohesion) typically in the 'private' realm of families. This process, in dominated or minority cultures especially, occurs through the agency of women, either male-controlled or active cooperators and culture-makers, through their child-bearing, child-rearing and language teaching (Vickers, 1984).

In the politics I need to understand, both as a Canadian and as a feminist, identity groups are organized in different ways and to different degrees. Dominant and minority communities have different access to state institutions in maintaining their cultural identities. Individuals of different communities pay different 'prices' for identity maintenance. Moreover, while the members of some groups can choose to integrate into the dominant culture, others are marked off from this option by race, language or custom.

The 1980s project in Canada of entrenching a Charter of Rights and Freedoms (with equality rights guarantees) revealed the profound relationships between sex and power and the conflict this could generate among feminists in a multicultural, multinational state. Initiated by then Prime Minister Trudeau, the project was not initially attractive to most Canadian feminists.[7] Many francophone feminists in Quebec have conceptualized their project as using the state instruments of an autonomous Quebec to achieve their goals (the feminist project of the state). Most anglophone, alophone (non English-speaking and non French-speaking) and immigrant women eventually adopted Trudeau's Charter and fought for a sex equality clause in it (Kome, 1983). When the Charter was lodged in a new Constitution patriated from the UK, many francophone feminists in Quebec rejected the Charter as an anglophone imposition and continued to support Quebec's collective right to self-determination and a distinctive Quebec Code of Rights.

The francophone nation lodged in Quebec historically employed patriarchal sex/gender arrangements to maintain population, language and cultural cohesion.[8] From an era of large families and a culturally protective religiosity, francophone Quebec moved very quickly through the 'Quiet Revolution' after the Second World War to an era of modernity. Indeed, the province entered the 1970s with the lowest birthrate of any province and experienced only a slight (6 per cent) post-war baby boom (McLaren and McLaren, 1986). For women, the sex/gender regime went from traditional to modern very quickly. Indeed francophone women in Quebec now exhibit levels of post-secondary education, paid workforce participation, marriage avoidance and feminist organization higher than in most of the anglophone provinces.

This remarkable transition seems to have 'freed up' many francophone women in Quebec to participate in the nationalist project of building a new, unitary, autonomous nation-state on a feminist basis. For Quebec feminist organizations,[9] however, the concerns of other feminists living within the territory claimed by the francophone nation constitute a proverbial 'fly in the ointment'. Like the rest of Canada, post-war Quebec experienced a huge rainbow wave of immigration. Although many newcomers are francophone, they are sharply distinguished by their race and culture. Whereas some immigrant women have adopted the autonomous feminist state project, most reject the collective rights claims of Quebec nationalists in favour of the Charter protections of the federal constitutional regime. Such women are also in conflict with francophone majority women over issues reflecting the newcomers' concerns with family re-unification, mother-tongue maintenance and the use of Charter guarantees in relation to these concerns.

Many First Nations women have also advanced their own project asserting inherent collective rights to self-government. While anglophone, immigrant and ethnic minority feminists have tended to support the Charter, aboriginal women seem divided on its value to their cause. Ovide Mercredi, now Chief of the Assembly of First Nations, has argued that it is premature to talk about individual rights until the collective rights of survival of the First Nations have been ensured. There is conflict among aboriginal women and between aboriginal men and women on whether the Charter, on which the Supreme Court relied in striking down Canada's abortion law, would apply within First Nations territory once self-government is re-established. To some members of the First Nations, communal survival requires policies concerning adoption, abortion and the treatment of batterers and child abusers different from those espoused by majoritarian feminists based on doctrines of individual rights.

The re-creation of Canada on a new constitutional basis threatens potential disruption of the sex/gender arrangements for each of the communities discussed. In each case, a political conflict has a sub-structure of sex/gender issues and the conflicts within women's movements are also expressed within a framework of racial, linguistic, ethnic, class and national politics. Therefore we are not dealing with two separate realms – sexual politics and 'real' politics. What we need is a theoretical map to link the realms of sex and power in a more meaningful way.

Note II: About the Trouble with Gender and the Power of Reproductive Sex

Currently, extensive work is being done to understand sexualities leading to an emphasis on gender, gender relations, 'the gender order' and 'gender regimes' (Connell, 1987) understood in a social constructionist framework. In this note, I will outline the problems of a focus on gender alone for the development of a theory of politics which does not marginalize reproduction.

I take as my starting point Mary O'Brien's proposition that biological reproduction is the sub-structure (or deep structure) of history (O'Brien, 1981), although I do not accept her account of male and female reproductive consciousness as a universal process because it fails to *contextualize* for different groups the significance of the 'moments' of reproductive sex. O'Brien's account alone cannot help us understand the role of sex/gender in class or race struggle or in the struggles of language and ethnicity or between tribalisms or nationalisms. Nor can it reveal the relationships between gender solidarity and the absence or presence of other communal solidarities.

The value of O'Brien's account is well captured, none the less, by Bev Thiele: 'O'Brien does not begin with a redefinition of the body as a social and political object but with a redefinition of biology *as process*' (1989a: 10, emphasis in original). O'Brien rejects a dualism between the biological and social aspects of reproductive sex and seeks to dissolve the conceptual gap between 'biological' and 'social'. As Thiele argues, 'Seeing reproduction as a process makes it possible to accommodate questions about social construction, cultural meaning and historical variability without making "biology" marginal or redundant' (1989a: 10).

Why has O'Brien's brilliant insight failed to provoke further theorizing about the history of reproductive sex and gender struggle? Her account emerged against a backdrop of a left feminist debate about the material cause(s) of women's oppression. Her purpose was to put *birth* on the same plane as work, sex and death as bases for political theorizing. Her gynocentric version of dialectical materialism, therefore, raised the question of whether birth (or reproductive sex) is more significant to women's oppression than work. (I reserve the term 'labour' to describe the physical act of giving birth.)

The debate has now shifted so that the key question is whether sexuality is more significant to women's oppression than work or reproductive sex, in the sense of conception, gestation, giving birth, lactating, and so on. Indeed, Thiele argues that the history of sexuality is now being written at the expense of the history of reproduction (Thiele, 1989b). Although for many women a distinction between sexuality and reproductive sex is largely theoretical, for gays, many heterosexual men and some heterosexual women, the distinction has an importance which justifies a distinctive theoretical field. None the less, a struggle exists between what Thiele calls 'reproductive materialism' and discourse theories of sexuality as witnessed by Somer Brodribb's argument that: 'Post-structuralist theories of gender and sexuali*ties* construct psychoanalyzed bodies without sexes. Yet power is based on sex not gender' (1991: 140, emphasis in original).

What is a non-combatant to make of this struggle? Is power lodged in sexuality? Or is it located in procreativity; in the power to give birth? The simple shift from the term 'sex' to the term 'gender' could mean that cultural exchanges will be stressed to the exclusion of biosocial processes.

Because my focus is on sex/gender as the deep structure of political conflicts, I cannot 'side' with an approach which displaces the link between power and reproductive sex. Important though the exploration of sexualities is, therefore, I must question whether 'gender' can be reformulated to encompass the sociobiological moments of sexual reproduction. As Bev Thiele notes, it is 'reproduction which feminists most often sacrifice in their rush to describe women's bodies as social constructs' (1989a: 10). In particular, 'gender' must be a suspect concept to the extent that it makes us evasive about the biology of sexual reproduction for fear of being accused of being biological determinists.[10]

Bob Connell, by contrast, in his remarkable synthesis *Gender and Power*, clearly believes gender, understood as a fully social construct, *can* bear the weight of theorizing reproductive sex, as well as sexualities and the other aspects of what he calls the gender order. He argues 'in the reality of practice the body is never outside history, and history never free of bodily presence and effects on the body' (Connell, 1987: 87). Connell describes gender alternately 'as a process' and as a 'linking concept which is about the linking of other fields of social practice to the modal practices of engendering, childbirth and parenting' (1987: 140).

While the O'Brien-like emphasis on process is encouraging, it is revealing that few aspects of physical reproduction even merit a mention in Connell's text. Hence eroticism appears in the index; erection does not. Sexual intercourse is dealt with in two short passages which marginalize 'the simple bodily logic' and orgasm is discussed only as 'satisfaction'. The social inscription of menstruation is dealt with briefly but not menstrual cramps, P.M.S or the taxation of tampons. 'Nursing' appears in the index but the discussion in the text is about the profession not about lactation. Suckling is discussed in relation to social bonding but neither its relation to language acquisition nor its eroticism is mentioned. In fact, one of the only mentions of the biosocial 'facts' of reproduction is this revealing comment: 'The biological differentiation of sex in reproduction, is a *passively suffered condition*' (Connell, 1987: 81, emphasis added).

While Connell's text captures far more of women's lived experience of reproductive sex than most social constructionist works, it reveals clearly the shortcomings of an exclusive emphasis on gender. Women's power of reproductive creativity has been too often the basis of their political power to marginalize the sociobiological moments of reproductive sex. The fact that the greatest conflicts, both within feminism and in conventional politics, revolve around issues of reproductive sex, moreover, should also alert us to the need to retain it firmly within our theoretical field of vision. Therefore, I have chosen to use the complex term *sex/gender* rather than either 'sex' or 'gender' alone. The term has two parts: the fact of sex, which means that women are the physical reproducers of the species and of identity groups, and the fact of gender, which encompasses social roles, sexualities and personalities assigned, with differing content, to women and men in different societies and, often, also differently within different identity groups in the same society.

This construction does not follow a biological/social divide. It also rejects Connell's premise that 'reproductive biology is historicized in gender' (Connell, 1987: 79). As Mary O'Brien argued:

> The low value of reproductive labour is not necessarily immanent in that form of human labour, but may well be assigned to it by those who are excluded from it . . . The low social and philosophical value given to reproduction and to birth is not ontological, not immanent, but sociohistorical, and the sturdiest platform of male supremacy. (1981: 75)

At the basis of both the physical work which feeds and shelters us and the physical labour through which we are reproduced is a form of power generally denigrated and undervalued. The power to sustain, create and nourish life has been associated with 'necessity', 'brute nature' and 'mere' physicality. Almost without exception, the powerful have been men whose food, shelter and reproduction have been gained by appropriating the labour of others. Power, therefore, came to be understood as the ability to appropriate from others the work and labour to sustain and reproduce oneself and the ability to use others for various purposes.

Power in political science has a conventional meaning consistent with this history and most feminist theorists have adopted this meaning uncritically (Hartsock, 1983). Feminist discussions of power have focused mainly on male *power over* women. Hence patriarchy is easily defined as 'a political system in which the balance of power and authority between men and women favours men' (Vickers, 1984: 37). Among the experiences which have mobilized women in gender struggle are rape and battering, which illustrate aspects of men's bodily power to harm and coerce women. Women have also mobilized to break the monopoly of male power in the coercive state institutions of the police, the courts and the military.

Power, as the capacity of men to oppress, dominate, exploit and subordinate women, therefore, is well explored in feminist accounts. But they rarely explore women's *power over* children, other women or, more rarely, men. Gerda Lerner's account (1986) of the 2500-year process of creating a specific historical patriarchy does outline women's activities as co-exercisers of power in class and race oppression and as collaborators in the construction and maintenance of patriarchal institutions, but it is an exception. What has received even less attention is the other dimension of power understood as the ability or capacity to create, guide (or lead) and the ability to perform other valuable tasks (Vickers, 1980). Most politically profound of women's powers is the *power* of procreation. To understand power in a way useful to my project, therefore, I must understand more about how this potential power is linked to political power and how it is harnessed in patriarchal sex/gender arrangements.

Clearly this is potentially dangerous ground which requires a delicate balancing act theoretically. As Frieda Forman argues, 'As feminists, while not disowning our very real bond to the natural world, we must continue to resist the definition of women as nature: that is, we must live in the world as subjects whose transcendence is grounded in a generative temporality' (Forman and Sowton, 1989). This means giving ontological significance to birth (and to the other moments of reproductive sex) and restoring our collective memory of our potential powers of procreation. It means understanding birth, potentially, as a profoundly political act while also allowing ourselves to understand that 'what we share with other lactating mammals – bringing forth and suckling our young – is perfectly compatible with being human, indeed is part and parcel with it' (Pfeufer Khan, 1988: 30).

It is useful to learn from Gerda Lerner that a central purpose of the patriarchal control of women through the institutions of kinship, slavery, the law and the state in her case study was control of women's power of procreation. Intuitively, Zillah Eisenstein also defined patriarchy as 'a political structure [which] seeks to control . . . women so that their possibilities for making choices about their sexuality, childrearing, mothering, loving and laboring are curtailed' (Eisenstein, 1981: 14). While I reject the universalism inherent in this definition, Eisenstein's assertion points to the historical fact that all known states have been patriarchal in organization and many pre-state communities also display patriarchal sex/gender arrangements. Women's power of procreation, therefore, historically has been the target of men's collective (and often coercive) power to control.

Women's powers of creation can extend far beyond child-bearing and child-rearing. Patriarchal sex/gender technologies, however, harness women's powers to bear, nurture and rear children, reducing them from autonomous historical acts in which we *choose* to reproduce our values for our purposes. So long has this power been harnessed to the wills and purposes of others, that women (including many feminists) have denied the powers of giving life, language and identity an ontological status equal to work, sex or death. Since biological explanations were used to 'justify' women's assignment to non-autonomous reproduction, moreover, we have feared to explore biological powers for fear of giving credence to such 'justification'. Now that women have rediscovered our capacity to choose to give birth for purposes we share as autonomous, historical actors, we can reject the devaluation of our potential power to reproduce classes, races, tribes and nations even if we choose never to realize it.

Hence, I end this note where I began, with Mary O'Brien's proposition that biological reproduction is part of the sub-structure of history. Patriarchal sex/gender arrangements, which are highly varied technologies of social organization and control, are so deeply based and developed over such a long period of time as to be nearly invisible. In these arrangements, communal power and individual male power are employed to control women's procreative power so that identity groups are reproduced.

Note III: About Technologies of Patriarchal Sex/Gender Arrangements

I suggested in the introduction that conceptualizing arrangements for social organization and control as technologies is a useful first step in developing a general theory to explain oppression, exploitation, domination and subordination of all forms within a common schema without decontextualizing the unique aspects of each (and without the pointless discussions of whose oppression is worse, came first or is more fundamental). Although I am not yet able to outline all of the elements of such a theory, in this brief note I will unpack the idea of viewing sex/gender arrangements as technologies.

In this text, I have used the term *sex/gender arrangements* to identify the technologies used to organize and control reproductive sex, sexualities, sex roles and gendered personalities. While the 'sex/gender' part comes from the work of Gayle Rubin (1975), I have not adopted her full usage of the sex/gender *system* because it suggests the possibility of a universal form and because it can be taken to mean that sex/gender arrangements constitute a natural system (Vickers, 1991). Since I am clear that sex/gender arrangements are not natural, although they are 'naturalized', I use the term *technology* to signal that they are highly variable artefacts of human invention.

Mary Douglas (1986) offers important insights into the nature of the technologies of human organization we create as a species. She argues that institutions are composed *both* of structures *and* their legitimizing myths (like lichen which requires both algae and fungi living in symbiosis). Douglas also demonstrates that the legitimizing process always involved *naturalizing* the structure, in the sense that a structure has been institutionalized when people view it as 'natural'. These institutions and the technologies of which they are part, however, can take on lives of their own in that they can be borrowed, imitated or imposed, recombined and refurbished.

Patriarchal sex/gender arrangements are composed of varying sets of institutions including kinship, sexualities, sex roles and gendered personalities which are naturalized. These technologies have a greater 'space–time extension' than that attributed by Giddens to institutions (Giddens, 1984); that is, they have the power of great longevity. We know, for example, that the institution of kinship that survived after it was gutted of many of its functions over time as they were assumed by the institutions of the archaic states (Lerner, 1986).

Bob Connell adopts the concept of 'the gender order' from Jill Matthews (1984) to capture a 'historically constructed pattern of power relations between men and women and definitions of femininity and masculinity' (Connell, 1987: 99). He also uses the concept of the 'gender regime' to capture the structural inventory around the sexual politics of a single institution. Neither usage allows us to understand the extent to which whole and highly varied technologies can be and have been transferred between societies through migration and colonialism, imitation and force. Nor do they allow for significant disjunctures between the technologies used by dominant, majority cultures (which include state instruments) and those of marginal, oppressed or divergent communities within the same territory.

Finally, I view states as sets of institutions which also can usefully be thought of as technologies. As our ability to understand the mechanisms of social organization and control increases, it will be possible to integrate this conception into our theories of oppression, exploitation, domination and subordination.

Note IV: About the Political Power of Reproduction

Patriarchal sex/gender arrangements are central to the maintenance of many political forms because male groups cannot reproduce themselves without 'their' women being committed to reproduction. As Thomas Hobbes observed in *De Cive*, 'in nature, the birth follows the belly'; that is, men must control or have the cooperation of mothers if they wish to control 'their' children's labour, values, loyalties, energies and attachments. The conflicts of caste, class, race, tribe and nation are all waged initially through the womb and through battles of the cradle and the nursery. The black woman who chooses a white partner; the Algerian woman who 'collaborates' by bearing children for the colonial enemy; the Jewish woman who no longer 'keeps Kosher': each reveals the centrality of women as reproducers to the conflicts which prevail in patriarchal politics. Likewise, the working-class woman who teaches her children to respect picket lines; the French Canadian woman who ensures that her children speak French; the upper caste woman who teaches her children to abhor untouchables: each reflects the centrality of women as reproducers of stable identity and as agents of cultural cohesion. Only mothers are so central to the dynamics of patriarchal political conflict and reproduction, generally viewed as a private, 'natural' act, is revealed to be profoundly political.

For many communities, collective autonomy, cohesion, continuity and identity have been maintained by limiting severely the autonomy, freedom of choice and social adulthood of individual women. This technology of bonding and identity transmission is based on an imitation of the blood-tie such that notions of shared blood, ancestors, shared territory and a language learned 'at his mother's knee', or breast, bond men together as if they were kin. Patriarchal technologies were one solution devised to address the human dilemma of crafting enduring forms of social organization and identity.

Not all groups have the same stake in reproduction as the crucible of identity. Groups facing cultural disruption and not in control of state institutions are especially dependent on patriarchal forms and the men in such groups tend to scapegoat the women in response to men's loss of status and power in the public realm (Sanday, 1981). Franz Fanon, in *The Wretched of the Earth* (1963: esp. 254–9) identifies a 'need' developed by Algerian men under French colonialism to act out their hostility against 'their' women who had 'collaborated' by embracing the colonizers as partners or their attitudes towards women. Viewing their families as their only remaining arena for identity and assertion, they interpreted all French efforts to change the status of 'their' women as a scheme to undercut their last bastion of status, identity and culture.

Fertility research also reveals that geographically concentrated minority groups, which feel themselves in a struggle to maintain their autonomy and identity, pursue a pronatalist fertility strategy often with stricter enforcement of patriarchal sex/gender arrangements than other groups in the same territory (Bouvier and Rao, 1975; Chamie, 1981; Day, 1968; Golscheider and Uhlenberg, 1969; Long, 1970; McLaren and McLaren, 1986; Ritchey, 1974). Majority cultures, however, can also respond to threatened cultural disruption with a pronatalist strategy and the strict enforcement of patriarchal sex/gender arrangements which usually goes with it. English-Canadian Protestants, at the turn of the century, for example, experienced anxieties 'exacerbated . . . by both the fertility of the [immigrant] Irish and Quebec's successful "revanches des berceaux," and later by the influx of non-British migration' (McLaren and McLaren, 1986: 17). They responded with a profound fear of 'race suicide' which coloured views about changes in women's status and made reproductive issues especially touchy in Canadian politics. (The francophone majority in Quebec has responded similarly to the huge post-war influx of immigrants despite the fact that many are francophone.) Hence nationalisms which feel embattled may adopt pronatalist strategies even when they control state instruments of coercion, media and education. The pronatalism associated with the 'white Australia' policy and the 'Babies for Botha' campaign in South Africa, both directed at white women, are instances of such situations.

Feminism has frequently been seen as a 'foreign plot' to woo women away from the mission of reproducing threatened minority groups. Nor are these fears entirely unreasonable or baseless. Especially when there is state support for policies which may 'emancipate' individual women or 'educate' individual children but which may also disrupt a community's sex/gender arrangements, resistance is not surprising. Gregory Massell's account (1974) of Soviet policy to recruit women in Soviet Central Asia against their natal groups outlines the most tragic example in his text *The Surrogate Proletariat: Moslem Women and Revolutionary Strategies in Soviet Central Asia, 1919–1929*. A comparable policy was undertaken by the federal government in Canada in its forced incarceration of Indian children in residential schools.

In each case, the overt purpose was for the benefit of the individuals involved: an 'emancipated' life for the Moslem women of Soviet Central Asia and a 'civilized' life for aboriginal children in Canada. In each case, however, death, cultural dislocation and its associated disorders were often the result for individuals with severe cultural disruption the 'cost' for the communities involved. Other policies which threaten cultural cohesion are mandatory sterilization, mandatory abortion and 'incentives' for both of these acts offered to women (and men in the case of sterilization) for food or the retention of welfare services. These are more frequently imposed on women of colour, poor women and women of cultural and linguistic minorities although girls and women with disabilities are also often targets.

Women and men of secure, dominant cultures who have access to state institutions, therefore, understand reproduction and its links to political power differently from members of threatened minority communities. Similarly, majoritarian feminists can afford to be forgetful and 'coy' about the links between reproduction and political power in ways which minority feminists cannot. If we wish to transcend the conflicts around reproductive issues which threaten the effectiveness of women's movements, therefore, women differently linked to reproductive sex must struggle together to truly comprehend the meaning of the links between reproduction and power for each other.

Conclusion

In this chapter, I have demonstrated our need to understand the connections between sex and power as they are manifested in political conflicts within women's movements and in state and international politics. I have argued that patriarchal sex/gender arrangements are part of the deep structure of many political conflicts. Given this approach, I argued that the marginalization of the biological dimension of reproduction means we fail to illuminate this basis of women's power and of men's interest in controlling reproduction. Consequently, I proposed a conception of sex/gender arrangements as technologies of social organization and control which vary historically and contextually within the territory of the same state.

I also argued that reproduction has a different significance for women and men located in secure, dominant cultures than it does for those located in minority or threatened communities. Understanding this is the key to comprehending the differences among feminists around questions related to reproduction. And while understanding difference does not dissolve it, it is an important step to helping us transcend its effects.

We must listen more to the voices of women for whom procreation, in all of its moments, is a way of being historic actors and of exercising politically significant power. We must not assume that women who value birth and child-rearing are always 'dupes' of men or inferior to those whose projects do not include reproduction. We must not accept patriarchy's denigration of procreation as 'mere animality' or 'brute nature'. Although all women must be free to explore their full range of capacities, we must finally accept our power of giving life and nurturing identity as a fully human power.

Notes

1 This usage is discussed in detail in Note II.

2 The *'revanche des berceaux'* of the French Canadian nation against its British conquerors is the most familiar in my society.

3 This is a term adopted by many aboriginal peoples in Canada to locate their claim to inherent collective rights of self-government on the same plain as Quebec's claim.

4 The accusation against black South African women locked with their menfolk in struggle against a repressive white state is especially offensive.

5 NAC is an umbrella organization of more than 500 feminist groups, largely from English Canada.

6 In Canada, both anglophone and francophone women occupy majority cultures: francophones in relation to Quebec. The francophone nation, however, is insecure and minorized in anglophone North America.

7 Feminists were initially more interested in which level of government would have responsibility for laws governing marriage and divorce. Francophones favour a provincial regime; anglophones a federal one.

8 Faith was also an important 'glue' until the 1960s and a significant minority of men and women went into the church, increasing the reproductive responsibility of their secular kin (McLaren and McLaren, 1986).

9 The Federation des Femmes du Quebec (FFQ), for example, is a multicultural umbrella organization like NAC.

10 Our difficulty in theorizing disability from a feminist perspective, especially around issues of abortion and reproductive technology, may also reflect this trend.

References

Bouvier, Leon F. and Rao, S.L.N. (1975) *Socio-religious Factors in Fertility Decline.* Cambridge, Mass.: Ballinger.

Brodribb, Somer (1991) 'Discarnate desires: thoughts on sexuality and post-structuralist discourse', *Women's Studies International Forum*, 14(3): 135–42.

Chamie, Joseph (1981) *Religion and Fertility.* New York: Cambridge University Press.

Connell, R.W. (1987) *Gender and Power: Society, the Person and Sexual Politics.* Stanford, Ca.: Stanford University Press.

Day, Lincoln, H. (1968) 'Natality and ethno-centrism: some relationships suggested by an analysis of Catholic–Protestant differences', *Population Studies*, 22 (March): 17–50.
Douglas, Mary (1986) *How Institutions Think.* Syracuse, NY: Syracuse University Press.
Eisenstein, Zillah (1981) *The Radical Future of Liberal Feminism.* New York: Longman.
Fanon, Franz (1963) *The Wretched of the Earth.* New York: Grove Press.
Forman, Frieda Johles with Sowton, Caoran (eds) (1989) *Taking Our Time: Feminist Perspectives on Temporality.* Toronto: Pergamon.
Giddens, Anthony (1984) *The Constitution of Society.* Cambridge: Polity Press.
Golscheider, Calvin and Uhlenberg, P.R. (1969) 'Minority group status and fertility', *American Journal of Sociology* 74(4): 361–72.
Hartsock, Nancy (1983) *Money, Sex and Power: Toward a Feminist Historical Materialism.* London: Longman.
Kome, Penny (1983) *The Taking of Twenty-Eight: Women Challenge the Constitution.* Toronto: Women's Press.
Lerner, Gerda (1986) *The Creation of Patriarchy.* New York: Oxford University Press.
Long, Harry H. (1970) 'Fertility patterns among religious groups in Canada', *Demography*, 7(2): 135–49.
Massell, Gregory (1974) *The Surrogate Proletariat: Moslem Women and Revolutionary Strategies in Soviet Central Asia: 1919–1929.* Princeton, NJ: Princeton University Press.
Matthews, J.J. (1984) *Good and Bad Women: the Historical Construction of Femininity in Twentieth-Century Australia.* Sydney: George Allen and Unwin.
McLaren, Angus and McLaren, Arlene Tigar (1986) *The Bedroom and the State: the Changing Practices and Politics of Contraception and Abortion in Canada, 1880–1980.* Toronto: McClelland and Stewart.
O'Brien, Mary (1981) *The Politics of Reproduction.* London: Routledge and Kegan Paul.
O'Brien, Mary (1989) *Reproducing the World: Essays in Feminist Theory.* Boulder, Co.: Westview Press.
Pfeufer Khan, Robbie (1988) 'Women and time in childbirth and during lactation', in Frieda Johles Forman with Caoran Sowton (eds), *Taking Our Time.* Toronto: Pergamon, pp. 1–10.
Ritchey, Neal V. (1974) 'The effect of minority group status on fertility: a re-examination of concepts', *Population Studies*, 29(2): 249–57.
Rubin, Gayle (1975) 'The traffic in women: notes on the "political economy" of sex', in R.R. Reiter (ed.), *Toward an Anthropology of Women.* New York: Basic Books.
Sanday, Peggy (1981) *Female Power and Male Dominance.* New York: Cambridge University Press.
Thiele, Bev (1989a) 'Dissolving dualisms: O'Brien, embodiment and social construction', *Resources for Feminist Research*, 18(3): 7–12.
Thiele, Bev (1989b) Review of her PhD thesis 'Reproduction in socialist accounts of the woman question: Britain 1880–1900', *Resources for Feminist Research*, 18(3): 125–6.
Vickers, Jill McCalla (1980) 'Coming Up for air: feminist views of power-reconsidered', *Canadian Women's Studies*, 2(4): 66–9.

Vickers, Jill McCalla (1984) 'Sex/gender and the construction of national identities', *Canadian Issues/Thèmes Canadiens* (Fall): 34–49.

Vickers, Jill McCalla (1987) 'At his mother's knee: sex/gender and the construction of national identities', in G.H. Nemiroff, *Men and Women*. Montreal: Fitzhenry and Whiteside, pp. 478–92.

Vickers, Jill McCalla (1988) *Getting Things Done: Women's Views of their Involvement in Political Life*. Paris: CRIAW/UNESCO.

Vickers, Jill McCalla (1991) *An Examination of the Scientific Mode of Enquiry in Politics with Special Reference to Systems Theory*. New York: Garland Publishing.

9

Problematizing Pleasure: Radical Feminist Deconstructions of Sexuality and Power

Celia Kitzinger

Sexuality is socially constructed – the phrase has become a truism in some circles with the increasing proliferation of 'social constructionism' literature. But, as Catherine MacKinnon (1987) points out, rarely specified is what, exactly, sexuality is socially constructed *of.* This chapter explores the nature of socially constructed sexuality, and the role of power in that construction. I argue that power does not simply prohibit certain sexual activities, and shape social representations of sexuality. More than this, power is implicated in the 'doing' of sex, such that both heterosex and sex between two people of the same gender is constructed of eroticized power differences.

The Construction of Sexuality

Sexual pleasure – the cycle of arousal, desire and orgasm – is often seen, in Western society, as basic, 'natural' and pre-social. Sexuality is, in our post-Freudian construction, at the core of the individual, rooted in childhood oral and oedipal fantasies, expressive of primitive human longings, revealing the 'true self' stripped of the trappings of civilized social etiquette. In the industrialized Western world, individuals no longer find support, sustenance and meaning from the public symbols of institutional roles, but retreat instead into 'private' worlds of sex and relationships for life-enhancing meanings. This was not always the case: sociologists have linked this shift from 'social' to 'privatized' selves with the demise of the concept of 'honour' as a central principle in identity construction, and its replacement with the concept of individual dignity.

> The concept of honour implies that identity is essentially, or at least importantly, linked to institutional roles. The modern concept of dignity, by contrast, implies that identity is essentially independent of institutional roles. To return to Falstaff's image, in a world of honour

the individual *is* the social symbols emblazoned on his escutcheon. The true self of the knight is revealed as he rides out to do battle in the full regalia of his role; by comparison, the naked man in bed with a woman represents a lesser reality of the self. In a world of dignity, in the modern sense, the social symbolism governing the interaction of men [sic] is a disguise. The escutcheons *hide* the true self. It is precisely the naked man, and even more specifically the naked man expressing his sexuality, who represents himself more truthfully. (Berger et al., 1973: 84, emphasis in original)

The modern construction of sex, then, means that it has come to represent key aspects of individual functioning.

If the kinds of sexual things a person does are seen as reflecting the kind of person he or she is, then sexual activity is translated into sexual identity. Before the rise of sexology in the late nineteenth and early twentieth centuries, for example, romantic friendships between women were commonplace and did not attract any opprobrium. Many middle-class women 'had relationships with each other which included passionate declarations of love, nights spent in bed together sharing kisses and intimacies, and lifelong devotion, without exciting the least adverse comment' (Jeffreys, 1985: 102). In North America it was still possible, until as late as the first decade of the twentieth century, for passionate tales of love between women to be related in periodicals like *Ladies' Home Journal* and *Harpers* totally without self-consciousness or awareness that such relationships might be considered unhealthy or taboo (Faderman, 1980: 298). On the rare occasions when sex between women was discussed in medical textbooks, it was presented as an extension of masturbation or as studious preparation for marriage (Cook, 1979). Male indulgence of love between women ceased abruptly with the first wave of feminism as the early sexologists (Bloch, 1909; Forel, 1908; Ellis, 1934; Krafft-Ebing, 1882[1965]) pathologized lesbianism and/or glorified heterosexuality for women. Sex between same-sex partners was constituted as a 'master status trait' (Hughes, 1945); that is, it was assumed that homosexuality was a powerful character trait; that to do homosexual things required a certain kind of psychological history, and that this history, combined with homosexual experience, was powerfully influential on the whole range of a person's non-sexual activities. Sexual activity is translated into identity.

To be more precise, *homo*sexual activity is translated into *homosexual* (or lesbian, gay etc.) identity. *Hetero*sexual activity *per se* is generally seen as having no particular implications for identity, and most heterosexuals find it extremely difficult to talk about themselves *as heterosexuals* (cf. Wilkinson and Kitzinger, 1993). Like other privileged identities ('white', 'Western,' 'able-bodied'), 'heterosexual' is a silent term, a submerged and taken-for-granted aspect of the self, which is rarely consciously articulated. Few heterosexual women have ever before been forced to consider the kind of questions we raised in the 'Call for Contributions' for our Special Issue of *Feminism and Psychology* on heterosexuality (Wilkinson and Kitzinger, 1993): 'What is heterosexuality and why is it so common? Why is it so hard for heterosexuals to change their "sexual orientation"? What is the nature of heterosexual sex? How does heterosexual activity affect the whole of a woman's life, her sense of herself, her relationships with other women, and her political engagements?' Heterosexual women responded to these questions with surprise, and their answers were hesitant and uncertain. Most lesbians, by contrast, have considered in depth the parallel questions relating to our own sexual experience and identity, and have well-rehearsed answers ready for the casual enquirers who so frequently interrogate us in this way.

In sum, then, sexuality has been prioritized as reflecting fundamental aspects of the 'true self', and sexual activity is held to have major identity implications for those who deviate from heterosexual norms. The social power serves to control and shape our purportedly 'basic' sexual activity, by forcing us to confront questions about who we 'really' are on the basis of what we do in bed. Historically, the major psychological theories about people who do homosexual things was that they were pathologically disordered, suffering from abnormal hormone levels, faulty parenting, traumatic early experiences, or psychological immaturity. Most contemporary psychological theories about people who do homosexual things are rooted in liberal humanistic ideology (cf. Kitzinger, 1987). Such theories prescribe lesbian and male gay identities which replace 'sickness' with 'personal choice', 'sexual preference', 'alternative lifestyle' or 'true love'. Power does not simply repress and deny same-sex sexual activities. It also actively constructs the form those activities take, and the identity implications they invoke.

Lesbian Representations of Sex

Lesbian pleasure is not constructed in a heteropatriarchy-free zone. There is nothing 'pure', 'unsullied' or inherently revolutionary about the lesbian orgasm. Under heteropatriarchy, a system within which lesbian pleasures are specifically crushed and denied, anything which gives us pleasure, or from which we are able to 'take' pleasure (especially *sexual* pleasure) can seem like a Good Thing – even, inherently revolutionary. Some feminists appear to be suggesting that even the use of heterosexual-male-authored pornography for lesbian pleasure can be subversive (Segal and MacIntosh, 1992). But far from 'subverting' or 'transgressing' heteropatriarchal norms, lesbian 'erotica' and pornography often reinscribes them. The lesbian porn magazine, *Quim*, for example, is heavily reliant on the traditional pornographic paraphernalia of sadomasochism: whips, chains, studded belts, black leather boots, stiletto heels, corsets, Nazi-style caps, fists and pierced nipples. Far from 'transgressing' traditional representations, they reinscribe them: the dominatrix, the bound woman on a rack, the huge (albeit detachable) dick. In the London heterosexual club Night of the Living Ultra Vixens, women dance provocatively in cages for male pleasure: in the London lesbian club Venus Rising, the women in cages dance for other women. All the trappings of sadomasochism are commonplace on the heterosexual scene among middle-aged business men (cf. *Sunday Express*, 7 June 1992). Nor is the allegedly 'transgressive' fascist symbolism beyond the bounds of social acceptability in today's repressive right-wing climate. 'Nazi Chic' (Norman, 1992) is part of contemporary fashion: a Chelsea boutique decorates its carrier bags with a Nazi double-headed eagle, framing Hitler's aphorism, 'The strength of the country is in its youth', and T-shirts are on sale in London with a giant swastika on one side, and the words 'Keep Britain Tidy' on the other. Lesbian appropriation of the symbols of domination does not alter their oppressive meanings, but merely puts those meanings at the service of a new group. Taking pleasure in sex scenes which enact power struggles, or which play with the symbols of fascism, may reflect the measure of our complicity in our own and other people's oppression (Lorde, 1987). (For a more detailed discussion of the ethics and politics of lesbian representation of sex, see Kitzinger and Kitzinger, 1993.)

Heterosexual Sex and Power

The intimate relationship between sex and power is not limited to lesbian relationships. Indeed, it has been far better documented and analysed by feminists concerned about the role of male power in the practice of heterosexual sex. Rape, sexual harassment, the sexual abuse of girls, prostitution and pornography are acts of dominance expressed through sexuality. These forms of male sexual violence against women are not rare, aberrant, or deviant behaviours. Only 7.8 per cent of United States women are *not* sexuality assaulted or harassed in their lifetimes (Russell, cited in MacKinnon, 1987: 66). About a third of men say that they would rape women if assured that they would not be punished (Briere and Malamuth, 1983; Tieger, 1981) and each year, in the United States, 30 per cent of all women murdered are killed by their husbands or male lovers; and at least 1.8 million women are beaten by husbands or male lovers annually (Uniform Crime Reports, 1987, cited in Caputi, 1989). Men routinely use violence against their lovers, and use sexuality as a way of 'doing power' over women.

More than this, ever since Adrienne Rich's groundbreaking article, 'Compulsory heterosexuality and lesbian existence' (1980), feminist theorists are increasingly exploring the violence done to women through the enforcement of heterosexuality as the normal 'sexual preference' of most women. Heterosexuality in and of itself is a cornerstone of male power. 'Only in the system of oppression that is male supremacy does the oppressor actually invade and colonise the interior of the body of the oppressed', says the Leeds Revolutionary Feminist Group (1981: 5), arguing that 'the heterosexual couple is the basic unit of the political structure of male supremacy'. Onlywomen Press suggest that 'heterosexuality is an institution . . . created, maintained and enforced upon women by men, for their purposes, one of which is to oppress all women, everywhere'.

Viewed from this perspective, it is hardly surprising that many women dislike heterosexual sex. Psychology and sexology have usually constructed women's disgust for or refusal of heterosexual intercourse as a problem: the sex therapy industry is devoted to the 'cure' of women who do not enjoy or do not have orgasms during sex with men (Jeffreys, 1985) – and the sheer size of the industry suggests that this is an enormously common problem. Many women, whether or not they identify themselves as heterosexual, and whether or not they have been on the receiving end of overt male violence, derive little or no pleasure from sexual encounters with men. In an article called 'Love Hurts', published in a British national newspaper in 1989, an anonymous woman describes how she dreaded sex with her husband:

> Sometimes I lie in bed and think of all the women who might be crying tonight. Crying because they know they'll have to 'do it' tomorrow, crying because they can 'feel him' coming towards them, crying because he is grunting there on top of them, crying because their bodies aren't their own any more because they promised them away twenty years

ago and it doesn't seem possible to get them back (*Guardian*, Women's Page, 22 November 1989)

The newspaper was immediately deluged with letters (two-thirds written anonymously) from women who clearly identified with this writer. A marriage guidance counsellor read through all the letters and commented:

> Most of those who wrote seem to find sex with their husbands anything along the scale from boring to repugnant, clenching their teeth or digging their nails into their palms to get them through the whole horrible process ... Many speak of husbands with such revulsion and dread ...

'In two columns, a picture of my life has been described', wrote one woman. Another said, 'After 21 years of marriage, these feelings are my feelings. If it were possible to sleep nearer the very edge of the bed I would'. A third wrote of her fear that 'one day I may not be able to take it any more and shall be forced to leave my home and children simply because I want control over what happens to my own body' (all in *Guardian*, 30 November 1989).

These women experience heterosexuality in precisely the manner one would expect if one accepts radical feminist theories about the relationship between heterosexuality and male power. Such theories offer insight into women's resistance of and disgust for heterosexuality. When women submit to intercourse it is often, as Andrea Dworkin says, not for any intrinsic satisfactions it brings, but because:

> we are poorer than men in money and so we have to barter sex or sell it outright (which is why they keep us poorer in money). We are poorer than men in psychological well-being because for us self-esteem depends on approval – frequently expressed through sexual desire – of those who have and exercise power over us. ... We need their money; intercourse is frequently how we get it. We need their approval to be able to survive inside our own skins; intercourse is frequently how we get it. (1987: 150)

According to this argument, in so far as women submit to heterosexual sex, they do so because they are forced (financially, psychologically, or with fist and gun) into submission. We are forced into heterosexuality *because we are oppressed*. Our apparent collusion in intimate relationships with our oppressors is a measure of our powerlessness. Feminists have used the same argument to explain, for example, why battered women continue to live with men who abuse them – because they have no income of their own, nowhere to go, because they have to take care of children. Men force women into intolerable situations, and compel us to remain in them simply through the use of their own greater power. Any suggestion that women in these situations are making 'free choices' wilfully ignores the realities of power and oppression.

Important and politically useful as this argument is, there are problems when we apply it, as Dworkin does, to explain women's involvement in sexual intercourse. In particular, many women insist that they have *voluntarily chosen to engage in sexual intercourse, and that they enjoy it, and have orgasms through it* (or, at least, in contexts which include it). When radical feminists argue that heterosexuality is an exercise of male power, that it is degrading and humiliating for women, many women feel that their own personal experience is being negated. bell hooks claims that 'attacking heterosexuality does little to strengthen the self-concept of the masses of women who desire to be with men' (1981, quoted in 1984: 153) and argues that 'many women choose to be heterosexual because they enjoy genital contact with individual men' (1984: 154). In response to the 'political lesbianism' paper (Leeds Revolutionary Feminist Group, 1981: 5), which argued that 'serious feminists have no choice but to examine heterosexuality', several women wrote describing the pleasures of heterosexual sex:

> I am the only authority on what I am experiencing when I make love . . . When they come, don't they get that sort of whoosh of overwhelming feeling coming up from inside, so that for a while you don't know where you end and your partner begins? . . . The Leeds sisters, like many sexist men, seem to fail to distinguish between rape and pleasurable heterolovemaking. (Cloutte, 1981)

Or, a more blunt response: 'I like fucking. Aren't women allowed to enjoy themselves?' (Attar et al., 1981). The responses to the Leeds Revolutionary Feminist Group paper made clear that it is very difficult to persuade even politically conscious and actively involved feminists to give up sex with men, and a central part of the heterosexual counter-argument comes down to 'but I like it'. Heterosexual sex is experienced by these women as *enjoyable* or *pleasurable*.

Of course there are many times when heterosexual sex is decidedly *un*pleasant, but a radical feminist politics has also to deal with the fact that many women, at least some of the time, actively desire, seek out and derive pleasure from heterosexual sex. Reading the radical feminist literature until a few years ago, one might be forgiven for believing that heterosexual sex is always experienced by all women as violent and brutish, or at best clumsy and penis-centred. There is very little indication that any woman might ever *enjoy* it. To suppress (some) women's pleasure in heterosexual sex, to fail to incorporate it into our political theory, is to create an 'open secret'. The danger is that where we fail to theorize about areas of experience, we leave open space for others to construct theories we may well find politically unacceptable. Stanley and Wise (1983) cite, as an example of an 'open secret' that backfired on feminists, the case of battered women's refuges. Workers in battered women's refuges knew that some women went back to men who battered them even though alternatives *were* made available, but continued to present an 'approved' image of the battered woman as victim of nothing but material circumstances. In the absence of radical feminist theorizing, Erin Pizzy (1980) filled the gap with a theory purporting to explain women's 'compliance' in terms that many of us found anti-feminist. Similarly, we all know apparently self-confident, financially solvent, childless women who *could*, in principle, choose, as many lesbians have chosen under far more difficult situations, to refuse sex with men. Yet they continue to have intercourse with men and say they enjoy it. Why? If male power is conceptualized only as external coercion and explicit psychological pressure, then we are at a loss to answer this question. A different understanding of the operation of male power on female sexual experience is necessary.

Eroticizing Powerlessness

In acknowledging female sexual pleasure in heterosexual sex, we have to see male power as productive. Power does not simply deny and repress women's sexuality; it also actively constructs it (cf. Kitzinger, 1987, 1991). Power is not simply a force which acts on individual women from the outside to control and punish; it is intimately involved in the way a woman experiences her own 'private' personal sexuality. Heteropatriarchal power promotes, cultivates and nurtures heterosexual 'pleasure'. It is, as revolutionary lesbian feminist Sheila Jeffreys (1990) argues, a serious problem that, despite the conditions of women's oppression, women can have orgasms in heterosexual sex.

Recently, radical feminist theorists have begun to explore the meaning of women's desire for and pleasure in heterosexual sex: Sheila Jeffreys (1990), Andrea Dworkin (1987) and Catherine MacKinnon (1987) have all produced similar analyses. Heterosexual desire, says Sheila Jeffreys

> is desire that eroticises power differences. It originates in the power relationships between the sexes and it normally takes the form of

eroticising the subordination of women. In heterosexual desire our subordination becomes sexy for us and for men. (1990: 206)

According to Andrea Dworkin, woman 'learns to eroticize powerlessness and self-annihilation' (1987: 163), and Catherine MacKinnon responds to the question of how women come to want that which is not in our own interests by saying that 'sexual desire in women, at least in this culture, is socially constructed as that by which we come to want our own self-annihilation' (1987: 70). This answer addresses the issue of 'pleasure' in heterosexual sex, acknowledges women's experience, and then problematizes it. The legacy of sexual liberationist ideology means that, for many feminists, anything which gives pleasure is justifiable. To suggest that sexual pleasure might not always be good flies in the face of the so-called sexual liberation, which offered pleasure as a moral arbiter: 'whatever is right is what turns you on'. But some lesbian and feminist theorists are now advancing an ethical position which problematizes pleasure when it is contingent upon oppression.

For feminists for whom 'the personal is political', sexual pleasure must necessarily be problematized. A feminist colleague told me recently how attractive she found a male professor. When I objected that he was extremely sexist, she responded, 'but sexism in men is so sexy'. Despite her feminist analysis, the men who turn her on are (I quote her) 'strong silent powerful types – men who don't pander to feminism'. Some 'anti-sexist' men have described feeling hurt and baffled when women see them as 'wimps' and do not find them sexually attractive: their analysis of the situation is that women 'prefer' (are sexually attracted to) macho men (cf. Hunter's (1993) analysis of a 'sissy man'). Read any book describing women's sexual fantasies, and you will find many devoted to sexual activities rooted in the eroticizing of powerlessness. The chapter headings of Nancy Friday's (1973) book include: 'Pain and masochism: Ouch, don't stop'; 'Rape: Don't just stand there, force me'; 'Domination, or how humiliating, thank you!'; and 'The sexuality of terror'. These are sexual fantasies women use during masturbation or sexual activities with others to give them pleasure – fantasies of bestiality, rape, passivity, being looked at, tied up, beaten. As Sheila Jeffreys has said, 'If your oppression turns you on you have a much harder time fighting your oppression' (1990: 75).

Many heterosexual feminists express political concerns about their own erotic responses. In such circumstances it is not the *lack* of pleasure in sex which is the problem, but rather the nature of sexual pleasure itself. Heterosexual feminists Ros Gill and Rebecca

Walker (1993) describe what they call their 'deeply unsound fantasies' in which 'men "sweep us off our feet", wrap us in their "strong tanned arms" and, of course, adore us'. 'We live these desires,' they say, 'through the discourse of patriarchal romances, not feminism. And the irony is that *we know it* – but that does not make the desires go away.' Heterosexual feminist philosopher Sandra Lee Bartky describes her attraction to powerful men:

> I began to see that I was attracted only to certain kinds of men – men who were older than I, who were somewhat arrogant and occasionally tyrannical, men to whom I needed to ascribe, whether they really had them or not, qualities of talent and intelligence far superior to my own . . . Continuities began to suggest themselves between these men and the heroes of film and fiction that had most excited me in adolescence: the arrogant and sarcastic Rochester of *Jane Eyre*; the distant and melancholy Max de Winter of *Rebecca*; the cold and harsh combination guardian and piano-coach of *The Seventh Veil* and, of course, Rhett Butler. (Bartky, 1993)

Nice guys, 'new men' are apparently not attractive to many heterosexual women.

The 'problem', according to this analysis, is not how *few* orgasms, how *little* pleasure women derive from heterosexual sex – but how many and how much. Instead of arguing about whether or not, and to what extent, women enjoy heterosexual sex – and how to make it more enjoyable – these feminists recognize that many women *do* enjoy heterosexual sex, and that it is precisely this *pleasure* in heterosexual sex that is the problem. Instead of exploring why it is that some women do *not* enjoy heterosexual sex, proclaiming their 'right' to pleasure, and demanding sex therapies and male education to ensure it, these theorists ask how it is possible, given the conditions of female subordination, that some women *do* enjoy heterosexual sex, and what costs are associated with that.

In response to the 'political lesbian' paper, some women who no longer have heterosexual sex described their own pleasure in it as rooted in the eroticizing of powerlessness. In a letter headed 'Why I liked screwing? Or, is heterosexual enjoyment based on sexual violence?' one woman says:

> When I was 5 I played doctors and patients with my little girl friends. The *male* doctor, played by the eldest girl, 'made' the rest of us take our knickers off and bend down while she 'tortured' us. At 8 I played a gypsy girl; dressed only in a skirt I fantasised nameless horrors forced on me by some lord of the manor. A friend aged 7 fantasised herself as Roman Slave in the Market Place; naked and chained with legs wide apart for men to see.

> In 1969 aged 22 I read 'The Story of O' and my horror and disgust
> was deepened by the then unspoken-for-many-years, ultra guilty
> realisation that reading of O's total degradation was to me – a turn on.
> Passages from the book came unbidden to my mind when my
> boyfriend penetrated me and however fast I banished them they *worked*
> – I *did* enjoy it more.
>
> Never did I speak of this, even when women in sexuality CR groups
> revealed their own hated masochistic fantasies and dreams – how in
> order to come they had to think of the man in the raincoat who'd
> flashed at them in the woods when they were 15; how images of rape,
> beating, bondage came to their minds when masturbating ... Our
> sexuality has been constructed by male-dominated society. (Jones, 1985:
> 55–6)

Changing Sexuality

Changing our sexualities is not easy. We live in a culture in which
sex is defined in terms of dominance and submission. We know we
are having 'sex' and deriving 'sexual pleasure' when we act out the
relationship between power and powerlessness, oppressor and
oppressed. Lesbian sexuality is not immune. Recalling her past
involvement in butch/femme roles, Julia Penelope describes her
sexuality as a 'butch':

> Just as I based my own sense of power on making love to other wimmin,
> I perceived their willingness to let me make love to them as a 'giving up'
> of power. When they yielded to me, surrendered themselves to me
> passionately, made themselves 'vulnerable' to me, I became powerful. I
> was absorbed by the anticipatory thrills of the 'chase' and my sexuality
> was dependent on the sexual charge I experienced when I made a new
> 'conquest'. (quoted in Hoagland, 1988: 67)

There is a revival of butch/femme roles amongst lesbians today –
so much for our ideals of egalitarian relationships. Sadomasochism,
too, is being promoted by some lesbians – the deliberate eroticizing
of power differences. Lesbians have not escaped from male-defined
sexuality – although we have been reluctant to admit this. A recent
discussion of lesbian battering describes how women already
socialized to be passive and submissive take the role with another
woman, and how reluctant other lesbians are to see the intrusion of
power into lesbian relationships – the anger at lesbian survivors of
battering for breaking the silence that supports our dreams and
visions of a united, non-violent, celebratory lesbian community
(Lobel, 1986). Similarly, some of the anger directed against those
who speak out against lesbian sado/masochist, or butch/femme
roles, seems to come from this desperate hope that, as lesbians, we
can escape from the destructive patterns of male-defined sexual

practices – those who point out that we have not done so are the bearers of unwelcome news.

Lesbian psychologists and psychotherapists are often in the business of *promoting* sexual behaviour amongst lesbians based on dominance and submission – and in particular, sadomasochism. Lesbians come to them with the 'problem' that their sex lives are not very exciting any more (they are having 'vanilla sex'), or because they have stopped having sex with each other altogether, a phenomenon common in long-term lesbian relationships described by JoAnn Loulan (1984) as 'lesbian bed death'. In order to resurrect sexual desire, many lesbian psychologists explicitly recommend sexual practices built around eroticizing power and powerlessness. This is the analysis presented by Margaret Nichols of the Boston Lesbian Psychologies Collective:

> Sexual desire requires a 'barrier': some kind of tension, a taboo, a difference of some sort, a power discrepancy, romance, the excitement of newness or the thrill of the chase – some form of disequilibrium. This hypothesis has some important implications for lesbian relationships. First it helps to explain why our romanticism is a problem. Or romanticism can be seen as a type of barrier to create sexual excitement; that is, we are romantic because it is sexually exciting to be so. The problem is that this appears to be the only acceptable form of tension or barrier we have for creating sexual excitement. . . . Clearly, we need to expand our repertoire so that there are more tensions or barriers available to facilitate sexual desire . . . To find such ways of introducing new barriers, we can look to our gay brothers. By experimenting with new sexual techniques, through the use of sex toys and props, through costume, through S/M (which maximizes differences between partners), by developing sexual rituals with our partners, by introducing tricking into our relationships we may be able to find other barriers that enhance sexuality once limerance is gone. (Nichols, 1987: 106–8)

According to Margaret Nichols, sexual desire is fundamentally rooted in the eroticizing of power differences. Lesbians are at special risk of losing sexual desire because relationships between two women are not, by necessity, unequal, in the way that a man and a woman are. Teaching sadomasochistic practices to lesbians is apparently successful in restoring sexual pleasure and sexual desire. Many lesbians have been critical of this tactic:

> Sadomasochism is an institutionalized celebration of dominant/ subordinate relationships. And it *prepares* us either to accept subordination or to enforce dominance. *Even in play*, to affirm that the exertion of the power over the powerless is erotic, is empowering, is to set the emotional stage for the continuation of that relationship, politically, socially, and economically. (Lorde, 1987: 68)

In response to implied criticism of her position on the grounds that sadomasochism is rooted in women's oppression, Margaret Nichols responds: 'We fear that at this point in our culture, so much of female sexuality may be contaminated by heterosexism and patriarchal oppression that if we reject aspects of our sexuality upon this basis we will have little left' (1987: 106–8). Feminists who are passionate in our rejection of heterosexism and patriarchal oppression are offered a choice: sex or freedom? Such is the power of sexual liberationist ideology, that to choose freedom means being labelled with a clinical diagnosis of 'erotophobia'.

It seems that the problem is not just the abuse of male power through sexual violence (rape, sexual harassment, pornography and child sexual abuse), nor is the problem of male power limited to the institution of heterosexual intercourse. The problem is the construction of sexuality. Sex is constructed, sexual desire is constructed, as the eroticization of subordination. Heterosexual sex involves male power and female subordination (sometimes apparently reversed as a 'game'). Homosexual male sex frequently involves the eroticization of differences like age, race, class and explicit S&M. And in lesbian sex, butch/femme roles, sadomasochism, and, when equality threatens, the deliberate introduction of power differences to sustain our flagging sexualities.

The language we use around sexuality is riddled with images of dominance and subordination. The word 'passion' comes from the same root as 'passive'; we are 'overcome', 'overwhelmed', or 'overpowered' by desire, we 'submit to a loved one' who has 'captured' our heart. Violence and sex are explicitly linked; in women's and men's fantasy, in real heterosexual, gay and lesbian relationships. The comparison of the penis to an instrument of domination, a gun, is commonplace; for example, in the Beatles' song, at the height of the 'sexual liberation', 'Happiness is a warm gun'. Pornography perhaps most graphically displays this pervasive association between sex and violence, sex and power. Pornographic images of women reinforce and reiterate the eroticizing of powerlessness – with women bound and gagged, mutilated, murdered, stuffed head first through meat grinders. A series of photos with text in *Chic* magazine is headed 'Columbine cuts up'. Here Columbine is shown stabbing herself in the vagina with a large butcher's knife and cutting her labia with scissors. She is smeared with blood and on her face is a fixed smile. In a purported interview, *Chic* has Columbine say, 'I would much rather masturbate with a knife than a dildo. I guess because I've always had an inferiority complex and I think of myself as deserving to be stabbed and killed' (quoted in Caplan, 1987). Feminists have sometimes denied that women are masochistic in the fear that if we say we do in fact derive pleasure from such images, or from humiliating sexual practices, men will see this as justification for continuing such practices: to acknowledge women's masochism is seen as too dangerous an admission. Only if we problematize pleasure, and insist that it is *not* the arbiter of morality, can we both acknowledge that women *do* have masochistic sexual fantasies, and seek to change that.

Radical feminist deconstruction of 'sex' and 'power' make explicit the productive nature of power, its ability to generate and construct even the most 'personal', 'private' area of our individual lives, our sexualities. Sex, as it has been constructed under heteropatriarchy, seems necessarily to involve the eroticizing of power and powerlessness, dominance and subordination: that is what makes it erotic. 'Equality does not have this danger of intoxication or derangement or obsession' (Dworkin, 1987: 19). When it is not explicitly sadomasochistic in the sense that most people use that term, when it does not involve whips and knives and ropes, its eroticism is still built upon difference, power distinction, loss of control, a sense of being driven, possessed or overcome, a loss of self. The one question that surfaces most urgently for many people with whom I have discussed these ideas is, 'how then can we have sex without re-enacting power differences – how can we do sexual things free of the taint of dominance and submission?' I suspect that we can reshape sexual desire only be reconstructing the social and political conditions within which sexuality is defined. The really urgent question is not how we should be having sex, but how we can create social and political change.

Notes

I would particularly like to thank Sheila Jeffreys for her inspiring writing, and for some stimulating conversations on this topic. Thanks also to Sue Wilkinson for her comments on an earlier version of this chapter.

This chapter was written while I was in the Department of Psychology at the University of Surrey, UK.

References

Attar, Dena, Bainbridge, Penny and Maloney, Jan (1981) 'A reply from York', in Onlywomen Press (eds), *Love Your Enemy? The Debate between Heterosexual Feminism and Political Lesbianism*. London: Onlywomen Press, pp. 45–6.

Bartky, S.L. (1993) 'Hypatia unveiled', in Sue Wilkinson and Celia Kitzinger (eds), *Heterosexuality: a* Feminism and Psychology *Reader*. London: Sage.

Berger, P.L., Berger, B. and Kellner, H. (1973) *The Homeless Mind: Modernization and Consciousness.* Harmondsworth: Penguin.

Bloch, I. (1909) *The Sexual Life of Our Time*. London: Heinemann.

Briere, John and Malamuth, Neil (1983) 'Self-reported likelihood of sexually aggressive behavior: attitudinal versus sexual explanations', *Journal of Research in Personality*, 17: 315–23.

Caplan, Paula (1987) *The Myth of Women's Masochism*. New York: Signet.

Caputi, Jane (1989) 'The sexual politics of murder', *Gender and Society*, 3: 437–56.

Cloutte, Penny (1981) Letter reprinted in Onlywomen Press (eds), *Love Your Enemy? The Debate between Heterosexual Feminism and Political Lesbianism.* London: Onlywomen Press, pp. 14–16.

Cook, Blanche (1979) 'The historical denial of lesbianism', *Radical History Review*, 20: 60–5.

Dworkin, Andrea (1987) *Intercourse*. London: Arrow Books.

Ellis, Havelock (1934) *Psychology of Sex*. London: Heinemann.

Faderman, Lillian (1980) *Surpassing the Love of Men: Romantic Friendships and Love between Women from the Renaissance to the Present.* London: Junction Books.

Forel, Albert (1908) *The Sexual Question: a Scientific, Psychological, Hygienic and Sociological Study* (trans. C.F. Marshall). New York: Physicians and Surgeons Book Co.

Friday, Nancy (1973) *My Secret Garden*. New York: Anchor/Doubleday.

Gill, Ros and Walker, Rebecca (1993) 'Heterosexuality, feminism, contradiction: on being young, white, heterosexual feminists in the 1990s', in Sue Wilkinson and Celia Kitzinger (eds), *Heterosexuality: a* Feminism and Psychology *Reader*. London: Sage.

Hoagland, Sarah Lucia (1988) *Lesbian Ethics: Toward New Value*. Palo Alto, Ca.: Institute of Lesbian Studies.

hooks, bell (1981) *Ain't I a Woman*. Boston, Mass.: South End Press.

hooks, bell (1984) *Feminist Theory: From Margin to Centre*. Boston, Mass.: South End Press.

Hughes, E (1945) 'Dilemmas and contradiction of status', *American Journal of Sociology*, 50: 253–9.

Hunter, Allen (1993) 'Same door, different closet: a heterosexual sissy's coming-out party', in Sue Wilkinson and Celia Kitzinger (eds), *Heterosexuality: a Feminism and Psychology Reader*. London: Sage.

Jeffreys, Sheila (1985) *The Spinster and her Enemies*. London: Pandora.

Jeffreys, Sheila (1990) *Anticlimax: a Feminist Perspective on the Sexual Revolution*. London: The Women's Press.

Jones, Justine (1985) 'Why I liked screwing? Or is heterosexual enjoyment based on sexual violence?', in Dusty Rhodes and Sandra McNeill (eds), *Women Against Violence Against Women*. London: Onlywomen Press, pp. 21–4.

Kitzinger, Celia (1987) *The Social Construction of Lesbianism*. London: Sage.

Kitzinger, Celia (1991) 'Feminism, psychology and the paradox of power', *Feminism and Psychology: an International Journal*, 1(1): 111–29.

Kitzinger, Jenny and Kitzinger, Celia (1993) '"Doing it": representations of lesbian sex', in Gabriele Griffin (ed.), *Outwrite: Popular/izing Lesbian Texts*. London: Pluto Press.

Krafft-Ebing, R. (1882[1965]) *Psychopathia Sexualis* (trans. M.E. Wedneck). New York: Putnams.

Leeds Revolutionary Feminist Group (1981) 'Political lesbianism: the case against heterosexuality', in Onlywomen Press (eds), *Love Your Enemy? The Debate between Heterosexual Feminism and Political Lesbianism*. London: Onlywomen Press, pp. 5–10.

Lobel, K. (1986) *Naming the Violence: Speaking Out about Lesbian Violence*. Washington: Seal Press.

Lorde, Audre (1987) Interview with Susan Leigh Starr, in Robin Ruth Linden, Darlene R. Pagano, Diana E.H. Russell and Susan Leigh Starr (eds), *Against Sadomasochism: a Radical Feminist Analysis*. East Palo Alto: Frog in the Well, pp. 66–71.

Loulan, J. (1984) *Lesbian Sex*. San Francisco: Spinsters Ink.

MacKinnon, Catherine (1987) 'A feminist political approach: pleasure under patriarchy', in James Geer and William O'Donohue (eds), *Theories of Human Sexuality*. New York: Plenum Press, pp. 135–52.

Nichols, Margaret (1987) 'Lesbian sexuality: issues and developing theory', in Boston Lesbian Psychologies Collective (ed.), *Lesbian Psychologies: Explorations and Challenges*. Chicago: University of Illinois Press, pp. 97–125.

Norman, Philip (1992) 'Nazi Chic', *Weekend Guardian*, 30–31 May: 4–6.

Onlywomen Press (eds) (1981) *Love Your Enemy? The Debate between Heterosexual Feminism and Political Lesbianism*. London: Onlywomen Press, pp. 14–16.

Pizzy, Erin (1980) *Scream Quietly or the Neighbours Will Hear*. London: Penguin.

Rich, Adrienne (1980) 'Compulsory heterosexuality and lesbian existence', *Signs: Journal of Women in Culture and Society*, 5(4): 631–57.

Segal, Lyn and MacIntosh, Mary (eds) (1992) *Sex Exposed*. London: Virago.

Stanley, Liz and Wise, Sue (1983) *Breaking Out: Feminist Consciousness and Feminist Research*. London: Routledge and Kegan Paul.

Tieger, Todd (1981) 'Self-rated likelihood of raping and social perception of rape', *Journal of Research in Personality*, 15: 147–58.

Wilkinson, Sue and Kitzinger, Celia (eds) (1993) *Heterosexuality: a Feminism and Psychology Reader*. London: Sage.

10

Post-modernizing Gender:
from Adrienne Rich to Judith Butler

Lorraine Weir

'It is difficult to see,' Diana Fuss argues in *Essentially Speaking –
Feminism, Nature and Difference*, 'how constructionism can *be*
constructionism without a fundamental dependency upon
essentialism' (Fuss, 1989: 4). The two are set in a binary and
antithetical relation to each other such that the attempt of post-
modern feminists like Judith Butler to deconstruct this imbricated
relation via a theory of 'gender parody' (Butler, 1990: 138) is, in
part at least, to reconstitute one voice through the other. For
parody, as Mikhail Bakhtin amply demonstrated, is a mode of
'double-voiced discourse' in which one voice attempts to overthrow
the other at the same time as the reader hears both voices
sounding through the text (Matejka and Pomorska, 1971: 195).

In Bakhtin as in Butler, parody is a revolutionary strategy,
foregrounding change against a background of the voice of
convention. It is also a strategy of exile, othering, dislocation,
decentring, a strategy which makes on its 'implied reader' (Iser,
1974) a hermeneutic demand to decipher its encrypted voices, to
reveal its 'truth'. This is equally, as Butler's discussion of Foucault
indicates, our culture's demand that 'sex speak the truth' of our
selves, a demand which liberal feminists have often joyously
espoused and which now occasions much of the tension in the
debate deconstructed by Fuss. But that tension is an ironic one at
best, a division which seems to set, for example, Adrienne Rich
against Judith Butler, which seems to rest on a principle of
hermeneutic ambiguity where, in fact, there is remarkable
congruence.

To inquire into this dialogism, we need first to consider Rich's
explicitly hermeneutic lexicon of 'truth' and identity, and then to
consider both Foucault's genealogy of gender and Bakhtin's theory
of parody and heteroglossia in the context of Butler's deconstruction of sex and gender categories. In the process, we may
discover the dangers for feminism of a hermeneutic methodology

with its proclamation of truth and its drive towards revelation. Post-modernizing gender through the making of 'gender trouble' may, then, come to seem not only more like Rich's hermeneutics than we expected but also, in its metatextual overdetermination, more like those liberatory forms of feminism which have traditionally proclaimed that to change our language is to change our world. Rich's 'dream of a common language' becomes Butler's dream of 'gender parody', and Donna Haraway's similarly Bakhtinian dream of heteroglossia: revolutionary strategies grounded in hermeneutic proclamations of truth.

Adrienne Rich on Lies, Secrets and Silence

In 'Women and Honor: Some Notes on Living', Rich writes of the struggle to speak the complex truth of our experience and our situation as women. For her, this is also the struggle 'to extend the possibilities of truth between us' (Rich, 1979: 194). Feminism for her is a hermeneutic enterprise, a process of discovery of our identity as women, and a process undertaken within a community, whether of many or two or, for Emily Dickinson and Anne Bradstreet, alone, looking inward, inwardly seeking secret knowledge which

> Few women have grown up without . . . , lodged as it may be in some collective unconscious, disguised as it may be under codes of chivalry, domestic sentiment, biological reduction, or as it is revealed in poetry, law, theology, popular songs, pornography, or dirty jokes. Such knowledge – so long as women are not pressured into denying it – makes them . . . potentially the deepest of all questioners of the social order created by men, and the most genuinely radical of thinkers. (1979: 81)

Radical: rooted – 'in some collective unconscious' which influences, perhaps determines, one's daily experience. Working together 'in a genuine alliance of women with women, and of women with non-masculinist men' (p. 84), women release 'an incalculable new energy – not merely for changing institutions but for human redefinition; not merely for equal rights but for a new kind of being' (p. 155). That 'new kind of being' is generated out of the '*primary presence of women to ourselves and each other* first described in prose by Mary Daly, and which is the crucible of a new language' (p. 250, original emphasis). Our utopian instrument of transformation, that new language, is, for Rich, grounded in a feminist hermeneutics which posits identity as that which can be *discussed*, by the individual speaking in the context of her feminist community.

Spoken in words, truth emerges – whether of sex or identity – as both the movement past lying and the creation through imagination of a new world by those in the act of articulating themselves as new kinds of beings (p. 155). The task is the hermeneutic one of speaking the unspeakable and thereby *presencing* the new world. As Rich says in that extraordinarily courageous essay, 'It is the Lesbian in Us . . .':

> Whatever is unnamed, undepicted in images, whatever is omitted from biographies, censored in collections of letters, whatever is misnamed as something else, made difficult-to-come-by, whatever is buried in the memory by the collapse of meaning under an inadequate or lying language – this will become, not merely unspoken, but *unspeakable*. (p. 200)

In speaking our experience, we 'grasp' it and make of it 'a key to action' (p. 202). In denying our experience, we refuse its truth, we lie: 'lying is done with words, and also with silence' (p. 186). Thus 'The word *lesbian* must be affirmed because to discard it is to collaborate with silence and lying about our very existence; with the closet-game, the creation of the *unspeakable*' (p. 202). In rejecting silence, we reject heterosexual culture's attempt to disappear us and choose instead to shape our own discourse and thus our world.

From Heteroglossia to Parody

Rich's invocation of hermeneutics is not without its problems. Her appeal is to an 'interpretive community' (Fish, 1980: 322) of women bound into a hermeneutic circle of like-minded interpreters, a procedure which – however empowering to the individual – finally serves only to reaffirm the circle and proclaim its truth, or mystery, as the case may be. Essentialist in its assertion of lesbian and heterosexual *identities*, Rich's theory is grounded in the conviction that our sexual repression is in metonymic relation to our social and political oppression, and that to speak the truth of one is to begin to reveal the truth of the other(s). Seen not as a construction but, rather, as the foundation of subjectivity, Rich's concept of truth is what Butler describes as 'a prediscursive structure for both the self and its acts' (Butler, 1990: 142). In this concept of truth inheres precisely the *common*ality of women's language: a truth of lived experience, the language of the body.

Re-enacting Fuss's paradigm of the dialogical relation of essentialism and constructionism, Donna Haraway rejects Rich's dream and its other in her 'Manifesto for Cyborgs', writing that this, 'like all dreams . . . [of] a perfectly true language, of a perfectly faithful naming of experience, is a totalizing and imperialist one' (Haraway, 1990: 215). In its place, she argues, must be created 'a powerful infidel heteroglossia . . . an imagination of a feminist speaking in tongues to strike fear into the circuits of the super savers of the New Right' (1990: 223). If god is dead, says Haraway, 'so is the "goddess", and feminist ontotheology must make way for 'cyborg semiologies' (1990: 204) where once it championed mutuality and humanist subjectivity. Apparently subverting the anthropomorphism of the liberal essentialist paradigm, Haraway substitutes the cyborg – a 'cybernetic organism, a hybrid of machine and organism, a creature of social reality as well as a creature of fiction' – for the subject; in science fiction, a creature 'simultaneously animal and machine, who populate[s] worlds ambiguously natural and crafted' (1990: 191). A strategy for imagining beyond/around/outside Rich's essentialist hermeneutics, Haraway's cyborg 'is a kind of disassembled and reassembled post-modern collective and personal self' (1990: 205). So the hermeneutic circle of the 'common language' is broken in favour of polysemy, the collective, and heteroglossia.

Complicating the simple collation of truth and identity, sex and gender, notions of 'being' a woman, cyborgian heteroglossia anticipates Judith Butler's opposition of 'heterosexual coherence' to 'gender parody' (Butler, 1990: 138). Cautioning us that 'The notion of gender parody defended here does not assume that there is an original which such parodic identities imitate', Butler writes that 'the parody is *of* the very notion of an original . . .' (1990: 138). 'Gender meanings' are plural, multifarious, joyous, diverse and performative while still

> clearly part of hegemonic, misogynist culture, . . . [and] nevertheless denaturalized and mobilized through their parodic recontextualization. As imitations which effectively displace the meaning of the original, they imitate the myth of originality itself. In the place of an original identification which serves as a determining cause, gender identity might be reconceived as a personal/cultural history of received meanings subject to a set of imitative practices which refer laterally to other imitations and which, jointly, construct the illusion of a primary and interior gendered self or parody the mechanism of that construction. (1990: 138)

Thus, for Butler, 'identity' does not precede enactment but is performed in, by and through it (p. 128), and rendered 'permanently problematic' through the 'convergence of multiple sexual discourses at . . . [its] site' (p. 128).

According to Butler, then, 'The unproblematic claim to "be" a woman and "be" heterosexual would be symptomatic of . . . [the] metaphysics of gender substances' which

> tends to subordinate the notion of gender under that of identity and to lead to the conclusion that a person *is* a gender and *is* one in virtue of his or her sex, psychic sense of self, and various expressions of that psychic self, the most salient being that of sexual desire. (pp. 21–2)

If 'There is no gender identity behind the expressions of gender: that identity is performatively constituted by the very "expressions" that are said to be its results' (p. 25). Butler's aim is therefore 'to make gender trouble, not through the strategies that figure a utopian beyond, but through the mobilization, subversive confusion, and proliferation of precisely those constitutive categories that seek to keep gender in its place by posturing as the foundational illusions of identity' (p. 34).

Deconstructing heterosexual culture's construction of homosexuality and lesbianism as derivative, Butler notes that

> The replication of heterosexual constructs in non-heterosexual frames brings into relief the utterly constructed status of the so-called heterosexual original. Thus, gay is to straight *not* as copy is to original, but, rather, as copy is to copy. The parodic repetition of 'the original' . . . reveals the original to be nothing other than a parody of the *idea* of the natural and the original. (p. 31)

Gender post-modernized is, then, gender without origin, gender as performative in that ceaseless parodic movement in which, as Butler says, the doer is not *behind* the deed but, rather, 'is variably constructed in and through the deed' (p. 142).

What Butler is attempting may then be seen as no less than a Heideggerian destruction of a feminist fundamental ontology, a destruction which is a deconstruction hinging on *difference* and articulated in terms of a Bakhtinian theory of parody which produces a 'proliferating [of] gender configurations, destabilizing substantive identity, and depriving the naturalizing narratives of compulsory heterosexuality of their central protagonists: "man" and "woman"' (p. 146). In Bakhtin, parody is classified as 'double-voiced' discourse (Matejka and Pomorska, 1971: 181) in which 'The second voice, once having made its home in the other's discourse, clashes hostilely with its primordial host and forces him to serve directly opposing aims. Discourse becomes an arena of battle between two voices' (Bakhtin, 1984: 193). Like the struggle of gender codes imbricated in each other, the parodic agon exhibits elements of heteroglossia as well, particularly when found in the genre of the novel to which both are crucial. As Bakhtin writes in *The Dialogical Imagination*, 'the novel begins by presuming a verbal and semantic decentering of the ideological world, a certain linguistic homelessness of literary consciousness, which no longer possesses a sacrosanct and unitary linguistic medium for containing ideological thought' (1981: 367). Bakhtin's concept of the novel as parodic, heteroglossic form thus becomes Butler's world of 'gender meanings taken up' in the 'parodic styles . . . of hegemonic, misogynist culture' (Butler, 1990: 138). Our task as readers of this polyvocal text is thus precisely to recognize its strategies and foreground them for 'As credible bearers of those attributes, . . . genders can . . . be rendered thoroughly and radically *incredible*' (Butler, 1990: 141, original emphasis) by skilled (Bakhtinian) readers. Thus where, in Rich, we *speak* our transformation process, in Butler we *read* it. No less textual for that, the language game of gendering still attaches only to the language game of performance. As Butler stresses, gender *is* performative.

Foucault, Butler and the Naming of Sex

What is performed is woman's 'hysterization', the 'truth' of her sex. Here Butler's deconstruction relies on Foucault's *History of Sexuality* with its distinction among the 'four great strategic unities which, beginning in the eighteenth century, formed specific mechanisms of knowledge and power centering on sex' (Foucault, 1978: 103). Of these four unities – the 'hysterization of women's bodies', the 'pedagogization of children's sex', the 'socialization of procreative behavior', and the 'psychiatrization of perverse pleasure' (Foucault, 1978: 104–5) – the first is the most important for Butler's analysis. Foucault maintains that 'hysterization' is

> a threefold process whereby the feminine body was analyzed – qualified and disqualified – as being thoroughly saturated with sexuality; whereby it was integrated into the sphere of medical practices, by reason of a pathology intrinsic to it; whereby, finally, it was placed in organic communication with the social body (whose regulated fecundity it was supposed to ensure), the family space (of which it had to be a substantial and functional element), and the life of children (which it produced and had to guarantee, by virtue of a biologico-moral responsibility lasting through the entire period of the children's education): the Mother, with her negative image of 'nervous woman', constituted the most visible form of this hysterization. (1978: 104)

Foucault's problematization of the naming of 'sex' and the 'production of sexuality' (1978: 114), his articulation of a 'discourse of power, and opposite it, another discourse that runs counter to it' (1978: 101) is focused in this passage in terms of hysterization as pathology, and pathology as 'truth'. To be hysterized is to 'become' woman but not in de Beauvoir's sense of encountering a culturally determined appeal which shapes one's 'identity'. Nor does one encounter one's 'concrete reality' as a woman from which this process of hysterization springs. Neither a transcendental principle of 'Being' nor a biology is at issue here. As Foucault writes of the construction of sex as identity:

> we demand that sex speak the truth (but, since it is the secret and is oblivious to its own nature, we reserve for ourselves the function of telling the truth of its truth, revealed and deciphered at last), and we demand that it tell us one truth, or rather, the deeply buried truth of that truth about ourselves which we think we possess in our immediate consciousness. We tell it its truth by deciphering what it tells us about that truth; it tells us our own by delivering up that part of it that escapes us. From this interplay there has evolved, over several centuries, a knowledge of the subject; a knowledge not so much of his form, but of that which divides him, determines him perhaps, but above all causes him to be ignorant of himself (1978: 69–70).

To 'speak the truth' of 'hysterization' is, in Foucault's terms, to enter the discursive system of one's own repression and oppression whether one is anatomically male or female. It is to participate in the 'deployment of sexuality' (Foucault, 1978: 152) which, since the nineteenth century, has elaborated the notion that 'there exists something other than bodies, organs, somatic localizations, functions, anatomo-physiological systems, sensations, and pleasure; something else and something more, with intrinsic properties and laws of its own: "sex"' (Foucault, 1978: 152–3). As Butler summarizes this condition of being 'sexed', it

> is to be subjected to a set of regulations, to have the law that directs those regulations reside both as the formative principle of one's sex, gender, pleasure, and desires and as the hermeneutic principle of self-interpretation. The category of sex is thus inevitably regulative, and any analysis which makes that category presuppositional uncritically extends and further legitimates that regulative strategy and a power/ knowledge regime. (1990: 96)

Thus the category 'woman' is regulative within the power/ knowledge regime of Western culture in which to be anatomically female is to be gendered as female, and, potentially, to be hysterized. Precisely in terms of the uterus, *hyster*, woman is defined and regulated, constituted as 'Mother', and the institution of motherhood constituted as telos. Through the hermeneutics of 'identity', then, woman is produced *as* woman, has her 'being' defined in terms of normative and regulative presuppositions about binding relations among – to use Butler's categories – anatomical sex, gender identity and gender performance (Butler, 1990: 137). The 'dream of a common language' becomes, then, a reclaiming of hysterization, a revisioning of the patriarchally encoded term to reveal its truth – not the truth of sex but that of woman; not the cyborg but the voice as summons to conversion and belief.

That summons, whether in Rich or in Butler, is a call to change *language* and thereby change the world. Rich's hermeneutics of truth is one frame in Butler's heteroglossic parody, and a frame which retains its ontological grounding in humanist understandings of the subject, of – as Butler says – 'heterosexual coherence', which, arranged differently, becomes the model for homosexual/ lesbian (in)coherence and for feminist truth-telling. What motivates both *Gender Trouble* and *On Lies, Secrets and Silence* is the still necessarily utopian dimension of feminism at the intersection of gender and power. Butler's 'subversion of identity' is, finally, an attempt to subvert liberal feminism's essentialist assumptions about woman. By making 'gender trouble', she seeks to deconstruct a politics grounded in ontotheology and to disseminate the processes of sexual signification across a broader cultural grid. However, the new dream of a post-modernizing of gender leaves us in much the same place as the old one: conversion, whether its mode of enactment is the 'subversive laugh' of Butler or the call to presence of Rich. One requires the other, one is implicated in the other, and both are formed through the technology of herme-neutics which, as successfully as ever, winds its prophetic skein around the truths it was designed to capture. Thus it evades the grasp of those who, using rhetorical tactics to deconstruct the text, succeed inevitably in construing the world as a language game.

References

Bakhtin, M.M. (1981) *The Dialogic Imagination – Four Essays* (ed. Michael Holquist, trans. Caryl Emerson and Michael Holquist). Austin: University of Texas Press.

Bakhtin, M.M. (1984) *Problems of Dostoevsky's Poetics* (ed. and trans. Caryl Emerson). Minneapolis: University of Minnesota Press.

Butler, Judith (1990) *Gender Trouble – Feminism and the Subversion of Identity*. New York: Routledge.

Fish, Stanley (1980) *Is there a Text in This Class? The Authority of Interpretive Communities*. Cambridge, Mass.: Harvard University Press.

Foucault, Michel (1978) *The History of Sexuality*, vol. 1 (trans. Robert Hurley). New York: Pantheon.

Fuss, Diana (1989) *Essentially Speaking – Feminism, Nature and Difference*. New York: Routledge.

Haraway, Donna (1990) 'A manifesto for cyborgs: science, technology, and socialist feminism in the 1980s', in Linda J. Nicholson (ed.), *Feminism/Postmodernism*. New York: Routledge, pp. 190–233.

Iser, Wolfgang (1974) *The Implied Reader – Patterns of Communication in Prose Fiction from Bunyan to Beckett*. Baltimore, Md: Johns Hopkins University Press.

Matejka, Ladislav and Pomorska, Krystyna (eds) (1971) *Readings in Russian Poetics – Formalist and Structuralist Views*. Cambridge, Mass.: MIT Press.

Rich, Adrienne (1979) *On Lies, Secrets and Silences: Selected Prose 1966–1978*. New York: Horton.

11

Over Dinner: Feminism and Adolescent Female Bodies

Michelle Fine and Pat Macpherson

The experience of being woman can create an illusory unity, for it is not the experience of being woman but the meanings attached to gender, race, class, and age at various historical moments . . . that [are] of strategic significance.

(Chandra Mohanty, 1987: 39)

When we invited four teenagers – Shermika, Damalleaux, Janet and Sophie – for a series of dinners to talk with us about being young women in the 1990s, we could not see our own assumptions about female adolescence much more clearly than we saw theirs. By the end of the first dinner, we could, though, recognize how old we were, how dated the academic literatures were, how powerful feminism had been in shaping their lives and the meanings they made of them, and yet how inadequately their feminism dealt with key issues of identity and peer relations.

Only when we started to write could we see the inadequacies of our feminism to understand the issues of female adolescence they struggled to communicate. In this space of our incredulity, between our comprehension of their meanings and our *in*comprehension of 'how they could call themselves feminist', we are now able to see the configuration of our own fantasies of feminism for female adolescents. The revision that is central to feminist process gets very tricky when applied to adolescence, because our own unsatisfactory pasts return as the 'before' picture, demanding that the 'after' picture of current adolescent females measure all the gains of the women's movement. Our longing is for psychic as well as political completion. Michael Payne (1991: 18) describes the fantasy of the Other: 'What I desire – and therefore lack – is in the other culture, the other race, the other gender' – the other generation, in our case. In the case of these four young women, to our disbelief, the desired Other is 'one of the guys'.

Our analyses of power lie revealed and problematic in two

intellectual spaces. First we worry about the hegemonic frames that we import as researchers to/on/over their stories (Lather, 1991). And second, in more Foucauldian fashion, we write on *their* strategies of resistance and negotiation with boys and men, girls and women, and the social representations of gender, race and class that litter their lives (Brodkey and Fine, 1988). We presume that power floats across relations, institutions and bodies, constructing and resisting asymmetries displayed materially and discursively.

We grew convinced that we needed to construct an essay about these young women's interpretations of and struggles with the discourses of adolescence, femininity and feminism in their peer cultures. Barbara Hudson explains the incompatibility of femininity and adolescence:

> femininity and adolescence as discourses [are] subversive of each other. All of our images of the adolescent – the restless, searching teen; the Hamlet figure; the sower of wild oats and tester of growing powers – these are masculine figures ... If adolescence is characterized by masculine constructs, then any attempt by girls to satisfy society's demands of them qua adolescents is bound to involve them in displaying notably a lack of maturing but also a lack of femininity. (1984: 35)

Adolescence for these four young women was about adventures of males and the constraints on females, so their version of feminism unselfconsciously rejected femininity and embraced the benign version of masculinity that allowed them to be 'one of the guys'. They fantasized the safe place of adolescence to be among guys who overlook their (female) gender out of respect for their (unfeminine) independence, intelligence and integrity. For them, femininity meant the taming of adolescent passions, outrage and intelligence. Feminism was a flight from 'other girls' as unworthy and untrustworthy. Their version of feminism was about equal access to being men.

When we scoured the literatures on adolescent females and their bodies, we concluded that the very construction of the topic is positioned largely from white, middle-class, non-disabled, heterosexual adult women's perspectives. The concerns of white **elite** women are represented as *the* concerns of this age cohort. Eating disorders are defined within the contours of what **elite** women suffer (for example, anorexia and bulimia) and less so what non-elite women experience (for example, overeating, obesity). The sexual harassment literature is constructed from **our** age perspective – that unwanted sexual attention is and should be constituted as a crime – and not from the complicated perspectives of young women involved. The disability literature is saturated with images produced by **non-disabled** researchers of self-pitying or embarrassed 'victims' of biology, and is rarely filled with voices of resistant, critical and powerfully 'flaunting' adolescents who refuse to wear prostheses, delight in the passions of their bodies and are outraged by the social and family discrimination they experience (Corbett et al., 1987; Fine and Asch, 1988; Frank, 1988).

We found that women of all ages, according to this literature, are allegedly scripted to be 'good women', and that they have, in compliance, smothered their passions, appetites and outrage. When sexually harassed, they tell 'his stories' (Brodkey and Fine, 1988). To please the lingering internalized 'him', they suffer in body image and indulge in eating disorders (Orbach, 1986). And to satisfy social demands for 'attractiveness', women with and without disabilities transform and mutilate their bodies (Bordo, 1990).

We presumed initially that the three arenas of adolescence in which young women would most passionately struggle with gendered power would include eating, sexuality and outrage. And so we turned to see what these literatures said, and to unpack how race, class, disability and sexuality played with each of these literatures. In brief, within these literatures, we saw a polarizing:

1. Eating disorders appear to be a question studied among elite white women in their anticipated tensions of career vs mother identities.
2. Sexuality is examined disproportionately as problematic for girls who are black and underprivileged, with motherhood as their primary identity posed as 'the problem'.
3. Finally, young women's political 'outrage' simply does not exist as a category for feminist intellectual analysis.

The literature on adolescent women had thoroughly extricated these categories of analysis from women's lives. So, in our text we decided to rely instead upon the frames that these young women offered as they narrated their own lives, and the interpretations we could generate through culture and class.

Our method was quite simple, feminist and, ironically, anti-eating disorder. We invited the six of us to talk together over pizza and soda, while Sam – Michelle's 4-year-old – circled the table. We talked for hours, on two nights two months apart, and together stretched to create conversations about common differences; about the spaces in which we could delight together as six women; the moments in which they bonded together as four

young women who enjoy football, hit their boyfriends, and can't
trust other girls – Not Ever!; and, too, the arenas in which the
race, class and cultural distances in the room stretched too far for
these age peers to weave any common sense of womanhood.
Collectively, we created a context that Shermika and Sophie
spontaneously considered 'the space where I feel most safe'. We
were together, chatting, listening, hearing, laughing a lot and truly
interested in understanding our connections and differences,
contoured always along the fault lines of age, class, race and
culture, bodies, experiences and politics.

But we each delighted in this context differently. For Michelle
and Pat, it was a space in which we could pose feminist
intellectual questions from our generation – questions about
sexuality, power, victimization and politics – which they then
turned on their heads. For Shermika (African-American, age 15) it
was a place for public performance, to say outrageous things,
admit embarrassing moments, 'practise' ways of being female in
public discourse, and see how we would react. For Damalleaux
(African-American, age 14) it was a place to 'not be shy' even
though the room was integrated by race, a combination that had
historically made her uncomfortable. For Sophie ('WASP', age
17), it was a 'safe place' where perhaps for the first time, she was
not the only 'out' feminist in a room full of peers. And for Janet
(Korean-American, age 17), like other occasions in which she was
the only Asian-American among whites and blacks, it was a time
to test her assimilated 'sense of belonging', always at the margins.
In negotiating gender, race/ethnicity and class as critical, feminist
agents, these four women successfully betrayed a set of academic
literatures, written by so many of us only twenty years older. Our
writings have been persistently committed to public representations
of women's victimization and structural assaults, and have
consequently ignored, indeed misrepresented, *how well young
women talk as subjects*, passionate about and relishing in their
capacities to move between nexuses of power and powerlessness.
That is to say, feminist scholars have forgotten to take notice of
how firmly young women resist – alone and sometimes together.

The four young women began their conversation within this
space of gendered resistance. Shermika complained, 'Boys think
girls cannot *do* anything', to which Sophie added, 'So we have to
harass them'. Shermika explained, '[Guys think] "Long as they're
takin' care of em [girls will] do anything they want." And if I'm in
a relationship, I'm gonna take care of you just as much as you
take care of me. You can't say "I did this" – No: "We did this."
... Guys think you're not nothin' – anything – without them.'

Janet sneered, 'Ego.' Shermika recruited her friend into this conversation by saying, 'Damalleaux *rule* her boyfriend [Shermika's brother].' Damalleaux announced her governing principle, 'Boys – they try to take advantage of you . . . As far as I'm concerned, I won't let a boy own me.' Janet provided an example of the 'emotionally messed up guys' she encounters: 'I didn't want to take care of him. I didn't want to constantly explain things to him . . . I want to coexist with them and not be like their mother . . . It happened to me twice.' And Sophie explained: 'I'm really assertive with guys [who say sexist stuff]. If they have to be shot down I'll shoot them down. They have to know their place.' The four expressed their feminism here as resistance to male domination in their peer relations. They applied the same principle in discussing how they saw careers and marriage, when Michelle asked about men in their future plans. Shermika laid it out in material terms: 'I imagine bein' in my *own* house in *my name*. And then get married. So my husband can get out *my house*.' Sophie chimed in, 'Seriously,' and Shermika nodded, 'Yes, *very important*. So I won't end up one of them battered women we were talkin' about. I'm not going to have no man beatin' on me.' Sophie offered her version: 'You have to like be independent. You have to establish yourself as your own person before some guy takes you – I mean . . .' Janet asserted her standard of independence: 'I wouldn't follow a guy to college.' Their feminism asserted women's independence from men's power to dominate and direct.

Class and cultural differences entered the conversations with their examples of domination and resistance. Shermika's example of guys materially 'takin' care of girls to establish dominance, and Damalleaux's resistance to male 'ownership' reflected the practice of gift-giving as ownership, a norm of their local sexual politics (see Anderson, 1990). Damalleaux explained that *respect* could interrupt this dominance structure: 'How much respect a guy has for you – especially in front of his friends . . . If a boy finds out you don't care how they treat you, and you don't have respect for your*self* . . . they won't have respect for you.' Damalleaux turned to Shermika and said, 'You try to teach me.' Shermika's talk was full of lessons learned from her mother, and examples of their closeness. 'My mom and me like this. Cause she understands.' Not talking '*leads* to problems. My Mom tells me so much about life.'

Sophie and Janet defined their resistance within their 'professional class', peopled by 'individuals', not relationships, who suffer from the dilemmas of 'independence', typically explained in terms of psychology. Their isolation from their mothers and female friends enabled them to frame their stories alone, as one-on-one battles across the lines of gender and generations.

Ways of Talking: on Cultures of Womenhood

> Herein lies a cautionary tale for feminists who insist that underneath or beyond the differences among women there must be some shared identity – as if commonality were a metaphysical given, as if a shared viewpoint were not a difficult political achievement . . . Western feminist theory has in effect . . . [demanded that] Afro-American, Asian-American or Latin American women separate their 'woman's voice' from their racial or ethnic voice without also requiring white women to distinguish being a 'woman' from being white. This double standard implies that while on the one hand there is a seamless web of whiteness and womanness, on the other hand, Blackness and womanness, say, or Indianness and womanness, are discrete and separable elements of identity. If . . . I believe that the woman in every woman is a woman just like me, and if I also assume that there is no difference between being white and being a woman, then seeing another woman 'as a woman' will involve me seeing her as fundamentally like the woman I am. In other words, the womanness underneath the Black woman's skin is a white woman's, and deep down inside the latina woman is an Anglo woman waiting to burst through the obscuring cultural shroud. As Barbara Omolade has said, 'Black women are not white women with color.'
>
> (Elizabeth Spelman, 1988: 13)

At this moment in social history, when the tensions of race, class and gender couldn't be in more dramatic relief, social anxieties load onto the bodies of adolescent women (Fine, 1988; Halson, 1991). Struggles for social control attach to these unclaimed territories, evident in public debates over teen pregnancy, adolescent promiscuity, parental consent for contraception and abortion, date rapes and stories of sexual harassment, as well as in women's personal narratives of starving themselves or binging and purging towards thinness. For each of these social 'controversies', there is, however, a contest of wills, a set of negotiations. Young women are engaged with questions of 'being female'; that is, who will control, and to what extent can they control, their own bodies?

Threaded through our conversations at the dining room table, culture and class helped to construct (at least) two distinct versions of womanhood. It became clear that the elite women, for instance, constructed an interior sense of womanhood out of oppositional relations with White Men. They positioned white men as the power group White Men (Baker, 1989), and they positioned themselves in an ongoing, critical, hierarchical struggle with these men. Sophie, for example, often defined her feminism in relation to white boys; instead of 'reinforcing guys all the time, I BUST on guys. Because if you don't bust em they'll get ahead. You have to keep em in their place'.

It was quite another thing to hear the sense of womanhood constructed horizontally – still in struggle – by African-American women, situated with or near African-American men. Given the assault on Black men by the broader culture, it was clear that any announced sense of female superiority would be seen as 'castrating', and unreconcilable with cross-gender alliances against racism (Giddings, 1984: hooks, 1984). So, the construction of Black womanhood was far less dichotomized and oppositional toward men, and far richer in a sense of connection to community.[1]

In the context of being 'deprived' of the traditional (oppositional to White Men) feminine socialization, women of colour, like women of disabilities, may construct womenhoods less deeply repulsed by the traditional accoutrements of femininity, less oppositional to the cardboard White Male, and less assured that gender survives as the primary, or exclusive category of social identity.

Among these four, then, we heard two quite distinct constructions of 'being female'. From the African-American women, both living in relatively impoverished circumstances, we heard a 'womanhood' of fluid connections among women within and across generations; maturity conceived of as an extension of self with others; a taken-for-granted integration of body and mind; a comfortable practice of using public talk as a place to 'work out' concerns, constraints and choices; and a nourishing, anchored sense of *home* and *community*. bell hooks describes home as a site of nurturance and identity, *positive in its resistance* to racist ideologies of black inferiority:

> Despite the brutal reality of racial apartheid, of domination, one's homeplace was the one site where one could freely confront the issue of humanization, where one could resist. Black women resisted by making homes where all black people could strive to be subjects, not objects, where we could be affirmed in our minds and our hearts despite poverty, hardship and deprivation, where we could restore to ourselves the dignity denied us on the outside in the public world. (1990: 42)

As the words of Damalleaux and Shermika reveal to us, however, the drawback of this centredness in community is in its fragility, its contingent sense of the future, terrors of what's 'across the border', and the lack of resources or supports for planned upward mobility.

Indeed, when we discussed future plans, Shermika 'joked' she would be a custodian or bag lady. She 'joked' she would like to be dead, to see what the other world was like. She said she would like to come back as a bird – 'Not a pigeon, I hope,' said Sophie – 'Dove or peacock,' Shermika decided, 'something nobody be kickin' around all the time.' Shermika finally confided – in an uncharacteristic whisper – that she would like to be a lawyer, even the D.A. (the district attorney). What Shermika can be – could be – would like to be – and will be – constitutes the terrain of Shermika's and Damalleaux's dilemma. Shermika does not worry that education would de-feminize her, or that her parents expect more or different from her career than she does. She quite simply and realistically doubts she will be able to get all the way to 'D.A.'.

Nevertheless, Damalleaux and Shermika, on the other hand, expressed the connections with and respect for mothers found in Gloria Joseph and Jill Lewis's African-American daughters when they write, 'A decisive 94.5% expressed respect for their mothers in terms of strength, honesty, ability to overcome difficulties, and ability to survive' (1981: 94). Shermika's many examples of respect for her mother, and Damalleaux's mother calling her 'my first girl' suggest 'the centrality of mothers in their daughters' lives' (Joseph and Lewis, 1981: 79). In their stories, active female sexuality and motherhood are everywhere 'embodied', while 'career' is a distant and indistinct dream, marginal, foreign and threateningly isolated.

In contrast, from the two privileged women, both living in relatively comfortable circumstances, we heard a 'womanhood' struggling for positive definition and safe boundaries; a sharp splitting of body and mind; maturity as a dividing of self from family and school to find individual identity; an obsessive commitment to using privacy – in body, thought and conversation – as the only way to 'work out' one's problems; all nourishing a highly individualized, privatized and competitive sense of home and community as sites from which they would ultimately leave, unfettered, to launch 'autonomous' lives as independent women. Materially and imaginatively these two women recognized an almost uninterruptable trajectory for future plans. Their 'womanhood' was built on the sense of *self as exception*, 'achievement' meritocratically determining how 'exceptional' each individual can prove herself (away) from the group. Self-as-exception, for women, involves 'transcending' gender. Rachel Hare-Mustin describes the illusion of gender-neutral, 'individualistic' choices:

The liberal/humanist tradition of our epoch assumes that the meanings of our lives reflect individual experience and individual subjectivity. This tradition has idealized individual identity and self-fulfilment and shown a lack of concern about power. Liberalism masks male privilege and dominance by holding that every (ungendered) individual is free. The individual has been regarded as responsible for his or her fate and the basic social order has been regarded as equitable. Liberal humanism implies free choice when individuals are not free of coercion by the social order. (1991: 3)

The invisibility of women's 'coercion by the social order' came out most clearly in Janet's and Sophie's relationships with their working mothers. They did not analyse their mothers' lives for power.

Sophie: 'My mom doesn't like her job but she has to work so I can go to college.' Janet and Sophie said they were afraid of becoming their mothers, unhappy and overworked in jobs they hate, their workloads doubled with domestic responsibilities. 'I fear I might be like her. I want to be independent of her', white middle-class women said of their mothers in the research of Joseph and Lewis (1981: 125). Janet and Sophie said they did not talk much, or very honestly, to their mothers, and did not feel they could ever do enough to gain their mothers' approval. Janet said: 'My mother [says] I really have to go to college . . . be a doctor or a lawyer . . . That's her main goal . . . job security . . . then she wants me to get married and have a nice family . . . preferably Catholic . . . Mom's got my life mapped out.' Ambition and career 'embody' this mother–daughter relationship, in a sense, while the daughter's problems with sexuality and power, and the mother *as woman*, are absent in the relationship Janet describes.

When discussing who they would tell if they had a problem, Shermika immediately said 'My mom' and Damalleaux said 'I tell Shermika almost everything before I tell my mother'. Sophie and Janet agreed only in the negative. It would not be their mothers: 'Don't talk to my mom.'

> *Janet:* I can't tell my mother anything. If I told her something she would ground me for an entire century.
> *Sophie:* Once you tell them one thing, they want to hear more, and they *pry*. I keep my home life and school – social – life so separate.
> *Janet:* . . . I'll be non-committal or I won't tell her the truth. I'll just tell her what she wants to hear.
> *Sophie:* I wish I could talk to my mom. It'd be great if I could.
> *Shermika:* It's the wrong thing to do [not talking], though . . . It always *leads* to problems. My mom tells me so much about life.

Janet said her mother stares at her complexion [her acne] and says,

'You're not going to get married, you're not going to have a boyfriend.' 'I get so mad at her,' Janet says. She tells her mother either 'I'm leaving, I'm leaving' or 'Stop it! Stop it!' Later when Pat asked whether self-respect was learned from her mother, Janet said her self-respect had 'nothing to do with my mother. I used to hate myself, partly because of my mother. But not anymore. My mother's opinion just doesn't matter to me.' Sophie said,

> My mother . . . nitpicks . . . I'm sure it was like her mom [who] never approved anything about her. I get self-respect from my mom because she wants me to respect myself . . . I don't think she respects herself enough. I respect her more than she respects herself. Her mother belittled her so much.

Later Sophie said, 'I have the feeling that no matter what I do, it's not enough.' Janet said her mother makes her and her sister feel like her mother's 'racehorses':

> My mom *lives* through her kids. Two daughters: two *chances*. My sister wants to be an actress and my parents hate that [dykey] way she looks . . . My mom: 'You're just not *feminine* enough!' I'm just like, 'Mom, grow up!' . . . She compares her daughters to everyone else's. [One example is] a straight-A student on top of all her chores . . . I know there's things in her personality that are part of myself . . . We're just like racehorses . . . 'My daughter has three wonderful children and a husband who makes a million dollars a year.'

Janet and Sophie described their mothers as supports you get over, central to the life these daughters wished to escape, and to revise, in their own futures. Within their liberal discourse of free choice, the inequalities of power determining their mothers' misery were invisible to them – and their own exceptional futures also unquestioned.

The Body: Boundaries and Connections

Over our dinners we created a democracy of feminist differences. That is, all four, as an age/gender cohort, introduced us to the female body in play within gendered politics. These young women consistently recast *our* prioritizing of sex at the centre of feminist politics into *their* collective critique of gender politics. Using a language that analysed dominance and power, they refused to separate sex from other power relations. Perhaps even more deeply Foucauldian than we assumed ourselves to be, they deconstructed our voyeurism with examples of sexuality as only one embodied site through which gendered politics operate. All four shared a distrust of men – 'they think they have power . . .'. But they also distrusted female solidarity – 'they back stab you all the time'. Their examples overturned our notions of sisterhood by showing us that both young women and young men proficiently police the borders, and tenets, of masculinity and femininity among today's teens. They are often reminded of their bodies as a public site (gone right or wrong), commented on and monitored by others – male and female. But as often, they reminded us, they forcefully reclaim their bodies by talking back, and by talking feminist. 'It'd be harder not to talk,' Sophie thinks, 'It'd be harder to sit and swallow whatever people are saying.'

Resonating much of feminist literature, when these four young women spoke of their bodies, it was clear that they found themselves sitting centrally at the nexus of race, class and gender politics. **Gender** determines that the young women are subject to external surveillance and responsible for internal body management, and it is their gender that makes them feel vulnerable to male sexual threat and assault. **Culture and class** determine how; that is, the norms of body and the codes of surveillance, management, threat, assault, and resistance available to them.

Susan Bordo (1990) writes about body management as a text for 'the controlling'/'controlling the' middle class. Reflecting both elite material status and a pure, interior soul, this fetish of body management, operated by the 'normalizing machinery of power', produces a desire to control flesh otherwise out of control, as it positions individuals within an elite class location. The tight svelte body reflects material and moral comfort, while the loose sagging body falls to the 'lumpen'. Bordo's cultural analysis of the representations and experiences of women's bodies and women's revulsion at sagging fat, captures and yet too narrowly homogenizes what the four young women reported.

Each of the four, as Bordo would argue, was meticulously concerned with her body as the site for cataloguing both her own and others' 'list' of her inadequacies. Indeed, each body had become the space within which she would receive unsolicited advice about having 'too many pimples', 'being too chocolate', 'looking chubby', 'becoming too thin', 'looking like a boy', or in the case of a sister, dressing 'very butch'. The fetish to control, however, was experienced in ways deeply classed and raced. While the more privileged women were familiar with, if not obsessed by, eating disorders now fashionable among their status peers, the African-American women were quite literally bewildered at the image of a young woman binging on food, and then purging. Therein lies a serious problematic in white feminist literatures – class and culture practices are coded exclusively as *gender*, reinforcing hegemonic definitions of (white) womanhood, while obscuring class/culture contours of the body.

For these women, the female body not only signified a site of interior management *vis-à-vis* male attention/neglect. It was also a site for gendered politics enacted through sexual violence. Celia Kitzinger (1988), in an analysis of how 2,000 young women and men frame their personal experiences with 'unfairness', found that 24 per cent of interviewed girls spontaneously volunteered instances of body-centred unfairness, including sexual harassment, rape and/or abuse. So too, violence stories were offered by all four of the young women, each particular to her social context:

> When I got my first boyfriend [he] pressured me to have sex with him. That's why I didn't never go over his house. (Damalleaux)
>
> I feel safe nowhere. (Sophie)
>
> When he pulled a gun on me, I said, 'This is over.' (Shermika)
>
> I know it's unlikely, but I am terrified of someday being date raped. It's always been something I've been afraid of. (Janet)

For Janet, violence is imagined as possible because of the stories of her friends. For Sophie, violence is encountered as harassment on the street. For Damalleaux and Shermika, violence is encountered or threatened in relations with boyfriends.

> *Michelle:* Is there any place where guys have more power than you?
> *Damalleaux:* In bed.
> *Shermika:* In the street. In the store, when he has all the money.
> *Damalleaux:* And all the guys can beat girls. But I don't think it's true.
>
> *Michelle:* Are you ever afraid that the hitting will get bad?
> *Shermika:* Yeah, that's why I don't do so much hitting.
> *Damalleaux:* When I go out with a boy I hit him a lot to see if he's going to do anything . . . You hit me once, I don't want anything to do with you.
>
> *Shermika:* Sometimes you can get raped with words, though. You feel so slimy . . . The guy at the newspaper stand, I speak to him every morning. Then one day he said, 'How old are you? I can't wait till you 16.' And I told my mom, and she came [with me and told him off]. He lost respect. He didn't give me none. And that day I felt bad, what was I, bein' too loose? .. You just can't help feelin' like that [slimy].

Liz Kelly offers this definition of sexual violence:

> Sexual violence includes any physical, visual, verbal or sexual act that is experienced by the woman or girl, at the time or later, as a threat, invasion or assault, that has the effect of degrading or hurting her and/ or takes away her ability to control intimate contact. (1988: 41)

We found that the fear and/or experience of surviving male violence was indeed central. But its expression was, again, classed and raced. These fears and experiences were deeply traumatic to all the women, and yet the African-American women more frequently and publicly, if uncomfortably, related them in the context of conversation. For the more elite women assaults and fears were privatized and so left relatively unanalysed, un-challenged and in critical ways 'buried'. For example, Janet's story of a friend's date rape contrasts radically with Shermika's stories of male violence and female resistance.

> *Janet:* That happened to one of my friends.
> *Sophie:* A date rape?
> *Janet:* Sort of . . . He'd been pressuring her for a long time, and she's just 'no no no no'. She's at this party, her [girl] friend says, 'Why don't you just do it?' and she says, 'Because I don't *want* to.' . . . She was drunk, puking. She fell asleep, and the next thing she knows she wakes up and he's on top of her and she's not really happy about it but she didn't do anything about it so she just let it happen. And . . . she was upset about it, she was really angry about it, but there was nothing she could *do* about it? [*Janet's voice rises into a kind of question mark.*] It didn't really bother her, but after that she totally knew who her friends were . . .
> *Sophie:* She could've done something about it.
> *Janet:* . . . I guess we didn't talk about how she really really felt about it. She seemed really comfortable with it after it. She was upset for while. After she –
> *Sophie:* There's no way she was *comfortable* with it.
> *Janet:* She's dealt with it in a way. She's gotten to the point where it doesn't really make her cry to talk about it.

Earlier in the conversation Sophie complained that the popular crowd got drunk at parties and had one-night stands. Somewhat defensive, Janet said aside to Sophie, 'Hey, *I*'ve done that.' Janet's story of the rape included Janet's anger at the girl's girl friend. 'Her *friend* was the hostess of the party and gave her the condoms and told her to go do it.' Betrayal by the girlfriend and the boyfriend, a rape Janet calls 'sort of' a date rape, in a party situation Janet has been in many times, anger and helplessness, talking about it finally without tears: this worst-case scenario of women's sexuality and powerlessness is 'dealt with' by *not* 'talk[ing] about how she really felt about it'. Janet's story was about the social and interior limits on one girl's control, before and after 'sex' she did not want.

In sharp contrast, Shermika offered a story of embodied resistance, through public talk. Michelle asked, 'Have you ever been in a relationship where you felt you were being forced to do what you didn't want to do?' Shermika's answer was immediate and emphatic, 'Yeah, I quit 'em, I quit 'em.' She followed with a story about what happened when she 'quit' the boyfriend who was getting possessive:

> *Shermika:* I almost got killed. Some guy pulled a gun on me . . . He put the gun *to my head*. I said, 'You'd better kill me cause if you don't I'm gonna kill you.' Then he dropped the gun . . . I kicked him where it hurts . . . hard, he had to go to the hospital. I was scared . . .
> *Janet:* What happened – have you ever seen him again?
> *Shermika:* I see him every day.
> *Michelle:* Did you call the cops?
> *Shermika:* Yeah . . . He had to stay in jail [two weeks] till I decided not to press charges . . . Don't nobody around my way playin' like that with them guns . . .

Shermika's examples of male threats and violence all show her and her mother talking back, striking back or disarming the man. The woman is embodied as her own best protector. Shermika followed up her first story (which stunned her audience into awed silence) with a second, another jealous boyfriend: 'He told me if I went with anybody else he'll kill me. And he pulled a knife on me . . . "Stab me. Either way, you ain't gonna have me."' Later she tells a story about her mother:

> My stepfather and my mother were fightin' – it's the only time they ever fought. And he stepped back and hit my momma with all his might. And he thought she was gonna give up. She stepped back and hit *him* with all *her* might – and he fell asleep. She knocked the mess outta him. He never hit her again.

And another about herself, with her mother as model:

> A guy tried to beat me with a belt, and I grabbed it and let him see how it felt to get beat with that belt. My mom wouldn't even take that.

The scars of actual and/or anticipated sexual violence were clear for each of the young women, and always culturally specific as encounter, resistance and recounting.

As with the violence of gender, the violence of racism on the female body was painfully voiced by the three women of colour. Fears of attending a white prep school 'where they'll ignore me', stories of fleeing an integrated school after three weeks and retrospective outbursts of anger at being 'the only woman of colour in my class!' showed a kind of agoraphobia which kept Shermika and Damalleaux in their wholly Black communities, and inversely, created in Janet deep assimilative wishes to disappear into the white suburbs. For Janet the 'white church' in her elite suburban neighbourhood – not the Korean church her parents attend – was the 'safest place' she could imagine.

For Damalleaux and Shermika, the neighbourhood and its school are clearly the only safe place. Damalleaux reported that she had lasted three weeks at an integrated school: 'It was OK but I didn't feel right. I didn't know anybody. I don't like introducing myself to people, I'm too shy ... I came back to the neighbourhood school.'

Shermika was offered a scholarship to go to a 'fancy' private school in a white suburb. When discussing what scares us about the future, Shermika admitted she fears 'being neglected. Not fitting in ... One time I'm goin' in and nobody likes me.' When Michelle asked if that was her fear about the prep school, Shermika said, 'Not as far as the people. But I don't like travelling. And I'm not staying on the campus ... I ain't stayin' away from home, though.' By the time of our second interview, Shermika had convinced her mother to delay her going to prep school, from mid-year till the next fall. Shermika said she feared she would not be able to keep her grades up in the new school. Shermika's reliance on non-standard English meant she would have to manage a major cultural shift both academically and socially. Her only envy of Sophie and Janet's school was what she called its 'socializing' function, that taught them 'how to get along, socialize, fit in, knowin' the right thing to say and do'. Shermika said that when she has a job she wants to stay in her neighbourhood 'where it all happenin' [not] where you won't fit in'. Racial identity, segregation and racism combine to reinforce the boundaries of Shermika's and Damalleaux's lives and futures, by defining where and who is 'safe'.

Shermika evidently decided our dinner table was a 'safe' enough place to explore our own racial (and maybe racist) differences. Shermika asked Janet, 'Are you Chinese?' and Janet said, 'No, Korean', and launched into a story about Japanese racism, including the sale of 'Sambo' dolls in Japan, and then a story about a 4,000-year-old hatred of Koreans for the Japanese. Shermika responded, 'Well, I don't understand that. I mean, I'm supposed to hate somebody white because somebody I know was a slave?' Then Shermika put race and racism right on our dinner table:

Shermika: I walk into a store and Chinese people be starin' at me. [*Shermika was mistaking Korean for Chinese for the third time.*]
Janet: My *mother* does that – I hate that, my *mother* does it. [*Her mother runs a dry cleaner.*] And I'm just like, 'Mom, STOP it.'
Damalleaux: I leave [the store].

Janet: How do you feel when you're the only minority in a room?
Damalleaux: I don't care.
Shermika: I make a joke out of it. I feel like a zebra.

Unlike Janet's experience, the assaultive nature of Shermika's and Damalleaux's encounters with the white world had given them little encouragement to isolate themselves among a white majority. Shermika said her 'darkness' meant she 'looked like a clown' when they put on make-up for her local TV interview about the scholarship programme she is in; then her pride and excitement about the video of herself on TV was clouded by family jokes about her dark skin making her 'invisible' to the camera. Shermika reported plenty of harassment about her dark skin, from girlfriends and boyfriends, even those as dark as herself. 'Choc-late!' was the common, hated term, and Shermika was troubled by its implied racial hierarchy and self-hatred. Atypically, she had no easy 'come-back' for that one.

Race in Sophie's (WASP) experience is about being privileged, and feeling harassed for her blonde and blue-eyed good looks. Janet, for instance, annoys Sophie by calling her the 'Aryan Goddess'. Sophie is harassed on public transportation on her daily commute, where she is in the minority as a white woman (Janet, in contrast, drives from suburb to school). Sophie became exasperated in our interview when she felt targeted for white racism, and said she did not 'notice' race half as often as race identified her in public situations in which she is made to represent WASPhood or white womanhood.

Just as these women co-created for us a shared, if negotiated, sense of body politics, they separated along culture lines in their expressed reliance on social connections and surveillance of bodily borders. The African-American women, for instance, detailed deeply textured and relational lives. They not only care for many, but many also care for them. They give much to others, and received much in return, but do not call it volunteer or charity work – simply 'what I do'. When they receive favours (from mothers and boyfriends), they feel neither 'guilty' nor 'obligated'. Held in a complex web of reciprocal relations, they contribute, easily assured that 'What goes around comes around'. They resonate the writings of Robinson and Ward:

> Nobles' conception of 'the extended self' is seen in the value structure of many black families. Willie (1985) argues that many African American children are encouraged to employ their own personal achievements as a means to resist racism. The importance of hard work and communalism is viewed threefold: as a personal responsibility, as an intergenerational commitment to family, and as a tie to the larger

collective. A resistant strategy of liberation, in keeping with African American traditional values, ties individual achievement to collective struggle. We maintain that in the service of personal and cultural liberation, African American adolescent girls must resist an individualism that sees the self as disconnected from others in the black community and, as it is culturally and psychologically dysfunctional, she must resist those who might advocate her isolation and separation from traditional African American cultural practices, values and beliefs. (1991: 94)

The elite women, in contrast, deployed a language of bodily integrity, patrolled borders, social charity, obligation and guilt. As for any favours of gifts or time from mothers and boyfriends, they felt a need to 'pay back'. Bearing often quite deeply hostile feelings toward their mothers, they nevertheless both feel obligated to repay her sacrifices by fulfilling her expectations, often a professional career in return for a gigantic tuition bill. As vigilantly, they monitor their social and bodily boundaries for what and how much comes in and leaves – food, drink, drugs, exercise, money, sacrifices and gifts. And they give back to community in the form of 'charity'. They live their connections almost contractually.

Related to these contrasting forms of body-in-relation, these two groups performed quite differently within our *public talk*. That is, they parted sharply in terms of how much they hibernated in privacy, how much they revealed themselves through talk. In numerous instances, the white and Korean teens deferred to a 'cultural privacy' in which 'personal problems' were rarely aired. 'Personal grievances' were typically suffocated. 'Personal disagreements' were usually revealed 'behind our backs'. They often withheld juicy details of life, safe only in diaries or other private writings. Their bodies absorbed, carried and embodied their 'private troubles'. These elite girls made it quite clear that their strategies for survival were interior, personal and usually not shared. The costs of 'privilege', as they revealed them, were in internalizing, personalizing and de-politicizing gender dilemmas. Research makes evident these costs in anorexia, bulimia, depression, 'talking behind each other's back' and even the 'secrets' of rape or abuse survival stories. Socialized out of using public talk to practise varied forms of womanhood, these women recognized collective gender power struggles, and retreated from women. They embodied their resistance alone, through feminist individualism.

The individualism from which modern feminism was born has much to answer for but much in which to take pride. Individualism has decisively repudiated previous notions of hierarchy and particularism to declare the possibility of freedom for all. In so doing, it transformed slavery from one unfree condition among many into freedom's antithesis – thereby insisting that the subordination of one person to any other is morally and politically unacceptable. But the gradual extension of individualism and the gradual abolition of the remaining forms of social and political bondage have come trailing after two dangerous notions: that individual freedom could – indeed must – be absolute, and that social role and personal identity must be coterminous.

Following the principles of individualism, modern Western societies have determined that the persistence of slavery in any form violates the fundamental principle of a just society. But in grounding the justification in absolute individual right, they have unleashed the specter of a radical individualism that overrides the claims of society itself. To the extent that feminism, like antislavery, has espoused those individualistic principles, it has condemned itself to the dead ends toward which individualism is now plunging. (Fox-Genovese, 1991: 240–1)

In contrast, the African-American women were publicly playful as well as nasty to each other, and about others, 'because we love each other'. Shermika told wonderful, vivid, outrageous tales, in part to 'test' what the others would do, including, we believe, testing whether she was being classified as exotic/sexualized/other/ specimen for the white women and the evening's analysis. Their school context made their bodies a matter of public talk. Exposed.

> *Shermika:* I don't like my rear end. Guys are so ignorant. 'Look at all that cake.'
> *Pat:* Maybe it's their problem.
> *Shermika:* No it *is* my problem. Because you see my butt before you see me.

Public talk could be aggression as well:

> *Damalleaux:* I wouldn't talk to him [a stranger] and he got mad.
> *Shermika:* I hate when they constantly talk to you and they get closer and closer.

The African-American women used and experienced conversation, public disagreements, pleasures and verbal badgerings as ways to 'try on' varied ways to be women.

During the second evening the four young women discovered and explored these differences through the metaphor of the 'private' and 'public' schools they attend.

> *Janet:* I've got a question. At [your school, Shermika] are there kids who are like by themselves? Loners . . . who don't sit with anyone else? . . . who nobody wants to sit with?

Shermika: Yeah but they can't because there's somebody always messin' with 'em, tryin' to get 'em to do something. So if they wanted to be by themselves they couldn't.

Janet: At our school it's so easy to get shut out when you're by yourself.

Sophie: You just kind of – disappear.

Janet: They don't say it [criticism or insult] in front of your face.

Sophie: You insult someone by not considering them . . . You don't consider their existence . . .

Shermika: . . . Sometimes people need you to tell them how you feel . . .

Janet: . . . for the most part when I'm mad at someone I don't say it to them.

Sophie: Only one on one. You don't say it to them in front of others unless you're joking. It's more private.

Shermika: But if you say it *to* the person, you avoid fights . . . If they hear you saying it behind their back, they wanna fight.

The four pursued this discovered difference between the 'private' and the 'public' school.

Shermika: Ain't nothin' private at my school. If someone got gonorrhoea, everyone knows it.

Sophie: Everything's private at my school.

Janet: Cause nobody really cares about each other at our school . . .

Shermika: In our school, when I found out I had cancer, I heard about it on the loudspeaker. And everybody come and offer me help. When you're havin' problems in our school, people talk. That's why they're more mature at my school – excuse me. Say somebody poor, need name brand sneaks, they'll put they money together and give 'em some sneaks. And teachers do that too, if someone need food.

Sophie: We like to pretend that we're good to the neighbourhood and socially conscious.

Over time, we came to see that 'the facts' of these young women's lives were neither what we had invited them to reveal in our conversations, nor what they were giving us. Rather, we were gathering their interpretations of their lives, interpretations which were roaming within culture and class.

On Good and Bad Girls: Prospects for Feminism

'I consider myself a bad girl,' Shermika explained, 'but in a good sorta way.' Feminist scholars as distinct as Valerie Walkerdine, Carol Gilligan and Nancy Lesko have written about polarizations of good girls and bad ones; that is, those who resist, submit or split on the cultural script of femininity. Gilligan's essay 'Joining the Resistance' (1990) argues that at the outset of adolescence, young women experience a severing of insider from outsider knowledge, such that 'insider knowledge may be washed away'. Gilligan and her colleagues have found that young women at early adolescence begin to submerge their interior knowledge, increasingly relying on 'I don't know' to answer questions about self. They say 'I don't know' at a rate amazingly greater the older they get – an average of twice at age 7, 21 times at age 12, 67 times at age 13. Gilligan and colleagues conclude: 'If girls' knowledge of reality is politically dangerous, it is both psychologically and politically dangerous for girls not to know . . . or to render themselves innocent by disconnecting from their bodies, their representations of experience and desire' (1988: 33).

Nancy Lesko (1988) has written a compelling ethnography of gendered adolescents' lives inside a Catholic high school, where she unpacks a 'curriculum of the body', mediated by class distinctions. In this school female delinquency was sexualized and 'embodied'. The genders segregated in high school by class, and created categories of behaviours to hang on to within these class groups. The rich and popular girls at her school paraded popular fashions, spoke in controlled voices, muted their opinions and worked hard at 'being nice'. If they pushed the boundaries of wardrobe, it was always in the direction of fashion, not 'promiscuity'. The 'burnouts', in contrast, were young women who fashioned their behaviours through smoking and directness. They rejected compulsions towards being 'nice' and excelled at being 'blunt'. Refusing to bifurcate their 'personal' opinions and their public stances, they challenged docility and earned reputations as 'loose' and 'hard' (like Leslie Roman's (1988) working-class women who displayed physicality and sexual embodiment). Social class, then, provided the contours within which a curriculum of the body had its meaning displayed, intensifying within gender oppositions, and undermining possibilities for female solidarity.

Departing somewhat from Gilligan and Lesko, Valerie Walkerdine (1984) sees adolescence for young women as a moment not to *bury* the questioning female 'self', but a time in which young women must *negotiate* their multiple selves, through struggles of heterosexuality, and critiques of gender, race and class arrangements. In an analysis of popular texts read by adolescent women, Walkerdine finds that 'heroines are never angry; most project anger onto others and suppress it in self, yielding the active production of passivity' (1984: 182). She asks readers to consider that 'good girls are not always good, [but] when and how is their badness lived?' Interested in the splitting of goodness and badness we, like Walkerdine, asked these young women that question.

When Shermika said, 'I consider myself a bad girl, but in a good sorta way,' she was positioning herself in our collectively made feminist context where *good girls* follow femininity rules, and *bad* girls do not. This good kind of bad girl plays by male rules of friendship, risk, danger and initiative.

Within five minutes of our first meeting, the four girls discovered they all liked (American) football, *playing* football, and they eagerly described the joys of running, catching the ball, tackling and being tackled. Only Janet drew the line at being tackled, citing a '300-pound boy' in her neighbourhood. As an explanation for their preferred identities as 'one of the guys', football exemplifies 'masculine' values of gamesmanship. It is a game with rules and space for spontaneous physicality, with teamwork and individual aggression in rule-bound balance, and with maximum bodily access to others of both sexes, without fear about sexual reputation or reproductive consequences. When asked why they trust and like boys over girls, they cited boys' risk-taking making them more fun, their ability to 'be more honest' and not backstab, 'be more accepting', 'You can tell when a guy's lyin'.' 'First of all they won't even notice what you're wearing and they won't bust on you.' Shermika bragged that all of her boyfriends said they valued her most as a friend, not merely a girlfriend. The behaviour, clothing and values associated with such identification with boys and sports suggests both a flight from the 'femininity' they collectively described as 'wearing pink', 'being prissy', 'bein' Barbie', and 'reinforcing guys all the time' – *and* an association of masculinity with fairness (vs cattiness), honesty (vs backstabbing), strength (vs prissiness, a vulnerability whether feigned or real), initiative (vs deference or reactionary comments), and integrity (vs the self-doubt and conflicting loyalties dividing girls). The four's risk-taking behaviours – driving fast, sneaking out at night – reinforced identities as 'one of the guys'. Such are the Bad Girls.

But being 'one of the guys' makes for a contradictory position of self versus 'other girls'. Sophie mocked the femininity of good girls, at its worst when she said dismissively, 'You should sit and wait in your little crystal palace' rather than 'chase after guys'. This constructed difference between self – the good kind of good girl – and other girls – the bad kind of good girl – is an essential contradiction of identity that all four girls were struggling with. Valerie Hey in her study of adolescent female friendships calls this 'deficit dumping': all the 'bad' bits of femininity, social and sexual competitiveness, placed upon the 'other', that is, other girls (1987: 421). Sophie, like the girls in Valerie Hey's study, excepted her best friend along with her self from the generality of femininity:

'It's different though with best friends. I mean like girls in general.' Shermika likewise excepted Damalleaux when Michelle asked whether *no* other girls were to be trusted. 'She a boy,' Shermika countered, raising a puzzled laugh. But when Shermika's boyfriend likened her to a bodybuilder when she was running track, she felt ashamed to 'feel like a boy . . . like a muscle man'.

Sophie confessed ruefully, 'I'm certainly no bad girl,' and Janet taunted her, 'Sophie has a little halo.' Certainly Sophie's good grades, good works, politeness, friendliness, trustworthiness, were acceptably 'good' to both adults and peers, even if the popular crowd had not approved or welcomed her. 'I don't want that image,' Sophie told Janet about the halo. Goody-goodyism would be unacceptable to *all* peers. Good-*girl*ism – Sophie's uncomfortable state – seems 'good' for her conscience and adult approval, but 'bad' for approval by the popular set, whose upper-class drink-and-drug-induced party flirtations and sexual liaisons Sophie disapproves of. The meaning of Sophie's good-girl image is, however, quite class-specific, as Mary Evans describes in her analysis of middle-class schooling, *A Good School*:

> as far as possible a 'good' girl did not have an appearance. What she had was a correct uniform, which gave the world the correct message about her – that is, that she was a well-behaved, sensible person who could be trusted not to wish to attract attention to herself by an unusual, let alone a fashionable appearance. (1991: 30–1)

Signalling her acceptance of the career-class uniform, Sophie could not also signal her interest in boys. Indeed, she walked away from her body, except as an athletic court. 'Other girls' dressed either 'schleppy' (the androgynous or indifferent look) or 'provocative'. Sophie's neat, 'sporty' look – tights and a lean body made her miniskirt look more athletic than hooker-inspired – seems designed to be comfortable and competent as one-of-the-guys while ever-so-casually gesturing toward femininity (no dykey trousers). Her dress is designed to bridge the contradiction of middle-class education and femininity, as Mary Evans describes it in her own schooling in the 1950s:

> To be a successful [prep] school girl involved, therefore, absorbing two specific (but conflicting) identities. First, that of the androgynous middleclass person who is academically successful in an academic world that is apparently gender blind. Second, that of the well-behaved middleclass woman who knows how to defer to and respect the authority of men. (1991: 23)

Feminism has altered, over history, their terms of deference to men, their ability to name sexism and resist. But their feminism does not seem to have revised the categories of 'gender' or 'body' at all. What seems intact from the 1950s is their terms of respect for the authority of men as superior and normal forms of human being. What seems distinct in the 1990s is that these young women think they have a right to be young men too.

Damalleaux's example of her own good-girlism shares some of Sophie's dilemma of being a good student at the expense of peer popularity. But Damalleaux resolved this tension differently, as Signthia Fordham (1988) would argue is likely to happen among academically talented low-income African-American students:

> *Damalleaux:* I used to be a straight-A girl and now I'm down to Bs and Cs. I used to be so good it's a shame . . .
> *Pat:* What changed?
> *Damalleaux:* I couldn't help it any more . . . When I got straight As they'd call me a nerd and things. But I'd be happy because my mother would give me anything I want for it . . . Mom [would say to teasing brothers] 'Leave my first girl alone!' . . . [Then] I got around the wrong people, I don't study so much . . .
> *Pat:* Is it uncool to be a girl and get good grades?
> *Damalleaux:* Yes it is . . . I'll do my work and they'll say 'Smarty Pants! Smarty Pants!'

Janet gave an example of 'acting stupid' with peers, which seemed to be her manner of flirtation. Sophie pointed out that Janet could afford to because everybody already knew she was smart. Sophie clearly felt more trapped by being a smart and a good girl.

Girls can be good, bad or – best of all – they can be boys. This version of individualized resistance, or feminism, reflects a retreat from the collective politics of gender, and from other women, and an advance into the embattled scene of gender politics – alone, and against boys, in order to become one of them.

On Closings, or, The End of the Second Pizza

We heard these four women struggling between the discourses of feminism and adolescence. Perhaps struggling is even too strong a word. They hungered for a strong version of individualistic, 'gender-free' adolescence and had rejected that which had been deemed traditionally feminine, aping instead that which had been deemed traditionally masculine. Delighted to swear, spit, tell off-colour jokes, wear hats and trash other girls, they were critical of individual boys, nasty about most girls, rarely challenging of the sex/gender system, and were ecstatic, for the most part, to be engaged as friends and lovers with young men. But we also heard their feminism in their collective refusal to comply with male demands, their wish for women friends to trust, their expectations for equality and search for respect, their deep ambivalence about being 'independent of a man' and yet in partnership with one, and their strong yearnings to read, write and talk more about women's experiences among women. They appreciated our creation of a context in which this was possible. 'The women of Michelle's place', Shermika called us at the end of one evening, prizing our collectivity by re-using a black woman writer's novel title.

> The public terms of the discourse of femininity preclude the expression of deviant views of marriage, motherhood, and the public terms are the only ones to which girls have access. Part of the task of feminist work with girls is thus, I would suggest, giving girls terms in which to express their experiential knowledge, rather than having to fall back into the stereotyped expressions of normatively defined femininity in order to say anything at all about areas of life which vitally concern them. (Hudson, 1984: 52)

Through **critical and collaborative group interview** we evolved a form of conversation, what Hudson might call feminist work, with these four young women which allowed us to engage in what we might consider **collective consciousness work**, as a form of feminist methodology. Our 'talks' became an opportunity to 'try on' ways of being women, struggling through power, gender, culture and class.

With Donna Haraway's (1989) notion of 'partial vision' firmly in mind, we realized that in our talk, no one of us told the 'whole truth'. We all occluded the 'truth' in cultured ways. The conversation was playful and filled with the mobile positionings of all of us women. While we each imported gender, race, class, culture, age and bodies to our talk, we collectively created an ideological dressing room in which the six of us could undress a little, try things on, exchange, rehearse, trade and critique. Among the six of us we were able to lift up what had become 'personal stories', raise questions, try on other viewpoints and re-see our stories as narratives through power.

> As a critique of the excesses of individualism, feminism potentially contributes to a new conception of community – of the relation between the freedom of individuals and the needs of society. The realization of that potential lies not in the repudiation of difference but in a new understanding of its equitable social consequences. (Fox-Genovese, 1991: 256)

We could recount together how alone and frightened we have each felt as we have walked, and are watched, down city streets;

how our skin tightens when we hear men comment aloud on our bodies; how we smart inside with pain when we learn that other women define themselves as 'good women' by contrasting themselves with our feminist politics; how we fetishize those body parts that have betrayed us with their imperfection. Within the safety of warm listening and caring, yet critical talk, we attached each of these 'secret' feelings to political spaces defined by culture, class and gender contours of our daily lives. This method moved us, critically and collectively, from pain to passion to power, prying open the ideologies of individualism, privacy and loyalty which had sequestered our 'personal stories'.

After our last dinner, stuffed and giggly, tired but still wanting just one more round of conversation, we – Pat and Michelle – realized that the four young women were getting ready to drive away. Together and without us. Before, Pat had driven Shermika and Damalleaux to Michelle's and home. But now they were leaving us behind. Stunned, we looked at each other, feeling abandoned. We thought we were concerned about their safety. Four young women in a car could meet dangers just outside the borders of Michelle's block.

We turned to each other realizing that even our abandonment was metaphoric and political. These four young women were weaving the next generation of feminist politics, which meant, in part, leaving us. We comforted ourselves by recognizing that our conversation had perhaps enabled this work. No doubt, individual interviews with each of the four would have produced an essay chronicling the damages of femininity – eating disorders, heterosexual traumas, perhaps some abuse or abortion stories; that is, deeply individualized, depoliticized and atomized tales of 'things that have happened to me as an adolescent female'. What happened among us instead was that a set of connections was forged – between personal experiences and power, across cultures, classes and politics, and within an invented space, cramped between the discourses of a rejected *femininity*, an individualized *adolescence* and a collective *feminism as resistance*.

Resistance is that struggle we can most easily grasp. Even the most subjected person has moments of rage and resentment so intense that they respond, they act against. There is an inner uprising that leads to rebellion, however short-lived. It may be only momentary, but it takes place. That space within oneself where resistance is possible remains: It is different then to talk about becoming subjects. That process emerges as one comes to understand how structures of domination work in one's own life, as one develops critical thinking and critical consciousness, as one invents new alternative habits of being and resists from that marginal space of difference inwardly defined. (hooks, 1990: 15)

In our finest post-pizza moment, we – Pat and Michelle – realized that as these women drove off, they were inventing their own feminist legacy, filled with passions, questions, differences and power. We were delighted that we had helped to challenge four young women's versions of individualistic feminism, without solidarity, by doing the consciousness work of our generation. We taught, and relearned, feminism as a dialectical and historical discourse about experience and its interpretations, a collective reframing of private confessions. As we yelled, 'Go straight home!' to their moving car, for a moment we felt like the world was in very good hands.

Notes

'Over dinner: feminism and adolescent female bodies' by Michelle Fine and Pat Macpherson. Copyright by the University of Michigan 1992. Originally published by the University of Michigan Press. Reprinted with the permission of the University of Michigan Press.

Many thanks are due to Elizabeth Sayre for her patient assistance.

1 And, although not at the table, it is still another thing to construct a sense of womanhood by and for women whose disabilities socially and sexually 'neuter' them, propelling them out of any presumed relation with men, and depriving them of the many burdens of being female, including the privileges that come with those burdens in experiences such as sexual harassment, motherhood, sexually, having others rely on you, etc. Disabled women's identities are rarely positioned under, against or with men's. As Kathryn Corbett, Adrienne Asch and Michelle Fine, Harilyn Rousso and others have written (Asch and Fine, 1988), it is no blessing for the culture to presume that because you are disabled, you are not female; not worth whistling at; not able to love an adult man or woman; not capable of raising a child; not beautiful enough to be employed in a public space.

References

Anderson, E. (1990) *Streetwise: Race, Class and Change in an Urban Community.* Chicago: University of Chicago Press.

Asch, A. and Fine, M. (1988) 'Shared dreams: a left perspective on disability rights and reproductive rights', in M. Fine and A. Asch (eds), *Women with Disabilities: Essays in Psychology, Culture and Politics.* Philadelphia, Pa: Temple University Press, pp. 297–305.

Baker, H. (1989) Personal communication.

Bordo, S. (1990) 'Reading the slender body', in M. Jacobus, E. Fox Keller and S. Shuttleworth (eds), *Body/Politics: Women and the Discourses of Science.* New York: Routledge, pp. 31–53.

Brodkey, L. and Fine, M. (1988) 'Presence of mind in the absence of body', *Journal of Education*, 170(3): 84–99.

Corbett, K., with Klein, S. and Bregante, J. (1987) 'The role of sexuality and sex equity in the education of disabled women', *Peabody Journal of Education*, 64(4): 198–212.

Evans, M. (1991) *A Good School: Life at a Girl's Grammar School in the 1950s*. London: The Women's Press.

Fine, M. (1988) 'Sexuality, schooling and adolescent females: the missing discourse of desire', *Harvard Educational Review*, 58(1): 29–53.

Fine, M. and Asch, A. (1988) 'Disability beyond stigma: social interaction, discrimination and activism', *Journal of Social Issues*, 44(1): 3–22.

Fordham, S. (1988) 'Racelessness as a factor in Black students' school success', *Harvard Educational Review*, 58(1), 54–84.

Fox-Genovese, E. (1991) *Feminism without Illusions: a Critique of Individualism*. Chapel Hill, NC: University of Carolina Press.

Frank, G. (1988) 'On embodiment: a case study of congenital limb deficiency in American culture', in M. Fine and A. Asch (eds), *Women with Disabilities: Essays in Psychology, Culture and Politics*. Philadelphia, Pa: Temple University Press, pp. 41–71.

Giddings, P. (1984) *When and Where I Enter: the Impact of Black Women on Race and Sex in America*. New York: Bantam.

Gilligan, C. (1990) 'Joining the resistance: psychology, politics, girls and women'. Essay presented as the Tanner Lecture on Human Values, University of Michigan.

Gilligan, C., Wards, J. and Taylor, J. (1988) *Mapping the Moral Domain*. Cambridge, Mass.: Harvard University Press.

Halson, J. (1991) 'Young women, sexual harassment and heterosexuality: violence, power relations and mixed sex schooling', in P. Abbott and C. Wallace (eds), *Gender, Power and Sexuality*. London: Macmillan, pp. 97–113.

Haraway, D. (1989) *Prime Visions: Gender, Race, and Nature in the World of Modern Science*. New York: Routledge.

Hare-Mustin, R.T. (1991) 'Sex, lies, and headaches: the problem is power', in T.J. Goodrich (ed.), *Women and Power: Perspectives for Therapy*. New York: Norton, pp. 63–85.

Hey, V. (1987) '"The company she keeps": the social and interpersonal construction of girls' same sex friendships'. PhD dissertation, University of Kent at Canterbury, England.

hooks, b. (1984) *Feminist Theory from Margin to Center*. Boston, Mass.: South End Press.

hooks, b. (1990) *Yearning: Race, Gender, and Cultural Politics*. Boston: South End Press.

Hudson, B. (1984) 'Femininity and adolescence', in A. McRobbie and M. Nava (eds), *Gender and Generation*. London: Macmillan, pp. 31–53.

Joseph, G. and Lewis, J. (1981) *Common Differences: Conflicts in Black and White Feminist Perspectives*. Boston, Mass.: South End Press.

Kelly, L. (1988) *Surviving Sexual Violence*. Oxford: Basil Blackwell.

Kitzinger, C. (1988) '"It's not fair on girls": young women's accounts of unfairness in school'. Paper presented at the British Psychological Society Conference, University of Leeds.

Lather, P. (1991) *Getting Smart: Feminist Research and Pedagogy within the Postmodern*. New York: Routledge.

Lesko, N. (1988) 'The curriculum of the body: lessons from a Catholic high school,' in L. Roman, L.K. Christian-Smith and E. Ellsworth (eds), *Becoming Feminine: the Politics of Popular Culture*. Philadelphia, Pa: Falmer Press, pp. 123–42.

Mohanty, C. (1987) 'Feminist encounters: locating the politics of experience', *Copyright*, 1: 39.

Orbach, S. (1986) *Hunger Strike: the Anorectic's Struggle as a Metaphor for Our Age*. New York: Norton.

Payne, M. (1991) 'Canon: the New Testament to Derrida', *College Literature*, 18(2): 5–21.

Robinson, T. and Ward, J.V. (1991) '"A belief in self far greater than anyone's disbelief": cultivating resistance among African-American female adolescents', *Woman and Therapy*, 2: nos 3–4, pp. 87–104.

Roman, L.G. (1988) 'Intimacy, labor, and class: ideologies of feminine sexuality in the punk slam dance', in L. Roman, L.K. Christian-Smith and E. Ellsworth (eds), *Becoming Feminine: the Politics of Popular Culture*. Philadelphia, Pa: Falmer Press, pp. 143–84.

Spelman, E. (1988) *Inessential Woman*. Boston, Mass.: Beacon Press.

Walkerdine, V. (1984) 'Some day my prince will come: young girls and the preparation for adolescent sexuality', in A. McRobbie and M. Nava (eds), *Gender and Generation*. London: Macmillan, pp. 162–84.

Willie, C.V. (1985) *Black and White Families: a Study in Complementarity*. Dix Hill, NY: General Hall.

12

Separation, Integration and Difference: Contradictions in a Gender Regime

Wendy Hollway

Connell defines the term 'gender regime' as 'the historically produced state of play in gender relations within an institution which can be analysed by taking a structural inventory' (1990: 523). In this chapter I use his framework to analyse the gender regime in the Tanzanian civil service from the perspective of women managers.[1] Connell suggests three structures as a preliminary taxonomy of gender relations: a gendered division of labour, a structure of power and a structure of cathexis (Connell, 1987: 96–7; 1990: 523–6).

1 **A gendered division of labour.** This includes:
   organization of housework and childcare;
   division between paid and unpaid work;
   segregation in labour markets (women's and men's jobs);
   discrimination in training and promotion;
   unequal wages and unequal exchange.
2 **A structure of power.** This includes:
   hierarchies of state and business;
   institutional and interpersonal violence;
   sexual regulation and surveillance;
   domestic authority and its contestation.
3 **A structure of cathexis** or 'the construction of emotionally charged social relationships' (1987: 112). This includes:
   the patterning of object choice;
   desire and desirability;
   the production of heterosexuality and homosexuality and the relationship between them;
   the socially structured antagonisms of gender, trust and distrust;
   jealousy and solidarity in marriages and other relationships;
   the emotional relationships involved in child-rearing.

According to Connell, the first structure is based on the principle of separation and the second on the principle of unequal integration. He does not suggest a principle for the third. I suggest that it is the emotional investment in gender difference. Gender analyses have confronted the question of how subjectivity is fundamentally gendered and how structures and practices are reproduced or modified through subjectivity. Sex-role and socialization theories have been criticized for failing to provide an account which can explain the emotionally entrenched aspects of gender relations (Henriques et al., 1984). The structure of cathexis requires an analysis of the emotional investment in gendered subjectivity which reproduces gender-differentiated power relations.

According to Connell, structures constrain practice through providing a given form of social organization (1987: 92). However, practice provides the dynamic of change: 'practice, while presupposing structure . . . is always responding to a *situation*. Practice is the transformation of that situation in a particular direction. To describe structure is to specify what it is in the situation that constrains the play of practice' (1987: 95). My previous analyses have tended to use a Foucauldian framework of the relations among power, knowledge and practice; an analysis which might be assumed to be inconsistent with a 'structuralist' approach. However, by identifying multiple structures and sub-structures, rather than one monolithic structure of patriarchal dominance, and by Connell's emphasis on the dynamics of practice in the context of multiplicity and contradiction, the two approaches are consistent.

In this analysis therefore the structures of gender relations are conceived as multiple and potentially in contradiction and it is this assertion that I test out against the Tanzanian civil service data.

Contradictions between and among the three structures are not only important nodes for analysis but guides for practice. For example, the stipulated terms of service for women and men civil servants are identical. However, when it comes to postings around the country, wives are expected to follow their husbands and the converse is almost unheard of. Women's careers routinely suffer. In terms of the gendered division of labour (structure 1), the bureaucracy offers formal equality. In terms of authority, control and coercion (structure 2), men's interests win out. Men's authority is underpinned by emotional investments (structure 3), such that a husband would often feel not only his authority, but also his masculinity, threatened if his wife's career dictated his movements. Moreover, the wife would often regard it as her duty to follow his posting. As one woman told us 'I was not bitter at having to move because of my husband's posting because I believed that I had to make the sacrifice.'

In the following three sections, I document some of the phenomena which Connell classifies under the three structures (though these are not neatly separable). Connell's taxonomy refers to gender relations across all the institutions of society: it was not intended to be limited to work organizations. It is widely acknowledged that the splitting of knowledge into work and domestic spheres has hindered the understanding of women's positions and I make links across work and domestic life and across public and private spheres in this analysis. In the final section, I draw out the analysis in terms of the contradictions among and between these.

The Gendered Division of Labour

Tanzania is an agrarian country, with most people living in rural areas and more than four-fifths of the labour force engaged in agriculture. More than 70 per cent of women are engaged in small cash crop and food crop peasant production and they produce 70 per cent of all the food in Tanzania (Hollway and Mukurasi, in press).

Traditionally, authority rests with the older men of the community and the man, as husband and father, has head-of-household rights which have not been challenged by a wave of women's liberation as in the West. While women have virtually sole responsibility for childcare, men's legal rights to their children remain almost unchallenged.

In the Arusha Declaration of 1967 the Tanzanian government announced a policy of socialism and self-reliance. The public sector was intended to play a leading role in the development process. The government's recognition that the human resource needed to be the major force of development was important in encouraging the employment of educated women, because it provided women with legitimate grounds for claiming equal treatment, in contrast to their prior exclusion on the grounds of sex. Thus in the civil service there is no formal segregation of professional women. As elsewhere, however, most women's employment is in stereotypically women's fields, such as education and health. The government takes responsibility for placing all graduates who seek employment in the public sector. It tends to direct more women into the civil service than into the parastatals (government-owned organizations). Within the civil service more women are in personnel management and few are finance management officers.

The government enacted legislation and issued a number of policy directives aimed at eliminating gender discrimination in employment. For example a Civil Service standing order, applicable also to the parastatal sector, provides that 'all employment will be open to women who are suitably qualified, and there will be no difference between the salary and other terms of service of men and women officers of equivalent qualifications and experience' (Government Standing Orders D20). With regard to the civil service's employment of graduates, this is largely achieved in practice, so major inequalities under the headings of segregation of labour markets and unequal wages and exchange can be ruled out.

Organization of Housework and Childcare
Women are responsible for organizing, if not for actually doing, all housework and childcare. Labour-saving devices such as freezers, vacuum cleaners and washing machines are out of the reach of even most professional families. Graduate women tend to marry younger and have more children than graduate women in the West. There are no nursery facilities and working women rely heavily either on their mothers or, more frequently, on a 'housegirl', who may be a relative come to live with the family. In a low-wage economy, housegirls are paid less than unskilled men, and a family member may earn little more than her keep. A housegirl's reliability is an important factor in a woman's availability to commit herself to her job. The gender structuring of the unskilled labour market thus reinforces the domestic division of labour between professional couples, since it provides one means whereby women can sustain their dual responsibility.

Despite the fact that most educated women are from privileged families, the majority must work because the family's financial viability depends on it. None the less the domestic division of labour remains unchanged and virtually unchallenged.

The civil service provides for either parent to take time off to care for a sick child. However it is extremely unusual for a man to do so, unless his wife is away. Most men feel that it would be a slight on a husband's masculinity.

Discrimination at Work
It is impossible to separate out the discrimination which results from unequal power relations (see the following section on gendered power relations) from discrimination within the formal system. Here, however, I will briefly document the discrimination routinely experienced by women in access to training, allocation of work and promotions.

Training is vital for promotion and reduced access to training has probably had the greatest negative effect on women's chances of seniority. Women who have managed to get training have usually taken the initiative themselves and used whatever informal influences they have.

It was standard practice, though never official policy, to require husbands' permission for women to go for training. Applications without a husband's permission were treated as if permission had been withheld. In the following extract, the practice is described by a woman training officer:

> I would look for training opportunities, I would identify employees who were fit for that training and I would at least make sure there was a woman or girl on that programme. But when the list used to go to the Principal Secretary, he used to be very strict. He'd say 'there's no way I can send anybody's wife to training without the consent of the husband'. It was not official policy. I remember two women being put forward. He just put a big cross. I asked him what had happened and he said 'I'm not going to wreck marriages'. I asked him 'why don't you get these men to give permission?' and he said 'that's not my duty, it's for the girl to bring a letter from the husband'. So I used another trick. I used to send names without identifying whether they were male or female. So unless he knew the person personally, he would just approve the list.

Here the principle of equality on which the formal system is based is undermined by the dominant values of the wider culture, as mediated by a senior man. The values are not monolithic – the woman training officer does not subscribe to them – but the man concerned has an emotional investment in husbands' control over their wives, through identification with them as a man.

Many women gave accounts of how they had to find their own feet when they were first appointed. Surprisingly often we were told by women that they had never had a job schedule or job description. Of course men experienced this too, but it seems likely that lack of schedules interacts with the sceptical and defensive attitudes of many male bosses to produce a situation where women are given 'ad hoc' work which is routine, below their capacity and will later place them out of line for promotion. For example:

> I have a degree in Public Administration and have been here for the last eighteen years. When I started work I was given a work schedule that involved taking meeting minutes. I observed that with my qualifications, a man would not have been assigned such a schedule. I also observed that I was the only woman in a man's meeting and some of the men in the meeting were not as highly educated as I was. I refused to take the minutes but I did so informally. Then the work

schedule was given to a man with increased responsibility and an office imprest [budget] which he controlled. The job title was no longer Secretary to the Committees but he was called Protocol Officer. Then I was moved to another section. I was put under a man who held low qualifications. He only assigned me routine work. I was unwilling to work under him and aired my grievance to the Director of Manpower.

The practices involved here reflect an uneasy coexistence of the principles of separation and unequal integration.

Much of the criticism we heard from women concerning fair promotion opportunities centred on the system of staff appraisal. It is mandatory for certain designated officers at senior levels to ensure that, every year, subordinates and their bosses fill in the report. However, many women officers did not know that this was the case. According to most schemes of service, promotions should be given after three years to all members of the cohort who have performed satisfactorily, according to their appraisal.

We did not hear of a single case where women had been given feedback by their bosses on what was contained in their appraisals. Most women assumed that they were 'completely confidential' and yet the first paragraph on the form says that one of its purposes is to provide employees with information about their previous year's performance. (The second is to provide the system with accurate information on which to base transfers, promotions, training and salary increments.) The report specifies that 'it is the duty of the assessor to inform the person being assessed of the outcome of the appraisal'. The following position was typical:

I do not know what was said about me in all those reports for the twenty years of my service. If they would tell me my weakness, I would know how to improve. . . . I wouldn't say I've had any adverse reports, because I've never been given a letter of warning or anything.

While men may find themselves in this position, they often have more open informal access to their bosses for reasons to do with wider gender segregation and the construction of women's sexuality (see the next section on gendered power relations).

The result of the various malfunctions of the appraisal system is to create profound scepticism in the majority of women (and probably of men too). Most women see the appraisal system not only malfunctioning, but being subordinated to the informal system when it comes to promotion:

There are haphazard modes of promotion. A person may recommend his friend, his brother or a person who is really hard working. Which means promotion in the civil service is not necessarily based on an employee's performance. Even when one is promoted, one is never sure on what grounds one has been promoted. What is shown is that he has held such and such positions even if his performance had been suffering from major deficiencies. What if he has not been accountable or efficient, and what if he has not really contributed as is required of his position? But that is the malaise of the whole civil service system.

Government employees who reach a certain scale are appointed by the president, a procedure which depends in theory on a seniority list. Cases were continually cited to us of people who had got promotions through 'short cuts', rather than via the seniority list. None of the senior women to whom we talked had taken a short cut to her present position. For women, the move to presidential appointment is the most difficult in their career advancement, a move which is often achieved by networking, nepotism and corruption. Most women felt that while the formal system is so comprehensively undermined by informal influence, men will have a wide margin of advantage in getting into top positions in the civil service. The discrimination which exists with regard to promotion of women into senior-most positions is one of the most obdurate worldwide. The gender regime can tolerate integration lower in the hierarchy, but top positions are still firmly based on the principle of separation.

It is already clear from these examples that a formal bureaucracy which is based on principles of gender equality is undermined in practice by the gendered power relations of the organization and its wider cultural context. Bureaucratic organization usually provides a site of contradiction between the two. In the following section, I go on to explore the way that gendered power relations are expressed at home and at work and how these things impinge on women managers' positions.

Authority, Control and Coercion

It is in connection with the structure of authority, control and coercion – what I call gendered power relations – that the wider culture is manifest in conjunction with the power relations of hierarchy. There exists a gradient of control, which may have physical violence against wives and daughters at one end and policing of everyday behaviour at the other. In the domestic sphere the two are intimately connected, since transgressions can lead to the threat or reality of physical violence against women. At work, sexual harassment, common as it is, is the most coercive form of control. Rumours about sexual behaviour can lead to restrictions on professional relationships which diminish a woman manager's effectiveness.

Sexual Harassment

Sexual harassment makes life difficult for women in several ways. First, most of the women we talked to had been sexually harassed. Secondly, however they behave in practice, their success will provoke rumours that they have achieved their position through sleeping with some man in a powerful position. Thirdly, married women's husbands' behaviour is premised on sexual jealousy, at times obsessive, which limits their freedom of movement in ways that impinge seriously on their job. If they are not married, on the one hand they are considered fair game (lacking husbands with sexual rights over them) and on the other, their freedom of movement is policed in a more indirect way by assumptions about proper and improper behaviour.

One married man, when asked, 'How would you react if a new, attractive, woman started work in your department?', replied: 'I would seduce her and what we agree is our affair and has nothing to do with work.' This response exemplifies some common approaches by men to the question of sexual harassment, all of which help to legitimate it. The first is that it is perfectly natural that he should wish to 'seduce' her; that an attractive woman is automatically an object of a man's sexual attentions. Secondly, he assumes that she could make a free choice as to whether they have a sexual relationship; that power does not enter into consideration. The third, linked, assumption is that sex is separable from work. Each of these assumptions is problematic for women.

Sexual relationships cannot be separated from power, and in a hierarchical organization, a sexual relationship derives its meaning from the relative ranks of the pair involved:

> I'm very comfortable with junior male officers because it's very rare they'll suspect a senior woman of running around with junior males. It's not common. But it's very common for male officers to go with junior female officers. So they can only suspect me with senior male officers.

When men harass women, they almost always harass women who are junior to them, since these are the women over whom they have power. For junior women, sexual harassment is a constant hazard. As one man expressed it, 'in principle a woman can refuse without repercussions, but in practice she cannot'. The repercussions can easily affect a woman's career.

For example, one woman described her predicament as follows (she was employed in a parastatal organization):

> I was a personnel manager of my company and my superiors said I was good in my job. Armed with this knowledge I was very confident and I enjoyed my work. My educational background was good by any standard. I held a Masters degree in Personnel Management.
>
> One day the Chairman of the Board was visiting and he invited me to dinner. I assumed I had been asked to dinner as part of the whole management team. As the chairman was staying in a self-contained suite, I had no hesitation in knocking at his room. Surprisingly only the two of us were there. I was shocked and a bit uncomfortable at being alone with him but I convinced myself I could control the situation. I quickly recalled my lessons about having mentors and forging networks that helped one in career advancement and I began to conduct what I though was an intellectual discussion with him along those lines. However I could detect some impatience as we talked.
>
> By 8.30pm I could see that there was no dinner preparation and my sense of unease increased. I held on until 9pm and then told him that I wanted to leave. All of a sudden he moved from his chair, came to my side and started telling me how he admired me and whether I can grant him a favour of taking me to bed. Personally I was not attracted to him and I had to find a way of getting gracefully out of this predicament. Two thoughts crossed my mind. If I refuse him, I am doomed because he could affect my career. If I accept him, I am doomed because he will think I am a cheap woman and there for the taking. After all I had come voluntarily to his room. I decided not to give in.
>
> In 1985 when the cost-reduction exercise was carried out in my parastatal, I was the first person to be sacked. He was still the Chairman of the Board. How could I tell anyone that I was being victimized on sexual grounds. What evidence did I have?

In such cases, women have to be prepared to sacrifice a job opportunity if they refuse a man. Yet men use informal channels for jobs and promotions without these hazards.

The following example suggests that a sexual approach was premised on power which also involved the power relations among men. The woman described a time of family crisis when her husband lost a job:

> Maybe that is also the time I was exposed to sexual harassment, because more senior people, they took advantage of that and thought I should give in because of my problems. I said no. Yes, during that time I got a lot of sexual harassment. A lot of people, very senior, in political positions. Because they thought I would say, now I'm helpless I'll go with them.

This implies that women may be protected from sexual harassment if they have powerful husbands. We asked one man would a man try to seduce a woman who was the wife of a senior officer? The answer was threefold: 'not unless she was willing' (which implies that in other cases, a woman's willingness is irrelevant); 'one has to think twice' and 'only young girls are vulnerable'. As women get older, especially if they become senior, they generally experience less sexual harassment. One senior woman could be quite relaxed about it:

> I've had colleagues [make sexual advances]. I've always been very open with men. I've said I'm not interested. And I've made a joke with them. I've said if I want to have some funny business, I'll go with a man who is higher than me. What benefit would I draw with a colleague?

Even in jest, the power relations are clear. The premise of the joke is that women consent to sex with superiors because they get benefits.

Whatever their behaviour and their relative power, senior women are subject to rumours about their sexual liaisons. Indeed, their high profiles, and the resentment many men feel about their success, make it virtually inevitable that rumours will abound. The common thread running through these rumours is that women have slept their way to their present positions. As one old hand put it 'by lying horizontally, they rise vertically'. All these rumours need is that a woman and man have developed a friendly professional relationship. It seems beyond the male cultural imagination that this might be possible without involving sex:

> Once I heard a nasty rumour about myself – that my boyfriend was the Minister of —. Now my work involved looking after this man and arranging various things for him when he came in. He was nice, we used to talk. If he said let's go for a beer —. I think I gave people reasons to think that I was running with that man, but I have never done it. . . . One rumour was circulating that all of us senior women officers [she mentions five women] were sleeping with Principal Secretary —. It was soon after we'd been promoted.

Sexual Surveillance

It seems that any social relation between a woman and a man sparks off assumptions that sex is at the root of it. Women are inadvertently sexualized by a combination of male colleagues' sexually predatory behaviour and husbands' lack of faith in them. It does not need all men to behave in this way, either as husbands or colleagues, for this sexualization to pervade the organizational culture and disadvantage women.

Good working relations with women colleagues did exist. One man explained: 'It is difficult to work genuinely with a woman for fear that people might have the wrong ideas. But the women I work with, I know their husbands and they have a great trust in me. But this varies from man to man.' This illustrates that the primary relation is between men. In one case, although 'most of the time I could feel that my colleagues were conscious that they had a female around', through working well together 'we succeeded in becoming colleagues and in the end they were not deeply conscious of my presence'.

As a result, all contact between women and their male bosses or peers (male subordinates is a separate issue, which I shall discuss below), is deemed to be at risk and consequently the limits imposed on women in their informal work relations are strict. The principle of segregation ring-fences the organization, even when it is not sustainable at professional levels within. Women are expected to go straight home after work, and only to go out socializing in their husband's company. Bosses may fear to ask women to work late or at weekends because of the minority of husbands who object. One woman director explained that, if she needed to ask one of her woman subordinates to stay late, she sent a note in advance to the husband. Of course men who are uncomfortable with having women in equal positions to them will use this as a reason for stopping all women from moving to jobs where this might be required of them. Thus one man said, 'We have not tried to recruit women because they might have problems in the field, domestic responsibilities. My wife does not give me trouble when I go to do fieldwork.'

Husbands do sometimes give their wives trouble:

Once I was required to go to two different districts in my region to do some work. As usual my boss informed me in advance and, knowing the type of husband I have, I decided not to ask him permission, but to tell him that I was leaving my station for the districts on an official duty. When I told him about this, he kept quiet. The next day I went to my office and got my imprest ready for the trip. At this time, my husband had been dismissed from his job and he was just at home. When I got back home, I gave him the money from the imprest so that he could purchase provisions when I was away. The next day I left in a Ministry Landrover. When I was in the meeting I received a call from the boss asking me if everything was fine when I left home. Since I had no worries about this, I answered in the affirmative, only to be told that my husband had gone to the boss's office to inquire about my whereabouts claiming that he had not seen me for two days. I became furious and told my boss not to take any note until I came back.

As if this embarrassment was not enough, after two days my husband went again to my boss and told him that he wanted me back, otherwise he would take a legal action against me. Being terrified, my boss dispatched another (junior) officer to meet me so that I could come back. I came back to find my boss worn stiff. From that day on they have never tried to give me assignments outside my station.

Given the tendency of male officers to generalize from single cases to all women, this sort of story, which circulates energetically through the networks, begins to provide a rationale for any men who have financial reasons for not allocating travelling jobs to women. In one of the men's groups, other examples came up:

One man used to tell his wife which route to take home. Another used to phone her up three or four times a day. X's husband used to deliver her to the office and pick her up. She was not allowed to get a lift. Then, he bought her a car and she was forbidden to give anyone a lift.

One woman's tactic for challenging her male boss's assumption that her husband's permission was required for travelling played on the contradictions between male authority in the domestic and work spheres: 'He would ask if I've had permission from my husband. I'd always tell him I had permission from my boss and I don't ask permission from my husband, because he's not my boss in my job'. She did not question his status as boss at home. This woman's husband never complained about her travelling, but none the less, she pointed out that:

I've never given him cause for alarm. I'm very particular before I travel. If I know well in advance, I try to put my house in order. If I'm going to travel, I never give him surprises. So I try as much as possible to respect him as the head of the household. Sometimes it's difficult to satisfy these African men, you might do a little thing. So I try and be extremely careful.

The care with which this senior woman exercised her relative freedom to travel in connection with her work indicates the power relations on which their arrangements are premised. He is head of the household and any inadvertent 'little thing' might upset him. It is left implicit what he might do if upset, but it is enough to make her extremely careful.

While the right to travel is contested because of the accompanying financial benefits, restrictions on women's freedom of movement are much broader and affect their access to informal networks which operate after working hours where information and influence is traded. After-work restrictions on informal socializing, usually even with fellow women colleagues, were observed by every woman who was interviewed:

Being an African society, there's limited movement for women in association just for the sake of it. If I want to meet a woman friend, there's no way I can nip out of my house and just meet her unexpectedly, like my husband can. Just after taking a shower 'OK, I'm going out to meet my friends', simple as that. There's no way I can do that and I do think that meeting friends in social clubs is very relevant to your career, exchanging ideas and so on.

For an unmarried woman: 'Networking for women like me who are singles is not easy, because people might misunderstand you.' However, married women felt the same, only they are also worried about their husbands misunderstanding them: 'I do not see why I should push it [networking], and I do not like such things to interfere with my relationship with my husband.' In the case of either a married or an unmarried woman, the boss and his wife would assume a sexual motive:

I know a man who actually networks seriously by taking gifts to the boss to get recognized. Men do it and women cannot do that because there'll be misunderstanding from the boss and from the wife of the boss. The boss would think you wanted a relationship . . . and the wife would be scared, if you're not a friend of the wife. But if the subordinate was a man, the wife would not be shocked. She would think they were discussing office things.

These restrictions affect women's access to information:

In our society, if you're a female officer, you have to think twice before going to a pub. With my husband it was OK, but we thought it was best for me to keep in. My husband had a lot of interaction, yes, he was always going off to the pub with the boys. What they said about me outside, I never knew; whatever plans they made outside, I never knew. I relied on the information my husband brought back home. Sometimes I got it. Sometimes he would keep it to himself.

One senior woman occasionally goes out with her husband and his friends, who do not work in the civil service:

Sometimes when I go out with my husband, I sit with his group, but even then, there are some things I can benefit a lot from, just sitting listening. There are lots of gossips – things about this Ministry which I personally don't know, yet it's where I work.

The Structure of Cathexis

I have suggested that the structure of cathexis is based on the principle of emotional investment in gender difference. In previous work I have explored the psychodynamic forces involved in the reproduction of gender difference in the sphere of heterosexual couple relations. Splitting, for example, is a concept from psychoanalytic object relations theory which provides insight into early defence mechanisms through which as infants – and later as adults – we project unacceptable parts of ourselves on to others. Traditionally, psychoanalytic theory did not locate these parts in the discourses and practices of gendered power relations. In my analysis of interview material with heterosexual couples I have shown how splitting works according to gender difference, for example such that a man may remain 'in charge of patriarchal reassurance' while a woman partner expresses needs and anxieties for both (Hollway, 1989: ch. 5). Such discursive practices reproduce gender difference at the level of subjectivity; men feeling reassured in their masculine positions in ways which protect deeper vulnerabilities:

> Often men do not separate emotionally from their mothers. Rather they suppress and later displace these desires on to another woman. The consequent vulnerability is not an effect of a woman's 'real' power but rather her misrecognized power as the 'psychic' object – object of desire for the mother/Other. Normally men's power in other spheres makes the relationship safe. In addition they have available to them discourses concerning sexuality which confer power on them and produce women as weak. Their investment in these positions (and therefore their reproduction of them) counters women's 'sexual' power – a power that is not about 'sex', but about desire for the Other. (Hollway, 1984b: 68)

Similar dynamics are evident in the workplace, reflecting the power relations of the formal hierarchy. They are manifest in the harassment of junior women, a practice which reproduces heterosexuality and, importantly, thereby rehearses masculinity and femininity. Sexual harassment rehearses masculinity and femininity, as well as reproducing heterosexuality. Connell argues that 'hegemonic masculinity is always constructed in relation to various subordinated masculinities as well as in relation to women' (1987: 183). Sexual success provides a pecking order amongst men through the criterion of masculine heterosexuality. While some men negotiate their masculine status with each other through the vehicle of women as sex objects, some women compete in the stakes of sexual attractiveness through the attentions of men. The organizational culture, dominated by men who see men's sexuality as a natural drive (Hollway, 1984a), does not aspire seriously to control sexual harassment in the workplace.

There was other evidence of the need to rehearse masculinity, not routed through sexuality. Most obvious were the occasions when women's authority was refused by men, despite their level in the hierarchy, because they were women. For example:

> I am working with a male officer who is anti-women. I once went for special duties in the region and left written handing-over notes on what

was supposed to be covered while I was out. When I came back, everything was untouched. When I inquired, he said that he did not touch anything because he will not take instructions from a woman.

Here the requirements of the formal bureaucracy are clearly contradicted by a structure of gender relations which is underpinned by an emotional investment in gender difference which is experienced at the level of masculine identity.

Usually the effects are more covert and, I came to see, worked through identification between the sphere of the family and that of the organization, creating an automatic alliance between male decision-makers in organizations (who are almost invariably husbands themselves) and the husbands of the women who depend on the decision-makers for fair treatment. Occasionally male superiors' identification as a husband was explicit. One woman said: 'When I was doing my MSc, I had a young infant. I sacrificed my studies abroad and went locally. The Professor told me that while I was struggling hard, his wife, who did not have a BSc, was contented.' The effect was to position this young woman as equivalent to his wife, over whom his patriarchal authority was, in principle, firmly established. Similarly when the director of training said 'there's no way I can send anybody's wife to training without the consent of the husband', he was identifying with the husbands and not with his women professional colleagues.

While younger women are more likely to be emotionally positioned in the same power relations as wives through such projective identification,[2] older women are more often positioned as mothers. This is often quite overt and is facilitated by the linguistic convention in parts of East Africa of calling married women 'Mama —'. 'Mama' functions as a title like 'Mrs', but defines a woman's identity as that of a mother.[3] One senior woman experienced this as comprising her organizational status:

X: A lady is supposed to act like a mother. She's supposed to be kinder 'Mama, please . . .'
Q: How do you handle it?
X: First of all I tell all male officers, don't call me Mama, I don't want to be called Mama. I'm not Mama, I'm Mrs —. I'm not here as a woman, I'm here as an officer. If they don't get what they want, they'll say 'she's not a woman, not a motherly-like woman'.

In such ways the patriarchal model of family relations enters the gender relations of the organization. It is anchored through the emotional connections which go back through a person's history to their early object relations. Men's motivation for its continued rehearsal and reproduction is the superiority which gender difference affords them. As soon as a woman's status is equal to her husband's, his identity is put on the line.[4] This was a well-recognized dilemma for graduate women, who expect their husbands to need to be more successful then they are themselves in their careers. This is said to affect a graduate woman's marriageability:

> *X:* You graduate at 25, and people think why isn't she getting married? There weren't so many unmarried girls of my age. You can be misinterpreted – one is loitering. People thought it was particularly difficult for graduate girls to get husbands. Most graduate boys don't want to get married to graduate girls. They would rather marry girls who are of slightly lower education, for reasons that I guess are obvious. Most of them don't tolerate discussions and things like that.
> *Q:* What about your husband?
> *X:* He didn't mind at all. He was a Masters, maybe that's what gave him more confidence. . . . He's five years older.

In two instances women reported that their husbands had opted out of the same career as them, into the private sector, when the woman had become more senior. In neither case was it made explicit that their wife's seniority was the reason, but in one: 'Most of my friends and male colleagues said your husband must have been upset [and thought]; why should I work at a job that is lower than my wife's job?'

One interview with a married couple (whom I have called Salim and Fatma) exemplified these dynamics in greater detail and introduced the element of class status into the equation. Salim, from a poor rural farming family, had married a bourgeois, light-skinned woman of Arab parentage from the town. As Salim put it 'I'm trying my level best not to let her down because the main problem was on her side. My parents were just farmers.' Fatma had had the chance of being sponsored to go to Europe to do a Masters degree in Public Administration, when their first child was one year old. She went, and graduated one year later. Soon after her return, she was promoted to a high post in the civil service. Salim was a general manager in a parastatal company. Salim is three years older than Fatma. He has been away twice on short courses abroad, but not for a Masters degree.

> *Q:* How did you feel when Fatma was going abroad for training?
> *S:* I was very very uneasy at that time, I must be frank. [Pause] It was a very very hard time. But you see, I had development ideas and I was not contented with the life we had at that time and I found that

there was no way to be out of that situation without going for further education.

When you get the chance to go for education abroad, you are going to get two things. First you are going to get education. This education will enable you for promotion in your career, and secondly definitely you will benefit materially. Per diem is handsome, so you can bring back a lot of luxury items – a vehicle, a refrigerator, a blender – very very useful things in everyday life. So when she told me that she got the chance, then I said OK, just proceed and I will try my level best to handle the family.

Q: What about you Fatma?

F: Yes, I wanted very much to go for further studies. But it was a decision that you have to think of the future and the future of your kids. I wanted something better for my kids. So the only way was to go for further studies and get promotion and it has materialized.

As other respondents also pointed out, economic pressures make it necessary for husbands to support their wives' careers. 'Development ideas' won out over Salim's masculine anxieties, helped by their good communication and trust in each other, and the fact that Fatma did not treat him any differently just because she had a higher qualification. In his words 'she was still in my command':

Q: Salim, how did you feel about Fatma's promotion?

S: I was very much encouraged and very very proud, when I was informed that she had been chosen for further studies. I must confess at that time I was a little bit afraid that this girl, my wife, when she gets Masters degree, when she comes back, she may decide to [pause] quit me, because at that time she'll be having higher education compared with mine. But fortunately she was very very dedicated to me and the communication between us while she was away was so good, that when she came back, she never showed anything against me, so this encouraged me very much.

Q: [*to Fatma*] And you?

F: [*laughs*] No, we have trust, that's the important thing and what I was doing was for the future of our home and our kids and, much as I missed him, I was consoling myself that I was doing the right thing. I had faith that my husband was waiting for me and we would have a better life.

Q: It didn't change you as a person?

F: No of course, I came back.

S: And she was still in my command [*both laugh*].

Q: Does she change? As she gets more senior?

S: No, she has never changed her attitude to me.

Salim felt ambivalent about the possibility of Fatma getting a Masters degree when he did not have one. On the one hand, he felt insecure. If she were more highly qualified, would she still want to remain with him? This derives from many men's fear, often not consciously articulated in the way that Salim does, that if he is not superior in status to his wife, he is not in control of her, she is not dependent and he cannot be sure of keeping her. On the other hand, Salim had 'development ideas', and these won out. Such anxieties are usually irrational, produced by the exigencies of masculinity, rather than by women's feelings. Despite Fatma's higher educational and job status, Salim was still the boss at home. As long as the patriarchal principle in family life remained unchallenged, the contradiction was sustainable, by separating the two spheres.

Contradictions

Connell's three structures refer specifically to gender relations. The data presented here has required that I analyse these in relation to the formal organizational structures, even though this is never purely reflected in organizational practice. The principle on which the formal organization is based, at least in relation to its graduate employees, is that of equal integration. The contradictions which I have identified involve this principle of equal integration, under-mined by gender difference, with power and emotional investment reproducing each other.

For example, when the older woman officer was positioned as motherly by male subordinates, she identified the contradiction by saying 'I'm not here as a woman, I'm here as an officer.' The emotional construction of gender difference makes it impossible to maintain such a clear distinction in practice, but the principle on which she wishes to insist, the one that supports her managerial authority, is that of gender-equal integration. It is these contradictions which afford most support for changes in practice for women because they can call on the principles of the formal bureaucracy for support.

The multiplicity of power is central to the analysis. On the one hand, power is an expression of the formal bureaucratic hierarchy. On the other, it is an expression of patriarchal structures, such as the gendered division of labour. Women, like men, will use the sources of power available, whether these be gendered or otherwise. As well as deriving power from their formal position in the hierarchy and their qualifications, some women derived it from their ethnic group connections and the class status of their family of origin. As well as having their power undermined by the gender regime, some women used it, for example by exploiting their sexuality or their husbands' political status. Being married was a source of power as well as constraint, for example:

The fact that I was married to the regional Party boss was important. I was promoted to Regional Community Development Officer as a result of my husband's position. Then when we moved to Dar es Salaam, my husband was no longer a regional Party boss, without the power, but with the contacts previously made. I was promoted. My boss was a man. He was capable of listening to me. I took initiative on a lot of things and I always got his approval. He was also my husband's friend.

As the following examples show, multiple sources of power provide locations of contradictions where practice becomes open to change. The fact that in principle women have equal access to training bore no relation to practice until recently. Power relations were clearly in evidence since access to training is one of the civil service's most highly valued resources. This also makes it a site of contestation by women. The practice of requiring husbands' permission required several conditions. It required a person with the authority to implement the non-formal criterion of husbands' permission and who believed in it sufficiently to take the initiative. The Principal Secretary in question identified not with women as fellow colleagues, but with their husbands. The practice required collusion at higher levels, where all were men. It required acquiescence by the women, either through ignorance or through gendered power relations in the household. In the case of the latter, a woman who took up a training place without her husband's consent might risk losing her children. The final requirement was therefore that men occupied a sufficient position of authority in the household. It is clear from the foregoing discussion that they usually did.

However, organizational change did take place without change in all these conditions when a woman was appointed as director of training. Since the position controlled such valuable resources, this was a struggle and only happened because a woman was head of the relevant Ministry. Once a woman occupied the job of director of training, she identified, not with the husbands, but with the women.[5] At that point, the formal provision of equal access to training could prescribe practice, at least at one level of the organization.

The provision that parents are equally able to take leave to look after sick children is virtually invisible in practice: if the mother is available, she will be the one to do it. The example differs from training in the sense that there is no obvious workplace privilege attached to avoiding childcare responsibility. However, women's childcare responsibilities are habitually used against them when it comes to promotion and responsibility. The practice of men avoiding equal childcare responsibility seems more directly associated with their wish to remain distant from women's roles; that is, it is a way to reproduce gender difference. The association of childcare with women is so strong that most men feel that taking on this work would compromise their masculinity: masculinity is defined in relation to women's role, in this case as mother. The formal symmetry of organizational provision has almost no bearing on practice and it is an area – negotiated between wife and husband – on which organizational intervention is likely to have little leverage.

In the example of job schedules, the contradiction once again is between the formal organization and a combination of the three structures. The absence of job schedules may affect men as well as women, but the allocation of more menial tasks to qualified women is gendered. It is primarily to do with power relations, with male bosses who do not find it comfortable to relate with women in authority. But the power dynamic is inseparable from investment in gender difference: such men reproduced their superior masculine status by automatically allocating women inferior tasks; by treating them as if they were not equally competent. This dynamic is beneath many of the daily difficulties in social relations experienced by women in positions of authority at work. Women's formal qualifications are the strongest counter-weapon at their disposal (hence the importance of training). They also stand to profit when the formal rules of the bureaucracy work optimally: if job schedules, job allocation, appraisal and promotion criteria were set down more precisely, it would be more difficult to discriminate against women.

The following commentary on networking exemplifies the connections between the general culture of gender segregation and its anchorage in gender-differentiated identities for both women and men, husbands' power, the sexualization of women and informal influence bordering on corruption.

> *X:* It is hard [to network]. That is why some of us are never remembered when promotions are being discussed. There is a club for civil servants called the Leaders' Club. But it is a beer club where people drink alcohol and eat roasted meat. It is not customary for Tanzanian women to go to the club just to drink beer and eat meat. It would be a good club if it was designed to cater for families. You could then go there as a family. But the way it is designed, it is a pub. Women here do not go to pubs. I do not frequent there but the few times I have been there the main activity is drinking.
>
> *Q:* How about clubs such as Gymkhana?
> *X:* Yes such clubs are good, but I am not a member. When I tried to join the club, my husband became suspicious. My husband works

with the army and they have a mess, which is like a club, but it caters for families. So we meet there as families, and women meet in their roles as housewives of the senior officers in the army. But as a senior civil servant, I would prefer to be a member of the Leaders' Club.

I know that networking is important, but you cannot merely depend on it. Even men do not use it so simply. No. There are other accompanying elements. In my experience I know people who give out bribes, for example, a sackful of tomatoes, chicken and so forth. I have seen people give cars, video.

Now how can a woman afford these things, unless I take it to a fellow woman? But as you know, leadership is dominated by men. They are the people who make recommendations and they also are the people in our administration. Another thing in clubs men buy beer for each other. But can I buy a man a beer? It is unbecoming, I cannot do that.

The gender regime manifests here in several ways. First, there exists a male club, based on the principle of separation, which is supported by the norms of comportment which say that women's participation is inappropriate (eating roast meat, drinking alcohol and buying others' drinks are unbecoming for a woman). This is consistent with the wider prohibition on women's access to certain kinds of public spaces (another example of the principle of separation). Second, the husband's suspicion, an example of structure three, based on the principle of emotional investment in gender differences, reproduces the specific and more general prohibitions. It is implied, though not stated, that his suspicions involve her sexuality. Like the senior woman who has to be careful to prepare in advance for travelling, this woman said that she did not want to jeopardize her relationship with her husband. Her husband would be happy for her to go to the mess which is for wives and families, where she would not be exposed to men as a professional but be in her role as wife. However, this is inconsistent with her professional status. Finally, as a woman she cannot take gifts to influential people, most of whom are men, because a sexual motive would be assumed. Here too a woman's sexualization is a strong force in the reproduction of gender-differentiated power relations.

The main principle at work here is gender separation. It is supported by conventions which work at the level of identity (for example, it is unbecoming for women to buy a man a beer) and also by the husband's jealousy, suspicion and policing of his wife's movements. These forces at the emotional level are conditional on his power to dictate to his wife, however unreasonable, and even when it is against her professional interests. Again the contradiction is between her status as a senior civil servant on the one hand and the three structures on the other.

This is a major site of contradictions which can provide arenas of practice for women. With their professional status go gender-equal variants of the three structures: equal access (structure 1); power, authority and control based on the organizational hierarchy (structure 2) and identities which have primarily to do with professional status and responsibilities (structure 3).

The evidence suggests that the main point of resistance to changes towards equality is husbands: the domestic division of labour which they carefully uphold; their cultural status as master of wife and children; the threat or reality of violence if their authority is challenged; their emotional need to reproduce their superiority through gender difference and their masculinity through policing their wives as sexual objects. These same power relations are manifest between men and women at work, but there it is contradicted by the formal bureaucratic principle of equal treatment. In the domestic sphere in Tanzania, no equivalent principle yet exists.

Notes

1 The research was funded by the British Overseas Development Administration (Hollway and Mukurasi, 1991). I directed it and worked with a team of Tanzanian researchers, three of whom were employed in the civil service. The research was conducted in order to find out why there were so few women in senior positions in the Tanzanian civil service. It used a minimally structured interviewing method. Interviews were with individuals and groups, with women and men.

2 'In projective identification the ego projects its feelings into the object which it then identifies with, becoming like the object which it has already imaginatively filled with itself' (Mitchell, 1986: 20 and quoted in Hollway, 1989: 71).

3 This is underlined by the fact that the title 'Mama' can be followed, not by the woman's family name (which anyway may be her husband's), but by that of one of her children.

4 I have noted the same dynamic in a British heterosexual couple:

When I first met him, he had a Degree and I had a Certificate. And I wanted a Degree and he encouraged me. But I actually got far higher qualifications than he did. So that also made him feel unconfident . . . It didn't occur to *me* it was a problem. Of course it was a problem for him. (Hollway, 1984b: 65)

5 This identification is not a foregone conclusion: in a different climate a woman Director of Training might reproduce old practices, but it is none the less far less likely, because of the common experience of gender which promotes identification. I have analysed the relation of gender difference and identification in detail elsewhere (Hollway, 1989: ch. 7).

References

Connell, R.W. (1987) *Gender and Power*. Cambridge: Polity Press.

Connell, R.W. (1990) 'The state, gender and sexual politics: theory and appraisal', *Theory and Society*, 19: 507–44.

Henriques, J., Hollway, W., Urwin, C., Venn, C. and Walkerdine, V. (eds), (1984) *Changing the Subject: Psychology, Social Regulation and Subjectivity*. London: Routledge.

Hollway, W. (1984a) 'Gender difference and the production of subjectivity', in J. Henriques, W. Hollway, C. Urwin, C. Venn and V. Walkerdine (eds), *Changing the Subject: Psychology, Social Regulation and Subjectivity*. London: Routledge, pp. 227–63.

Hollway, W. (1984b) 'Women's power in heterosexual sex', *Women's Studies International Forum*, 7(1): 63–8.

Hollway, W. (1989) *Subjectivity and Method in Psychology: Gender, Meaning and Science*. London: Sage.

Hollway, W. and Mukurasi, L. (1991) *Tanzania: Obstacles to Women's Advancement in the Tanzanian Civil Service*. Report to the Civil Service Department of the Government of Tanzania and the UK Overseas Development Administration. British Council report no. 3813.

Hollway, W. and Mukurasi, L. (in press) 'Women managers in the Tanzanian civil service', in N. Adler and D. Izraeli (eds), *Women in Management Worldwide*, 2nd edn. New York: Sharpe.

Mitchell, J. (ed.) (1986) *The Selected Melanie Klein*. Harmondsworth: Penguin.

13

Women in Women's Organizations: Power or *Pouvoir*? A Case Study of Leadership in the National Council of Jewish Women in Canada

Eliane Leslau Silverman

The National Council of Jewish Women of Canada is nearly 100 years old. Throughout its history, it has been dedicated to identifying social, political and economic problems, and to seeking their solutions. The organization has been guided by a vision of social change for people in Canada, intending less than many other Canadian women's organizations to perpetuate the status quo, hoping instead to introduce alterations to Canadian social policy and changes in the fabric of people's lives. Because its goals have often been to ameliorate social conditions, it attracts a leadership intent on reform, and which thus understands that it must attain a public presence. This chapter will analyse several generations of those leaders' understandings of their actions with respect to power. Did they think of themselves as political agents and of their actions as political? Did they want power, within and outside the organization, or did their involvement in Council suggest rather the French infinitive *pouvoir*, to be able? Did they seek power or enablement?

Women, Power and Leadership

Women's groups provide the historian with a setting in which to connect gender with power. From within them, leadership emerges which reflects the members' understandings of power, expressed within the organization, or directed to the surrounding world. In those organizations, people interact, are invested in one another, and negotiate with one another to achieve their goals. Leadership tends, in women's organizations, to be a process of collective effort, rather than the efforts of one person who leads others. In groups like the National Council of Jewish Women, we have the opportunity to observe such collective expressions over the course of the twentieth century, with successive generations of leaders interacting in different ways with the membership, responding to, even as they create, political and cultural changes in the country.

Views of power, as we shall see, change over time, in a dialectical exchange between members and their world, the one always interacting with the other. Women in such groups, and their views of power, are not 'affected by' the politics around them – for that would imply them to be separate from it – but are part of its making, part, in short, of political history. The women whose own words comprise the evidence for this study are enmeshed in gender arrangements, religious and cultural precepts, and twentieth-century political realities. From these they derive not only a vision of power, but a place in the history we must rewrite to include women's presence.

Nobody achieves a public presence alone. Birth and family connections, party affiliation, accumulated wealth, the prestige of professional standing, the support of dedicated followers – any or all of these are prerequisites to a presence in the public realm. Most women who have had such assets have not usually been able, alone, to transform them into political power. Instead, from the late nineteenth century, organizations like the National Council of Jewish Women have served to set the stage for women's exercise of agency in local and national communities. In these groups they identified issues, studied them, made recommendations, and acted on them. Organizations were often successful in bringing about the changes they intended, sometimes on their own and sometimes enlisting the support or funding of local and national governments. In formalized groups, councils and organizations, women succeeded in putting new issues, new strategies and new solutions on the public agenda. Activist Jewish women found expression for their desires to participate in making a Canadian culture in the National Council of Jewish Women of Canada.

The search for historical evidence of women's quest for power can begin with the perceptions offered by the participants themselves. Canadian women's history is not yet extensive or elaborate enough to allow us the multiplicity of insights we need into women's lives. Organizational histories and the records of women's groups help to locate the political questions posed by women's groups, and thereby to begin an analysis of how they understood the communal, public world and their own place in it.[1] We need to extend our analysis as well to individual women's motivations for joining those groups, and then staying within them to effect change. Women's groups became vehicles to political action elsewhere denied them, but in which they played a role none the less.

The National Council of Jewish Women

While historians creatively resurrect written evidence from the nineteenth century and tease out its meanings, they can add oral data to the twentieth to locate women as active agents in the national story. Council women's testimony in interviews can direct us to women's understandings of their political roles – political in respect of the alterations they sought in power relations – and of their social activism, which they hoped would come to comprise part of the national agenda. I was fortunate in being able to interview about fifty leaders of the National Council of Jewish Women of Canada. From the 1920s to the 1980s they were national and local officers of an organization founded in Montreal in 1897. Its national office is in Toronto, and employs a small staff. Council now has eleven sections in as many cities, many of which also contain a large number of affiliates, each with its own officers. Thus, its organization is traditionally hierarchic, its leaders formally acknowledged and deriving authority from their offices. The national executive meet frequently in Toronto, sometimes visiting the sections to bring them a sense of organizational unity and in turn to bring the membership's concerns to the national level. Sections' contacts with National, especially at the biennial national meetings, said a leader who was president in the 1960s, gives members 'that strength, that feeling of power, that we are a force in this country. Not that one is better than another, but that together we are better'. Hierarchical or authoritarian practices are not encouraged, despite the formal structure of the organization.

The women whom I interviewed were hospitable and open. They told me about their motivations for joining Council, their perspectives on leadership, their inner and outer conflicts. They shared personal histories, political perspectives and organizational records. Their terms of office both antedated and succeeded the contemporary women's movement. It is difficult not to fear misinterpreting them, more difficult to leave their accounts untold. I hope that I transmit their perceptions of their power and their place in the political world faithfully, even as I acknowledge that the questions I asked them emerge from my feminist under-standings, not necessarily their own, of the political culture.

Female and Jewish

As Jewish women, few of them religious but all of them dedicated to social justice, the leaders were united in their belief that social problems can be identified and solutions found. As a Calgary leader said, 'We saw voids and we would fill them.' She continued, 'You can't accept things as your just due. I can't accept the thought of not having left something on this earth.' Most of them shared a sense of their marginality as Jews in a Christian culture.[2] One leader spoke of having been raised in the only Jewish family in a small Ontario town – 'everybody was nice to us, but I felt we were different'. An American-born immigrant remembered her family's being the only Jews in a New Jersey town where they were not allowed to buy a house. An Alberta leader born in the 1930s, a student when there was only thirteen Jewish students at the University of Alberta, never came to feel comfortable in what she called 'Christian settings'. Many of them brought their sense of marginality to their activities: 'maybe the Jewish people feel a little more emotional. Jewish people have not been affluent that long; we remember these things.'

Some of the younger leaders from Vancouver, where Jews arrived only recently, felt more assimilated. Even for them, their Jewish identification was not unconflicted. One of them told me that when a speaker addressed the 1983 national biennial meeting on the exploitation of women working in the garment factories, the comments at the session divided between members who felt defensive, identifying with husbands who had financial interests in the industry, and those who felt that, 'Given that two generations ago Jewish women were those being exploited, they should identify with the subject.'

The women of the earlier generations of leadership, those women of 'two generations ago', organized relief efforts for the unemployed during the Depression, lobbied their governments for welfare and health care legislation in the 1920s, urged for fair employment practices in the 1940s, and for equal pay legislation in the 1950s. Different needs were identified in different cities. The 1960s found the Winnipeg section organizing hostels and meals for hippies and a nursery school for Indian and Metis children. The leaders who succeeded them in the past two decades have involved Council in providing services to immigrant children, such as a library and after-school care centre in Montreal; to people with mental and physical disabilities; and to senior citizens. They tended to agree that 'Jewish women have to be strong for practical reasons, to get things done'; Council's policy of identifying a problem, creating its solution, and then often passing the project on to another group or agency suited them well. 'Do one project, then move on; I hate things that go on and on.' Young and old, the leadership all saw a place for Council in their lives, praising its contributions to social amelioration.

Stewardship

Among Council leaders, benevolent activity was highly regarded. They saw it as a vehicle to carry out their responsibilities to people in Canada. Most of the women I interviewed stressed that their allegiance lay with Council, rather than with other Jewish women's organizations like Hadassah, because of its long tradition of working in its immediate community, not fundraising for Israel. They saw themselves as 'stewards', to use the phrase of the physicist Ursula Franklin, taking care of things they do not own, enabling other people to carry out their own lives.

Throughout the twentieth century, Council women observed the demoralizing, dispiriting effects of social and economic dislocation on people – 'you have to fight these things, or you can't sleep at night'. They created institutions like summer camps for poor girls, clubs for old people, second-hand clothing stores, English classes for immigrants, day care centres in working-class neighbourhoods, sexual assault awareness programmes for children. 'Let's face it, dear, the women know what they're doing.'

They did not merely fund these projects; they worked in them, volunteering as teachers, counsellors, babysitters, drivers. Their sense of stewardship derived from a very personal connection, a close, hands-on identification, to their work and their world. They offered their labour to the projects, seeing activism in the community much as if it were involvement in their family, and rewarding in the same way. A woman who joined Council in 1925 and held a number of national offices made the analogy. She said that her mother lived with her in her old age, weak and unable even to comb her hair. 'She'd say "My darling daughter, your blessing will be that your daughter will do the same for you as you do for me." And she was right.' The Toronto section president who brought two young camp survivors to her dentist in 1946, only to be told that he was too busy to do free work, never returned to him. Council work was not usually an abstraction; principles had to be translated into action. 'Leadership is about demonstrating by doing – and that included sweeping the floor at Council House.' The stewardship that many of the women expressed included benefits to themselves – 'Council was a learning thing' or 'You get more out of it than you put into it' – as well as to people unknown to themselves but to whom they felt responsible: 'Your neighbour was the whole world.' They envisioned their community as a network of social relationships in which they were fortunate enough to be able to act as catalysts for change.

Many of them agreed that it was Council that provided them

with the skills to create change. They saw their volunteer work in the organization to be a commitment quite as serious as paid labour, where they could turn their sense of stewardship into action. 'There was growth; there was working with kindred women, intelligent, open to ideas, and who cared enormously; there was learning how to lobby, like setting up Cool Aid for troubled teenagers; there was learning how to do public speaking.' They measured their success both by what the projects * accomplished and by what they derived from their work. 'Council has been the instrument in moulding my personality,' said a leader of Montreal section. 'I spoke five languages, and couldn't say a thing in any of them. Council gave me a philosophy of life so I do the most I can every day.' They offered Council their skills. A Calgary section leader with a Masters degree in Social Work provided unpaid services for five years, three days a week, at Jewish Family Services, a counselling agency founded by Council. A Toronto leader, now over 80, became the third national president in the 1940s, and told me that, 'Through organizations you acquire skills, and suddenly realize you have a great potential. You do things you want to do, and then you get a reward because you see how you've grown. Council gave me the potential. The first trip across Canada [in the 1940s] was very frightening to me: radio interviews and two-engine planes with the oxygen thing and the hose along the floor. But it made me more interesting, and more interesting to my family.' Another national president in the 1950s, constantly visiting sections, 'always had an airplane ticket in my purse.'

While Council leaders were clear that their benevolence was to be extended both to the Jewish and non-Jewish communities, they were not united in their need to ally with non-Jewish organizations. A Montreal section president, later a president of International Council of Jewish Women, who joined in 1927, invited non-Jews to Council meetings, and invited other organizations' officers to hear about their work. Like several other leaders, she was active on civic boards, hospital boards and Women's Canadian Club, and chuckled that the pastor of the Catholic Church, the rabbi, and the mayor of Westmount were all present at her ninetieth birthday. A Vancouver leader, on the other hand, criticized the insularity of Jewish women who were unwilling to be involved in non-Jewish groups. The older leaders whom I interviewed were less likely to be active outside Jewish groups, while the younger ones tended to do more volunteer work outside the Jewish community, less fearful of the anti-Semitism that might await them. They were more willing to negotiate their goals with members in organizations that had different histories from their own. They volunteered with Planned Parenthood, Girl Guides, theatre associations, museums, or the Council of Christians and Jews.

Leadership and Authority

As Jewish women in Canada, Council leaders were heirs of a complicated history and tradition. They expressed their activism, and their assessment of success, in consonance with their personal and communal pasts. The women who foregrounded Council's emphasis on family and the Jewish community understood power in certain ways; those who stressed individual responsibility, women's activism, and feminism understood power in other ways. The latter sought to ameliorate social and economic circumstances in Canada, implicitly believing change to be more promising than order. They wanted to be among the forces for change. Still, depending on what they drew from their histories, the generations had different perspectives on power.[3]

Most women joined the organization just after marriage. Until the 1960s, they normally joined the Brides' Group. 'You met Prince Charming, got married, but then the books didn't tell you what to do, so you had to join something. Then you got pregnant, but still had to feel active and participating.' They usually met in the evenings, when husbands looked after their children, and became 'a self-help group. We talked about our kids, how to cope, and gave strength to each other.' A 50-year-old Vancouver leader said, 'It became a place where I could use my mental abilities, and there was no stigma attached to being able to do things well.' Some women joined Council to learn skills, as many sections and branches offered courses like French, art appreciation, and cooking; 'I didn't know how to boil water, not Jewish style or any style.' Others joined because their mothers, members of the synagogue, or their friends had been involved; yet others joined literary or religious study groups which led them toward projects like collecting toys for hospitals during the Second World War. Many leaders indicated that joining Council served their need 'to do not frivolous but serious things when I went out'. 'I joined to prove myself to myself.' A 30-year-old section president whose parents had divorced, 'joined because I needed that belonging that I didn't have before; I needed someone to pat me on the back and say you're OK'. A Vancouver member vowed that 'when my kids grow up, this community is going to know who I was, know who their mother was'.

For these women, the sense of fitting into the organization grew stronger as they discovered their own capacities, as they launched successful community projects. Leadership and authority within the organization came to them. Some leaders offered the capacity to 'get things done', others were best at strategizing, while many employed both kinds of skills. A section president described working in the pre-school for children of low-income families in Toronto, staffed by volunteers who had teacher training. 'But then I thought, what would be the purpose of bringing these children to school every day, then letting them go home to more of the same? Why don't we bring the mothers at the same time?' They learned how to involve parents who had previously feared school personnel; at present they teach English to the immigrant mothers. These kinds of initiatives were valued and rewarded with greater power and visibility within the organization because, as a former national president said, 'You need a leadership that will raise the level of the whole organization.'

Generational Tensions
In the years since 1970, leaders have sometimes transferred their organizational strategizing skills from the volunteer sector to the paid labour force and to feminist organizations like the Women's Legal Education and Action Fund, Elizabeth Fry Society, and Match International. Less motivated solely by their Jewishness, more by their feminism, some of them joined Council specifically to address women's issues like equal pay and access to abortion. Marrying later, if they married at all, feminist women joined Council after they already had a larger sense of their potential power than younger brides once had. Sometimes finding insufficient response to their initiatives on issues like the prevention of child abuse, 'the sort of project that would appeal more to younger women', they sought membership, and power, elsewhere. Council leadership is concerned that they are losing these women for lack of an overtly feminist orientation, despite its pro-choice position on abortion. Many of them were adamant about the organization's need to be relevant to younger women, while continuing to provide a 'smorgasbord of opportunity' to older members.

Some leaders recognized the irony of their own daughters' not working for Council, since 'they learned by watching their mothers that there were things to do in life'. The women now aged between 50 and 60 had combined their activism with their domestic lives. Public and private activities went together, although sometimes the combination was demanding. Women of that age always left meals in the freezer for their families when they went out of town, even though their husbands and children inevitably went out for dinner. 'Whatever I did was never in the way.' Their husbands, they said, usually supported their Council activity. These women were thankful, recognizing that other men in the Jewish community with different ideas about women's appropriate activities felt comfortable only if their wives were 'doing the stuff that men won't do, like teas and bake sales'. Their parents helped out too. When a Winnipeg member whose baby was only 6 months old was invited to a national conference, her father told her, 'When you get asked to something like this, you go. We'll manage here.'

On the other hand, this generation of leaders also had to appease parents who sometimes disapproved of their extensive public involvement; some of those who entered the political sphere heard, 'Don't you think that's for men?' They had their moments of anxiety, these women. A western leader wondered if it was 'good to teach our daughters that you shouldn't settle for just marriage? Do they become unmarriageable?' And yet she was proud: 'we're rocking the boat'. Some of these women read de Beauvoir in the mid-1950s, 'which caused our anger to emerge, but still we stretched, and realized that the trivia like the colours of napkins at a luncheon was only a means to an end.' They were sometimes torn between 'the stuff that men won't do' – the activities that were extensions of domesticity – and a newfound desire for a public presence.

The interactions among generations of leaders could be difficult, power within the organization being the sticking point following out of their knowledge and perceptions of a changing culture. A 90-year-old woman, formerly a national president, complained, 'Even though people know you have experience they never ask your opinion'; another resented the recipient of an honorary membership 'who only arrived in the 50s; and that's a long way from 1923'. A former section president said that 'leaders need a view from the top. A view from the middle out is not going to help you', with others agreeing that their knowledge of the organization's history should be solicited. A younger leader was sympathetic to their complaints. 'There comes a time in their lives when they don't have the energy to run around so much, and at that point they'll know they'll be a nothing, that they won't count any more'. Another section president disagreed: 'lots of presidents don't know there is nothing so past as a past president'. As the issues changed with changing time, as leadership changed, some women felt their power usurped and their authority challenged.

Perceptions of Power and Leadership

There has evidently been a shift in women's perceptions of power within the organization, reflecting the changed emphases among the age cohort most influenced by the women's movement. The older leaders emphasized their capacity gently and persuasively to bring people to work for the organization. They saw their strength as leaders to lie in identifying and encouraging talent and action in other people. Their vision of power in the organization derived from the parallel they experienced between the organization and a family. 'We'll work together on it, and as long as each person feels a responsibility, that's the key. I don't want to see one person do everything.' Another stressed the importance of 'dynamic people. If someone dynamic can bring people together, and let them know they're doing a good job, they should do it.' Dynamism could serve to valorize other people's efforts. The younger leaders stressed their efficiency in the interest of getting things done, even if single-handedly. A few contemporary leaders in their thirties and forties expressed comfort with power in a way that the older women did not, causing, perhaps, some of the resentment that the latter expressed. One young western section president said, 'Yes, I want power. Yes, I want some of the things that come with it, and I'm not ashamed of it. It fills the void that I need to be recognized; it's the basic drive to be part of something, to be up there.' Another's desire for power was driven by her commitment to the projects. 'I can get people to do the work. I tell people, I don't care if you don't love me. Just do it; I have to get the job done fast and with little fuss.' Paradoxically, the younger leaders who considered themselves feminists were also more concerned with efficiency than their predecessors, and thus less likely patiently to elicit leadership from others. More prepared to use their positions of power, less likely to negotiate, they also considered themselves more professional.

These candid expressions of the use of power were not universally admired. Ambition was not a quality that all leaders appreciated in their colleagues. Several section and national leaders complained about a former leader who was 'a different breed from other Council women. She doesn't care who she's going to step on.' 'When I was president she said to me, "you're the boss and you make the decisions". I said to her, "I don't make decisions that way".' A Toronto section former president wryly observed that Council had not in the past been a politically ambitious organization; 'now that women are more ambitious, it's easier to get officers.'

Ambivalence over power in the organization also emerged in

sometimes irritated discussions of national versus section power. Section leaders who went to national events invariably returned excited and inspired, 'in awe of the national executive', hoping, frequently unsuccessfully, to convey their enthusiasm over projects to section membership. Sections felt either neglected or overwhelmed by the national office, complaining that 'they forget there are others out there'. National, on the other hand, feared that sections were too often ignorant of Council history and their connections with each other, and attempted to bind them together through newsletters, national biennial conventions, and visits from national officers and staff. Some of this competition derived from age-associated disagreement over the utility of the organization to themselves and their visions of power in the local community, the younger leaders hoping for less direction from National, greater autonomy for themselves and their sections. They saw Council's policy recommendations as 'motherhood statements so sections can interpret them in many ways', while not losing the benefits of Council's good reputation inside government. The older leaders tended instead to merge themselves, their sections and National into a kind of family, its parts intimately connected. Territorial struggles were another sign of varied understandings of power and its purposes.

The older cohorts tended to see their leadership as 'sharing responsibility, being able to delegate and trust that she will carry through, and allowing people to make their mistakes'. A president of Montreal section in the 1950s believed that leadership consisted in 'a willingness to serve', to the extent of taking the bus to three meetings a day. 'Responsibility,' she said, 'falls on the shoulders where it can be assumed.' A Winnipeg leader believed her strength as a leader to be her lack of dogmatism – 'I really believe in the group and what the group can do.' 'Everyone has something to offer. People know what they do well. You need to put the right people in the right places,' said a Vancouver section president. A national president who became president of another Jewish organization wondered whether she could 'thump on the table and tell people what to do [as was the custom in her new group]. I come from a different background where I listen to the group and use the group for implementation. I decided that I couldn't act their way. I had to do it my way. I found it earned a great deal of respect and a great deal of cooperation.' 'A leader has to know how to pour oil on troubled waters, has to be a hand holder.'

The younger leaders, influenced by the women's movement and reconfiguring roles in their families and their work places, understood their leadership differently. They were less diffident about using power in the organization. An Ottawa section president in her thirties said, 'I can make a decision fast and act on it.' She was also prepared to accept its consequences. 'I learned to admit I had made a mistake and to apologize.' Still, she did not always welcome leadership's outcomes: 'I hate when people are mad at me.' Another section president from the west liked her leadership role because 'I can be in the limelight, and it gives me something to work for, because it makes me different from the next person.' She admitted that 'I'm not patient with people who screw up, and I don't encourage leadership in others. It's easier to do it myself than go out there and find somebody who perhaps can do it better than I.' These are women of a transitional generation, working within the constraints, which include a tradition that decries authoritarianism, of an organization they admire, yet seeking a public persona of their own. They are also of a generation that began to solicit government funds for some of their projects, which necessarily implied assigning priorities and manifesting efficiency and professionalism to satisfy the requirements of funding bodies.

Former leaders do not necessarily approve. A past president was concerned that people who want power were self-centred, seeking only adulation. Thus, feeling unwelcome, some potential leaders looked elsewhere, some to feminist organizations, speaking in the name of women for altered power arrangements, others to elected and appointed political office. They were less wary than their older colleagues of claiming power. Others among the younger leaders still tended to seek power within Council's long-standing tradition of community service, staying connected to their predecessors. As a 75-year-old leader observed of them, 'A good leader must have the ability to inspire others. She has imagination and conviction, she sees the changes needed, and she has the courage to make the changes.' She was pleased that the younger leaders evinced these qualities. A Vancouver section president was grateful that younger women were joining other organizations that stimulated them, offering them intellectual stimulation and political mobility. 'It's via those women you'll get clout in government,' she said.

Many contemporary Council leaders were aware of the changes taking place in the organization and in the country. An Ottawa section past president, now active in politics, wondered whether the relatively wealthy women who were once the leadership 'can still be in the forefront of social change. They do have an interest in equality, but feminism is not just equal pay but a power sharing that would turn society upside down.' She thought it possible that, even while embracing Jewish social ideals, the older leaders 'might not be prepared for the logical consequences of feminism. But the younger ones are less affluent, more forward-looking.'

Youth alone did not determine Council women's quest for political power, nor did wealth necessarily prevent it. In fact, one of the wealthiest national presidents, who encountered feminism in the late 1960s, recounted, 'I wanted to head where the power was. Not for a bread-and-butter need, but for a self-independence need. I came from a home where I felt like a prisoner waiting to get out. I feel a responsibility to myself to set up the kinds of paradigms where I can function on my own' – not relying solely on her wealth. Other women of her age, in their fifties and sixties, the generation which witnessed both their mothers' perceptions of power and their daughters', were neither as reticent as the one nor as ambitious as the other. A national president in the 1980s 'made a concerted effort to attend every government meeting in Ottawa that I was invited to', but would not herself run for office. Her vice president said, 'Council work is small "p" political, because you deal with government and policy. We're non-partisan, but we are political, making a contribution to the social policy of our country.' They did not say, as did a past president in her nineties, that 'politics was so full of graft, and if you were honest, you'd end up giving up a lot of your principles'; since those were the terms as she saw them, she clearly had no interest in entering the political sphere. Nor did they echo the sentiments of an 80-year-old past president who equated running for office with the search merely for personal fame. Rather, they hesitated to engage their energies directly in politics because they feared that they could not fit their experience of collective activism in Council into political structures, which they thought were insensitive to individual needs, either politicians' or electorate's. 'Politics is not people-oriented enough.' They continued instead to agitate for change through the organizational vehicle they found both comfortable and efficacious.

The leaders' view of power was an outcome of their under-standing of the human ability to act as individuals – to make a decision that action in the world was their human responsibility. However, young or old, they also manifested their cerebral and visceral knowledge of the human capacity to act in concert. They fully understood that groups of people can have power which individually they would not have. In this way, all Council leaders sought power – not for accolades (although they did not despise them) and certainly not for domination, but to enhance their own ability, and their memberships', to act together, to interact, in

order to improve lives. Power for them meant enhancing each
other's capacity to interact.

It is clear that underlying their desire to create the setting, in
Council, for such interaction, was a conscious or unconscious
belief in a multitude of individual capacities – social, intellectual,
emotional, aesthetic, sympathetic – or individual powers. They
took these to be the power that is released and enlarged by
interaction with others. Thus, their leadership was a quest to
identify that kind of power, and to play a role in releasing it, to
interact in magically creative ways in concert with other women.

They further assumed that members can use and develop their
capacities in the Council setting, where impediments to their
development have no place, where domination would not serve.
Domination there could mean only the disempowerment of
individuals' capacities for growth, for change, for action. In this
respect, then, *pouvoir* (to be able) and power come together in the
leaders' understandings of their role. All are able, if all can act
together. Like all of us, they understood power as dominance
perfectly well. However, they also understood power as individual
capacity, and power as the capacity to work and act in concert
with each other.

Summary and Conclusions

At the time of the interviews, women continued to see the
organization as a route towards developing skills and confidence,
in order to effect political and cultural changes. Clearly, they did
not intend to do so solely through 'big "p" politics'. Women of all
ages, whose leadership spanned five decades, from the 1930s to the
1980s, located themselves within the Jewish tradition and gave it
expression in their domestic lives and their organizational activities.
It remains to the historian to discern how they combined their
changing experiences of the private and public realms.

The oldest leaders, active between the 1930s and the 1950s,
experienced membership in Council as an extension of their roles
as wives. They joined the Brides Group upon marriage as a matter
of course and, as long as they were able, continued to do Council
work with the 'girls' they met there, often relatives and friends
from childhood. They experienced no dissonance between their
responsibilities at home and their volunteer work with children,
mothers and the poor from the Depression and well after the
Second World War. They married upon reaching adulthood; being
an adult also implied working in the community. They responded
unhesitatingly to the needs they identified, many of them

prompted by national and international crises. Issues of gender did not much concern them; they simply asserted that married Jewish women had always done such things. 'I just followed by mother.' National Council of Jewish Women offered them the vehicle for *pouvoir*; it enabled them to act collaboratively and simultaneously in the public and private realms.

The leaders who followed them in the 1950s and 1960s were more conflicted. The post-war messages urging them towards unmitigated domesticity did not inspire them; on the contrary, they began covertly resisting those messages by forming study groups examining political issues, by beginning to lobby governments for equal pay and fair employment practices, and by discussing women's roles in public life at meetings and in newsletters. While continuing Council's work with the elderly, children and the poor, some of them also read the early feminist literature. Its political contents forced them to think about domestic relations; they were more torn at leaving the house in the evenings than their mothers, although they insisted that neither their children nor their husbands were deprived by their activism. Certainly, they appreciated their husbands' support, while recognizing that their public lives were beginning to have a momentum that did not necessarily conform to their household responsibilities. None the less, they did not hesitate. This generation of women saw the beginnings of new roles for themselves, and they began to express them within the organization, demanding greater professionalism and education in political issues. Their understandings of women's roles changed as they perceived, albeit remotely, the possibility of acting in their own names. No longer did they sign themselves 'Mrs Abraham Gold'.

Their daughters, now in their thirties, inherited their mothers' activism. Some of them delayed and even disavowed marriage, and became professionals for whom the private and public realms, not unlike their grandmothers, were not in conflict. Their priorities were reversed, though; the former would serve the latter. A few of these single women joined Council, organizing study groups for professional women and urging the organization to take up feminist issues. Others worked directly for feminist organizations. Most of them, however, married, joined Council, bore children, worked for pay, and began to move into leadership roles. For this generation, issues of gender were central to their understanding of their own roles and the work of Council. While they recognized the need to offer a 'smorgasbord of opportunity', they also recognized that the choices must grow to attract young women who wanted power, in the family and in the culture. They accepted their husbands' participation in the household as normal, just as they intended to take their own places in the public world, the world of power.

These changes are not taking place easily. The young women, like their mothers and grandmothers, are far from certain of their direction. While acknowledging their feminism, they also recognize that when seeking funding they need to nurture professionalism and assign priorities, whether by negotiation or by the use of their authority as leaders. The older women sometimes accuse them of brashness and excesses of ambition, and sometimes feel marginalized by the quest for efficiency. The political culture they hope to enter, whether within government or as spokeswomen for their causes, has yet to accept them. But all of them have inherited values of loyalty to their organization, assurances of its presence, support from its membership who are their friends and relatives, and fidelity to the hope for change. They know their histories. They recognize that as they were formed by the social and political issues of their time, so too will they play a part in changing them. Not just enabled themselves, but enabling others, they will attain a place in our common world.

Notes

I appreciate the financial assistance of the Social Sciences and Humanities Research Council. I am truly grateful for the hospitality and help of the national office of the National Council of Jewish Women of Canada, and for the openness of the women across the country who talked to me about themselves and the organization.

1 Such studies include Bennett et al., 1986; Black, 1989; Dennison, 1987; Kealey and Sangster, 1989; Mitchinson, 1987; Razack, 1991; Sangster, 1989; Silverman, 1986; Strong-Boag, 1977.

2 Only a few works locate Canadian women in religious organizations which are not mainstream Protestant expressions. For a few recent examples, see Danylewycz, 1986; Marks, 1986; Simmons, 1986.

3 For analysis of these themes in nineteenth-century American history see Berg, 1978; Blair, 1980.

References

Bennett, John, Kohl, Seena and Sherburne, Dan (1986) 'Northern Plains Culture History'. Interim Report No. 3, unpublished.

Berg, Barbara (1978) *The Remembered Gate: Origins of American Feminism*. New York: Oxford University Press.

Black, Naomi (1989) *Social Feminism*. Ithaca, NY: Cornell University Press.

Blair, Karen J. (1980) *The Clubwoman as Feminist: True Womanhood Redefined, 1868–1914*. New York: Holmes and Meier.

Danylewycz, Marta (1986) 'In their own right: convents, an organized expression of women's aspirations', in Veronica Strong-Boag and Anita Fellman (eds), *Re-Thinking Canada*. Toronto: Copp Clark Pitman, pp. 160–81.

Dennison, Carol (1987) '"Housekeepers of the community": the British Columbia Women's Institutes, 1909–46', in Michael Welton (ed.), *Knowledge for the People: the Struggle for Adult Learning in English-Speaking Canada, 1828–1973*. Toronto: OISE Press, pp. 52–72.

Kealey, Linda and Sangster, Joan (eds) (1989) *Beyond the Vote: Canadian Women and Politics*. Toronto: University of Toronto Press.

Marks, Lynne (1986) 'Working-class femininity and the Salvation Army: Hallelujah lasses in English Canada, 1882–1892', in Veronica Strong-Boag and Anita Fellman (eds), *Re-Thinking Canada*. Toronto: Copp Clark Pitman, pp. 182–205.

Mitchinson, Wendy (1987) 'Early women's organizations and social reform: prelude to the welfare state', in Allan Moscovitch and Jim Albert (eds), *The 'Benevolent' State: the Growth of Welfare in Canada*. Toronto: Garamond Press, pp. 78–92.

Razack, Sherene (1991) *Canadian Feminism and the Law: the Women's Legal Education and Action Fund and the Pursuit of Equality*. Toronto: Second Story Press.

Sangster, Joan (1989) *Dreams of Equality: Women on the Canadian Left, 1920–1950*. Toronto: McClelland and Stewart.

Silverman, Eliane Leslau (1986) 'The National Council of Jewish Women: private lives, public people', *Canadian Woman Studies*, 7(4), 49–51.

Simmons, Christina (1986) '"Helping the poorer sisters": the women of the Jost Mission, Halifax, 1905–1945' in Veronica Strong-Boag and Anita Fellman (eds), *Re-Thinking Canada*. Toronto: Copp Clark Pitman, pp. 286–307.

Strong-Boag, Veronica (1977) '"Setting the stage": National organization and the women's movements in the late 19th century', in Susan Trofimenkoff and Alison Prentice (eds), *The Neglected Majority*. Toronto: McClelland and Stewart, pp. 87–103.

14

On Oppressing Hypotheses: or Differences in Nonverbal Sensitivity Revisited

Marianne LaFrance and Nancy M. Henley

Power has figured prominently in debates surrounding why women and men differ on a host of nonverbal behaviours, including how they respond to the nonverbal behaviour of other people. For example, research has shown that women are better than men at deciphering the meaning of another person's facial expressions or vocal intonation. This superior ability of women to read accurately others' subtle communication behaviour has engendered controversy not over whether it exists but why it exists. One thesis, sometimes labelled the 'oppression hypothesis', is that women's superior nonverbal sensitivity or decoding skill originates in their subordinate standing in society. In short, the argument is that people possessing relatively little power need to be able to discern the meaning of others' expressions and especially the expressions of those possessing higher power. Despite its surface cogency, the hypothesis for gender differences in decoding skill based on differential power has been found wanting or at least, one conspicuous programme of research has apparently shown that it has no empirical support. In what follows, we provide a detailed study of the evidence against and for this power-based interpretation. Our conclusion is that power is clearly implicated in why women are better decoders and that its rejection as a viable explanation is both uninformed and incorrect.

The Power of Nonverbal Behaviour

Nonverbal behaviour has long been a topic of the social and behavioural sciences (Darwin, 1872) and empirical research on it began in earnest nearly three decades ago. Anthropologists like Birdwhistell (1970) and E.T. Hall (1959, 1966) proposed that becoming enculturated involved learning not only the verbal language of one's group but the nonverbal language as well. Sociologists like Goffman (1959, 1967) demonstrated that everyday face-to-face encounters were actually made possible by an elaborate system of subtle yet well understood nonverbal signs. Ethologists like Eibl-Eibesfeldt (1972) and psychologists like Ekman et al. (1972) have established that the face is capable of registering the full range of human emotions, and social psychologists like Sommer (1969) and Exline (1972) have examined how and when people manage interpersonal distances and employ eye contact. Today, many academic and popular books dealing with political, business and interpersonal transactions include information stemming from research on nonverbal communication; professional meetings in psychology frequently address the role that nonverbal behaviour plays in the management of emotions, in the development of personality, in effecting change in relationships, and in the monitoring of therapeutic progress. The field even has its own journal, the *Journal of Nonverbal Behavior* which is in its fifteenth year of publication.

The aspects of behaviour called 'nonverbal' are rather extensive but most accounts include messages conveyed by the face, such as facial expression and gaze behaviour; messages communicated through body movement (kinesics) such as gesture, posture, and orientation; messages reflected by people's use of space (proxemics); an array of messages carried by the act of touch; and a large set of messages conveyed by vocal intonation and voice quality (paralinguistics). Dress, body type, smell, and use of physical objects are examples of nonverbal cues less often studied.

Research in all these areas has confirmed longstanding intuitions that nonverbal behaviour is a significant human activity and that its import is neither redundant or extraneous to words. But what empirical research has added to intuition is delineation and depiction of the various functions that nonverbal behaviour plays. For example, the expression of feeling is more typically conveyed nonverbally than verbally; one's standing in one's community may be revealed quite literally by how one carries oneself; turn-taking in conversations is negotiated nonverbally as is evidence of listening; development, maintenance, and change in personal relationships are often handled nonverbally; and nonverbal channels are regularly called upon when there is need to decipher whether a verbal statement is meant to be taken as fact or fabrication. The present chapter addresses another significant face of nonverbal behaviour, namely its role as a marker of power.

Women and men do different things with their eyes, faces, voices and bodies. In fact, it has been alleged that to be recognizably female or male requires being able to perform a complicated nonverbal script. Our focus here involves taking a close look at one aspect of this extensive nonverbal script. The particular effect is a controversial one and has to do with accounting for why women show greater ability to 'read' the nonverbal behaviour of other people than do men. A recurring question is whether this well-documented gender difference in nonverbal sensitivity is best understood as stemming from deep-seated differences between the sexes or whether it is due to structures that create power inequities between women and men. As will become apparent, the resolution of this dispute is handled in the social science literature not primarily by recourse to reflection or argument or illustration (although all can be compelling), but rather through a painstaking process that involves methodological critique, valid measurement and objective scrutiny of reliable data. We follow this latter course not only because we are social scientists but also because we believe that close examination of the processes behind the 'facts' often allows us to grasp what is really going on.

Accounting for Nonverbal Sex Differences

Interestingly, there is little controversy in the literature concerning whether there are gendered aspects of nonverbal behaviour. Differences in the nonverbal behaviour of women and men are now well established (Aries, 1987; Frieze and Ramsey, 1976; Henley, 1977; Hyde, 1990; LaFrance and Mayo, 1979). Although varying with the nature of the situation, the differences sometimes being quite substantial and other times non-existent, nevertheless the data tend to indicate that women and men display different kinds and degrees of nonverbal behaviour. For example, females engage in more mutual and non-mutual gaze at others than males and they smile more than males. Early on, the favoured explanation was that such differences reflected basic gender-stereotypic personality variables. That is, women's greater eye contact was due to their greater affiliative need or more pronounced field dependence (Exline, 1963; Exline et al., 1965) and their tendency to smile more than men was the result of their greater propensity towards social affiliation. Other researchers, however, looked at these same results and saw different forces operating. For example, Henley (1977) noted the tendency to gaze and smile was also shown by the lower-power person in status-discrepant relationships. Thus a substantial number of nonverbal gender differences might be attributable to power inequities rather than personality differences. In other words, instead of seeing a person's facial expression or body gesture as solely indicative of some underlying trait such as sociability or emotionality, the conjecture based on a power analysis was that many expressions and gestures are also called for by one's social position or lack thereof. Their role is to signal one's compliance with the social order rather than reflect one's individuality.

The hypothesis that men and women demonstrate different nonverbal behaviours because they possess unequal power grew out of work in the early 1970s which started to document other inequalities in the small stuff of everyday life, including dynamics within familial and close relationships (Gillespie, 1971; Safilios-Rothschild, 1970), in language used by women and men (Kramer, 1977; Lakoff, 1975; Thorne and Henley, 1975), and in other microsocial domains. More specifically, feminist scholarship had begun to identify power as a significant component of male–female relationships and thus scrutinizing the subtle realm of nonverbal behaviour between women and men for the workings of power was a natural outcome. Among those who looked at nonverbal sex differences in the 1970s and considered a power explanation were Frieze and Ramsey (1976), Goffman (1979), J.A. Hall (1979), Henley (1973a, 1973b, 1977), LaFrance and Mayo (1979), Weitz (1976) and Wex (1979).

Thus, another function was added to those already identified with nonverbal behaviour. Nonverbal cues could act in such a way not only to embody hierarchical relations but perhaps more importantly, to uphold and to justify them. Men's greater social power relative to women is reflected again and again in portrayed interactions seen in the media. Goffman (1979) has provided numerous illustrations of this in a book appropriately entitled *Gender Advertisements*. When men are shown in home settings engaged in stereotypically 'feminine' activities, advertisements use nonverbal cues to convey a 'clowning' or frivolous flavour. So even if men are shown as doing at home 'what women do', and women at work doing 'what men do', the accompanying nonverbal messages indicate that the basic gender arrangements are intact.

Men's greater social power relative to women is also substantiated in the subtle yet pervasive nonverbal cues given and received between the sexes in actual everyday interactions. There is now evidence that males are less facially expressive than females (LaFrance and Banaji, 1992). Moreover, males report greater satisfaction with their dating relationship when the exchange has the male disclosing less about himself relative to his female partner than she to him (Millar and Millar, 1988) and males report being more attracted to a high-expressive female than a low-expressive female, especially if she is described as physically attractive

(Sprecher, 1989). So the norms call for women to be revelatory even while the men they associate with adopt a non-disclosing stance. In a related study among married couples, husbands' marital complaints were found to increase as their wives' expressive abilities decreased (Sabatelli et al 1982). No such relationship was found for wives.

A particularly interesting difference between the sexes has been the noted superior ability of females accurately to decode the nonverbal behaviours of others (Rosenthal et al., 1979). Here too, power has been used to interpret the differences (Henley, 1977; Henley and LaFrance, 1984; Snodgrass, 1985). The basic thesis is that it falls to persons of lower power to be able to read the cues of someone possessing higher power, because their ability to respond appropriately, if not their very survival, may depend upon it. But despite the intuitive appeal of a power explanation to account for the observed tendency for females to be more nonverbally sensitive than males, some published work reports failure to find corroborating evidence. Specifically, one oft-cited programme of research concludes that a power explanation of gender differences in decoding ability is without merit. In what follows, we provide a detailed review of the empirical evidence for and against a power explanation for nonverbal sensitivity.

Our rationale for scrutinizing this particular issue is based on several considerations. Just as literary and historical scholars see advantage in conducting extremely close textual readings, social scientists believe that intense examination of the data bearing on a particular behavioural phenomenon can reveal something essential about why there are differences. If God is not exactly in the details, then at least valid interpretation may be. Secondly, we examine this particular nonverbal behaviour because it illustrates more generally how psychologists have and have not dealt with power as a key dynamic in human relationships. We expect to show that some researchers have been too quick to dismiss a power explanation of gender differences in nonverbal behaviour in part because they have been insufficiently apprised of what a power explanation consists of. Hence, we will elaborate its key aspects, especially as they pertain to nonverbal relationships between the sexes. Finally, we tackle this particular issue because it is interesting on its own terms. It appears that people differ substantially in their ability accurately to read and understand what others are not saying but are none the less clearly communicating. It would be fascinating to understand why a lot of the people who are better happen to be women.

Power and Nonverbal Behaviour

As noted, the gender aspects of nonverbal behaviour are multiple. So, in tackling why there are sex differences in nonverbal decoding skill, we are necessarily being selective. Nevertheless, this particular issue is in many ways representative of work going on in other areas of nonverbal communication research. The attempt to account for women's greater nonverbal sensitivity taps into a more basic issue, namely whether the appearance of sex differences is rooted in power inequities.

A power analysis applied to nonverbal sex differences proceeds from two sets of ideas. First, there is the recognition that power constitutes a pervasive dynamic in social relationships whether those relationships take place in public or private spheres. Secondly, in the nonverbal communication literature, there are clear indications that power differences between people are expressed via an array of nonverbal cues, whose meaning, while tacit, is nevertheless transparent. For example, Ellyson and his colleagues have consistently found that high-power people (assessed by such measures as higher social rank or greater expertise) look at their conversational partner more when they are speaking than when they are listening but that the reverse is true for lower-power people who look more at the other when they are listening than when they are talking (Ellyson et al., 1981). Moreover, differences in visual dominance can be perceived by observers such that when individuals exhibit high ratios of look–speak to look–listen behaviour, they are rated as more powerful than when they demonstrate moderate ratios (Ellyson et al., 1981).

Thus visual behaviour appears to serve an important function in establishing and conveying social power. But visual behaviour is not the sole nonverbal behaviour that acts in this way. Other nonverbal cues such as facial expressivity, postural arrangements, licence to touch, and admissible space are also modalities through which power is exercised in the context of personal relationships. Context is important to keep in mind for it is a reminder that power thus conceived is not something that someone invariably possesses but rather it is an attribute of relations. As such, its concrete manifestations in one or more nonverbal behaviours will vary depending on the nature of a particular relationship. One can have more power with respect to a specific other but have less with respect to someone else even in the same context. Thus, in talking to a subordinate I may adopt the visual dominance pattern described above but would likely cease that pattern when communicating with my superior.

This relational nature also means that in a power-discrepant relationship, each party will display different nonverbal behaviour relative to the other, in contrast to equal-power relationships, in which both parties are likely to engage in reciprocal or symmetrical patterns of nonverbal behaviour (Henley, 1977). It is also the case that the nonverbal concomitants of power are not entirely arbitrary but are associated with psychological attributes that not only signal difference between individuals but also convey disparities in control. We hypothesized in an earlier chapter that these disparities would be manifest in four separate and significant interpersonal domains (Henley and LaFrance, 1984). The specific domains are as follows:

(a) Readability The hypothesis is that power inequity will show itself in how differentially 'readable' or nonverbally communicative individuals in a relationship are. Specifically, we predict that lower-power people will be more nonverbally readable, that is, be more nonverbally expressive than higher-power people. The basic idea is that power is sustained, in part, through the exercise of apparent composure and concealment. In contrast, lower-power people are expected to be more disclosing, which has the effect of making them more accountable and vulnerable.

(b) Accommodativeness We also predicted that power differentials would be manifest in the degree to which individuals show the tendency to modify their behaviour so as to accommodate the other party in an interaction. The specific prediction is that members of a lower-power group will be more nonverbally accommodating, in that they are more likely to adjust their nonverbal behaviours to fit with the behaviours of the higher-power group than the higher-power group will adjust in response to them. Having control means that others will have to adjust.

(c) Submissiveness A third prediction stemming from a power analysis of nonverbal behaviour is that members of a lower-power group will show more nonverbal signs which convey an attitude of submissiveness than will members of a higher-power group. For example, the submissiveness hypothesis proposes that females' greater smiling, gazing (and gaze aversion, such as eyelid-lowering), head canting and head lowering, lower or 'after' spatial positioning, smaller personal spaces, contracted postures, and higher rates of being spatially invaded and being touched are due to their subordinate status (Henley, 1977; Henley and LaFrance, 1984).

(d) Sensitivity   Finally, a power analysis suggests that members of lower-power groups will need to be more attentive to those possessing higher power than the reverse. As indicated previously, the specific prediction is that the lower-power group will show more nonverbal decoding skills, that is, will be better at reading the expressions of the higher-power group than vice versa.

The argument that certain nonverbal differences stem from power inequities means that situations of status differences other than sex would create similar differences in nonverbal behaviour. For example, there is parallel evidence of nonverbal behaviour differences in situations involving intercultural inequality (Henley and LaFrance, 1984) or experimentally created hierarchies (Leffler et al., 1982; Snodgrass, 1985).

Finally, it is important to note that the relationship between lower-power and higher-power groups is basic to the theory; the lower-power group's greater readability, accommodation, submissiveness and sensitivity are expected to be most manifest relative to the higher-power group. However, because of gender-based socialization, they may be manifested in other situations as well.

Decoding Skill and the 'Oppression Hypothesis' Controversy

Each of the hypotheses described above has received some empirical attention, but as we observed earlier, the hypothesis that greater sensitivity by women occurs *because* of their lower status remains controversial. In fact, Judith Hall and her colleagues (Hall, 1984, 1985, 1987; Hall and Halberstadt, 1981, 1986; Stier and Hall, 1984) have been at continued pains to refute a power explanation for gender differences in nonverbal decoding skill, an explanation which Hall has labelled 'the oppression hypothesis' (1984: 39). In what follows we undertake an extended examination of the theory and research bearing on it. Our reasons for probing Hall's conclusions are several. First, while there already exist reasons to question Hall's rejection of a power analysis (see, for example, the critiques offered by Henley and LaFrance, 1984; Kramarae, 1985; LaFrance, 1986, 1987), the more typical response, especially within the field of the psychology of women, has been to accept Hall's assessment (for example, Eagly, 1987b: 103ff; Matlin, 1987: 216–18; Wallston, 1987: 1035). Secondly, we take a close look at this work because for many psychologists Hall's conclusions seem to be the result of having employed a sophisticated and objective research methodology. We suggest, however, that there are flaws in that methodology which if left unearthed might lead others to conclude erroneously that Hall is on the right track. Finally, we undertake this critique in order to clarify the continued viability of a power analysis to account for nonverbal gender differences.

In the following section we begin our examination by attempting to track the origins of what has come to be called 'the oppression hypothesis' within the psychology of nonverbal behaviour. We consider the appropriateness of the term and then go on to describe the empirical research bearing on it.

Source and Appropriateness of the Term 'Oppression Hypothesis'

Origin The origin of the 'oppression hypothesis' to explain nonverbal sex differences has been variously attributed by Hall in her different writings:

1. Hall (1978) cites English (1972) and Weitz (1974).
2. Hall and Halberstadt (1981) cite both these references as well as Thomas et al. (1972).
3. Stier and Hall (1984) cite Henley (1973b).
4. Hall (1984) cites all these (changing the Henley reference to 1977) and adds Frieze and Ramsey (1976).
5. Hall (1985) cites Henley (1973b, 1977) as 'the major theorist' of this 'one prevalent interpretation.'
6. Hall and Halberstadt (1986) cite Henley (1977) as the author of the only hypothesis that 'has received any serious development' (1986: 138).

Henley in turn derived her (1973a, 1977) explanations of power-related nonverbal behaviour from the work of Goffman (1967) and Brown (1965), and of nonverbal decoding sensitivity as related to subordinate status from several sources, including Gitter et al. (1972), Rubin (1970) and Weitz (1974). Snodgrass (1985) attributes the 'subordinate role' explanation of interpersonal sensitivity to Hall (in Rosenthal et al., 1979), Miller (1976), Thomas et al. (1972) and Weitz (1974).

The interpretation of women's position as subordinate hardly needs justification, enshrined as it is in law, language and custom. In what is known as the first wave of feminism, writers like Virginia Woolf (1929) and Elizabeth Cady Stanton, Susan B. Anthony and Matilda Joslyn (1889) noted a correlation between the subordination of woman and how she behaved, as did writers like Friedan (1963), Millett (1969) and Firestone (1970) early in the second wave. This power-based analysis is now widely discussed among feminist scholars.

Naming the theory   As indicated, the title Hall gave to the idea that women's greater sensitivity might derive from their unequal status was the 'oppression hypothesis'. Although achieving some currency owing to repetition, the label is probably not the best choice for the phenomena it describes. The term 'subordination hypothesis' is preferable because gender variability is seen to stem from differences in power variously conceived. For example, subordination could result from possessing less social power (defined as influence based on control of resources), lower social status (defined as attributed esteem or importance) or restricted interpersonal dominance (defined as control over another individual's behaviour). Because a power-based analysis, while including oppression, also applies to a broader set of phenomena, we find the terms **subordination hypothesis** or **subordination theory** preferable.

Although Hall appears to accept the idea that women's lower standing might play some part in accounting for why they are more nonverbally sensitive than men, her basic argument rejects the notion that women's subordinate status is directly implicated. She writes:

> Girls and women could learn that as females they ought to be good decoders, not because they are actually oppressed in any sense of the word, but because society prescribes certain roles and behaviours for them . . . Though women's oppression may play a part in such sex-role expectations, in that such expectations reflect the earlier extreme circumscription of women's activities . . . it would nevertheless be an overstatement to claim that women's nonverbal skill stems from their oppression in any direct sense. (Hall, 1984: 42)

Subordination theory also takes account of sex role expectations and gender socialization but in a more contiguous and continual way. Patriarchal societies shape, establish and maintain gender roles that support male dominance. Moreover, patriarchal societies bring about and maintain gender roles drawing on several agencies such as religion, the media, education, public policy and the legal system. Because socialized roles constitute a significant part of the mechanism supporting inequities, pointing to their part in nonverbal gender differentiation does not diminish the power of subordination theory, as Hall (1984) implies, but rather supports its finer points.

Testing the Subordination Hypothesis of Nonverbal Decoding Ability

A good deal of evidence apparently refuting a power-based explanation of sex differences in decoding ability has used a test of decoding skill called the **Profile of Nonverbal Sensitivity (PONS)** (Rosenthal et al., 1979). The PONS was initially designed to measure individual differences in the ability accurately to 'read' someone else's communicative cues coming from the face, body and voice. Although various subtests have been spun off from the original test, the full PONS consists of 220 very brief (2-second duration) visual and/or vocal segments (without verbal content) enacted by one young Caucasian woman. The segments are presented in a regular order on a movie screen or television monitor to one or more test takers who have a few seconds after each segment to decide what each segment conveyed. Specifically, test takers must decide which of two possible situations presented in multiple choice format on a standard rating sheet best describes the presented segment. One's score on the PONS is a tally of how many choices correspond to what the test takers had initially established were correct responses.

In studies involving over 10,000 people, varying in age and nationality, the original investigators noted a small but consistent sex difference favouring females, that is, females had higher scores on the PONS than did males (Rosenthal et al., 1979). They reported that of 133 separate samples, 80 per cent showed difference in this direction, with a median effect size r of 0.20. It is important to note that the size of difference, while reliable, is quite modest. In addition, a cross-cultural set of data from forty-six samples from ten nations plus six from the United States showed an average female–male difference of about 2 percentage points. An r of 0.20 (found in both the total 133 samples and cross-cultural subsamples) indicates that sex differences account for only 4 per cent of the total variance in the results (Hall, 1984: 18).

Hall herself reviewed seventy-five studies of nonverbal decoding accuracy and concluded that 'the analyses revealed that more studies showed female advantage than would occur by chance' (Hall, 1978: 854). Sixty-eight per cent showed female superiority in decoding skill and 31 per cent showed statistically significant differences favouring women. When studies reporting no difference between the sexes were excluded, 84 per cent of the remaining studies showed female superiority. In 1984, Hall reported results of fifty additional studies, only one based on the PONS. Among these, 20 per cent showed a statistically significant difference favouring females although 52 per cent of the total showed a female advantage. When studies which found no sex difference were excluded, 81 per cent of the remaining number showed female superiority.

Thus, we concur with Hall and others that there is evidence for a small but consistent difference favouring females. The problem then becomes to account for this effect.

Hall and Halberstadt (1981): Refutation or Support of the Subordination Hypothesis?

Hall and Halberstadt (1981) purport to provide a test of 'the hypothesis that persons with less social power need to be especially alert to the behaviours and moods of more powerful others' (1981: 275). The empirical test of the hypothesis necessitated measuring two key components on the same set of female respondents. First, it required a way to measure decoding skill and secondly, there was need to measure individual differences in the degree to which a sample of women were 'oppressed'. This latter variable was derived based on the following reasoning. Based on 'the assumption that traditionality on questions of women's rights represents acceptance of an ideology of male domination', Hall and Halberstadt predicted that if the 'oppression hypothesis' had merit, then 'the more traditional, less egalitarian women would be the best decoders' (Hall and Halberstadt, 1981: 282). In other words, they inferred that women who espoused more traditional sex role views were more oppressed and as such they should, if lower power caused greater sensitivity, score higher on decoding skill than women who had less traditional sex role views.

They found the opposite relation, namely that those women who were *less* traditional had higher decoding scores, and therefrom concluded that the oppression hypothesis was unsupported.

However, closer inspection of their method indicates that they misinterpreted their own results. In fact, their own data may actually be seen as support for the subordination hypothesis (Henley and LaFrance, 1984; LaFrance, 1986). To understand how we arrive at this conclusion, it is necessary to study closely what Hall and Halberstadt (1981) did and what they found.

Hall and Halberstadt (1981) define 'oppression' at the individual level (as contrasted with a structural level) in terms of traditionality of sex roles and assess differences in traditionality in two ways: by measuring both attitudes and behaviours of female respondents. Regarding attitudes, they draw on three studies which used the short **Attitude towards Women Scale (AWS)** (Spence et al., 1973) or a children's version of the AWS. Regarding behaviours, they examined the relationship of decoding skill to married women's self-reported preference for traditionality in their own marriage and actual traditionality via division of labour in housecleaning and laundry. As they conceived it:

Thus, we operationalized the concept of 'oppressed status' both in terms of subjects' perceptions and their more objective estimations of their own sex-role-related behavior. Of course, these are not the only criteria of 'oppressed status' that one could employ, but they were reasonable ones to start with. (1981: 283)

With respect to the studies which used attitudes as a measure of oppression, Hall and Halberstadt found that females with more egalitarian views were actually better decoders than females holding more traditional views – exactly the opposite of what they argued would need to occur if the oppression hypothesis were to be supported (1981: 292). With respect to studies using behavioural measures of oppression, they also found that those who adopted less traditional marital division of labour showed higher decoding skill. However, it is important to note that their results differed with the sex of the *encoder*, that is, the target person who was being 'read'. For the two tests that measured sensitivity to a *female* encoder (the original PONS), they write:

the more 'liberated' type of woman – at least as indicated by these measures – was a *better* decoder of a woman's nonverbal cues than was the less 'liberated' woman. This is the opposite of the original prediction, as was the case with attitudes towards women. (1981: 284, emphasis in original)

In contrast, with the one test of decoding skill involving audio segments only, which used a *male* encoder, they report:

There was a tendency for a more traditional marriage (both actual and preference) and for performance of more housecleaning to be *positively* associated with ability to decode a man's voice. If this pattern is reliable, it would suggest that those who prefer and have traditional marriages are better at understanding a man's subtle messages than are less traditional women. (1981: 284, emphasis in original)

In other words, their own data indicate that there was a positive association between the tendency to be in a more traditional marriage and the ability to read a man's voice, results which seem entirely compatible with the subordination hypothesis. Their response to these data was twofold: first they worked to undermine the results, specifically: 'these correlations should be interpreted very cautiously since they are based on a single small sample . . .' (1981: 284). Then they re-interpret findings involving skill in reading female and male encoders as indicating not support for the subordination hypothesis, but support for what they call a salience argument. Their argument:

The overall picture . . . would suggest the possibility that women may become better nonverbal decoders of whichever sex is most salient to them – men in the case of more traditional women, other women in the case of less traditional women. (1981: 284)

In other words, the two obtained patterns – greater decoding skill of a female encoder for non-traditional women and greater decoding skill of a male encoder for traditional women – are rejected as reflecting support for the subordination hypothesis. They are construed instead as indicating 'salience', which given its proposed stance as an alternative explanation means that decoding skill is interpreted as being unrelated to power.

Both results are decidedly compatible with a power-based explanation. Had the authors taken feminist arguments seriously, they might have begun by focusing on the ability of women to read a *man*'s nonverbal cues and hypothesized greater sensitivity in more traditional women and directed their test there. As it is, with most of the evidence bearing on the subordination hypothesis coming from skill measured in response to a female, the results are tangential to the issue of subordination with respect to men. In fact the original developers of the PONS test wrote in 1979:

> From the start, we recognized that our observation of sex differences in nonverbal skill might be confounded by the fact that that PONS sender was a woman . . . Women and young girls may have special skill only at reading another female . . . We are also incapable of detecting a sender sex × receiver sex interaction, if one exists. (Rosenthal et al., 1979: 162)

Hall and Halberstadt eschewed this interpretive problem and proceeded to correlate scores on the PONS with another measure of oppression. This time, structural oppression was defined as indices of women's educational, occupational and cultural status relative to men's. Using these measures, they report no relationship between decoding skill and degree of oppression in general, although when the test was subdivided into separate channels, complex patterns emerged. For vocal cues, 'less ostensible oppression was associated with greater skill in women' but for visual cues, the correlations were negative, although 'only a few of these were significant' (Hall, 1984: 43).

Hall and Halberstadt's (1981) studies, properly interpreted, do yield relevant information. By finding greater sensitivity to a man's vocal cues in more traditional women, the findings appear to support the subordination hypothesis. By finding greater sensitivity to a woman's nonverbal cues in less traditional women, the findings do not directly bear on the subordination hypothesis because the relevant behaviour is not decoding skill in general but decoding of men in particular. Nevertheless, the findings are interesting in feminist terms, which might predict that less traditionally orientated women would be more attuned to other women.

Unfortunately, the procedures followed in the 1981 report were flawed in other ways. First, the authors rely almost exclusively on the PONS, which has been criticized as being a limited and artificial measure of nonverbal decoding skill.[1] The authors employ a range of measures of 'oppression' but do not call on the same range when measuring sensitivity. Secondly, the use of women's attitudes as a measure of oppressedness is problematic. In doing so, Hall and Halberstadt essentially assessed the strength of a relation between women's attitudes towards *women's roles* and their ability to choose a label for the posed emotions of a female that coincided with the emotion the female was attempting to project. Unfortunately, this ill-considered venture and attendant conclusions have been magnified by repetition by Hall (for example, 1984, 1985). Moreover, when these interpretative problems were pointed out in an otherwise positive review of Hall's book by LaFrance (1987), a published response defended Hall's general approach rather than giving consideration to the particular criticism (Eagly, 1987a).

Other Tests of the Subordination Hypothesis
Lamentably, there have been few other tests of the subordination hypothesis with respect to decoding skill, but two studies are suggestive. Looking at racial/ethnic differences, Gitter et al. (1972) photographed encoders, who were either Afro-American or white and female or male, as they conveyed seven different emotions. Perceivers of both sexes and races were asked to indicate which emotions were being portrayed. Afro-American respondents were found to be more accurate at decoding the emotions of both races and sexes than white perceivers, although no significant sex differences were found. In another study, Rollman (1978) tested both Afro-American and white decoders' abilities to read the nonverbal signals of a prejudiced (anti-black) or non-prejudiced white. He found that black perceivers were better judges of racial prejudice than whites. Given that Afro-Americans as a group are socially and economically oppressed by whites, both studies seem to support the subordination hypothesis.

Halberstadt (1985), however, reached a different conclusion after conducting a comprehensive review of studies examining the effect of race and/or socioeconomic status (SES) on nonverbal decoding skill. Her review found no significant difference in decoding skill in seven studies which compared black and white decoders. For seven studies which investigated the effect of SES, lower-class decoders were found to be less skilled than middle-class ones, with a moderate effect size, a pattern that at first glance fails to support a subordination explanation. However, the difference in decoding skill favouring middle-class decoders decreased as the decoders got older. Even though the age factor showed a large effect size, Halberstadt reported that it was 'non-significant because of the small N' (1985: 235). Halberstadt might have noted that limited range might have prevented a better test of the relationship, since *none* of the reported seven studies used an adult sample (in only one were the subjects even in high school). In summary, the author reports:

> All seven of the studies concur; lower class individuals are not as skilled at decoding as more privileged individuals. . . . Though using the highly conservative procedure of setting the zs for these studies at zero, the effect of an advantageous background on nonverbal decoding skill was apparent . . . lower class children are less skilled at decoding cues than middle-class children . . . the 14 studies . . . continue to suggest two clear patterns for race and class differences in nonverbal communication skill: (a) young white and middle-class individuals are better decoders than young black and lower class individuals and (b) these race and class differences are attenuated and possibly even reversed by adulthood. (1985: 234–5)

Again, a closer examination suggests some need for revision. First, for the race comparisons, the author points out (1985: 234) that for four of the studies only white encoders were used thus replicating the problem noted above with respect to encoder sex, namely the failure to compare skill across encoders who differ on the relevant dimension. In addition, five of the studies confounded race and SES. For the SES comparisons, Halberstadt notes that 'most, if not all, of the studies on skill employed middle-class senders only' (1985: 258). Thus we have few, if any, true comparisons of differential abilities across race/ethnicity and class lines, any more than we have across gender lines. Although Halberstadt concedes this deficiency, nevertheless she combines them in a meta-analysis which leads to her drawing inappropriate conclusions. It is our opinion that researchers who review a field and find studies insufficiently constructed to test a desired hypothesis, besides acknowledging and criticizing them, should not then do a meta-analytic conglomeration of them. To do so gives a false scientific gloss to the collection and leads to insupportable claims.

Despite these reservations, can anything be concluded from the available data? Since the encoders have tended to be white and middle class, this at least is the group for whom the subordination hypothesis would predict decoding superiority in black and poor subjects. Contradictory data would thus be damaging to the subordination hypothesis. Analogous to our re-interpretation of Hall and Halberstadt (1981) on gender, we submit that the findings reported by Halberstadt (1985) on race and SES are also not in conflict with a subordination explanation. The increasing skill shown by blacks and by lower-class children with age suggests gains due to social experience, which would be consistent with the subordination hypothesis. Indeed, the finding of no difference at early ages supports a learned rather than innate basis for the difference. However, scant study has been made of the older end of the age spectrum, which would be a better test of the subordination hypothesis.

An Appropriate Test of the Subordination Hypothesis

What then would be an adequate empirical test of the subordination hypothesis? First, an adequate measure of decoding skill should be used. Such a test of individual differences would do the following:

1. Incorporate spontaneous instead of or in addition to posed emotions.
2. Employ several as opposed to single encoders.
3. Include both female and male targets to be 'read'.
4. Allow more rather than two response options.

Some attempts along these lines have been made by Buck (1984) and Costanzo and Archer (1989).

Secondly, the design should incorporate appropriate contrasts. The subordination hypothesis posits that a subordinate group's ability to decode a superordinate group's nonverbal behaviour will be superior to the superordinate group's ability to decode the subordinate group's. Thus both groups, and in the case of gender hierarchy, both sexes must be represented as both senders and receivers of nonverbal signals. The comparison that tests the hypothesis is that of cross-group (cross-sex) decoding abilities. Within-group decoding competencies may be used for control comparisons. The question of whether there is a prediction of differential within-group decoding ability is taken up below.

Thirdly, the operationalization of superior/subordinate status should be consistent with a theory of subordination. This could be done in various ways, such as choosing subjects based on pre-existing differences in relative economic, social, political, or relationship power, or by creating asymmetric relationships in experimentally created groups. Using self-reported attitudes regarding gender equality, such as was done by Hall and Halberstadt (1981), is more risky as a measure of subordination because people in low power positions often hold the attitudes of the dominant group (Tajfel, 1984). Nevertheless, an attitudinal measure could conceivably be appropriate if it was independently shown to be a valid indicator of respondents' beliefs about their *own* status *vis-à-vis* members of an identified superordinate group.

Fourthly, the design should at some point test competing alternative explanations for the nonverbal sensitivity difference empirically and specifically, rather than seeking to refute the subordination hypothesis by integrative review, such as was done by Hall and Halberstadt (1981). Their method essentially amounts to an attempt to confirm the null hypothesis, which is at odds with the preferred strategy of attempting to disconfirm it.

Finally, an ideal test would probably entail an experimental design, in which individuals would be randomly assigned to superior and subordinate groups. By so doing, it would be possible to separate status from pre-existing individual differences. The work of Snodgrass (1985, 1992) represents just such an approach, although she measured sensitivity not as a trait-like ability to decode a stranger's nonverbally expressed emotions, but as sensitivity to the feelings of the other within a specific situation. In the first investigation, same-sex and cross-sex dyads interacted in a laboratory context. These research participants were asked four times during an interaction to use rating scales to indicate both their own feelings and the other person's regarding themselves, the other and the activity. Status asymmetry was established by randomly assigning subjects to be either teacher or student in an instruction situation. Following this session, the dyad engaged in both competitive and cooperative games.

The results supported predictions from subordination theory. First, there was no significant main effect for sex collapsed across context; that is, women were not more sensitive than men overall in judging the other's feelings and reactions when status was not considered. Secondly, there was a strong main effect for status position, such that lower-status people (learners) were significantly more sensitive to the feelings of the higher-status persons (teachers) than higher-status persons were to the feelings to the lower-status participants. Thirdly, there was a significant effect for gender composition, such that women's sensitivity towards men was greater than women's sensitivity towards women, but the reverse was not true for men (that is, men's sensitivity towards women was not significantly greater than their sensitivity towards men). Snodgrass (1985) also found a significant interaction of role, type of judgement and activity, and a significant contrast within it which indicated that, in the teaching–learning activity, female subordinates with male superordinates were more sensitive than all other combinations.

Snodgrass (1992) extended her examination of the relationship among gender, status, and sensitivity to an experimentally created boss–employee relationship. In this study, subjects were not only randomly assigned but also served in both capacities, twice as leader and twice as subordinate. Again, there was no significant main effect for sex; females were not more non-verbally sensitive than males. Again there was a significant effect for role, such that 'employees' were significantly more sensitive to how the 'boss' saw them (the employee) than vice versa. Finally, there was a significant statistical interaction among the three factors of subject sex, type of judgement and role which showed that the effect was more pronounced with female than with male subjects.

The subordination hypothesis has also to be tested with respect to other sex differences in nonverbal behaviour. In those domains, the subordination hypothesis predicts that the subordinate group's nonverbal behaviour will be more expressive, submissive and accommodating than that of the superordinate group. Interestingly, Hall and Halberstadt (1986) have also tackled these behaviours and have again found the oppression hypothesis to be without merit. Again, it is our position that there are clear indications that this rejection is also questionable on scientific grounds. We address these areas of research in a separate paper (Henley and LaFrance, 1992).

Explanatory Politics in Explaining Sex Differences in Nonverbal Sensitivity

Hall (1978) put forward three possible explanations for the finding of sex difference in nonverbal sensitivity. They are as follows:

(a) socialization to gender role stereotypes;
(b) women's oppressed status;
(c) genetic predisposition from adaptive evolution: that is, females may be 'wired' from birth to be especially sensitive to nonverbal cues or to be especially quick learners of such cues . . . because nonverbal sensitivity on a mother's part might

enable her to detect distress in her youngsters or threatening signals from other adults, thus enhancing the survival chances of her offspring. (Hall, 1978: 854)

Later, Hall (1984) expanded the possible explanations to include:

(a) sex-stereotypical masculinity and femininity, as measured by sex role self-concept scales;
(b) greater female empathy (also part of the gender stereotype), as measured by empathy scales;
(c) attention and practice focused on nonverbal decoding required by the female role;
(d) accommodation by women to politeness norms to attend to more controllable (less 'leaky') nonverbal channels;
(e) women's adaptation to oppression by special alertness to the behaviour and moods of the more powerful (men); and
(f) males' greater cerebral hemispheric specialization, which may inhibit processing of nonverbal information.

Hall finds the most promising of these explanations to be those based on practice/attention and accommodation. She also repeats the 'interesting suggestion' that 'girls are born with a predisposition to be responsive to nonverbal cues' as a result of biological adaptation toward 'maximizing reproductive success' (1984: 47).

As we have remarked earlier, subordination theory is not necessarily at odds with all these explanations; (a), (b), (c) and (d) above are not in fact competing explanations, but ways in which an explanation based on power inequities may be realized. Socialization to perform certain behaviours is quite likely implicated in these behaviours' association with one or the other gender, but we must ask *why* certain behaviours are associated with being male and some with being female, especially when these same behaviours are associated, respectively, with power and subordination? Why might females have greater empathy, attentiveness, accommodation and alertness? Why might women get more practice in various nonverbal skills? Taken separately, each of these factors provides part of the answer but they beg the question as to their cause. It is our contention that they frequently serve as the mechanisms by which subordination is achieved in face-to-face social interaction.

Finally, Hall offers the possibility of a biological cause, in which the observed sex difference in decoding skill results from males' greater cerebral hemispheric lateralization and females' evolutionary shaping towards nonverbal sensitivity. These processes are, of course, highly speculative.

Conclusion

Communication between the sexes is a complex business and that is especially true of nonverbal signals. Although nonverbal communication takes place typically out-of-awareness, it is none the less pervasive and potent. It carries many messages and supports many practices, an important one being the maintenance of power differentials between men and women. In the foregoing, we have presented the case that sex differences in nonverbal sensitivity derive in good measure from sex-based power inequities and we have tried to show that a particular programme of research aimed at disqualifying this conclusion is itself flawed. The research put forward as refuting the 'oppression hypothesis' has asked peripheral questions, employed questionable measures, made inappropriate comparisons, drawn unwarranted conclusions, and/ or reported results in a biased manner (downplaying unsupportive findings, overrating seemingly supportive ones).

In contrast, we have described some recent studies using appropriate and rigorous methods which find support for subordination theory as an explanation for women's greater nonverbal sensitivity. (It should be noted that several of these studies were unavailable to Hall and Halberstadt for their various reviews.)

It may appear to some that we are rejecting the use of meta-analytic techniques much favoured by Hall and her colleagues to deal with this issue. We have no quarrel with meta-analysis. When used appropriately, it is a most useful tool for integrating and evaluating the findings on a particular topic of research. But we must repeat the caveats that others (for example, Unger and Crawford, 1989) have raised about its utility: all the meta-analysis in the world cannot draw correct conclusions from poorly designed or inadequately conducted studies. As evaluators, consumers and citers of others' research we need to examine studies carefully and thoughtfully, to ask whether the question posed can in fact be answered by the research proffered.

Perhaps more critical in this debate has been the reluctance of psychology in general to address issues of power and status. Hierarchies of all kinds exist and psychological processes are implicated at all levels. Yet as a discipline psychology has slighted consideration of a dominant feature of everyday life, namely hierarchy. When group differences are found there is the lamentable tendency to attribute them to inherent differences (biological) or socialized differences without mention of power. When power inequities are noted in interpreting research findings, socialization is often presented as the culprit that needs to be changed in order to bring about equality. But we, with others, see socialization as the means for perpetuating society's values, beliefs, behaviours and power structures. Societal supports of inequality are what is basic and need to be changed. The phenomenon of gender will be more clearly understood in psychology only when power becomes a prominent item of the psychological agenda.

Notes

The second author wishes to thank Ann Leffler, undergraduate students Caroline Collins, Brian Doherty and Catherine Lerer, and graduate classes at the University of California, both Santa Cruz (1987–8) and Los Angeles campuses, for their stimulating discussion and/or investigation of the ideas contained herein, contributions to her thinking, and support.

1 The PONS is artificial in presenting posed displays of emotion and limited in having the poses of only one gender and race, and in having one actor of that gender and race, and in allowing subjects to choose from only two alternative responses. For brief critiques of the PONS, see Friedman (1980) and Archer and Akert (1977). Rosenthal et al. themselves also describe some of their test's shortcomings (1979: 17–22). Feldman and Thayer (1980) compared the PONS with two other nonverbal sensitivity measures and found no significant relationship among the three, leading one to be concerned about what aspect of decoding skill is being assessed.

References

Archer, D. and Akert, R.M. (1977) 'Words and everything else: verbal and nonverbal cues in social interpretations', *Journal of Personality and Social Psychology*, 35: 443–9.

Aries, E. (1987) 'Gender and communication', in P. Shaver and C. Hendrick (eds), *Sex and Gender*. Beverley Hills, Ca: Sage, pp. 149–76.

Birdwhistell, R.L. (1970) *Kinesics and Context*. Philadelphia, Pa: University of Pennsylvania Press.

Brown, R. (1965) *Social Psychology*. Glencoe, Ill.: Free Press.

Buck, R. (1984) *The Communication of Emotion*. New York: Guilford Press.

Costanzo, M. and Archer, D. (1989) 'Interpreting the expressive behaviour of others: the Interpersonal Perception Task', *Journal of Nonverbal Behavior*, 13: 225–45.

Darwin, C. (1872) *The Expression of the Emotions in Man and Animals*. London: John Murray.

Eagly, A.H. (1987a) 'On taking research findings seriously' [Comment on LaFrance, 1986], *Contemporary Psychology*, 32: 759–61.

Eagly, A.H. (1987b) *Sex Differences in Social Behavior: a Social-Role Interpretation.* Hillsdale, NJ: Lawrence Erlbaum Associates.

Eibl-Eibesfeldt, I. (1972) 'Similarities and differences between cultures in expressive movements', in R.A. Hinde (ed.), *Non-verbal Communication.* London: Cambridge University Press, pp. 297–314.

Ekman, P., Friesen, W.V. and Ellsworth, P. (1972) *Emotion in the Human Face.* New York: Pergamon.

Ellyson, S.L., Dovidio, J.F. and Fehr, B.J. (1981) 'Visual behavior and dominance in women and men', in C. Mayo and N.M. Henley (eds), *Gender and Nonverbal Behavior.* New York: Springer-Verlag.

English, P.W. (1972) 'Behavioral concomitants of dependent and subservient roles'. Unpublished manuscript, Harvard University.

Exline, R.V. (1963) 'Explorations in the process of person perception: visual interaction in relation to competition, sex and need for affiliation', *Journal of Personality*, 31: 1–20.

Exline, R.V. (1972) 'Visual interaction: the glances of power and preference', in J.K. Cole (ed.), *Nebraska Symposium on Motivation*, vol. 19. Lincoln: University of Nebraska Press, pp. 163–206.

Exline, R.V., Gray, D. and Schuette, D. (1965) 'Visual behavior in a dyad as affected by interview content and sex of respondent', *Journal of Personality and Social Psychology*, 1: 201–9.

Feldman, M. and Thayer, S. (1980) 'A comparison of three measures of nonverbal decoding ability', *Journal of Social Psychology*, 112: 91–7.

Firestone, S. (1970) *The Dialectic of Sex.* New York: Bantam.

Friedan, B. (1963) *The Feminine Mystique.* New York: Bantam.

Friedman, H.S. (1980) 'Scientists snatch body language' [Review of Sensitivity to nonverbal communication: the PONS test] *Contemporary Psychology*, 25: 123–4.

Frieze, I. and Ramsey, S.J. (1976) 'Nonverbal maintenance of traditional sex roles', *Journal of Social Issues*, 32: 133–41.

Gillespie, D.L. (1971) 'Who has the power? The marital struggle', *Journal of Marriage and the Family*, 33: 445–58.

Gitter, A.G., Black, H. and Mostofsky, D. (1972) 'Race and sex in the perception of emotion', *Journal of Social Issues*, 28: 63–78.

Goffman, E. (1959) *The Presentation of Self in Everyday Life.* New York: Anchor Books.

Goffman, E. (1967) *Interaction Ritual: Essays on Face-to-Face Behavior.* Garden City, NY: Doubleday.

Goffman, E. (1979) *Gender Advertisements.* New York: Harper and Row.

Halberstadt, A.G. (1985) 'Race, socioeconomic status, and nonverbal behavior', in A. Siegman and S. Feldstein (eds), *Nonverbal behavior in Interpersonal Relations.* Hillsdale, NJ: Erlbaum, pp. 227–66.

Hall, E.T. (1959) *The Silent Language.* Garden City, NY: Doubleday.

Hall, E.T. (1966) *The Hidden Dimension.* Garden City, NY: Doubleday.

Hall, J.A. (1978) 'Gender effects in decoding nonverbal cues', *Psychological Bulletin*, 85: 845–57.

Hall, J.A. (1979) 'Gender, gender roles and nonverbal communication skills', in R. Rosenthal (ed.), *Skill in Nonverbal Communication.* Cambridge, Mass.: Oelgeschlager, Gunn and Hain, pp. 32–67.

Hall, J.A. (1984) *Nonverbal Sex Differences: Communication Accuracy and Expressive Style.* Baltimore, Md: Johns Hopkins University Press.

Hall, J.A. (1985) 'Male and female nonverbal behavior', in A. Siegman and S. Feldstein (eds), *Nonverbal Behavior in Interpersonal Relations*. Hillsdale, NJ: Erlbaum, pp. 195–225.

Hall, J.A. (1987) 'On explaining gender differences: the case of nonverbal communication', in P. Shaver and C. Hendrick (eds), *Sex and Gender*. Beverly Hills, Ca: Sage, pp. 177–200.

Hall, J.A. and Halberstadt, A.G. (1981) 'Sex roles and nonverbal communication skills', *Sex Roles*, 7: 273–87.

Hall, J.A. and Halberstadt, A.G. (1986) 'Smiling and gazing', in J.S. Hyde and M.C. Linn (eds), *The Psychology of Gender: Advances Through Meta-analysis*. Baltimore, Md: Johns Hopkins University Press, pp. 136–58.

Henley, N.M. (1973a) 'Power, sex and nonverbal communication', *Berkeley Journal of Sociology*, 18: 1–26.

Henley, N.M. (1973b) 'Status and sex: some touching observations', *Bulletin of the Psychonomic Society*, 2: 91–3.

Henley, N.M. (1977) *Body Politics: Power, Sex, and Nonverbal Communication*. Englewood Cliffs, NJ: Prentice-Hall.

Henley, N.M. and LaFrance, M. (1984) 'Gender as culture: difference and dominance in nonverbal behavior', in A. Wolfgang (ed.), *Nonverbal Behavior: Perspectives, Applications, Intercultural Insights*. Lewiston, NY: C.J. Hogrefe, pp. 351–71.

Henley, N.M. and LaFrance, M. (1992) 'Sex difference in nonverbal behavior: putting power back into the analyses'. Unpublished manuscript.

Hyde, J.S. (1990) 'Meta-analysis and the psychology of gender differences', *Signs*, 16: 55–73.

Kramarae, C. (1985) 'Beyond sexist language', *Women's Review of Books*, 2(12): 15–17.

Kramer, C. (1977) 'Perceptions of female and male speech', *Language and Speech*, 20: 151–61.

LaFrance, M. (1986) 'Reading between the lines' [Review of Hall, *Nonverbal Sex Differences*], *Contemporary Psychology*, 31: 793–4.

LaFrance, M. (1987) 'On taking the oppression hypothesis seriously', *Contemporary Psychology*, 32: 760–1.

LaFrance, M. and Banaji, M. (1992) 'Towards a reconsideration of the gender emotion relationship', in M. Clark (ed.), *Emotion and Social Behavior: Review of Personality and Social Psychology*, vol. 14. Beverley Hills, Ca: Sage.

LaFrance, M. and Mayo, C. (1979) 'A review of nonverbal communication of women and men', *Western Journal of Speech Communication*, 43: 96–107.

Lakoff, R. (1975) *Language and Woman's Place*. New York: Harper and Row.

Leffler, A., Gillespie, D.L. and Conaty, J.C. (1982) 'The effects of status differentiation on nonverbal behavior', *Social Psychology Quarterly*, 45: 153–61.

Matlin, M.W. (1987) *The Psychology of Women*. New York: Holt, Rinehart and Winston.

Millar, K.U. and Millar M.G. (1988) 'Sex difference in perceived self- and other-disclosure: a case where inequity increases satisfaction', *Social Behavior and Personality*, 16: 59–64.

Miller, J.B. (1976) *Towards a New Psychology of Women*. Boston, Mass.: Beacon Press.

Millett, K. (1969) *Sexual Politics*. Garden City, NY: Doubleday.

Rollman, S.A. (1978) 'The sensitivity of Black and White Americans to nonverbal cues of prejudice', *Journal of Social Psychology*, 105: 73–7.

Rosenthal, R., Hall, J.A., DiMatteo, M.R., Rogers, P.L. and Archer, D. (1979) *Sensitivity to Nonverbal Communication: The PONS Test.* Baltimore, Md: Johns Hopkins University Press.

Rubin, Z. (1970) 'Measurement of romantic love', *Journal of Personality and Social Psychology*, 16: 265–73.

Sabatelli, R., Buck, R. and Dreyer, A. (1982) 'Nonverbal communication accuracy in married couples: relationship with marital complaints', *Journal of Personality and Social Psychology*, 43: 1088–97.

Safilios-Rothschild, C. (1970) 'The study of family power structure: a review 1960–1969', *Journal of Marriage and the Family*, 32: 539–52.

Snodgrass, S.E. (1985) 'Women's intuition: the effect of subordinate role on interpersonal sensitivity', *Journal of Personality and Social Psychology*, 49: 146–55.

Snodgrass, S.E. (1992) 'Further effects of role versus gender on interpersonal sensitivity', *Journal of Personality and Social Psychology*, 62: 154–8.

Sommer, R. (1969) *Personal Space.* Englewood Cliffs, NJ: Prentice-Hall.

Spence, J.T., Helmreich, R.L. and Stapp, J. (1973) 'A short version of the Attitudes toward Women Scale (AWS)', *Bulletin of the Psychonomic Society*, 2: 219–20.

Sprecher, S. (1989) 'The importance to males and females of physical attractiveness, earning potential and expressiveness', *Sex Roles*, 21: 591–607.

Stanton, E.C., Anthony, S.B. and Joslyn, M. (1889) *The History of Woman Suffrage*, 2nd edn. Rochester, NY: Charles Mann.

Stier, D.S. and Hall, J.A. (1984) 'Gender differences in touch: an empirical and theoretical review', *Journal of Personality and Social Psychology*, 47: 440–59.

Tajfel, H. (1984) 'Intergroup relations, social myths, and social justice in social psychology', in H. Tajfel (ed.), *The Social Dimension.* Cambridge: Cambridge University Press.

Thomas, D.L., Franks, D.D. and Calonico, J.M. (1972) 'Role-taking and power in social psychology', *American Sociological Review*, 37: 605–14.

Thorne, B. and Henley, N. (1975) 'Difference and dominance: an overview of language, gender and society', in B. Thorne and N. Henley (eds), *Language and Sex: Difference and Dominance.* Rowley, Mass.: Newbury House, pp. 5–42.

Unger, R.K. and Crawford, M. (1989) 'Methods and values in decisions about gender differences' [Review of Eagly, *Sex Differences in Social Behavior*], *Contemporary Psychology*, 34: 122–3.

Wallston, B. (1987) 'Social psychology of women and gender', *Journal of Applied Social Psychology*, 17: 1025–50.

Weitz, S. (ed.) (1974) *Nonverbal Communication: Readings with Commentary.* New York: Oxford University Press.

Weitz, S. (1976) 'Sex differences in nonverbal communication', *Sex Roles*, 2: 175–84.

Wex, M. (1979) *Let's Take Back Our Space: 'Female' and 'Male' Body Language as a Result of Patriarchal Structures.* Hamburg: Frauenliteraturverlag Hermaine Fees (first published in German).

Woolf, V. (1929) *A Room of One's Own.* New York: Harcourt, Brace and World.

Index